Adobe® Photoshop® Lightroom® & Photoshop® Workflow Bible

Mark Fitzgerald

WILEY

Wiley Publishing, Inc.

Adobe® Photoshop® Lightroom® and Photoshop® Workflow Bible

Published by
Wiley Publishing, Inc.
10475 Crosspoint Boulevard
Indianapolis, IN 46256
www.wiley.com

Copyright © 2008 by Wiley Publishing, Inc., Indianapolis, Indiana

Published simultaneously in Canada

ISBN: 978-0-470-30309-2

Manufactured in the United States of America

10 9 8 7 6 5 4 3 2 1

For general information on our other products and services or to obtain technical support, please contact our Customer Care Department within the U.S. at (800) 762-2974, outside the U.S. at (317) 572-3993 or fax (317) 572-4002.

Library of Congress Control Number: 2008933789

About the Author

Mark Fitzgerald is a Photoshop teacher and workflow consultant who specializes in helping professional photographers thrive in the digital age. He has taught hundreds of photographers how to smooth out their workflow and get the most from their important images — through private training, classes, and workshops. Mark is an Adobe Certified Photoshop Expert and an Adobe Certified Photoshop Instructor. He and his wife Julia (with their three dogs, Ruby, Hazel, and Sam) live in Portland, Oregon, where Mark owns a consulting business called The Digital Darkroom (www.ddroom.com).

Credits

Associate Acquisitions Editor
Courtney Allen

Project Editor
Martin V. Minner

Technical Editor
Mike Hagen

Copy Editor
Kim Heusel

Editorial Manager
Robyn Siesky

Business Manager
Amy Knies

Sr. Marketing Manager
Sandy Smith

Vice President and Executive Group Publisher
Richard Swadley

Vice President and Executive Publisher
Bob Ipsen

Vice President and Publisher
Barry Pruett

Project Coordinator
Erin Smith

Graphics and Production Specialists
Elizabeth Brooks
Stacie Brooks
Carl Byers
Nikki Gately
Andrea Hornberger

Proofreading
Christine Sabooni

Indexing
Sherry Massey

Cover Design
Michael Trent

Cover Illustration
Joyce Haughey

Preface

Back in the days before digital, when photographers shot film, few gave much thought to workflow. That's because the film-based workflow offered far fewer options than the digital workflow, and the way those options were executed was fairly straightforward. Even so, though most of them didn't realize it, all of these photographers had a two-part workflow.

The first part began right after the shoot. It consisted of processing all of the rolls or sheets of film. In the case of negative film, automated proofs, such as 4 x 5's or contact sheets, were printed from the negatives — usually by a photolab. The point with these proofs was to quickly create tools to use for further evaluation by the photographer — or the photographer's clients. Every effort was made to manage tone and color, but the point was to create proofs quickly and cheaply because they were merely tools used to identify the best photos. After those few best photos were identified, they were moved into the second part of the two-part workflow.

This second part of the film-based workflow was focused on fine-tuning these special images and preparing them for output. Every effort, and oftentimes much expense, was put into managing the strengths and weaknesses of each image. This was usually accomplished through a custom print that was handcrafted by a highly skilled technician. Retouching and artwork were often thrown into the mix when required to fix problems. The resulting image was a one-of-a-kind print that had little resemblance to the proof that was used to pick it from the original group of photos.

The modern digital photography workflow is much like the film-based workflow. It consists of the same two parts. The first part is focused on processing a group of photos from a shoot or event so that they can be used to identify the most important images from the group. One of the main differences is that digital photographers don't have to pay for every exposure, so they tend to generate lots of photos. These large numbers of digital files require software tools and procedures for using them that are streamlined and efficient. For that reason I call this first portion of the digital workflow the *Production Workflow*.

Like the film-based workflow, the second part of the digital workflow is all about the pursuit of perfection. This is accomplished by managing the strengths and weaknesses of the image. The same rules apply regarding what separates a good image from a great one. The difference is in the amazing amount of control possible with today's digital tools. Anything is possible for someone who understands how to use these new tools. Thousands of decisions can be made while editing a single image because the options are so open ended. That's why I call this second portion of the two-part digital workflow the *Creative Workflow*. The open-ended process allows the maker of the image to create a true personal expression of that image.

The most powerful aspect of digital photography is that the tools are now in the hands of the photographer. Though photo labs are still very useful for output, most of the important decisions are made by the photographer before the lab even comes into the picture.

Photoshop has been the foremost tool for executing the Creative Workflow for many years. But it has never been a very good solution for photographers managing large numbers of images in their Production Workflows. Adobe, the maker of Photoshop, solved this problem when it introduced Adobe Lightroom. Now Lightroom and Photoshop can be combined to offer the complete digital post-production workflow solution. In this book, I explain how both of these programs are used individually, and together, to manage your own digital two-part workflow. By the end of this book you'll be ready to begin making your workflow work for you.

What's in This Book?

This book is divided into five parts. Part I explores the workflow concept and how it's used to organize the digital photographer's post-production procedures. You take a closer look at the two-part workflow and the role each part plays. Then you take a peek at Lightroom and Photoshop and compare and contrast them, and how they're used in combination to create the total workflow. You finish this section by comparing different file types, how they're used for specific portions of the workflow, and how to keep them organized.

Part II is all about Lightroom and the Production Workflow. You take a close look at Lightroom's intuitive workspace and the five modules that comprise Lightroom. Then you cover best practices for importing new photos into Lightroom and organizing them with keywords and other metadata. The next chapter covers everything you need to know to process your photos in the Develop module so that you quickly make them look great. After that you look at the three output modules — Slideshow, Print, and Web — and how they're used to share and present your photos. You also look at how to export files so that you can take them to a lab for output if you prefer. Then you put it all together by looking at how a wildlife photographer handles his Production Workflow with Lightroom while photographing polar bears in the extreme conditions of the Arctic.

In Part III, you move into the Photoshop section of the book. In this section, I introduce Photoshop, Bridge, and Adobe Camera Raw and discuss how they work together to open files in Photoshop. I also discuss ways to insure that editing done in Lightroom is seen by these three programs. Then you take a close look at Photoshop and how its workspace is used. Next, I show you how to adjust tone and color in Photoshop and how those tools compare and contrast with similar tools in Lightroom. I finish this section with a chapter on one of the most important Photoshop concepts: layers.

Once you have the basic Photoshop concepts down, it's time to move beyond them. In Part IV, you explore the real power behind Photoshop: the selection tools, layer masking, and Photoshop's retouching tools. When you learn to use these three features together, you'll be able to accomplish just about anything. I finish this section by showing you how some of these special Photoshop procedures can be integrated into Lightroom during file export. This is one of the few ways that Lightroom and Photoshop are used together at the same time.

Part V puts all of the tools to work by looking at how they're used to solve specific problems. You explore the concept of retouching and define exactly what it is. Then you look at how Photoshop is used to solve several everyday portrait retouching problems from repairing missing eyes to removing braces. The next chapter covers burning and dodging, resolution, sharpening, and printing, as well as other finishing touches. In the final chapter, we work together on a hands-on project and take it through the entire Creative Workflow process.

As we explore Lightroom and Photoshop together, I demonstrate the practical applications with real-world images and step-by-step examples. I also make every attempt to explain the theory behind the steps so you understand the reasoning behind the process. In some cases, when feasible, I provide online practice files for hands-on projects so that you can work along beside me.

Who Should Read This Book?

Adobe Photoshop Lightroom and Photoshop Workflow Bible is intended for anyone wanting to know how to take control of his or her complete digital post-production workflow. You don't have to be an accomplished Lightroom or Photoshop user, but it is helpful if you have some experience with the software. With that said, even a beginner benefits from reading this book, especially when you consider that as a beginner you'll be starting out on the right foot with your digital workflow.

This book is not intended as a comprehensive guide to all things Lightroom and Photoshop. My intention is to give you the things you need to establish a bullet-proof workflow, without distracting you with what you don't need right now. There are times when I'd like to go into deeper detail, but I can't because those details are outside the scope of this book. If I don't cover a topic in detail that interests you and you want to know more about it, find a resource to help you explore it. Two of the most useful resources are the Lightroom and Photoshop Help menus, and Google. (Just type your question into Google to see if someone else has already asked it and posted an answer.)

How to Use This Book

To get the most from this book, start at the beginning and go through it sequentially. This allows you to experience the learning process in the way I envision it. In many cases, ideas in one chapter build on information introduced in previous chapters. This amplification process won't make as much sense if experienced out of order. Also, take the time to read each chapter, even if you think you already understand its subject. You never know when you'll turn up a nugget that will completely change the way you work with your images.

Download all the practice files from the Web site at this URL:

> www.wiley.com/go/workflow

Most of the practice files are fairly small. If you have a slow Internet connection, borrow a friend's connection and download them all at once. After we go through a hands-on process together, take the time to explore those new processes with some of your own photos. I know from my own experience that working with personal files makes a big difference in the learning process. This is where you'll find the time to go as deep as you need to go while exploring the content of this book.

After you've been through the book from front to back, you can use it as a reference guide to help you solve your own workflow issues. When a specific issue pops up, find the relevant references in the book and review them as needed.

Conventions Used in This Book

I'm big on using keyboard shortcuts in my own workflow, but I won't be stressing them much here because there are potentially hundreds of shortcuts in Lightroom and Photoshop and I don't want to confuse you with them. The other thing is that I think it's more important that you know where to find a command in the workspace, rather than the fastest way to execute it. After you're comfortable with the workspace, you can focus on speed.

With that said, I do think you should begin getting used to the idea of keyboard shortcuts. So I share some of the more useful shortcuts. When I first introduce the most common tools and commands, I give you their keyboard shortcuts in parentheses like this: the Lasso tool (L).

NOTE If you want to know all of Photoshop's keyboard shortcuts, choose Edit⇨Keyboard Shortcuts and click the Summarize button when the Keyboard Shortcuts and Menus dialog box opens. In Lightroom, check the Help menu of each module for module-specific shortcuts, as well as shared shortcuts or press Command+/ (Ctrl+/).

Because this book was written on two Macs, all the screenshots are from the Mac versions of Lightroom 2.0 and Photoshop CS3. That shouldn't make much difference, because almost everything is the same in the Mac and Windows versions of the software. (In fact, you can open a Lightroom catalog on either platform.) If you're using a Windows machine, the only real differences are the keyboard modifier keys.

Macs use the Option (Alt) key and the Command (Apple) key as modifiers, and Windows machines use the Alt key and the Ctrl key for the same functions. (This is all the more confusing because a standard Mac keyboard has a Control key on it that has a completely different function.)

- Mac Option (Alt) key = Windows Alt key
- Mac Command (Apple) key = Windows Ctrl key

Because every modern Mac keyboard I've seen has an Alt label on the Option key, I refer to this key as Alt, which should be straightforward. When I need to mention the other set of modifier keys, I say Command/Ctrl. The only reason I'm putting the Mac command first is to be consistent with the screenshots.

Should You Use a Mac or a Windows Machine?

This is a question many people, especially photographers, ask themselves. Back in the old days of digital photography, the answer to this question would have had a serious impact on a photographer's ability to do what he or she needed to do. At that time, the Mac was a superior platform to Windows primarily because of its more intelligent way of dealing with color. However, that difference disappeared long ago. When it comes to Photoshop CS3, a modern version of either platform works quite well.

I've used personal computers since their earliest days. Many of the computers I used during that time were Windows-based machines. For the last few years, I've used Macs because I work with many professional photographers who use the platform. I switched to it so that I would be more comfortable in their environment. (I would say that my current client base is split 50/50 on the platforms.) I have both types of machines in my office, and I commonly use both Mac and Windows machines during a typical day. I like some things about each platform. In a perfect world, I could combine all those things to create the perfect operating system.

The subject of Mac versus Windows comes up in my workshops and private training quite often. When it does, I explain it like this: Deciding between Mac and Windows is like choosing Canon or Nikon (or any other camera system). Both systems are great. If you buy a quality system from either manufacturer, you should be happy. Your decision as to which to buy should be based on how you like a particular system. Does it feel good in your hands? Are the controls easy to understand? Is it the same system your friends are using so that they can help you when you have questions? After you make a choice and begin buying lenses for one of those camera systems, you'll probably want to stay with it for a while. This is the same as software. After you spend a few thousand dollars on software for one platform, it's not likely that you'll want to switch anytime soon, because you'll have to buy all new software.

No matter which computer system you decide to go with, be sure that the system is up to snuff. If your system is more than five years old, you may be disappointed in the performance of Lightroom and Photoshop, especially when you begin doing some of the things you're going to do in this book. You may not even be able to have both programs open at the same time. Ideally, you should have a machine with a fairly fast processor. A dual processor is even better because Photoshop is designed to take advantage of two processors. Lightroom and Photoshop are real RAM hogs, so you'll want to have at the very least 1GB of system memory and preferably 2. If you have both these bases covered, then it won't matter if you're running a Mac or a Windows machine.

Which Version of Photoshop CS3?

When Photoshop CS3 was released, Adobe did something new. It introduced two versions of the software: Photoshop CS3 and Photoshop CS3 Extended. The Extended version has some added capabilities for people who work with animation, film, and 3-D objects. It also has some cool features that allow people like architects, engineers, and medical researchers to analyze images. Many of these features are in a menu called Analysis. Because I used Photoshop CS3 Extended to write this book, you may notice the Analysis menu in some Photoshop screenshots. Don't worry if you don't have it. Most of the photographers I know don't need the added features of the Extended version, so I usually recommend that they save money and purchase the standard version. (I would prefer to see a photographer purchase Lightroom and Photoshop CS3, rather than only Photoshop CS3 Extended.)

Products Mentioned in This Book

On several occasions I recommend products I use or like. I want you to know that I do not have relationships with any of the companies that sell these products. These companies do not sponsor me. The only reason I endorse these products is because I think knowing about them will make your digital workflow experience more enjoyable.

One Last Thing

I tried very hard to make sure everything in this book is 100 percent accurate. When writing the Lightroom chapters that became a tall order because Lightroom 2 — still in the beta development process — was often a moving target. If you notice any errors or omissions, please let me know by emailing me at books@ddroom.com. That way, I can fix them in future editions.

Acknowledgments

Once again, I would like to thank my family, my friends, and most importantly, my clients for allowing me to disappear into my cave while writing this book. Your understanding and flexibility took much of the stress out of my taking on another big project.

I also want to thank the following photographers for letting me use their images:

- Emily Andrews, Emily Andrews Portrait Design: `emilyandrews.net`
- Jerry Auker, Jerry Auker Photography: `net-seniors.com`
- Dan Christopher, Dan Christopher Photography: `danchristopherphotography.com`
- David Hitchcock, Hitchcock Creative Photography
- John McAnulty, Inner Focus Photography: `pro.corbis.com` (search for John McAnulty)
- Ted Miller Jr.: `mrmontana.blogspot.com`
- Carl Murray, Seattle Photography, Inc.: `seattlephotography.com`
- Jordan Sleeth, Jordan Sleeth Photography
- Natalia Tsvetkov, Natalia T Photography: `nataliaphoto.com`
- Denyce Weiler, Something Blue Photography: `somethingbluephotography.com`
- Mark Wilson, Hakuna Matata Photography: `hakunamatataphotography.com`

This book would have been difficult to write without the sample images these photographers so generously provided. Please visit their Web sites to see more of their work.

I also want to thank all the people who allowed me to use images of themselves. Most of them had no idea they'd end up in a book when they had their pictures taken.

Thanks to the editing team at Wiley: copyeditor Kim Heusel, who did such a great job of noticing small details that made big differences; technical editor Mike Hagen, who once again took time out of his busy schedule to lend his extensive expertise; and project editor Martin V. Minner, who did such a great job of coordinating all of us. (Marty, it truly was a pleasure working with you again.)

I especially want to thank Courtney Allen, Associate Acquisitions Editor for Wiley Publishing, who so kindly invited me into the Wiley fold. Without her, this book would not be a reality.

Finally, I would like to thank Barry Pruett, Vice President and Publisher at Wiley Publishing, for suggesting this format for telling the Lightroom and Photoshop workflow story.

Contents at a Glance

Contents

Contents

Part I

Understanding the Workflow

The most important word in the title of this book is *workflow*. That's because many photographers struggle with managing the countless options available during the digital post-production process. Before you can understand the process, however, you need to know exactly what workflow means. In Chapter 1, I answer that question and more as you explore the concepts behind the digital photographer's workflow.

The two other important words in the title are Lightroom and Photoshop. In Chapter 2, I compare and contrast these two Adobe products and show why one is preferable to the other for specific portions of the workflow. Once you get a better idea of how Lightroom and Photoshop are used, you'll understand why I consider the combination of these two products to be the perfect solution for the digital photographer's post-production needs.

In the last chapter in this section, Chapter 3, I discuss the different types of image files photographers use. I also cover why one type is preferable to another during specific portions of the workflow. I then explain how to create and manage an organizational system that makes sense so that you can quickly find the files you want when you need them. Finally, I take a moment to discuss one of the most important subjects in Part I: backing up and archiving techniques and strategies. Be sure to read this section even if you already have a strategy in place.

Chapter 1

Making Your Work Flow

Just a few years ago, when photographers were primarily shooting film, I rarely heard any of them mention the word "workflow." That's because post-production consisted of taking film to the lab and then picking it up when processing and proofing were completed. When they needed enlargements, they took their selected negatives or slides back to the lab for printing. Unless they were developing their own film and doing all printing in the darkroom, the film photographer's workflow was mostly over once the shutter clicked. Even for photographers who processed and printed their own film, the options were so limited that it wasn't necessary to spend lots of time thinking about them.

Now that digital photographers are taking control over the entire imaging process, the word *workflow* is a common word in their vocabulary. That's because products like Lightroom and Photoshop have opened the door to unlimited options in post-production. In this new photographic paradigm a shutter-click signals the beginning of a whole new creative process — rather than the end of one. The trick to unlocking the power of that process is to manage the countless possible options when editing digital files by designing and using a well-defined workflow.

So what do I mean when I say *workflow*? The underlying concept of a workflow is a tested system that yields consistent and reliable results in the shortest amount of time. One of the best examples of a complete workflow is a Starbucks coffee shop. Starbucks isn't successful because it serves the best-tasting coffee drinks. It's successful because the coffee it sells always tastes the same whether you're drinking a Caramel Macchiato in Seattle or San Antonio. That's because each coffee shop uses the same system to prepare the drinks it serves — as well as everything else done at the store. This system not only guarantees consistent quality, it also ensures that all Starbucks

IN THIS CHAPTER

What is a workflow?

Understanding the photographer's workflow

Ensuring that your workflow doesn't damage your files

employees operate at peak efficiency because they don't have to invent their own system. This workflow is the key to the success of Starbucks because once it was developed it was duplicated and adapted over and over, in radically different locations across the globe.

Even though you're not making lattes, you can learn something from Starbucks. If you take the time to systemize everything you do to your images, you'll know that each step is being performed efficiently and in the correct order. You'll know that each factor that affects the quality of your images is being managed in the best way, so you won't have to reinvent the wheel every time you edit an image. Additionally, if your system is flexible, you'll be able to adapt it to all sorts of imaging scenarios for the different kinds of photographic needs you have. However, before you can design that system, you must consider the variables that you need to manage in a typical digital photographer's post-production workflow.

Exploring the Digital Photographer's Workflow

There are almost as many digital post-production workflows as there are photographers. In general, these workflows begin at the moment of capture and end with final output of a retouched and refined file. However, if you look at most of those workflows, you soon notice that they share a common, two-part foundation. I call these two parts the *production phase* and the *creative phase*. Let's take a close look at each of these phases so that you can get an overview of the job ahead.

The production phase of the workflow

This first part of your workflow deals with managing large numbers of images. I call this part of the workflow the *production phase* because the focus is on speed and efficiency. It's similar to a film photographer who processes her film, prints some proofs, and uses them to choose the winners and losers from the shoot. Refining this first part of the workflow is especially important for digital photographers because of the large number of images we tend to capture. When I got married in 1980, our photographer covered the entire wedding with 120 exposures. Today, many wedding photographers shoot as many as 2000–3000 images at a wedding. With these high numbers it's possible to get buried in your workflow unless you have a well-designed system. Figure 1.1 illustrates the main steps in the production phase of the workflow.

FIGURE 1.1

When dealing with large groups of images there are certain fundamental steps that must be considered. After these steps are systemized they form the foundation for the production phase of the workflow.

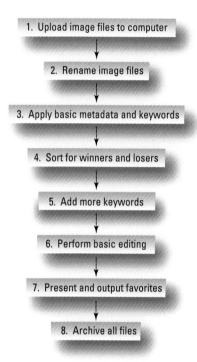

The Production Workflow

1. Upload image files to computer

2. Rename image files

3. Apply basic metadata and keywords

4. Sort for winners and losers

5. Add more keywords

6. Perform basic editing

7. Present and output favorites

8. Archive all files

Let's take a quick look at each of these steps:

1. **Upload image files to the computer.** This is where it all begins. Files are uploaded and imported into some kind of *digital asset management* (DAM) software. DAM software allows you to catalog images by creating a *database* (a structured collection of information), so that it's fast and easy to find the photo file you need when you need it.

2. **Rename image files.** This step is always a good idea so that your image files have unique and meaningful names.

3. **Apply basic metadata and keywords.** Basic metadata information such as the copyright holder's name and general keywords that describe the photos are added. This step, as well as the renaming step, takes place during the upload/import process. (I discuss metadata and keywords in detail in Chapters 5 and 6.)

4. **Sort for winners and losers.** During this process the good, the bad, and the just plain ugly are identified, labeled, and deleted if necessary. During this process important files begin to emerge. (These are the files that will eventually be moved to the creative phase of the workflow later.)

5. **Add more keywords.** More specific keywords are added to individual images and groups of images. The more specific this information is, the more powerful the search and filtering functions of the DAM software will be when it searches its database.

6. **Perform basic editing.** Qualities like tonality and color are modified, and functions like cropping are performed on the images. An important aspect of this step is to have the ability to apply the same adjustments to groups of similar images all at once.

7. **Present and output favorites.** This step allows you to share your favorite images with the rest of the world. There are several options here, depending on the form of the presentation. The usual options include slide shows, Web sites, e-mail, and prints.

8. **Archive all files.** After all of the work is done it's important to preserve it by backing up and archiving the image files as well as the DAM database.

NOTE Keep in mind that the final images from this phase are not yet highly refined, but they are ready for closer inspection. Think of them as the proofs a professional photographer would show to a client. All of the rejects have been removed and general edits have been performed so that these proofs are good enough to use as a sale tool.

It is useful here to visualize the production phase of the workflow as a funneling process. One of its main functions is to help you quickly identify important images. When you pour all of your photos into that funnel, only the best ones emerge from the other end. It's those few, special images that the second phase of the workflow, the creative phase, is designed to address.

The creative phase of the workflow

I call this portion of the workflow the *creative phase* because it focuses on creativity and quality rather than speed. Efficiency is important here, and efforts should be made to improve it. However, efficiency always takes a back seat to creating the best possible file for uses such as publication in a magazine or printing large wall prints for display.

This part of the workflow is like the film photographer who chooses a special negative from her proofs and then spends hours making a print in her darkroom. This is where the magic happens, as every aspect of the image is fine-tuned and perfected. Figure 1.2 shows the typical steps in the creative workflow.

FIGURE 1.2

These steps for the creative phase of the workflow begin after the steps in the production phase are completed. They are performed on a special, single image rather than a group of images.

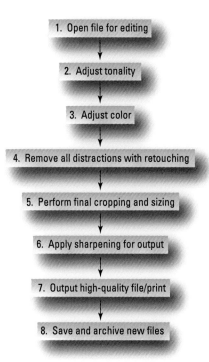

The Creative Workflow

1. Open file for editing
2. Adjust tonality
3. Adjust color
4. Remove all distractions with retouching
5. Perform final cropping and sizing
6. Apply sharpening for output
7. Output high-quality file/print
8. Save and archive new files

Let's break these steps down and take a closer look at them:

1. **Open file for editing.** This is where the creative part of the workflow begins. Files are opened with the editing software or directly from the DAM software.

2. **Adjust tonality.** If everything is done correctly during the editing process in the production phase of the workflow, then overall tonal correction is minimal here. Sometimes, though, specific areas of the image need to be darkened or lightened individually.

3. **Adjust color.** This is the same as the tonal adjustment step. Overall adjustment should be minimal. Special attention is given to specific areas of the image where color needs to be modified locally without affecting other colors in the image.

7

4. **Remove all distractions with retouching.** This is where most of the action occurs during the creative phase of the workflow. Retouching tools like Photoshop's Healing Brush and Clone Stamp are used to tone down or completely remove anything in the image that's distracting. Additional tools and techniques are used to ensure that the final image is designed to guide the viewer's eye through it in the way the image's maker intended.

5. **Perform final cropping and sizing.** After all the work is done, the image is prepared for its final use.

6. **Apply sharpening for output.** This step may seem basic, but it's one of the most crucial steps in the creative portion of the workflow. That's because final sharpening must be customized for the specific output size and use.

7. **Output high-quality file/print.** Now it's time for the payoff. Everything that's been done to the image since uploading it onto the computer comes together.

8. **Save and archive new files.** All new files created during this process are saved to specific locations and archived. Additionally, they're added to the DAM database with any additional keywords that may be necessary.

Where the production phase of the workflow is mostly concerned with speed and efficiency, the creative phase deals with high quality and creativity. Naturally, you want to have quality when working quickly in the production phase of the workflow, and you want to work as quickly as you can during the creative phase. But it helps to think about this division of the workflow so that you know when you should be moving quickly and when you should be spending extra time on an image. It also helps to know which tools and techniques you should be using at a particular time.

NOTE If you think about this division of the workflow, you soon realize that each of these workflow phases is actually a workflow in and of itself. Think of them as sub-workflows. Because of that I'm going to refer to them from now on as the Production Workflow and the Creative Workflow.

Building a Nondestructive Workflow

Speed and efficiency are always important in a digital workflow, especially when dealing with large numbers of images. However, another workflow issue that is just as important is flexibility. A flexible workflow allows you to keep your options open as you edit important files so that you can undo any editing at any time. To accomplish this you have to work with your files in a way that's *nondestructive* to the pixels in the image. That means that any changes made during the editing process do not have permanent effects on the underlying pixels unless it's absolutely necessary.

When pixels are altered in a destructive workflow the quality of the file is affected. For example, when tonal and color adjustments are made to a digital file, information is lost. If repetitive tonal or color adjustments are carried out, the data loss is cumulative. That means that making four tonal adjustments causes data loss four times. This loss of information can be subtle or it can be extreme, but it can't be undone.

> **NOTE** Nondestructive techniques are crucial if you're new to the digital editing process. That's because you'll be learning lots as you go through the learning curve over time. In six months you'll have new tricks that you might want to use on a special image. However, if the file has been edited destructively, you may not be able to use your new skills on it.

The workflow for the film photographer was mostly nondestructive. When she made prints from a negative, none of the qualities of the negative was altered. She could print a black-and-white 5 x 7 and a color 16 x 20, but the negative was still the same. The prints were merely derivative interpretations of the negative. There was nothing about the printing process that could alter the negative. Even if there had been, no one would have used it because the negative was considered the essence of the image and it was protected at all costs.

When many photographers first began to shoot digitally they didn't consider the destructive nature of digital editing. They even edited original files without considering the ramifications of making permanent changes to them. It wasn't until they went back to those images later on that they realized they had, in essence, destroyed important images.

This nondestructive editing philosophy is one of the most important aspects to consider when creating a digital workflow. Without it, you're like a trapeze artist who's working without a net. I stress the importance of a nondestructive workflow throughout this book — especially when you start working with Photoshop in Part III. That's because, as you'll see in the next chapter, by its very nature Photoshop is destructive to the pixels in an image file.

Summary

A workflow is a system that's used to codify each of the steps that are performed on digital image files. The main function of a digital workflow is to ensure that steps are being carried out in the correct order, in the most efficient way.

Digital photographers tend to work with a two-part workflow. The first part, the production phase, is focused on working with large groups of images. The idea is to use this production phase to identify important images so that they can be moved into the second part of the workflow, the creative phase. The creative phase of the workflow is where the magic happens. This is where speed and efficiency are not as important as quality and creativity. The creative phase is reserved for special images that are destined for uses that require the highest quality.

Because each of these two phases is a mini-workflow it's best to think of them as separate workflows. That's why I call them the Production Workflow and the Creative Workflow.

The most important thing about both these workflows, no matter what we call them, is that they must be designed to be nondestructive to the images. My goal throughout this book is to show you how to work nondestructively with your files throughout your total workflow so that you avoid any surprises when you revisit those images in the future.

Chapter 2

Comparing Lightroom and Photoshop

Photoshop is an amazing image editing software package. Ever since it was originally released in 1990 it has become the image editing industry standard for all sorts of users: from illustrators and designers to doctors and engineers. That's because it's loaded with powerful tools that do all sorts of interesting things to a wide variety of image files. However, very few Photoshop users make use of all of the tools in the program. They tend to use their own specific toolset to accomplish their particular needs, leaving as much as 80 percent of the program untouched. This is particularly true for many photographers.

Photoshop is like a huge toolbox full of every tool you can imagine. (Figure 2.1 shows the default user interface.) If it were a real toolbox it would be a lot like the toolbox I have in my garage, except it would be a lot bigger — maybe as big as my garage! It would be as if someone went to the hardware store and picked out one of each tool, and then filled the toolbox with them. This might seem cool, but for most people it's overkill. When a plumber goes to the hardware store he only purchases tools that a plumber needs. When a carpenter goes to the hardware store he only purchases the tools a carpenter needs. Sure, each may buy a hammer and a saw, but they will most likely be different kinds of hammers and saws because they'll be used in different ways.

In the right hands nearly anything can be done to modify and improve an image with Photoshop. However, in the untrained hands it becomes a confusing array of tools, commands, and palettes with few clues to which are best for a particular need. This becomes even more complicated when a nondestructive workflow is important. That's because most of the tools in Photoshop — such as the tonal adjustment, color-correction, and retouching tools — are all destructive in nature because they edit the image on the pixel level. If precautions aren't made to minimize this destructive nature with specific techniques, important image files can suffer a permanent loss of quality.

The Photoshop CS3 user interface provides few clues as to how the software should be used for a particular purpose. The default layout shown here has multiple hidden and nested tools and palettes. To get the most from Photoshop, a user has to remember where specific tools and commands are located.

Lightroom is different. It's as if someone went to Photoshop's giant toolbox and picked out only the tools a photographer uses the most. The rest of the esoteric tools are left in the Photoshop toolbox where they're saved for special projects. What's even better is that once all of the photographer's tools are gathered together in Lightroom, they're laid out in groups on the workbench in the order in which they are most often used. (Figure 2.2 shows the user interface for the Library module.) This intuitive nature allows the user to learn to use the tools more quickly and work much more efficiently once the workflow is learned.

FIGURE 2.2

The Lightroom user interface is much friendlier and intuitive. Five different modules are used for specific tasks. In this view, you're looking at the Library module. The tools within each module are placed up-and-down and left-to-right in the order in which they are typically used.

Photos by Denyce Weiler

Understanding the Purpose of Photoshop

Even though Photoshop can be confusing, it's one of the most powerful image-editing applications on the planet. When it comes to working with photography it can't be beat. The powerful tools in Photoshop allow photographers to do things that weren't possible with film photography. Figure 2.3 shows an original image and the new image that I created in Photoshop using advanced techniques, such as combining multiple images and layers, using special filters, and using custom layer blending styles. None of these techniques is available in Lightroom. When you're ready to set your creativity free, nothing compares to Photoshop.

FIGURE 2.3

This figure shows before and after images from an image in a series of dog portraits I created a few years ago. All of the editing was done in Photoshop. A finished image like this could never be created in Lightroom because it requires the advanced tools Photoshop is famous for.

The developers who originally created Photoshop could never have dreamed it would become the industry standard for all kinds of imaging professionals. That's because very few people were working with digital files when Photoshop was born. During the lifetime of Photoshop numerous improvements have been made in an effort to continue to supply imaging professionals with the tools they needed. Because of that, Photoshop has had ten major upgrades. The current version, CS3, barely resembles the earliest versions. Upgrades are good, but in the case of Photoshop, each time it's upgraded more tools are thrown into the toolbox. Sometimes these tools are useful to the average photographer, but many times they aren't.

Because of this growth, Photoshop has become a complex and often confusing piece of software. I have personally taught many photographers to use it and I know how difficult it can be to understand. What complicates this even more is that Photoshop is more than one program. It contains a file browser called Adobe Bridge, and a raw file converter called Adobe Camera Raw that's used to open raw files in Photoshop. These multiple applications compound the steep learning curve because photographers need to be trained in all three applications to get the most out of Photoshop.

CROSS-REF Chapter 3 discusses raw files in more detail.

Adobe Bridge

Photoshop's first file browser appeared in version 7 and was embedded in the Photoshop software. It allowed users to browse through files so that they could visually select which ones to open in Photoshop. The file browser was a huge improvement from the previous method of having to remember the name of the file to be opened and using Photoshop's Open command to open it.

When Photoshop CS2 was released, the file browser was replaced with a separate and independent piece of software called Adobe Bridge. Figure 2.4 shows the default Bridge interface. Notice that it resembles the Library module interface in Lightroom, as shown in Figure 2.2. The reason it's called Bridge is because it acts as a universal file browser for numerous Adobe products such as Acrobat, Illustrator, and InDesign. It serves as a bridge among these various applications because all the different files used by them can be viewed together in Bridge. This approach makes more sense than creating a separate file browser for each Adobe application.

FIGURE 2.4

Bridge is a very powerful file browser that comes with Photoshop. It's an independent piece of software that can be used outside of Photoshop. Notice that this figure resembles Lightroom's Library module.

Bridge takes the concept of a file browser to a whole new level. A huge number of things can be done to image files in Bridge, including sorting and managing large groups of images, adding metadata information (which I discuss in Chapters 3 and 5), and even creating Web galleries and picture packages. The problem is that many of these options are not apparent to the casual user.

> **NOTE** Adobe Bridge comes with Photoshop and is automatically installed when you install Photoshop.

Though Bridge is one of the most important parts of Photoshop for photographers, few seem to be aware of its power. I am often amazed at how many professional photographers I meet who use Photoshop but don't know how to launch Bridge. The main thing to understand now is that outside of Lightroom it's the primary conduit for managing and opening image files in Photoshop.

> **CROSS-REF** See Chapter 11 for an in-depth discussion of Adobe Bridge.

Adobe Camera Raw

In the last few years, serious photographers have begun to shoot in a file format called *camera raw*. Raw files are discussed in detail in Chapter 3. For now, I'll describe them as files that are captured in a special way so that they contain a huge amount of information. This extra information is extremely valuable for photographers seeking the highest quality. Most professional photographers I know use this format exclusively.

One of the problems with raw files is that they are not your usual image file. Each raw file needs to be converted to a standard type of file before it can be edited. This conversion process is handled by an intermediate software application called Adobe Camera Raw (ACR), as shown in Figure 2.5. That means that when a raw file is opened from Bridge it has to go through the conversion process in ACR before it can be edited in Photoshop.

Adobe Camera Raw allows the photographer to adjust settings like tonality and color, as well as reduce noise and modify esoteric qualities like noise and chromatic aberration during the conversion process. Because these edits are performed on raw files they are nondestructive due to the special nature of raw files. The ability to manage all of these features of a raw file while it's being converted for use in Photoshop is powerful. However, the fact that raw files required a different workflow has frightened many would-be raw shooters away from the file format because they don't understand how to use ACR.

FIGURE 2.5

The Adobe Camera Raw (ACR) interface allows raw files to be fine-tuned before they are converted for editing in Photoshop. ACR contains a large number of tools for modifying tone and color, as well as other, more esoteric file qualities.

Three in one

As you can see, Photoshop is more than a single piece of software. Bridge is used to manage groups of images and choose which ones to edit in Photoshop. Adobe Camera Raw is used to edit and convert raw files so that they can be opened in Photoshop. The main Photoshop program is used to retouch and fine-tune images that were selected in Bridge and opened through ACR.

This huge amount of complexity requires a real commitment to the learning curve because the workflow is not very intuitive and fluid for the casual user — especially the photographer who shoots raw. Adobe recognized this problem a few years ago and decided to come up with a novel solution. In the process, it revolutionized the approach to the photographer's workflow by introducing Adobe Photoshop Lightroom in the spring of 2007.

NOTE   The official name is Adobe Photoshop Lightroom. When referring to Lightroom in this book I leave out Photoshop to avoid any confusion while discussing these programs.

Understanding the Purpose of Lightroom

Because almost all of the tools in Lightroom are borrowed from Bridge and ACR it quickly becomes apparent that Lightroom isn't a replacement for Photoshop. Instead, it can be thought of as a replacement for Bridge and ACR. Photoshop is only used when an image needs more advanced editing than what's possible with Bridge and ACR. The good news is that only a small percentage of files need the full editing power of Photoshop.

Database management

With Bridge, it's possible to add all sorts of information to an image such as the location of where the photo was shot, the names of the people in the image, and any other information that may help to identify the image at a later date. This information is embedded in the image with something called *metadata*. The problem with doing this in Bridge is that the metadata system is clumsy and hard to understand. I know only a few of photographers who use it in Bridge to its fullest capability.

CROSS-REF   **Metadata is discussed in more detail in Chapter 4.**

When this feature was brought to Lightroom it was implemented in a very straightforward manner. Now it's easy to add metadata and use it to intuitively filter and track images so they can be located when necessary — even if they're on a hard drive that isn't connected to the computer. This ability is huge. It allows photographers to make sense of the thousands of images on their hard drives.

Nondestructive editing

Earlier I mentioned that editing raw files in ACR is nondestructive because of the special nature of raw files. When the ACR editing tools were added to Lightroom, this nondestructive philosophy was extended to all of the file formats Lightroom works with: JPEG, TIFF, PSD, and raw. That means when you're editing a JPEG photo in Lightroom none of the changes is permanent because none of the edits takes place on the pixel level. The image can be returned to its original state at any time in the future with a single click because all of the changes made to it are recorded in a separate file that keeps track of your changes.

CROSS-REF   **See Chapter 3 for a more detailed discussion of file formats.**

Figure 2.6 shows the Develop module of Lightroom, where most of the image editing in Lightroom occurs. If you compare it to Figure 2.5, you can easily spot the similarities between the Lightroom Develop module and Adobe Camera Raw interface.

FIGURE 2.6

The Develop module in Lightroom bears a striking resemblance to Adobe Camera Raw in Photoshop CS3.

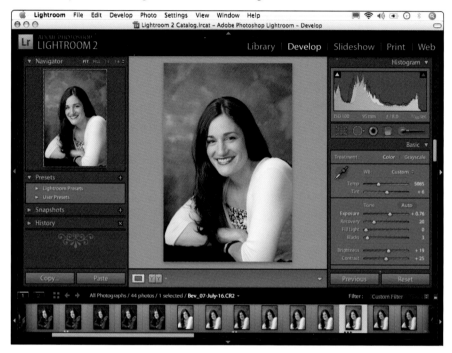

Sharing settings with other files

Another concept that's borrowed from Bridge and ACR is the ability to work quickly with groups of files. In Lightroom, it's possible to edit one image and then share those settings with other, similar images. With Bridge and ACR, this ability is mostly related to raw files. With Lightroom, the concept has been expanded to include all the file types that Lightroom uses. This ability allows photographers who don't shoot raw to work much more quickly with their images. Before Lightroom appeared, it was very difficult to share edit settings with multiple non-raw files. (I can't tell you how many times photographers have asked me how to do this in Photoshop.)

Output options

After images are edited they can be output in several ways. Customized slide shows and Web sites can be created, or images can be printed in a number of different layouts. Each of the various output options comes with templates that aid with the layout. Files can also be exported — individually or in groups — in a very intuitive and automated way so they're ready for e-mail or printing at a photolab.

The complete package

When you put all of these pieces together it's easy to see that Lightroom has three main functions: file management, nondestructive editing, and multiple output options. For many photographers this represents their complete workflow. However, for photographers who are interested in creating finished masterpieces it leaves something to be desired. But that's okay. That's where Photoshop comes into play. When an important image is selected in Lightroom, it can be opened in Photoshop with all of the Lightroom settings in effect so that it's ready for what I call heavy lifting in Photoshop.

Used together, Lightroom and Photoshop represent the complete digital workflow. Lightroom is used as a funnel to intuitively work quickly and efficiently with large groups of images. During this funneling process the most important images are identified. Once these images emerge, they're moved into Photoshop where special tools are used for the final polishing that turns these images into the special gems that they are.

Summary

Photoshop is one of the most powerful image-editing tools available. It's used by all kinds of people with diverse image-editing needs. This power comes at a price, however, that takes the form of a steep learning curve due to Photoshop's complexity and not-so-intuitive user interface.

Something that makes Photoshop even harder to learn for the photographer — especially if he is shooting in the raw format — is the fact that three separate software packages have to be mastered to get the most efficiency. They are Adobe Bridge, Adobe Camera Raw, and Photoshop itself. Each has its own toolsets and user interface.

Lightroom was designed to provide an intuitive and efficient workflow for photographers who are managing large numbers of images. It's perfectly suited to the digital workflow whether raw or non-raw files are being edited. However, Lightroom is not a replacement for Photoshop. It's more of a replacement for Bridge and Adobe Camera Raw. When a file requires serious editing Photoshop is still necessary.

Together, Photoshop and Lightroom offer the total post-production package for digital photographers. Lightroom is used for the production portion of the workflow where speed and efficiency are needed, and Photoshop is used to perfect special images individually during the creative phase where high quality is a must. This book is about this interplay between these two programs and how to effectively use each of them to create the complete digital workflow.

Chapter 3

Understanding Image File Basics

When you begin shooting digitally it's tempting to create a filing system I call the "bucket system." In this filing system you create individual folders for the main things you shoot. Every time you photograph one of those things you place the images into the appropriate bucket. Pictures of my wife get placed into a folder with her name, photos of the dogs are placed into folders with their names, photos of the mountains are place into a folder named Mountains, and on and on it goes. This system seems to make sense, but it really doesn't because photos from a particular shoot are spread all over the place. I can't look at a single folder and see the photos of my wife, the dogs, and the mountains that were all shot on the same backpacking trip. This problem is compounded when files for each bucket are created for the same original image.

This chapter looks at a more organized way of dealing with your images. Once you learn it, you'll find that it makes much more sense than the bucket system because it's based on the most common filing system there is — the filing cabinet.

IN THIS CHAPTER

Creating an organizational system that works like a virtual file cabinet

Understanding the file formats used in digital photography

Organizing the files that are created in a typical workflow

Protecting your work by backing up and archiving files

Creating a Virtual Filing Cabinet

Imagine a filing cabinet for a moment. Your filing cabinet has three drawers. Each of those drawers is used to store folders with specific information in them. Sometimes a folder contains subfolders inside of it. If you think about it, this is much the same way filing occurs on a computer. Images are placed inside folders and those folders are placed inside larger folders.

Figure 3.1 shows a typical filing strategy with the following file path: Photos ⇨ 2008 ⇨ Alice ⇨ individual files of Alice. The folder named Photos (in the first column) is my filing cabinet. It has three drawers named 2006, 2007, and 2008. Each of those drawers has a bunch of folders in it. The third column shows the folders inside of the 2008 drawer. The last column shows the individual images inside of the folder named Alice.

FIGURE 3.1

This image shows the file structure of a virtual file cabinet. The Photos folder represents the file cabinet. The subfolders titled for each year, in the second column, represent the drawers of the file cabinet.

The previous example uses three levels of organization:

- **One main folder contains all images.** This is incredibly useful when it comes to backing up photos because only one folder — with its subfolders — needs to be copied. (If you have an extra hard drive, it can be used instead of a folder.)

- **Subfolders are created for each individual year.** This level of organization prevents you from having to sort through folders from previous years unless you want to.

- **Shoot/Job folders are used to hold the files from an individual photo shoot.** This folder, as you'll see in a moment, is often divided into subfolders containing different kinds of files. Creating a filing system like this is the first step to becoming organized. The next step is to begin using a folder and file naming system that complements the kind of photography you do.

Folder naming strategies

When it comes to naming folders — and the files stored inside them — there are two predominant lines of thought. One is to name folders with dates and the other is to use descriptive names that describe the photos. Let's look at both of these strategies so you can determine which is best for you.

Naming folders with dates

Some photographers prefer to name all shoot/job folders with the date they were shot, or in some cases uploaded. That way every folder is listed in chronological order. Imagine that I go to the Oregon coast this weekend and shoot a bunch of photos over the three days that I'm there. When

I get back to my computer and upload the files I create three different folders — one When I upload the files I make sure that they go into their respective folders (that is tos into Friday's folder, Saturday's into the Saturday folder, and so on.).

At first, this naming strategy seems confusing because I have to remember when I went to the coast to find the photos later. However, if I use keywords to identify the contents of the photos, I can locate photos with specific image content whenever I need to.

NOTE A keyword is a descriptive term that you attach to a photo to describe something about it. These keywords are added to the photos file. For example, if I go to the coast I can use keywords such as "beach, seagulls, tide pool, and ocean" to identify the contents of various photos. Later, if I search for the keyword *seagulls*, I can find all photos with seagulls in them.

CROSS-REF Chapter 6 covers keywords in detail.

Part of the thought process behind this strategy is that using keywords allows photographers to find images when they need them, no matter which folder the images are in. If I keyword all of my photos from the coast correctly, I can use those keywords to locate them later. I don't need to give my coast folder a name that describes its contents. Instead, I can name it 2008_07_21. If I take the time to add keywords to each image, I'll be able to find them in a snap with Lightroom's powerful search and filter functions.

The key to using this naming strategy is to use the right date format so that folders are sorted in the correct order. The preferred method is Year_Month_Day. This way every file is sorted in the correct order, beginning with the year first, then the month, then the day. Some people like to make life easier by adding a descriptive name to the end of the date. So my folder earlier becomes 2008_01_21_Oregon_Coast.

NOTE Notice that I used an under bar (_), (Shift+-) to separate the numbers in the dates. This is better than leaving a space, especially if you plan to upload the photos to the Web because most Web servers replace a space with "%20". Some don't even accept files with a space in the name. You can also use a hyphen (-) or you can run the numbers together. I prefer to keep things easy to read.

CAUTION Mac users can use a slash (/) in a folder name instead of a hyphen, though Windows users may not be able to see the folder because / is an illegal character in a Windows environment.

One of the main drawbacks to using this system is that it tends to spread out similar images too much. In its purest form, all photos are placed into dated folders that represent the day they were created. If I take a trip to Europe for two weeks and then download all of my photos using the date naming system, I end up with a folder for every day. If I took pictures every day, then my vacation photos would be spread out into 14 folders. A better way to use this system is to create a main folder with a general date — such as the date the files were uploaded — and then add all files to this one folder instead of placing them into individual daily folders.

Naming folders with descriptive names

The other strategy is to use a descriptive name to identify a shoot. With this strategy, the folder from my coast expedition is named Oregon_Coast_08. If I took more than one trip to the coast in 2008, I would add the month after the year. An advantage to this strategy is that folder names have a more descriptive name. Another advantage is that all photos from the shoot are located in one main folder.

The main disadvantage is that folders are sorted alphabetically by your system, instead of chronologically. If that's important to you, then this system may not be the best choice. Another disadvantage is that a single descriptive name doesn't always describe everything in the folder. This happens when you allow lots of images to collect on your camera's media card before uploading them. One way to solve this is to do multiple uploads from the camera's card—placing groups of images into individual folders with descriptive names. Another way to solve this is to regularly upload your photos so they don't accumulate on the card.

Choosing a folder naming system

I know photographers who use each of these systems. The people who tend to use the date system are photographers who shoot lots of images like commercial and stock shooters. They also tend to be photographers who are highly organized with their keywording and DAM systems.

The photographers who tend to use the descriptive name method are mostly portrait and wedding photographers who are more oriented to locating jobs by the client's name. They don't always find it useful to spend lots of time organizing these jobs with keywords, because once the job is completed, they most likely won't be going back to those images very often. Also, if they use keywords with the client's name, then their keywords list becomes filled with keywords that are never used.

Photographers who don't fall into either of these camps tend to use a blend of the two naming systems. If the images in the folder can be categorized with a descriptive name—such as Hawaii 08, or Jones Wedding—then they use a name. When the images don't have a predominant theme, they use a general date for the name and then use keywords to identify the individual images.

Let's say you have some photos of the kids playing in the yard last month and some other photos you shot on a walk in the woods last week. These could be uploaded into separate folders named Kids_in_the_yard and Walk_in_the_Woods. The problem is that these names aren't too descriptive even if dates are added to the ends of the names. After you have a few dozen folders with names like these, you find that you need to use keywords to find them anyway. It would be better to put these images into a single folder with a date-style name. That way you cut down on meaningless names and all of those folders are in chronological order on the folder tree.

Naming original files

Digital cameras automatically create filenames for every photo you shoot. Sometimes those names are quite cryptic. A filename like MG9769 doesn't tell me much about the file, even if I understand why the camera created that name in the first place. That's why I always like to use descriptive names that tell me something about the image when naming original files. I might use something like Jane_Doe_123 instead of the name created by the camera because it makes more sense on a couple of levels. First, if I ever need to find Jane's photos using their names, I can do a system search with my computer's operating system for Jane_Doe. Without a descriptive name, this becomes impossible.

The second reason a descriptive filename makes sense is that eventually derivative files for editing and output will be created from some of the originals. It's easier to keep those files organized when you begin with a descriptive name.

Understanding File Formats

Now that you know something about file organization, let's look at some of the different types of files that get stored in your virtual filing cabinet. These various file types are known as file formats.

Think of file formats as different languages. When a book is printed in a particular language, only someone who reads the language can understand it. If the reader knows a second language, he can translate the book into that other language, making it available to other people. This is similar to the way file formats in Lightroom and Photoshop work. Certain file languages are used for different purposes. As an image moves through the digital workflow it's translated into the language that's most appropriate for that particular portion of the workflow.

When discussing how file formats fit into the workflow, it's useful to divide them into three groups — *image capture formats*, *editing formats*, and *output formats*. Image capture file formats are the file types that come directly out of a digital camera. Editing formats are file types that are typically created during the editing process in Photoshop. Output formats are used for specific output such as printing or Web.

Image capture file formats

Digital photographers tend to capture images in one of these two file formats: JPEG and camera raw. The decision between which of these two file formats should be used can have a huge impact on the possibilities of what can be done during the editing process. Let's compare and contrast these file formats so you can make your own decision as to which format is best for you.

JPEG

The JPEG file type (JPG when used as a file extension) was designed to be a space-saving file format. It was created in 1992 by a committee called the Joint Photographic Experts Group (JPEG). The committee's goal was to establish a portable standard for compressing photographic files that would be universal for all kinds of editing software. This compression results in smaller, more portable files.

JPEG files can be created with all digital point-and-shoot and SLR cameras. This is because of the space-saving ability of JPEG files. In the early days of digital cameras, memory cards were small and expensive, so the files had to be small so that more would fit onto the card.

File compression is a system of analyzing a file and looking for common strings of data. When several identical stings are located, they're replaced by a single representative string with references to all the places where it appears in the image. Compression can substantially reduce file size when images contain lots of the same tones, such as solid backgrounds. Images with lots of details and colors won't compress as much.

When saving a JPEG file you're presented with the option to determine the amount of compression that's applied to the file. Greater amounts of compression yield smaller file sizes. Let's look at an example to see this in action. Figure 3.2 shows the JPEG Options dialog box that appears when saving a JPEG file in Photoshop. In this case, an image that is 24.8MB becomes a 3.2MB JPEG with a compression quality of 12. If the compression on this file is lowered by two, to 10 instead of 12, the file size is reduced by two-thirds to 1.0MB without adversely affecting the image quality.

FIGURE 3.2

The JPEG Options dialog box lets you compress the size of your image. The higher the Quality number in the JPEG Options dialog, the lower the amount of compression. The saved file in this case will be 3.2MB, shown just below the Preview check box.

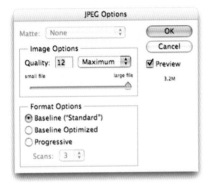

JPEG compression is a double-edged sword. Very small files can be created with high compression, but JPEG compression is *lossy*, meaning that information is lost during the compression process, affecting image quality. The amount of loss depends on the amount of compression. Additionally, whenever a file is resaved and compressed again, more data is lost. The key is to limit the total loss by compressing a JPEG file only once — not editing and resaving the file later on. That's why the JPEG file format is not considered an editing format. If you think you'll be reopening a JPEG and resaving it, choose the highest quality when saving — or better yet, save it as a TIFF until you're through editing.

JPEG is one of the most widely used file formats for digital imaging. Virtually any software that can open an image file can open a JPEG. What's more, nearly all the photographs you see on the Internet are JPEG files — at least the ones that look good. That's because JPEGs can be *compressed* to very small sizes, which is perfect for online delivery or e-mail where quality isn't as important.

> **NOTE** The JPEG file type is a capture file type and an output file type. The same is true for TIFF.

Camera raw

Camera raw files get their name from the kind of information they contain. When I point my digital SLR camera at a scene and click the shutter, the camera's chip captures a huge amount of information. If I have the camera set to capture JPEG files, the camera's onboard processor processes all that information into a JPEG file. The processor looks at all the settings I have dialed into my camera — sharpness, white balance, color space, contrast, and so on. Then it applies all these settings and creates the JPEG file from a small sliver of the data that the chip recorded. The rest of the information — most of what was captured — is ignored and deleted. Even if the JPEG is of the highest quality (least compression), it represents a fraction of what the camera actually saw.

The JPEG process seems easy because it allows the camera to make lots of decisions very quickly. If I'm working in a very controlled environment, or under extreme deadlines, this can be a fast way to work. The problem is that I don't get to look at all the information before it gets thrown away. When you shoot JPEG, you have to live with the data the camera selects to create the JPEG files. A great analogy is that shooting JPEG is just like shooting film and then taking the film to the lab and telling it to process a set of proofs and throw the film away.

Camera raw is the solution to this problem. It allows you to save most of the information that a camera's chip is capable of capturing. After you have this information in a file, you can selectively choose which information becomes part of the file by converting the data from the raw file into a working file that editing software like Photoshop can use.

The mechanics of a raw file

So what is *raw*? A raw file is a grayscale image. This means that qualities like color attributes and color space have not been assigned to the file. In fact, the only camera settings that are permanently part of a raw file are ISO, aperture, and shutter speed. Everything else is up for grabs during the conversion process. Decisions like color space or white balance settings can be made after the exposure was made. This is why you often hear raw files described as being "digital negatives." They are open to a great deal of interpretation during conversion, just like the process a film photographer goes through in a darkroom as she interprets a negative.

One of the big things to understand about raw is that digital capture is linear in nature. Without getting too technical, this means that it devotes more bits to capturing highlights than it does to capturing shadows. This is the opposite of the way humans see things. We're really good at distinguishing detail in the shadows and not very good at seeing detail in the highlights. Film was designed to mimic human vision, so it works in much the same way.

The way a raw file records information is different. A typical 12-bit raw file captures 4096 distinct tonal levels within a six-stop range. Because this is a linear capture, a full 50 percent (2048 levels) of the file's tonal information is devoted to the brightest stop of information. Only 1.6 percent (64 levels) of the file's tonal information is devoted to recording shadow detail, as shown in Figure 3.3.

FIGURE 3.3

A typical raw file covers about six stops of exposure with 4096 tonal levels recorded. Because raw files are linear, they devote a large amount of their capturing ability to recording highlights and a small amount to recording shadows.

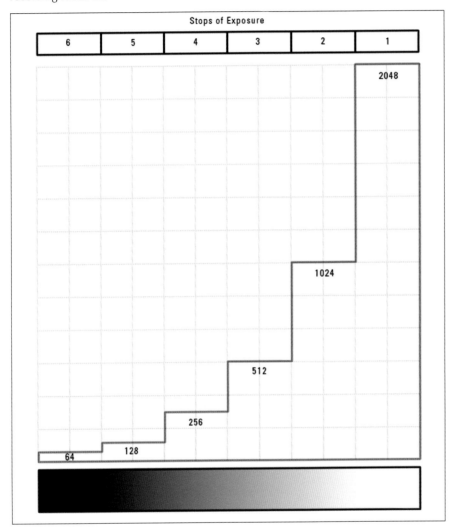

NOTE Some new, higher-end dSLR cameras are capable of capturing 14-bit raw files that capture 16,384 tonal levels.

When an image is underexposed, as shown in the first diagram of Figure 3.4, half of the levels in the file are wasted on information that wasn't captured in the brightest stop. If the camera is adjusted to move the histogram to the right by increasing exposure, then the brightest stop of information is used. Now it describes the highlights in the image, as shown in the second diagram of Figure 3.4. Because so much information describes these highlights, detail that seems lost at first can be recaptured. (Also, notice that twice as many levels are being used to describe the shadows.)

FIGURE 3.4

When a raw file is underexposed, half of the file's bandwidth is wasted on information that isn't recorded, as shown in the first diagram. When the brightest part of a scene is exposed correctly, you take advantage of the ability of a raw file to capture highlight detail. The correct exposure moves the rest of the image's tonal levels to the right, so that each gets twice as much information dedicated to describing it, as shown in the second diagram.

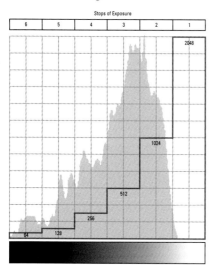 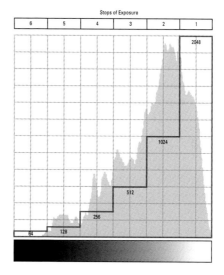

I know this flies in the face of conventional wisdom for a JPEG shooter. When you shoot JPEG, a highlight that is overexposed is gone forever. When you shoot raw, this isn't always the case. I shot the barn in Figure 3.5 when I was photographing flowers at a local tulip field. When I shot this picture, I forgot that I had a +2-stop bias dialed into my camera's exposure meter. When I got home and looked at the image, I realized that I had overexposed it, as shown in the first image in Figure 3.5. Fortunately, this was a raw file with 50 percent of its capturing bandwidth devoted to describing the highlights. I was able to recover all highlight detail, as shown in the second image of Figure 3.5. If this image had been shot in JPEG, the file would have been useless.

FIGURE 3.5

This barn photo was exposed two stops too bright. The first image shows how the image would have looked if it had been captured as a JPEG. The second image shows the amount of highlight detail that was hidden, ready to be revealed during the raw conversion process.

So here's the thing to remember: If you're shooting raw, be sure to fully expose for the highlights. Needing to darken an image and compress shadow detail is better than needing to lighten an image and spread out the shadow levels because there isn't much information to work with in the shadow tones. Additionally, most of the *noise* in a digital file is in the shadows. When you lighten shadow detail you reveal this noise. Naturally, nailing your exposures right the first time is always best. But if you're going to err on one side or the other of a perfect exposure, make sure that you err in the overexposed direction when shooting raw.

NOTE Noise in a digital file usually looks grainy. It's called *noise* because it's created by the operation of the system. It's similar to the light hum I hear on my speakers when no music is playing. When I turn the speakers up all the way, the noise becomes more noticeable. The same is true for digital noise. When you underexpose or shoot with a high ISO, any noise becomes more apparent. It's like turning up the volume on my speakers.

A true digital negative

Calling a raw file a digital negative makes sense because it shares another important trait of a film negative. Altering a raw file permanently while editing in Lightroom or Photoshop is virtually impossible. The file can be interpreted in many ways, but none of the conversions alters the underlying file. Instead, a set of metadata instructions is written to describe the way the raw file is meant to look while a new file for editing is created from the conversion.

When I convert a raw file and open it in Photoshop, it becomes something different than a raw file. Here's what I mean: My Canon shoots with the raw file format of .CR2. When I save an open file in Photoshop, the Save As dialog box doesn't include a format called CR2. This makes it impossible to overwrite the original raw file.

CAUTION You may notice an option in the drop-down list called Photoshop Raw. This isn't a camera raw file format. Photoshop Raw is used as a flexible file format for transferring files from one computer platform to another (Mac, PC, Unix, and so on) or between exotic applications.

The word *metadata* literally means data about data. Each digital camera file contains metadata about the file and the camera that created it, as well as information about any editing done to the file during the production phase of the workflow. (The keywords I discussed earlier are a form of metadata.) This means that no matter what you make a raw file look like when you convert it, you can always return the original file to the way it looked the day your camera created it. Any adjustments you make are simply written to a metadata file that can be overwritten at any time.

I imagine that you're starting to see lots of advantages to shooting raw. However, I'd be remiss if I didn't take a moment to warn you about some of the disadvantages.

Disadvantages of shooting raw

Camera raw allows you to make all sorts of interesting adjustments to an image post-capture, but that means that you have to take time to do something that the camera often does a pretty decent job of doing when it creates a JPEG. You have to convert every raw image into some other format for editing such as TIF or PSD. This conversion process used to be considered laborious. Fortunately that isn't the case anymore because Lightroom treats raw files and non-raw files virtually the same.

Another problem is that raw files are much bigger than JPEG files. They can run two to four times larger because lots more information is being saved. This means that raw files consume media cards and hard drives much faster than their JPEG cousins. I've spoken to many wedding shooters who shoot their first raw wedding without being aware of this size issue. In a panic, halfway through the wedding, they had to switch the camera to medium-quality JPEG because they had already consumed most of their media cards with large raw files. This problem can be solved with a little preparation. Media cards are cheap now. If you are shooting raw, buy some extras.

The biggest issue regarding the raw format is that there are many varieties of raw. Each camera company creates its own version of the raw format. In fact, these companies often have several slightly different versions that all have the same name. For example, my Canon camera shoots raw files with the extension of CR2. Other Canon dSLRs also share this format name, yet the files are different; different algorithms are used to convert them. Adobe estimates that at least 200 different versions of the raw file format exist. When a camera manufacturer comes out with a new camera, even though the raw format still has the same name, Lightroom and Adobe Camera Raw can't read the files until they have time to evaluate the new version. Adobe tries to keep up with this by releasing frequent updates to Lightroom and ACR.

If you think about this for a moment, a nightmare scenario emerges. Because these files are proprietary they're linked to the manufacturer that created them. What if that manufacturer goes out of business and stops supporting the product? Over time, all of the tools for opening its files could disappear. Imagine wanting to open an important photo file 15 years from now and not being able to. I doubt that this will happen, but who knows what the future holds.

NOTE   **Adobe is attempting to address this issue with the creation of a standardized raw format called DNG (Digital Negative). Adobe's goal is to get everyone using the same standard so that all these problems caused by different versions of raw go away.**

Now you know some of the main disadvantages to shooting raw. I hope you see that the advantages far outweigh the disadvantages, especially when using Lightroom for the production phase of the workflow. The only real downside is the size of the original files. With the low cost of hard drives, this disadvantage pales in comparison to the data-capturing capacity of a raw file.

Understanding metadata and XMP

Metadata is a standardized set of information that describes characteristics about a file. This information refers to details like copyright, resolution, color space, and keywords. For now the main thing to understand is that metadata is an important feature of a raw file. It prevents any editing from being destructive to the original file. In the case of JPEG, TIFF, and PSD metadata, information is saved inside of the file and becomes part of it. However, metadata in a raw file is handled in a completely different manner.

As stated earlier, there are many proprietary versions of raw. Because of that proprietary nature Adobe doesn't have access to the details of the math that's used to create these files. Understanding that this could lead to problems, Adobe made a wise decision a long time ago to prevent any of its products from altering raw files. Otherwise no one could guarantee that writing even basic information like keywords wouldn't produce unpredictable results and corrupt a file.

To get around this issue, a system called *sidecar XMP* is used to create a second XMP (Extensible Metadata Platform) file with the same root name. The new file containing only metadata is saved right next to the original raw file. For example, if I edit a raw file named `file123.cr2`, an XMP file named `file123.xmp` is automatically placed in the folder right next to it. These XMP files are tiny files, yet they not only contain information like copyright and keywords, they also contain all of the editing changes that have been made to the file like tonality, color, and cropping.

> **NOTE** If the XMP file is deleted, the original raw file reverts to what it looked like when it was uploaded from the camera.

The use of metadata and XMP files is why any editing done to a raw file is nondestructive. It's impossible to change the original file. Any changes made are recorded in the XMP file. Every time you view a raw file that's been modified you see it through the filter of the XMP file. Take a moment to absorb this because it's a huge concept to understand. Before Lightroom, when working in Photoshop this nondestructive ability only worked with raw files. When Lightroom was introduced, this use of metadata to describe every detail of a file without changing the original file was extended to JPEG, TIFF, and PSD files. Now, in Lightroom, the editing workflow for the two main capture file formats, JPEG and camera raw, are both nondestructive. This makes the editing workflows for each format virtually the same.

Advantages of using DNG for metadata

I mentioned earlier that Adobe created a universal file format called DNG in an effort to eliminate confusion and standardize an emerging format. There's another important feature of DNG files that I didn't mention. Because it created the DNG format, Adobe understands it perfectly. This allows it to place metadata inside of a DNG file instead of attaching an XMP sidecar file to it. (By the way, did I mention that Adobe also developed the XMP format?) This allows the DNG file to be more efficient because it eliminates the need for sidecar files.

Some high-end digital cameras are able to capture images in the DNG format. However, DNG files are usually created by converting proprietary raw files into the DNG format when importing files in Lightroom, which you learn about in Chapter 5.

Editing file formats

Earlier I stated that raw files cannot be edited with Photoshop during the creative part of the workflow. A conversion process must take place to convert the file into a format that's recognized by the editing software. In the case of Photoshop, the file formats are JPEG, TIFF, and PSD.

Though JPEG files can be edited in Photoshop, that's not really what they are best used for. The main attraction of the JPEG format is the ability to compress the file so that it consumes less space. Because that compression often comes with the price of reduced quality, it's best to only use JPEG files when file size is an issue — usually capture and output.

Another reason the JPEG format isn't very useful for the creative phase of the workflow is the inability to save *layers* in a JPEG file. A layer is just that — a segment of image information that's stacked on top of the original image. This ability to isolate different aspects of the image allows a great deal of control over the image as a whole. As you see in Chapter 14, the use of layers is the central concept behind creating a nondestructive workflow when editing in Photoshop.

TIFF

TIFF (or TIF when used as a file extension) stands for Tagged Image File Format. TIFF is a flexible format that's supported by virtually all image-editing and graphics software. Layers can be saved in TIFF, and the format supports a number of color models that JPEGs don't support like CMYK and LAB.

CROSS-REF See Chapter 13 for more information on color models.

A TIFF file can be compressed just like a JPEG file. Normally, a TIFF file is larger than a PSD file (Photoshop's native format, which is discussed in the next section) that's saved from the same image. That's because PSD files are compressed a bit by default to make them smaller when they're saved.

With a TIFF file, compression doesn't happen automatically, it's an option. It must be selected in the TIFF Options dialog box when the file is first saved, as shown in Figure 3.6. Photoshop offers three different types of TIFF file compression: LZW, ZIP, and JPEG. The main difference among these three compression methods is that LZW and ZIP are *lossless* compression methods and JPEG is a *lossy* method of compression — just like the compression used on JPEG files.

FIGURE 3.6

When a TIFF file is saved for the first time, four compression options are available: None, LZW, ZIP, and JPEG.

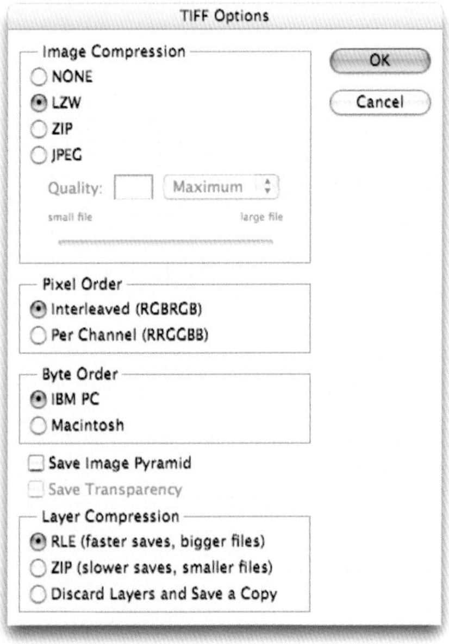

When an image is compressed, the data is generally handled in one of two ways:

- **Lossless compression:** All information is retained during the compression. This means that an image can be resaved and recompressed without compromising image quality.

- **Lossy compression:** During compression, data is permanently removed. Higher levels of compression result in greater data loss. Every time a file is resaved with lossy compression, more data is lost. This cumulative data loss can greatly affect quality.

When compressing a TIFF file, stick with lossless compression by selecting LZW or ZIP. They're fairly equal in performance, and Photoshop opens either of them. However, be aware that ZIP is not supported in older software. I compress a TIFF file only when I'm planning to e-mail or FTP it to someone and I want to save space. Many people compress all TIFF files to save room on their drives.

Another option with TIFF files in Photoshop is the ability to save layers. This seems pretty cool, except that few image-editing applications can open all of the layers of a layered TIFF file. If I'm saving a layered file and planning to use Photoshop to edit it, then I save it as a PSD file, Photoshop's native file format. If you're worried about hard drive space, go ahead and save your layered files in the compressed TIFF format. Just be aware that they will take longer to save and to open.

Because I don't use layered TIFF files I have Photoshop warn me when I forget to flatten a TIFF file before saving it. I select the Ask Before Saving Layered TIFF Files option in the Photoshop File Handling Preferences dialog box. (This dialog is shown in Figure 3.8.). When this box is checked, a warning, shown in Figure 3.7, appears to remind me that I'm about to save a layered TIFF file. When I see this warning I know I have to either flatten the file or save it as a PSD.

CROSS-REF Chapter 12 discusses Photoshop's preferences.

FIGURE 3.7

When you select the Ask Before Saving Layered TIFF Files option in the File Handling Preferences dialog box, Photoshop reminds you that the TIFF file you're about to save contains multiple layers.

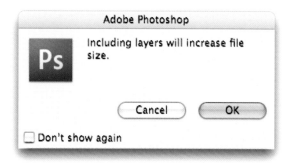

PSD

PSD is Photoshop's proprietary default file format. It supports more Photoshop features than JPEG or TIFF. One of the big advantages of working with PSD is that other Adobe products like Illustrator can open PSD files and access all the saved features. This makes life easier for people who move back and forth between those Adobe software applications.

A special option can be set in Photoshop's preferences that maximizes PSD file compatibility when saving a PSD. With this option turned on, a composite version of all the layers in the image is embedded in the file. It's like a little snapshot of the layered image. This composite can be read by other non-Adobe applications as well as earlier versions of Photoshop so that you can at least see what the file looks like. The downside to doing this is that the PSD file is larger because of the embedded composite. However, if you plan to catalog PSD files with Lightroom, you'll need this preview so that Lightroom can display the image. If it isn't present, Lightroom won't import the image. Instead, you get a warning that says, "The files could not be read. Please re-open the files in Photoshop and save them with the Maximize Compatibility preference enabled."

So it's a good idea to turn on Maximize PSD File Compatibility when Lightroom is part of the workflow. To learn how this is done, open Photoshop and follow these steps:

1. Go to Photoshop's Preferences:

   - Mac: Photoshop ⇨ Preferences ⇨ General
   - PC: Edit ⇨ Preferences ⇨ General

2. Choose File Handling from the menu on the left. The Preferences dialog box opens.

3. Under Maximize PSD and PSB File Compatibility, click the pop-up, as shown in Figure 3.8, and choose Always. Click OK.

   If you choose Ask, Photoshop asks you before saving a PSD file. This is a good way to make the compatibility choice on a case-by-case basis, but it adds an extra step.

TIP   The dialog shown in Figure 3.8 is also where you can choose to have Photoshop warn you when saving layered TIFF files by checking Ask Before Saving Layered TIFF Files.

One of the big advantages to using PSD is that all layer information is preserved and stored. When the image is opened, it goes to the state that it was in when it was last saved. All the layers are there, and the last active layer is still active. When you work extensively with layers, as you do later in this book, saving them becomes important.

FIGURE 3.8

The File Handling preference in Photoshop CS3 allows you to choose how Photoshop handles PSD file compatibility. The Ask option allows you to make the choice each time you create a new PSD file using the Save or Save As commands.

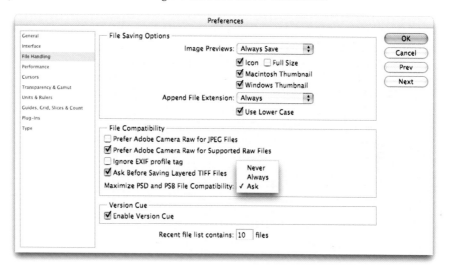

Output file formats

After all of the work is done some kind of file needs to be generated for output. This output often takes the form of a slide show, a print, or a Web site. The JPEG file format is the most common file type for all of these uses. In fact, when it's time to have prints made, you'll find that most photolabs only accept JPEG files because they take up less room on their servers and move through their workflow faster.

NOTE If you print with an inkjet printer you can print from any of the editing file formats.

Sometimes a TIFF is preferred when a file is being prepared for publication. This is because the publication workflow takes place in a CMYK color space, which cannot be used with the JPEG file format. When saving a layered TIFF file for this use, be sure to flatten it unless you have specific instructions from the graphic artist handling the project. Otherwise, she may not be able to see all layers of the image in her layout software.

CROSS-REF For more information on color spaces, see Chapter 13.

Now that you understand the different file formats, let's look at how those various formats are used in the workflow.

Organizing Different Kinds of Files

When you first get interested in digital imaging, you may not realize just how quickly the digital dream can become an organizational nightmare. In the days of shooting film, organization was just as important, though much more intuitive. After film was developed, it — and its associated proofs or contact sheets — was placed in a box or file cabinet. When a negative was needed for printing, there was a clear idea of where to find it.

With digital photography, organization is more complicated. For one thing, the place where image files are stored isn't quite so intuitive. Sometimes, files end up in cryptic places requiring three software engineers to find them. Second, working with digital images tends to create lots and lots of derivative files from some original files. When so many similar yet different files are created, organization takes on a whole new meaning. Finding a particular photo is important, but finding a particular interpretation of that particular photo is even more important.

Considering the nondestructive workflow

One of the other ways to limit the destructiveness of image editing is to avoid cropping and image-size adjustments in Photoshop whenever possible. If these changes are made and the file is closed, they become permanent. What if you decide tomorrow that you don't like the cropping you did, or what if you crop to a 5 x 7 but the client decides she wants a 16 x 20? These things happen all the time. You can protect yourself by always saving a master file before doing anything that permanently changes the image.

The problem is that you need to flatten and crop files at some point. You usually do this when you're giving someone else a copy of the file, taking it to a lab to be printed, or uploading it to a Web site. To solve this problem, save two separate files. Keep a master file (PSD) that retains all the flexibility possible in a PSD and a final file (JPEG or TIFF) that has been flattened, sized, and prepared for sharing or printing. Often, you'll prepare multiple final files from the same original image for different uses. These files begin to add up, creating a level of complexity that was never a problem when everyone shot film.

Three kinds of files

With the workflow in this book, you are working with three kinds of files: originals files from the camera, master files that contain as much information as possible (usually in layers), and final files for printing or display. Both a master file and any related final files are derivatives of the same original file. Let's look at these three kinds of file:

- **Original files:** These are the capture files from your camera that should never be overwritten. When you make changes to an original file, always save it with a new name that's based on the original. Original files need to remain pristine so you can go back to them when necessary — for example, when you learn a new technique. These files should remain in their original file format, which usually is raw or JPEG for dSLR captures. As I mentioned earlier, you can't overwrite a raw file, so this mostly pertains to JPEG files.

- **Master files:** These editing files contain all the flexibility and options that are built into the file as it is edited in Photoshop. Layers are used extensively, and permanent changes such as cropping or sizing are avoided at all costs. These files are almost always saved as PSD files, though they can be saved as layered TIFF files.

- **Final files:** These output files have been prepared for some final usage like print, Web, or e-mail. They have been cropped and sized to a final size and sharpened for output. In some cases, you may have quite a few of these originating from a single original.

> **NOTE** If you're doing your own printing on an inkjet printer, you don't need to flatten an image file or to save it as a JPEG. You can print straight from a layered PSD file. However, if you're going to crop and/or size the file before printing, save a master copy first.

When all these different files from the same image are stored in the same place, they become difficult to manage. They all look similar in Lightroom and Bridge, so you spend time sorting through them. In my workflow, I can't stand to see a bunch of similar images together. I waste too much time trying to figure out which file is the one I want — even when I use descriptive names. To minimize confusion, these three file types need to be organized in two ways: They need to have unique names based on the original file's name, and they need to be in special folders.

Building the system

One of the worst things to do when dealing with these three types of images is to use filenames that don't have the same base name. For example, suppose the original file is named ZOA6337.cr2 because that's what the camera automatically named it, the master file is named sarah_jones123.psd, and the final file for 8 x 10 printing is named girl_in_boat.jpg. This causes problems in two ways. First, if the files are all in the same folder and they're being sorted alphabetically, they're scattered all over among the other files. Second, if you learn some new tricks next year and decide to redo the girl_in_boat.jpg image, you may have trouble remembering from which original file it's derived.

I solve this problem by naming the original file early in the process. Then any new derivative file uses that name as a base. In the previous example, the original file becomes sarah_jones123.cr2, the master file becomes sarah_jones123_edited.psd, and the final file becomes sarah_jones123_8x10.jpg. This way, I know exactly what kind of file I'm looking at just by looking at the name. In the case of sarah_jones123_8x10.jpg I even know that it's been prepared for an 8 x 10 print.

After you establish a naming methodology, you must address the second level of file organization: filing different kinds of files in the appropriate folders. Figure 3.9 shows how I organize my file folders. When I begin a new project, I create a folder for it. In this case, the parent folder is titled Sarah Jones. I place it inside of a main folder called Photos that's used to store all my photo projects on my laptop. I then create three subfolders inside of the Sarah Jones (parent) folder:

- **Originals:** For all original files — JPEG or raw. (You can skip this folder by placing the originals in the parent folder, Sarah Jones, if you want to.)

- **Masters:** For all master files. These are multilayered TIFF or PSD files that are edited in Photoshop.

- **Finals:** For all final files. Sometimes, I break this folder into two subfolders titled Printing and Email so I can stay organized when I send e-mail versions to someone for approval before printing.

This shows how I organized the folder titled Sarah Jones into subfolders. This intuitive organizational system allows me to always know where to find the file I need when I need it.

My goal with this organizational system is to make it so intuitive that I know where everything is without looking. Even though I never do it, I want to be able to call my assistant back at my office and ask her to send a particular file to me if I need it. I can do that because I know exactly where the file should be, and so does she.

Your system doesn't have to look exactly like mine. If necessary, create something that makes more intuitive sense to you because you're the one who needs to understand it. The thing that's most important here is to get a system in place and begin using it now.

Backing Up and Archiving

Why organize all your photos if you don't take the time to back up all of your work? Digital photography offers all kinds of creative opportunities that have changed the way we work with images. Unlike film, though, digital files can disappear in an instant when a hard drive crashes. If proper archiving measures aren't used, a bad hard drive crash can be catastrophic. Let's explore some archiving options and strategies.

Hard drives

One of the easiest ways to create a backup is with a separate hard drive that backs up all image files. In its more sophisticated form, this is often an array of hard drives that are set up to act as one. This kind of array is called a *RAID* — Redundant Array of Independent Disks. Several different schemes are used to protect file integrity on a RAID. Here are the two main ones:

- **Mirroring:** Identical data is written to more than one disk. If a disk in this array crashes, identical data is recovered from the mirrored disk.

- **Striping:** Information is spread out across multiple disks. This greatly enhances performance because several disks are doing the job of one disk when reading and writing. However, unless some form of *redundancy* is built into the system, there is no data protection as in mirroring. Setting up some form of redundancy allows for striped data to be recovered after a crash. One method of doing this is by having software that can reconstruct missing data by analyzing data that wasn't lost.

All the workings inside a RAID, mirroring and striping, happen in the background. The best part is that it happens automatically. The RAID just looks like a big hard drive to the computer's operating system. After a RAID is set up, it does its job whether you think about it or not. With the low cost of hard drives today, a RAID is a great option if you're dealing with lots of files.

A less sophisticated hard drive solution is to have a secondary hard drive that's used for storing backup copies. These backups can be created automatically with specially designed software, or they can be created manually by dragging and dropping files. Of these two schemes, the automatic solution is by far the best. With backup software like ChronoSync by Econ Technologies (for Mac) and Microsoft Sync Toy (for Windows), multiple auto-backup scenarios are easy to set up so that you never have to think about them again.

Hard drive storage is a great solution for storing backup files, but this also can lead to a false sense of security. A few years ago, shortly after relocating my office, I had three hard drives crash within months of each other. They were all from different manufactures, and they weren't in a RAID. One of those drives was my main drive that had lots of data files on it. One of the other drives was a backup drive of that same data. Unfortunately, I hadn't taken the time to restore all the backed-up data, so when the second drive crashed, everything was gone.

TIP I solved my crashing hard drive problem by purchasing an uninterruptible power supply (UPS). A UPS is little more than big battery that you plug your computer into. If the power goes out unexpectedly, the UPS kicks in, giving you time to close important files and shut down your computer. Most UPS units also do something else: they clean up the incoming power so it's more stable. That's what solved my crashing problem.

A more extreme nightmare scenario with hard drives is fire and theft. Either of these events can wipe out years of work. You have to think about all these possibilities when you consider the storage of image files. I know several photographers who locate a backup drive or RAID in a hidden portion of their home or office in case of theft. With some of the wireless hard drive solutions appearing today, this is an even more viable option. In the case of fire, the best protection is to have a backup of important data that's stored off-site. This is something you couldn't do back in the days of film because there was only one copy of the original.

TIP Many photographers are beginning to use online storage options for backing up image files. This can be a great solution, too. But if you use online storage, make sure it's not your only backup. We all know what happened to many Internet companies a few years ago when the economy took a dive.

CD/DVD

Another system for backing up and archiving images are CDs and DVDs. CDs and DVDs are cheap, and almost any computer can read them. If handled properly, they'll faithfully preserve data for many years.

NOTE **A debate is currently raging concerning the longevity of CDs and DVDs. Some people say that they can't be trusted, while others say they'll last 100 years. In my own experience, I've seen more hard drives fail than CDs or DVDs. However, some people recopy their CD/DVD archives every few years to ensure longevity.**

CDs and DVDs are not as easy and seamless as using a hard drive, and they don't offer quick access to data. In my mind, they're best used as an adjunct to a hard drive backup — more of an archive that can be pulled out anytime a file needs to be resurrected. In a well-designed workflow, they should be used at two different times. Here's what I recommend to my clients:

- As soon as you finish sorting and renaming a new job or project in Lightroom, burn a CD (or DVD if necessary) of all original files and store it in a safe place. In the case of a professional photographer, that would be in the client's folder.

- After all work for the job or project is done, burn a DVD(s) of all related folders — originals, masters, and finals folders. File this DVD with the first CD/DVD backup you created. If the job or project is important, burn a second copy and store it off-site. Now everything is completely covered. You will probably never need these discs, but it's comforting to know that they are there in case you do. If the job or project is a big one that takes lots of time, then intermediate DVD backups are a good idea. You can use rerecordable media for this.

When working with plastic discs, you need to observe some basic ground rules regarding handling. They scratch easily when dragged across rough surfaces, so they should be in some sort of acid-free sleeve at all times. Keep these additional things in mind when working with CDs and DVDs:

- Try to avoid writing on the top surface. These discs are read by a laser beam that shines up from the bottom through the lower layers of plastic, reflects off the shiny layer on top, and bounces back down. If anything is done to degrade the reflective nature of the surface on the top of the disc, the laser won't be able to read it. Sometimes the acid in a pen's ink can destroy the shiny layer on top.

  If you have to write on a disc, try to do it on the inner circle where the plastic is clear. Another option is to purchase printable CDs and DVDs. These are designed to be printed on with an inkjet printer, so they have a more durable surface.

- Only use labels that are approved for CDs and DVDs. These use adhesive that's acid-free. You really don't know what kind of adhesive is used on a standard mailing label. Besides the adhesive issue, mailing labels can cause a different set of problems. A couple of years ago, a client dropped off a CD with files he wanted me to work on. He labeled the CD with three small, rectangular labels. Each label had a different set of information. I was unable to read this disc on any of my systems because when it was spinning at 10,000 RPM in the disc drive, the labels threw it out of balance.

- Store disks in proper, acid-free sleeves or envelopes. Keep them out of the sun, preferably in the dark. Store them lying flat if possible, rather than upright.

In a perfect world, hard drives and CDs/DVDs are used together with the hard drive acting as an up-to-date backup that can be easily accessed and the plastic discs acting as long-term storage. You don't need a sophisticated backup and archiving system, but you do need a system. Working without one is like a trapeze artist working without a net. When things come crashing down, it can be a real showstopper.

Summary

When working with digital files it's extremely important to get organized. One way to get your head around the organizational structure is to envision a filing cabinet where every image is stored in a special folder. There are a couple of systems for naming these folders — dates and descriptive names. Find which system works for you and use it faithfully.

Photographers use four different file types in their workflow. JPEG and camera raw are file types that are used by digital SLR cameras to capture images so they are called image capture formats. In the workflow described in this book, Lightroom is used for managing and editing these capture formats. When files are opened in Photoshop for advanced editing, master versions are saved in the TIFF and PSD formats to avoid lossy compression and to preserve individual layers that are added in Photoshop.

When you examine the capture file formats it's easy to see that the raw format is superior in every way, except for overall file size. It contains a vast amount of information that is used to interpret the image during the conversion process. Also, raw files are considered to be true digital negative files because it's impossible to change the underlying data in the file while editing in Lightroom or Photoshop. There are a few disadvantages to shooting raw but the opportunities far outweigh the downside.

Metadata refers to information that's embedded inside of digital image files. It is generated by the camera during capture and can be added during the editing process. Metadata with editing information, stored in sidecar XMP files, is what allows raw file editing to be nondestructive. When changes are made none of the original pixels that describe the image is changed.

Adobe's DNG file format is a special type of raw file. In some cases DNG files are created in the camera during image capture. Usually, though, they're created by converting proprietary file format raw files into DNG when importing new files into Lightroom. One of the biggest advantages to DNG is the ability to embed metadata into the file, rather than creating a separate sidecar XMP file.

Because different kinds of image files are used during the complete workflow, it's important to keep them all filed in appropriate folders. This is central to a well-designed organizational system, and the key to sanity when organizing large numbers of derivative files. Think about the analogy of a real file cabinet as you design your own system. Be sure to use a naming strategy that fits the type of photography you do.

After you build your organizational system, take the extra step of backing it up onto auxiliary hard drives and plastic discs. That way, if your system has a hard drive crash, you can quickly be back in the saddle with no serious loss of important files.

Part II

Using Lightroom to Manage Your Production Workflow

Now that we have some of the basics out of the way, it's time to start having some fun. In this part, I show you how easy it is to use Lightroom to quickly move groups of photos through the production phase of the workflow.

We begin by taking a closer look at the modular design of the Lightroom workspace. Then I take you, step-by-step, through the processes of importing new photos, organizing them, editing and fine-tuning them, and outputting them as a slide show, inkjet print, or Web gallery. I also show you how to export all sorts of files, from Adobe's Digital Negative (DNG) format for raw files to JPEGs for e-mail.

Though the emphasis is on efficiency in this phase, there are also many opportunities to easily add creative touches. I point out some of those creative effects along the way and show you how to save them as presets so they'll be ready to apply next time with the click of the mouse.

By the end of this part you'll know everything you need to know to create a Production Workflow with Lightroom that's fast and efficient. That way you'll be able to allocate more of your time for working with special images in the Creative Workflow that comes later.

Chapter 4

Understanding the Lightroom Workspace

Before you begin using Lightroom, take a few moments to orient yourself to its intuitive workspace. This user interface, with its consistent look and feel throughout all modules, is one of the best things about Lightroom. Understanding the consistency is the key to learning to use Lightroom in your workflow because it allows you to move quickly from one module to the next.

As powerful as Lightroom's consistent workspace is, there's one drawback — the workspace isn't as flexible as some other editing programs such as Photoshop. The user can't rearrange key elements by dragging them to different locations. With that said, there are a number of things you can do to quickly change the Lightroom environment and the way images are viewed to make the workspace fit your particular needs.

The least intuitive part of Lightroom is the way preferences are handled. The problem is that they aren't located together in the same place. In this chapter, I guide you through Lightroom's most important preferences. By the end of this chapter, you'll be ready to start off on the right foot when you begin using Lightroom in the next chapter.

Getting a Bird's-Eye View

One of the first things to notice about Lightroom is the simplicity of the overall layout. Figure 4.1 shows the workspace in the Library module. This simple interface consists of panels that are arranged on each side of a central viewing area with a filmstrip running across the bottom. In this image, all of the panels, with the exception of the Navigator, Folders, Histogram, and Quick Develop panels, are collapsed.

FIGURE 4.1

This image shows Lightroom's Library module. All of the major components labeled here are present in each the five modules, although they may look a little different in each module.

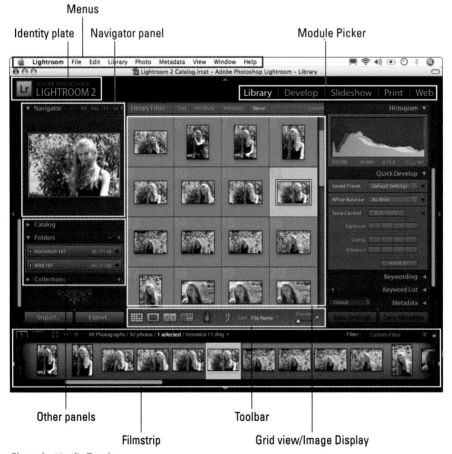

Menus

Identity plate   Navigator panel   Module Picker

Other panels   Toolbar

Filmstrip   Grid view/Image Display

Photos by Natalia Tsvetkov

NOTE   A panel is like a drawer in a toolbox. Each is filled with tools that are used for specific purposes. If you use some of these tools often, you tend to leave the drawers open for easy access. If you don't use a specific toolset much, it's more efficient to keep the drawer closed, opening it only when needed.

One of the reasons this interface is so intuitive is because it does such a great job of placing all of the important tools in just the right places. Something else that helps is that this intuitive interface is used throughout Lightroom, no matter which area you're working in. There are variations in the tools that are available, but the underlying structure is always the same. Following is a breakdown of some of the key features:

■ **Menus:** Lightroom has the usual strip of menu commands across the top of the screen. Something to notice about the menus is that some of them only appear in certain modules. For example, the Library and Metadata menus only appear in the Library module. You visit the menus occasionally in this book, though not as often as you might think, because of Lightroom's well-designed workspace.

■ **Module Picker:** Links to the five main modules: Library, Develop, Slideshow, Print, and Web. These individual modules are part of the genius of Lightroom. They're used to divide the Production Workflow into smaller, more manageable steps.

■ **Panels:** Panels are arranged in two sets on the right and left sides of the screen. You navigate through these panels by using the up and down scrollbars beside them. Panels are opened and closed by clicking the *twirly* next to them, but they cannot be moved or rearranged like the tool palettes in Photoshop.

> **NOTE** A twirly is the small triangular-shaped icon that appears next to the name of the panel. When this triangle is pointed sideways, the panel is collapsed. When it's pointing downward, the panel is open.

■ **Navigator:** This panel provides zoom and navigation features in the Library and Develop modules and also functions as a preview window in all modules.

■ **Grid View/Image Display:** This is the main viewing area in all of the modules. Keep in mind that groups of thumbnails (Grid View) can only be viewed in the Library module.

■ **Toolbar:** The Toolbar contains context-specific tools. These tools vary depending on the module that's currently active. Tools are added and removed from the Toolbar by clicking the twirly on the right-hand side and choosing tools from the menu.

■ **Filmstrip:** A row of images runs across the bottom of the screen in all modules. Figure 4.2 shows a detail of the left side of the Filmstrip. The thumbnails in the Filmstrip give you a second way to view and select images. This is quite useful when the main screen is occupied with a single image. You scroll across images on the Filmstrip using the scrollbar at the bottom of the screen or the arrows at each end of the Filmstrip. (You can also use the right and left arrow keys on your keyboard.) When you position the cursor over an image, the image is previewed in the Navigator panel. When you click an image in the Filmstrip, it becomes the selected image.

FIGURE 4.2

This detail of the left side of the Filmstrip shows a couple of useful items. The Back and Forward arrows allow you to move between views. The Source Indicator provides information about the source of the images that populate the Filmstrip.

- My favorite part of the filmstrip is the set of arrows on the left side of the header. These arrows function just like the back and forward arrows in your Web browser. If you want to move back to a previous view of images, click the Go Back arrow on the left. Naturally, the Go Forward arrow on the right moves you forward.

  Just to the right of these arrows is information about the images being displayed in the Filmstrip. This is called the Source Indicator. It shows the source of the images in the Filmstrip. In this case it's a folder named Photos, and the file path to that folder.

TIP   Click the downward-pointing arrow just after the filename to open a drop-down menu that allows you to quickly jump to a previous view.

All of the features in the previous list appear in each of the five modules. Once you learn to work with these features in one module, you'll be able to apply that learning to the rest of the modules.

Exploring the Five Modules

The five modules in Lightroom divide your workflow into smaller, more manageable pieces, allowing each workspace to be set up for specific uses. The best way to visualize this idea is to imagine a woodworking shop with five work areas arranged next to each other. Each workspace is laid out similarly with the same kinds of tables and benches — only the tools are different because they're specific to the job a particular workspace is used for. The carpentry area has lots of saws, drills, and hammers, while the finishing area has sandpaper and painting supplies. Because all of these work areas are in the same building it's easy and efficient to move a project from one space to the next as it moves through the shop's workflow.

Let's quickly explore the modules in your Lightroom workshop so you get a better idea of what they're used for:

- **Library:** This is one of the most powerful features of Lightroom because it's where all of the digital asset management takes place. The Library module acts as a true database. When image files are properly entered into this database they can be located in a variety of ways, making image sorting and location fast and easy. If your images are cataloged correctly, you'll always be able to find the image you need when you need it.

- **Develop:** This module is the other key feature to Lightroom. This is where nearly all of the nondestructive image editing takes place. Modifications to image qualities such as tone, color, and cropping can be undone at any time. Edits are performed on individual files, as well as groups of files. When a file exits this portion of the workflow it's ready for advanced editing in Photoshop, or output in one of the three output modules (Slideshow, Print, and Web).

- **Slideshow:** The Slideshow module is designed for creating and outputting a wide variety of slide shows. Though this module has some limitations, it's one of the easiest ways to share images with other people. Several design templates are included, and you can also create and save your own.

- **Print:** Like the Slideshow module, the Print module comes with a number of predesigned templates that give you lots of options from fine-art layout to contact sheets. This module is great for outputting quick prints or printing multiple images on the same page, but I don't use it for serious inkjet printing. I still use Photoshop for that.

- **Web:** This is my favorite of the three output modules. It allows you to quickly create Web galleries from your photos. Templates are included for Flash and HTML-style Web pages — and like the Slideshow and Print modules, you can create and save your own templates as presets. If you already have a Web site and want an easy way to upload groups of images to it, this is the way to go because Web galleries can be uploaded directly to your Web site from the Web module.

The Library and Develop modules are the core workspaces and account for most of the average user's Production Workflow. The Slideshow, Print, and Web modules are all oriented to creating different kinds of output near the end of the production phase of the digital workflow.

Looking at Things in Different Ways

Though much of the workspace in Lightroom is static — meaning that the pieces cannot be rearranged — there are still a number of things you can do to change it and the way you view your images. The following sections explore some of these features so you'll know how to make the best use of your screen real estate.

Primary viewing modes

When using the Library module there are two basic views: Grid view and Loupe view. You can move between these views by clicking the Grid View and Loupe View buttons on the left side of the Tools panel or by using the shortcut keys.

- **Grid view (G):** Displays several thumbnails inside of the Image Display, as shown in Figure 4.1. The size of these thumbnails is changed by using the Thumbnails slider located on the right-hand side of the toolbar just below the display area. If you don't see the Thumbnails slider, click the twirly on the right side of the toolbar and make sure Thumbnail Size is checked. If it is, and you still don't see it, you may have to uncheck one of the other tools to get it to fit onto your toolba (You get a closer look at Grid view in Chapter 6.)

 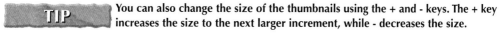

You can also change the size of the thumbnails using the + and - keys. The + key increases the size to the next larger increment, while - decreases the size.

- **Loupe view (E):** Any time a single image is displayed in the Image Display area you're in Loupe view, as shown in Figure 4.3. A loupe is a type of magnifying glass used by film photographers to view film up close. The Loupe view in Lightroom works in a similar way — it magnifies the image in the main viewing area. The best thing about the Loupe in Lightroom is the magnification can be changed by zooming in or out.

FIGURE 4.3

When an image is viewed in Loupe view it's the only image visible in the image display area. It can be viewed at different zoom magnifications by clicking one of the circled presets. When the image is magnified a box appears in the Navigator window indicating which part of the image is being displayed.

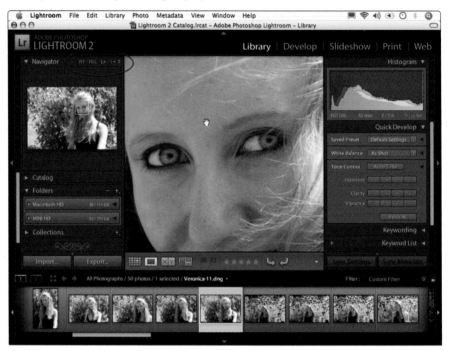

Changing magnification

There are a couple of ways to zoom in and out while in the Library and Develop modules. The first way is to use the zoom presets at the top of the Navigator panel, which is circled in Figure 4.3.

The following list explains what each of these presets does:

■ **Fit:** This zoom preset fits the selected image inside of the Image Display area. The complete image is visible on all sides.

■ **Fill:** Fills the display area with the shortest dimension of the image. When you do this, parts of the longer dimension are hidden from view.

■ **1:1:** This is the same as zooming to 100 percent, as shown in Figure 4.3.

■ **Other:** The fourth preset is selected by clicking the up/down arrows to the right of the presets and selecting a zoom preset from the pop-up menu. In Figure 4.3, a zoom ratio of 1:4 is selected.

Another way to change zoom magnification is to click on the image in the image display area. If the image is in Thumbnail view (refer to Figure 4.1), a click zooms to the most recently used zoom preset. If the image is already Loupe view, clicks cycle the view back and forth between the two most recently used zoom presets. (Pressing the Spacebar also cycles between the two most recent zoom presets.) Double-click to go back to Thumbnail view.

TIP When you click on an image in Loupe view to zoom in closer, the zoomed image is centered on the place where you click. When I zoomed in on the girl in Figure 4.3 I clicked between her eyes.

When an image is zoomed you navigate around it (pan) in two ways. You can use the Hand tool (refer to Figure 4.3) to drag the image in the display area. Or you can click and drag the zoom indicator box in the Navigator panel to select the area being displayed in the main view.

TIP To temporarily zoom in, click on the image in the display area and hold the mouse button down. You can pan as long as the mouse button is depressed. Release the mouse button when you're ready to zoom back out.

Comparing multiple images

There are two other ways to view images in the Library module, called Compare view (C) and Survey view (N). Both of these viewing modes allow you to compare multiple images in the main viewing area. The buttons for these view settings are on the left side of the toolbar by the Grid View and Loupe View buttons.

Compare view

Compare view is used to view two images at the same time so you can compare them side-by-side. First, the images are both selected in the Grid view or on the Filmstrip. Figure 4.4 shows the Compare view in action. The image on the left is labeled "Select" and the image on the right is labeled "Candidate." If you look at the Filmstrip, you notice that the Select thumbnail has a black diamond on the upper-left corner. The Candidate has a white diamond on it.

To select a different candidate, click the candidate image so that it has a white outline around it that shows that it's active. Then click a different thumbnail from the Filmstrip below to replace it. You can also use the arrow keys on your keyboard to move through images on the Filmstrip. To change the Select image, click it to make it active and choose a new image from the Filmstrip.

If you like the new Candidate more than the Select you can make the images trade places by clicking the Swap button on the right side of the toolbar. The Candidate becomes the Selected image and the Selected image becomes the Candidate.

NOTE The lock icon (Link Focus) keeps the zoom and pan settings consistent in both images. If you want to zoom or pan only one image, click the lock to unlock the images.

Compare view allows you to view two images simultaneously. The thumbnail in the filmstrip with the black diamond is the selected image. The thumbnail with the white diamond is the candidate image.

Photos by Natalia Tsvetkov

Survey view

Survey view is even cooler than Compare view because it allows you to view several images at once. To enter Survey view, select some thumbnails and click the Survey view button on the left side of the toolbar.

Figure 4.5 shows what the Survey view looks like when four images are selected in the Filmstrip. Images are added to the view by selecting multiple thumbnails on the Filmstrip by Shift-clicking or Command/Ctrl clicking the images to display. To remove an image, hover the mouse over it, as shown in Figure 4.5, and click the X that appears in the lower-right corner. You can also Command/Ctrl-click either the image or the thumbnail in the filmstrip.

The Survey view is another great way to compare similar images because it allows you to view all of the candidates at once. You can use this view to zero in on the best images by eliminating weaker shots from the selection. Both Compare view and Survey view are also useful for making presentations to clients, as you see in Chapter 8.

FIGURE 4.5

In Survey view, all images selected on the Filmstrip are displayed in the main viewing area. The image on the left is the most selected image because it has a white box around it.

Hiding panels

Sometimes you don't need to see a whole set of panels on one of the sides of the workspace. To temporarily hide a group of panels, click the twirly beside that group near the outside of the frame. This twirly is called the Show/Hide Panel button. When you do this, the twirly spins and the panel slides out of sight. To reveal the panel again reclick the twirly. To temporarily reveal a hidden panel, move the cursor into the area where the panel is supposed to be. The panel slides into view, allowing you to use it. When you move the cursor away, it goes back into hiding. You can use the twirly at the top of the screen to hide the Module Picker and the twirly at the bottom of the screen to hide the Filmstrip.

NOTE   You can change the width of the panels by clicking the line between the panel and the Grid view/image display area and dragging inward or outward. This also works for expanding or contracting the size of the Filmstrip. Click the line that separates it from the bottom of the toolbar and drag upward or downward.

You can hide both sets of side panel groups by pressing the Tab key. Press the Tab key once more to reveal them again. When you want to hide the side panels, the Module Picker, and the Filmstrip all at once press Shift+Tab. To reveal all of them again, press Shift+Tab once more.

The last thing you can do to get the most amount of screen area is to use the F key to cycle through three different screen modes. Pressing F once hides the header at the top of the screen. This is called Full Screen with Menu Bar. Pressing F a second time hides the menu bar, too. This is called Full Screen mode. Press F a third time to get back to Normal mode. Refer to Figure 4.6 to see what Lightroom looks like when you press Shift+Tab and the screen mode is set to Full Screen.

FIGURE 4.6

This is what the Grid view looks like when the side panels, Module Picker, and Filmstrip are hidden and the view is in Full Screen mode. The Show/Hide Panel buttons are circled, though they're hard to see.

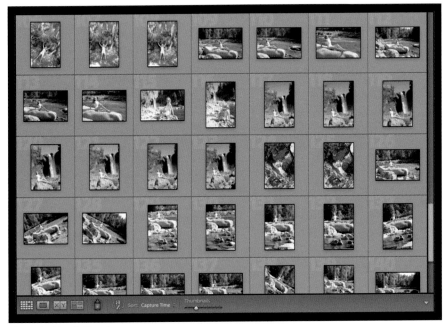

Photos by Natalia Tsvetkov

I use the Tab and Shift+Tab options often, but I don't find Full Screen mode to be extremely useful because it doesn't buy me much room. I already work with a large display so I tend to stay in Normal mode. If you go into Full Screen mode, remember that you'll have to go back to Normal to close Lightroom without using a menu command or a keyboard shortcut.

Turning the lights out

Another cool viewing feature that works in all five modules is the ability to highlight a single image by dimming the others. To do this, press L for what's called Lights Out. The first time you press L, the lights are dimmed by 80 percent on everything except for the selected image. This is called

Lights Dim. The panels are still slightly visible in the background so you can still access them. Pressing L again changes the amount of dimming to 100 percent, completely hiding everything except for the selected image. This is called Lights Off. When the lights are off you can still navigate through images on the Filmstrip by using the right and left arrow keys on your keyboard. Press L a third time to turn the lights back on.

> **TIP** Combine panel hiding and Full Screen mode with Lights Out to get the best effect.

Lights Out is useful when you first review newly imported images because it lets you focus on each image without any distractions. This viewing mode is also useful when you're doing presentations, which I discuss in Chapter 8.

Using multiple monitors

Many photographers use dual monitors to increase the amount of information they can view. A cool new feature in Lightroom 2 allows these users to take advantage of their second monitor by placing an auxiliary Lightroom window on the second monitor by clicking the Second Window icon on the left of the toolbar's header. If a second monitor is not attached to the system, the new window opens on the single monitor.

The secondary window, shown in Figure 4.7, is set to display in Loupe mode. The magnification is adjusted using the zoom presets at the bottom right, or by clicking on the image. When Loupe view is selected a set of viewing mode options is displayed on the top right of the window. These modes affect what is shown in this second window:

- When **Normal mode** is selected the image displayed in the second window changes whenever the selected image is changed in the main window.

- **Live mode** continually updates the secondary window whenever the cursor is hovered over an image in the main window. You can zoom to 1:1 to check focus on images in the second window while hovering over thumbnails in the Grid view of the main window.

- **Locked mode** locks the secondary window to the currently displayed image. This image does not change until you select the Normal or Live mode.

> **TIP** The secondary display has its own set of keyboard shortcuts. To view them go to Window ➪ Secondary Display.

If you work with a dual monitor setup, the secondary window is very valuable. It allows you to keep a Grid view open on the secondary monitor while working in modules that don't support the Grid view. For instance, if you're working in the Develop module, you can use the secondary display to make quick image selections. It's also quite useful when you're making presentations to a client because you can turn your second monitor toward the client and control it from the main window.

FIGURE 4.7

A new feature in Lightroom 2 allows dual monitor users to open an additional window on their second monitor. Note that this window has limited features.

Setting up Preferences

One of the few things about Lightroom that isn't very intuitive is the way various preferences are scattered throughout the program. This has caused some confusion with a number of my clients. This section looks at three areas where preferences are set: the main preferences, Catalog Setting, and the Identity Plate Editor.

CROSS-REF Another set of preferences called View Options is covered in Chapter 6.

The main preferences

Like most modern software, Lightroom's main preference dialog box is located in the usual place. Choose Lightroom ⇨ Preferences on a Mac and Edit ⇨ Preferences on a PC.

These preferences are broken down into the six groups. Each group is opened by clicking its tab at the top of the Preferences dialog box. The following list focuses on the most important settings:

- **General:** This dialog box, shown in Figure 4.8, allows you to modify some overall preferences. Make sure that the Automatically check for updates option is selected so you'll know when updates are available.

Another point of interest is the Default Catalog section. This is where you specify which catalog you want Lightroom to open when you launch the software. If you work with multiple catalogs, you can have Lightroom ask which one to use by selecting the Prompt me when starting Lightroom option.

The Go to Catalog Settings button at the bottom of the screen is used to access a different set of preferences. This is explained in a moment.

FIGURE 4.8

The main preferences dialog box allows you to work with six sets of preferences by clicking their names at the top. This view shows the settings in the General tab.

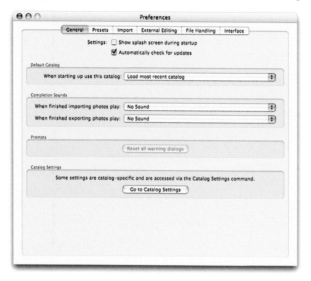

- **Presets:** One of the nicest features of Lightroom is the ability to create and store presets. (In some ways a preset is similar to an Action in Photoshop, though much simpler to create and use.) A preset allows you to store special settings that can be reused another time. For example, if I have a special black-and-white conversion formula I like, I can save it as a preset so it can be used again on other images, which saves me the time of having to remember and duplicate the formula. Lightroom is chock-full of presets. They show up in all kinds of places and are discussed often in this book.

Figure 4.9 shows the Presets tab Preferences dialog box. There are two areas of interest in the Presets tab. The first is the Default Develop Settings area at the top. I recommend that you leave the Apply auto tone adjustments option unchecked. I don't like Lightroom making adjustments automatically. However, I do recommend that you select the Apply auto grayscale mix when converting to grayscale option because it does a decent job of creating an initial grayscale mix when you create a black-and-white image.

FIGURE 4.9

The Presets preferences allow you to manage how presets are handled in Lightroom.

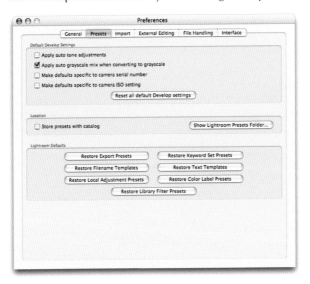

Because most of the default presets that come with Lightroom can be modified, Adobe developed a system for restoring groups of those presets to their default settings. This is the other thing to pay attention to here. To restore a group, click the appropriate button in the Presets area at the bottom of the screen.

■ **Import:** The Import tab governs the import process. I like to have the Show Import dialog when a memory card is detected option selected so that the Import dialog box opens automatically.

When importing new files it's possible to convert them to DNG during import. The Import DNG Creation section controls the type of file that's created.

CROSS-REF   **DNG files are discussed in more detail in Chapter 5.**

■ **External Editing:** Sometimes a file has to be edited outside of Lightroom. In fact, that's what the second half of this book is about. The External Editing tab controls the type of file that's opened in Photoshop when it's opened directly from Lightroom. For now, leave these settings at their defaults.

■ **File Handling:** The settings in this tab allow you to modify some of the nuances of the way Lightroom handles certain file-naming idiosyncrasies. About the only time you would need to modify these is when you're attempting to import a database that was created with other software. For now, leave them as is.

■ **Interface:** This tab allows you to slightly modify the look and feel of the Lightroom interface. Feel free to explore it to see if you prefer to use any of the settings here.

Catalog settings

A *catalog* in Lightroom is similar to a card catalog at a library. The card catalog has references in it that describe each of the books that have been cataloged. The Lightroom catalog functions very much like the library's system. It stores information about every image you import, making it the card catalog for your library of images.

The important thing to understand about the Lightroom catalog is that it's separate from the images themselves. This means that the only information contained in the catalog is metadata about the images and previews of those images. The images themselves are not contained in the catalog. Again, it's like the library. Information about the books is in the library's card catalog, but the books themselves are on the shelves. With that in mind, look at the Catalog Settings dialog box (see Figure 4.10). It can be opened from the General Preferences Dialog box (refer to Figure 4.8). Another way to open the Catalog settings is by choosing File ⇨ Catalog Settings. The Catalog Settings dialog box has these three tabs:

FIGURE 4.10

The Catalog Settings dialog box allows you to modify important things like the location of your catalog and how often Lightroom makes a backup of it. Here, Lightroom is set to make a backup once a day when Lightroom is launched. Remember, this only backs up the catalog, not the images themselves.

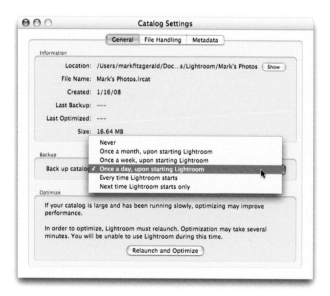

- **General:** The General tab, as shown in Figure 4.10, is the most important tab in this dialog box. The Information section shows you everything you need to know about the name, size, and location of your catalog. The Backup section is where you specify how often the Lightroom catalog is backed up. I like to have it ask me daily.

NOTE It's important to back up the catalog to a second hard drive if you have one. What's the use of having a backup of the catalog if it's on the same drive as the catalog? If that drive crashes, both are lost. (You can burn your backup to CD/DVD if you don't have a drive.)

The Relaunch and Optimize button at the bottom of the General tab of the Catalog Settings dialog box is useful if Lightroom starts responding sluggishly. I've seen this happen after long keywording sessions. When it happens, click Relaunch and Optimize to give Lightroom a moment to do some housecleaning.

■ **File Handling:** This tab, shown in Figure 4.11, controls some of the things that happen to files when they're being imported. Because the original images are not inside the Lightroom catalog, some kind of visual reference to them needs to be placed inside the catalog so that you can see what they look like. This system is much faster than having Lightroom go find a file every time you want to take a quick peek at it. It also means that you can view images in a catalog even if the image files themselves are not immediately available, such as on a different hard drive that isn't connected to the system. The previews are small JPEG files that are compressed to save space. They're like someone taking pictures of the books in the library and placing them into the card catalog so that you can see what the book's cover looks like.

FIGURE 4.11

The File Handling tab of the Catalog Settings dialog box allows you to specify the size and quality of the JPEG previews stored inside the catalog.

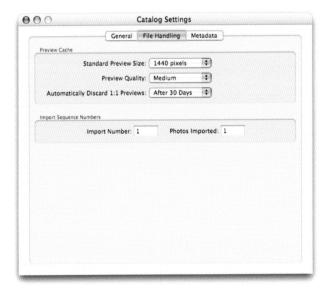

The settings in the Preview Cache area control the type of JPEG preview that's placed inside the catalog. The reason it's important to manage these previews is that they are the main contributor to the size of a catalog. The bigger these files are, the larger the catalog becomes. That's why it's a good idea to leave these settings at their defaults, as shown in Figure 4.10. If you increase the settings of Standard Preview Size or Preview Quality, the size of the JPEG previews increases.

When you zoom to the 1:1 view in either the Library or Develop modules a second preview is created. That's why you often see a message that says "Rendering: Larger Preview." After this preview is created, it's stored in the catalog. This second 1:1 preview is even larger than the original preview. That's why it's important to automatically discard these large files often. The default setting of After 30 Days works fine for most people. If you're having problems with storage space you may want to consider reducing the time period to weekly or daily.

■ **Metadata:** The Metadata tab of the Catalog Setting preferences dialog box, shown in Figure 4.12, allows you to control how metadata is handled. I recommend that you select the Include Develop settings in metadata inside JPEG, TIFF, and PSD files option so that any cataloging or editing is recorded inside the image file's metadata instead of in the catalog.

FIGURE 4.12

The Metadata tab in the Catalog Settings dialog box gives you some control over how metadata for your files is stored.

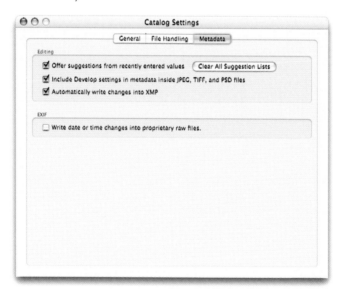

NOTE When you open a file into Photoshop directly from Lightroom all edits are automatically applied. However, sometimes you may want to open the file in Photoshop without using Lightroom. If the Develop settings are a part of the file, no matter which opening method you use, the file will look the way it did in Lightroom.

Including the Develop settings inside the file is also useful when you want to transport files to another computer. Say you want to take some files over to a friend's studio so you can work with them in Lightroom on her computer. If the metadata isn't part of the files, your Develop settings will be lost because they'll still be sitting inside your Lightroom on your computer. As soon as you move them, the connection is severed. When the Develop information is part of the file, that severance doesn't occur.

This is also why it's a good idea to select the Automatically write changes into XMP option. When you do this, sidecar XMP files are created for all of your raw files except DNG. You may recall from Chapter 3 that a raw file's XMP file is a container for all of the metadata that describes that file. If you select this option when you want to transport the files to your friend's studio, the original files and their associated XMP files are copied.

CAUTION If your catalog is large, the first time you select the Automatically write changes into XMP option your system may become unresponsive while the task is being completed.

Making it personal

I saved the preference that's the most fun for last. It's called Identity Plate Setup. Like the main preferences, it's located in the usual place. On a Mac, this preference is located in the Lightroom menu. On a PC, it's located in the Edit menu. The Identity Plate is the title that shows at the top left of Lightroom workspace. The Identity Plate Editor allows you to customize the Identity Plate and make it personal. This is a nice feature for professional photographers who use Lightroom as a presentation tool because it allows them to brand it with their business name.

Figure 4.13 shows the Identity Plate Editor. In this example, I typed my name into the text display box. I then highlighted the type and changed the font, the size, and the color. Finally I checked the Enable Identity Plate check box to make my new Identity Plate take effect. You can also use this dialog box to change the titles in the Module Picker so that they have a complementary font and color.

One more option here is to use a graphic, such as a logo, instead of type for your Identity Plate. To do so, select the Use a graphical identity plate option. Be aware that a graphic for this use has to be sized so that it's no larger than 57 pixels in height. It also has to be saved in a file format, such as GIF, that supports transparency.

FIGURE 4.13

The Identity Plate in Lightroom is totally customizable through the Identity Plate Editor. Be sure to check "Enable Identity Plate" to make your changes take effect.

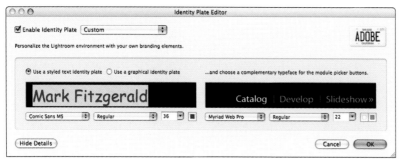

Summary

Lightroom is like a workshop with five workrooms called modules. The workspace in each module is set up for a particular workflow task. The Library module is used for tracking and managing images. The Develop module is where most of the nondestructive editing takes place. The Slideshow, Print, and Web modules are designed to create different kinds of output from edited files.

One of the best things about Lightroom is the clarity of the user interface design that's shared by all five modules. One of the main features of this design is the panels located on each side of the interface. These panels contain tools that are specific to that particular module. Panels can be opened or closed just like the drawers of a real toolbox so the tools you use most often are in plain sight.

Something that keeps the Lightroom user interface simple is its rigidity — the inability to rearrange the workspaces in each of the five modules. However, there are a number of things you can do to enhance your Lightroom experience. These include zooming, hiding panels, Full Screen, and Lights Out viewing modes. Take some time to explore these various ways of viewing your images so you'll be comfortable using them when appropriate.

The least intuitive part of Lightroom is the preferences. That's because they aren't all located in the same place. In this chapter, you explored several sets of preferences, including the main Preferences, Catalog Settings, and the Identity Plate Editor. The most important preferences you looked at were in the Catalog Settings, controlling where on the system the Lightroom catalog is stored, and where backups are stored. It's also where you specify file handling preferences that control the size of the catalog, and metadata preferences that control how metadata is stored for your files.

Chapter 5

Importing Images into Lightroom

The import process is the beginning of the Production Workflow in Lightroom. This is the process of adding information about your images to the catalog. Two types of files are imported into Lightroom — preexisting files that are already stored on your computer and new files that need to be transferred onto your system as they're imported into the catalog. These new files usually come from a camera's media card (that is, CompactFlash or SmartMedia), though they are also imported from CDs and DVDs.

The biggest difference between these two types of files is how their location is handled during the import process. Preexisting files are usually left in their current location when importing. This way your filing structure is maintained in the Lightroom catalog. Lightroom adds information about the images to the database, but the images stay where they are. New files need to be transferred from the media card to the computer hard drive as they're cataloged. The process for importing both file types is very similar.

NOTE Unlike Bridge, which sees all image files, Lightroom only knows about the files you tell it about by importing them.

The easiest way to open the Import dialog box is to click Import in the Library module. It's located just below the panels on the left. When a card reader is connected to the computer and you click Import, Lightroom asks where you want to import files from, as shown in Figure 5.1. If you want to import from your camera card reader, click USB Reader. If you want to import files that are already organized on your hard drive, click Choose Files.

IN THIS CHAPTER

Importing preexisting photos from the hard drive

Importing new photos from the camera's media card

Creating your own copyright preset

Converting camera raw to DNG during import

FIGURE 5.1

When you click Import and a card reader is connected to the system, you get a choice. Click USB Reader to import new files; click Choose Files to locate files on your hard drive.

Importing Files from Your Hard Drive

When setting up a new catalog from existing files, it's important to make sure your current organizational structure is preserved in Lightroom. The best way to ensure that happens is to import all photo folders at once, beginning with the main folder that contains all of them. The following steps illustrate how I do it for my system where photo folders are divided into subfolders for each year, which themselves are located inside a main Photos folder — my filing cabinet.

1. Figure 5.2 shows the Import dialog box that opens when you click Choose Files from the Import dialog box in Figure 5.1. When I click the main Photos folder, three subfolders — one for each year — are displayed to the right, indicating that they, and all of the files and folders inside them, will be imported.

NOTE   I could import those subfolders individually, but my goal here is to replicate my organizational system so I leave the Photos folder highlighted and click Choose.

2. Figure 5.3 shows the Import Photos dialog box that opens after clicking Choose. This dialog box presents options in the File Handling section that control how incoming files are handled. The second image in Figure 5.3 shows what these options are. In this case, I don't want to move my files; I just want to catalog them. I leave this set to Import photos to catalog without moving. If there are any folders I don't want imported, I uncheck their names.

I leave all other fields in the Information to Apply area with the default presets, as shown in Figure 5.3. (You look at what they do in just a moment.)

FIGURE 5.2

I want to import all of my existing photo folders, which are all located in a main folder named Photos. In this figure I have the Photos folder highlighted. If I only want one of those subfolders, I choose that folder from the list on the right.

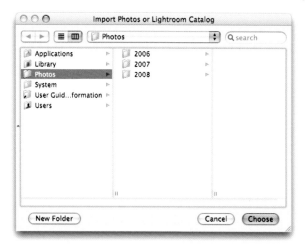

FIGURE 5.3

The Import Photos dialog box gives me the option of deselecting individual subfolders so they won't be imported.

3. When I click Import, Lightroom goes to work cataloging all of my folders. Any existing metadata is imported and added to the catalog. When this process is complete, all of my photos become part of Lightroom's catalog, as shown in Figure 5.4. It's that easy!

FIGURE 5.4

This image shows the Folders Panel in Lightroom after all of my photos files are imported together. Notice that the organization matches the folder structure on my system, as shown in the second image.

NOTE   Lightroom can't catalog some files. File types other than the four recognized types (raw, TIFF, JPG, and PSD), as well as Photoshop files that don't have an embedded preview, won't be imported.

A new feature in Lightroom 2 is the Volume Browser. Essentially it's a label for each hard drive that images are imported from. (Volume is a different name for a hard drive.) In Figure 5.4 you can see my laptop's main hard drive, Macintosh HD, listed above the Photos folder. This is a great feature for people who use more than one hard drive because it allows them to keep track of exactly where imported folders reside on their system.

Click on a volume's header to collapse it and hide all of the folders in it. Right-clicking on the header allows you to change the information that's displayed to the right. In this case I chose Disk Space so that I can see how much space is being used on the hard drive. Other options are Photo Count, Status (is the hard drive online or offline), and None.

Importing from a Camera Card

Figure 5.5 shows the default import dialog box that opens when files are imported from a USB card reader. This dialog box has a few more fields than the dialog box in Figure 5.3. These new fields mostly relate to where uploaded files are placed and how they're renamed. The options here may seem overwhelming at first, but after they are broken down you'll have a much better idea of what you're supposed to do with this dialog box.

NOTE   If you selected the Show import dialog when a memory card is detected option in the Import section of the main preferences, then the Import dialog box opens when you insert a card into your card reader. If it isn't checked, you have to click Import in the Library module.

FIGURE 5.5

When photos are imported from a card reader some new fields are added to the Import dialog box. They're mostly concerned with the new folder location and how the uploaded files are renamed.

TIP   Check Show Preview to display the preview pane on the right side of the Import dialog box if it isn't currently displayed.

Let's go through these settings one by one so that you can see how I set this dialog box up for this import:

- **File Handling:** This is where you choose how your files are handled as they're imported. When importing with a card reader you're presented with two options: Copy photos to a new location and add to catalog, and Copy photos as Digital Negative (DNG) and add to catalog. (Importing as DNG is discussed in detail later in this chapter.)

- **Copy to:** This is how you tell Lightroom where on the hard drive you want the imported files to be placed. The default goes to a user folder called Pictures, which I don't use. I prefer to keep all of my photos in a separate folder named Photos. This folder is in the main directory of my hard drive, making it easy to find. I click Choose and select the Photos folder in the pop-up menu.

■ **Organize:** This setting has a great deal of impact on how files are stored. By default, it wants to separate all files into folders that are arranged by date. If you have photos that were shot on different days, individual folders for each of those days are created. This can be very confusing unless you're already organized by date. I prefer to place all files like this into one folder, unless there's a reason to separate them. So I click the pop-up menu beside Organize and select Into one folder. (The other options allow you to modify how dates are displayed if you choose to use dates.)

■ **Put in subfolder:** When Into one folder is selected, the dates disappear and a new box appears. This one says Put in subfolder. Selecting this allows you to create a subfolder with a meaningful name during import. This folder is placed inside of the folder specified in the Copy to section. I select the check box and type Smith Family for the folder name.

■ **Don't re-import suspected duplicates:** It's a good idea to select this option so you don't inadvertently import multiple versions of the same file during different import sessions.

■ **Eject card after importing:** This saves time by automatically ejecting the media card.

■ **Backup to:** This setting allows you to back up your files as they're imported. Because I shoot only raw files, and I usually convert them to DNG files during import, I use this setting to make a backup of the original raw files.

I click Choose and select a folder I created on my desktop called Import Backup. This folder acts as a temporary holding spot. After the import process is complete, I burn the files in this folder onto CD/DVD for filing and then delete the files from the Temporary Raw Files folder. This way I have the original raw files put away in a safe place and the DNG files on my system for cataloging and editing.

■ **Template:** This setting allows me to rename my files as they're imported. The default setting Filename indicates that the files will retain their original camera-generated filenames. I click the pop-up to change it, as shown in Figure 5.6, and choose Custom Name - Sequence so that I can choose a custom name and let Lightroom add sequence numbers.

When this option is selected a text box appears that allows me to type the name I want to use for the files. Another box titled Start Number also appears, allowing me to choose the starting sequence number that's placed after the filename. This way, if I'm uploading more than one card for a shoot, I can choose to have the files from the second card begin with the next number in sequence after the first card. Naming changes are previewed just above the Template box so that you get an idea of what the new filenames look like.

NOTE   **Files can be renamed after they're imported by selecting them and choosing Library ⇨ Rename Photos (F2).**

■ **Develop Settings:** This pop-up menu gives you the opportunity to apply editing presets from the Develop module to the images as they're imported. Because it's so easy to apply develop settings later on, I leave this set to None.

■ **Metadata:** This setting allows you to add all sorts of metadata to the files as they're imported. I recommend that you use this field to add your copyright information to all files you import. I show you how to do it in just a moment. For now, I'm going to go ahead and use a template I already created called Mark's Copyright.

Lightroom provides several different renaming strategies. I prefer to use a custom name with a sequence after it.

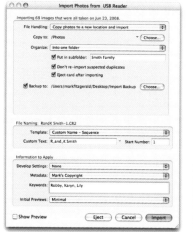

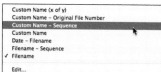

- **Keywords:** Keywords are informational tags that are added to images. These tags help to identify and find those images later. Using keywords allows you to get the greatest benefits from the powerful database capabilities behind Lightroom's Library module.

CROSS-REF Using keywords for sorting and searching is covered in Chapter 6.

During the import process it's important to think about keywords in the most general sense. You want to use only keywords that describe every image being uploaded. For example, if you just returned from a trip to Europe, you can use a general keyword such as Europe 08. After all of the files are imported you can select groups of images and add additional keyword like London, Paris, and Amsterdam.

For the import I'm doing here, I add the keywords Robby, Karyn, and Lily. I add the people's names because they're friends. The dog's name was also added because it's a friend's dog. If these people were clients, I would leave the names out because I don't want my Keywords tags list getting filled with keywords I won't need down the road. Using their names in the folder title and individual image titles is enough.

- **Initial Previews:** This is where you can override the Preview Quality setting in the File Handling preference inside of the Catalog Settings dialog box (shown in Figure 4.10 in Chapter 4). I leave this set to Standard.

■ **Show Preview:** When you select this option, thumbnails of the images to be imported appear in a window on the right. Use the slider at the lower right to change their size. To prevent an image from being imported, deselect it by unchecking it.

> **TIP** Use the check boxes in the Preview pane to selectively import groups of images from your camera card. Quite often a professional photographer has images from different sessions on the same card. To make life easier it's best to upload the jobs one at a time so the files are placed into the appropriate folders, with the appropriate filenames and keywords.

Figure 5.6 shows what this dialog box looks like after I've filled it out for this import session. When I click Import, all of the files are uploaded to the correct folder on my system and cataloged. I keep track of the import by watching the Activity Monitor that pops up over Lightroom's Identity Plate. I can cancel the import by clicking the X beside the progress bar. The Activity Monitor appears whenever Lightroom is busy with a task. Let's quickly review the main Import steps:

1. When the Import dialog box opens, choose the destination of the files to be imported — files on a hard drive or a camera's media card through the USB card reader.

2. Select the appropriate type of file handling. You can leave the files in place or move them to new location.

3. Select your main folder (your file cabinet) in the Copy to section.

4. Choose the type of folder organization you prefer — individual folders titled with dates or all files into one folder.

5. If you choose Into one folder under Organize, select the Put in subfolder option and type a name for the new folder.

6. Choose Custom Name - Sequence in the Template section so the files are renamed during import. Type a name in the Custom Text box and select a Start Number if necessary.

7. Add appropriate keywords that describe all images being imported.

8. Click Import.

> **NOTE** Something that's nice about this dialog box, as well as most other dialog boxes in Lightroom, is that the settings are. That means the next time you import from your camera card, all of the settings will be where you left them. The only fields that usually need changing are the subfolder name, the filename, and keywords.

Creating Your Own Copyright Preset

I want to back up for a moment and go over how to create your own metadata preset so that, at the very least, your copyright information is added to every uploaded image. Here's how you do it:

1. While the Import dialog box is open, click on the pop-up menu next to Metadata. The menu shown in Figure 5.7 appears. Click New.

FIGURE 5.7

The Metadata pop-up menu in the Import dialog box allows you to choose which meta-data preset you want to use. To create a new preset, click New. Click Edit to modify an existing preset.

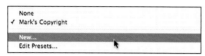

2. When the New Metadata Preset dialog box opens, as shown in Figure 5.8, find the Copyright Name field and type your name.

FIGURE 5.8

All sorts of information can be added to the metadata preset. Try to keep it simple because this preset is applied to everything you import as long as it's selected in the Metadata pop-up menu.

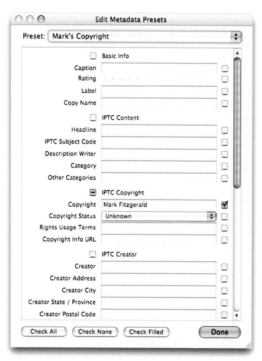

3. Give the preset a meaningful name in the Preset Name box at the top and click Create.

That's all there is to it. Whenever you import images, choose your preset to add your copyright information to all imported images. This copyright information is embedded inside of the file. It doesn't show on the image itself, though it can be overlaid on top of files when they're exported or output.

TIP When two or more people share a system, they can create their own metadata presets. When they upload images they select their own copyright preset to apply it to the photos.

Converting Camera Raw to DNG

If you're shooting in the camera raw format, you may want to consider converting to DNG when you import files. As you may recall from Chapter 3, there are some advantages to using the DNG format. The primary advantage is that unlike proprietary raw formats metadata is stored inside the DNG file so there's no need for sidecar XMP files.

Before you begin converting your imported images as DNG files, it's a good idea to set up how that conversion process is managed. Figure 5.9 shows the Import tab of the main Preferences dialog box. (To open this dialog choose Lightroom ➪ Preferences on a Mac, or Edit ➪ Preferences on a PC, and then select the Import tab.) The Import DNG Creation section on the lower half of the screen gives you control over the type of DNG files that are be created during import.

FIGURE 5.9

The Import DNG Creation section of the Import tab of the Preferences dialog box allows you to control the DNG conversion process. All DNG conversions done during import follow the rules established here.

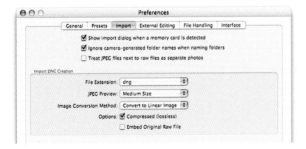

Let's take a closer look at these options:

- **File Extension:** The only difference here is in lower- and uppercase. Go ahead and leave it set to the default setting of lowercase, although it makes little difference with modern computer systems.

- **JPEG Preview:** Previews are embedded inside of DNG files so software that can't read the raw file can see what's inside it. The options are None, Medium Size, and Full Size. I prefer to leave this set to Medium, instead of Full Size, to keep file size down.

- **Image Conversion Method:** Leave this set to Preserve Raw Image to ensure that you retain the most information from the original camera raw file.

- **Compressed (lossless):** Selecting this option compresses the new DNG files to save storage space. The only downside is that compressed files take longer to open and save.

- **Embed Original Raw File:** Selecting this option does just what it says. Your file will be large, but you'll have the original and the DNG. I don't do this because I make a backup of the originals at the beginning of the process, but I know people who embed the original because they want to have easy access to the original raw file in the future.

NOTE   You can also convert existing Raw files by selecting them in the Grid view of the Library module and then choosing Library ▷ Convert Photo to DNG. A dialog box similar to the one in Figure 5.9 opens, giving you the added option of preserving or deleting the original raw files.

TIP   It's possible to convert JPEG and TIFF files to DNG also, but I see little advantage to doing this. I would prefer to know that all DNG files are true raw files.

DNG files give you the greatest amount of flexibility when using Lightroom and Photoshop/Bridge together. If you shoot raw, I recommend that you explore the DNG option and consider making it part of your Production Workflow in Lightroom.

Summary

Lightroom allows you to import preexisting files and new files. Preexisting files are generally left in the current location during the import process, while new files are transferred to the computer and placed in a unique folder during import. The biggest difference in how these files are handled is whether they're left in their original location or transferred onto the computer during the import process, though you can move preexisting files if you want to.

The Import dialog box is slightly different when you're moving files to a new location, as opposed to importing preexisting files. The dialog box may seem overwhelming at first, but after you set it up, you won't have to change many settings the next time you import.

It's a good idea to create your own metadata preset so you can add copyright information to the metadata in your images. Other contact information can also be added. Just remember that this information is applied to all of your photos unless you choose a different preset or no preset. Make the information general enough that it covers all images you import.

If you're shooting in the raw format you should consider the advantages of converting images to DNG during import. The Import section of the main preferences is where you control how this conversion is handled. Remember that you can also choose to convert your raw files to DNG at a later date.

Chapter 6

Getting Organized with the Library Module

Importing new photos into Lightroom is the first step in the Production Workflow, but the real fun begins after importing. That's when you begin the funneling process that leads to your most important photos. This initial funneling process consists of three parts — viewing the photos; organizing them with information such as keywords, labels, and stars; and using that information to quickly locate them when you need them using various filtering schemes.

In this chapter, you explore each of these parts in detail so that you know exactly how this process is best carried out on your photos. You also look at how these three parts fit together to form this portion of the workflow. By the end of this chapter, you'll be ready to create an organizational system that helps you easily manage all of your photos.

Surveying the Library Module

If you've read earlier chapters to this point, you've already looked at the Library module a couple of times. This chapter presents a more in-depth look. Figure 6.1 shows the Library module with its main components. This view is a little different because the Navigator, Histogram, and Quick Develop panels are collapsed to give more room to show panels underneath them. Also, the Collections panel below the Folders panel and the Metadata panel below the Keyword Tags panel are hidden from sight.

This overview shows the key players in the Library module. They are the side panels, the image display area (shown in Grid view), the Library Filter Bar at the top, and the toolbar and Filmstrip below.

Exploring the panels

The panels in the Library module allow access to all of your photos and the keywords and meta-data associated with them. Some of these panels are used to help you navigate through your cata-log, while others allow you to focus on individual photo details.

Catalog panel

This panel gives you quick access to all of the photos in the catalog. To display every photograph in your entire catalog, click All Photographs. Clicking Previous Import displays the most recently imported photos. (Quick Collection is discussed in a moment.)

Folders panel

The Folders panel gives you access to each of the folders that are imported into the catalog. When you click on a folder its contents are displayed in the image display area. If you select a folder with subfolders, all photos from every subfolder are displayed along with the contents of the main folder.

If you look closely at the organization here, you can see my virtual filing cabinet. The cabinet itself is the Photos folder at the top of the Folders list. There are three drawers in this filing cabinet: 2006, 2007, and 2008. One of those drawers is open. (You can tell it's open because its twirly is pointed downward.) You can see the list of folders inside of it, starting with Alice. If I click my top-level folder, Photos, I can see all of my photos — just as if I clicked All Photographs in the Catalog panel.

 The plus (+) and minus (-) signs on the header of the Folders panel are used to add or remove folders. When you click the plus sign the pop-up menu shown in Figure 6.2 opens. This menu has two functions. You use it to create new folders and to change the way current folders are displayed. Here's the breakdown:

- **Add Subfolder:** This adds a subfolder to the currently selected folder.

- **Add New Root Folder:** When you choose this option the Choose or Create New Folder dialog opens, allowing you to select an existing folder or create a new one in the desired location. If you select an existing folder the Import dialog box opens, allowing you to import the folder into Lightroom.

The Root Folder Display options change the way root folder names are displayed. A root folder is the highest folder in the hierarchy. It often contains other folders and can contain files as well. In Figure 6.2 the root folder is Photos.

- **Folder Name Only:** Displays only the folder name for root folders.

- **Path from Volume:** Displays the root folder and any subfolders.

- **Folder and Path:** Similar to Path from Volume, except that the path is reversed.

FIGURE 6.2

The pop-up menu in the Folders panel, accessed by clicking on the plus sign in the panel's header, allows you to manage your folders.

When a folder is active and the minus sign is clicked, the selected folder is removed from the Lightroom catalog, but it isn't deleted from the hard drive.

Moving folders and individual images is easy; just click and drag them to a new location. Folders can be dropped inside other folders, or they can be moved out of a containing folder. Photos are dragged and dropped into new folders from the Grid view or Filmstrip. Be aware that whenever folders or files are moved in Lightroom, they are also moved on the hard drive. Lightroom reminds you of this with one of the two dialog boxes shown in Figure 6.3.

TIP Seeing dialog boxes like the two shown in Figure 6.3 gets old after a while. If you get tired of them, select the Don't show again option.

FIGURE 6.3

These two dialog boxes are Lightroom's way of reminding you that when files and folders are moved in Lightroom, they're also moved to the corresponding place on the hard drive.

Collections panel

Sometimes you want to gather various files together so they can be seen as a group. Say you want to have one place where all of your best photos can be viewed together so you create a folder named Portfolio. If these files are located in different folders, you can't move them all to the Portfolio folder without wreaking havoc on your organizational system. What you need is a folder that allows you to collect photos without actually moving them.

This is exactly the idea behind collections. They allow you to create virtual groups of files. When a photo is placed inside of a collection the original isn't moved; instead, a reference to it is placed into the collection. Because of this, the same photo can be in different collections. When a file is deleted from a collection, it isn't removed from the catalog. Only the reference to it in the collection is removed. You look at how collections are created a little later in this chapter.

Keywording panel

A photo's keywords are managed in the Keywording panel. When a photo is selected in Grid view its keywords are displayed in the main window of the Keywording panel. When multiple images are selected all of the keywords that apply to them are shown. Keywords that are common to all of the selected photos display normally. Keywords that only apply to some photos have an asterisk after them. (We cover this panel in detail in a moment.)

Keyword List panel

The difference between this panel and the Keywording panel is that this is a list of all keywords that are currently in use for this catalog. These keywords are either created when files are imported or they're added later. This list grows as your catalog grows. It becomes unmanageable very quickly if you don't pay attention to organization. You come back to the Keywording panel in a bit. The Metadata panel (not shown) is also covered then, so it is skipped for now.

Library Filter Bar

This new panel, located directly above the viewing area, is one of the cooler upgrades to Lightroom 2. It consolidates the various filters that are used to sort through your catalog when you're searching for files based on specific information such as date or filename. This panel is only visible in Grid view. I show you how to use it later in this chapter.

NEW FEATURE The Library Filter Bar, right above the image display area, is new in Lightroom 2. It offers a much more intuitive way of searching and filtering for photos in the catalog.

CROSS-REF For a closer look at the Histogram and Quick Develop panels see Chapter 7.

Exploring the Grid view

When you're in the Library module, photos are viewed in the Grid and Loupe views. Chapter 4 looks at different ways of viewing photos while in the Loupe view, but it doesn't say much about what you see in the Grid view. Let's take a closer look now.

When you look at the Grid view (refer to Figure 6.1), you see rows of thumbnails. All four of the photos in the top are selected because they're all highlighted. The first photo on the left is the most selected photo of the four because it's the most highlighted. Notice also that the same four photos are selected in the Filmstrip along the bottom. Selecting multiple thumbnails is useful when you want to speed up the workflow by doing something to all of them at the same time. You can select multiple thumbnails by doing one of the following:

- **Select contiguous thumbnails.** Select thumbnails that are side-by-side by clicking the first thumbnail then Shift+clicking the last thumbnail.

- **Select noncontiguous thumbnails.** Select thumbnails that are not side-by-side by pressing Command (Ctrl) while clicking the thumbnails you want to select. You can also Command+click (Ctrl+click) selected thumbnails to deselect them. Both of these techniques work with thumbnails in the Grid and Filmstrip views.

TIP To select all thumbnails press Command (Ctrl)+A. To select no thumbnails press Command+D (Ctrl+D). You can also invert a selection of thumbnails — making unselected thumbnails become selected, and selected thumbnails become unselected — by choosing Edit ⇨ Invert Selection.

The thumbnails in the Grid view can be sorted in a variety of ways. Some of the most common are sorting by capture time, import order, filename, and file type. (File type is especially useful when you want to separate different kinds of files, but still view all of them in Grid view.) To change the sorting order, click the pop-up next to the Sort button on the toolbar and choose from the menu. To change the direction of the sort — from low to high, or high to low — click the A/Z button.

Move in closer and look at an individual thumbnail. Figure 6.4 shows a close-up of a thumbnail that's in the Grid viewing style called Expanded Cells (View ⇨ Grid View Style ⇨ Expanded Cells). This viewing style places lots of information on the thumbnail. If you don't need to see all of the information, you can choose Compact Cells, which allows you to fit more thumbnails into the display area. You can also press J to cycle through these views. (When you use the keyboard shortcut, a third option shows the compact thumbnails without any informational badges or extras such as labels and stars on them.)

FIGURE 6.4

When thumbnails are viewed in the Expanded Cell view a great deal of information is visible on the thumbnail. Some of this information is changed by clicking on it.

Sequence number   File base name

Pixel dimensions | File extension

Rating stars   Thumbnail badges

When thumbnails are viewed in the Expanded view, information about the photo is also displayed. The following list describes some of these features and how they're used:

■ **Thumbnail header labels:** The upper portion of the thumbnail in Figure 6.3 shows four labels that describe characteristics of the file. They are sequence number, file base name, pixel dimensions, and filename extension. Any of these can be changed to show different information by clicking on it and selecting from the pop-up menu.

- **Thumbnail badges:** At the bottom right of the thumbnail is another set of icons that indicate that photos have keywords, cropping, or image adjustments applied. Clicking the Keyword badge opens the main view of the Keywording panel. Clicking the Crop or Develop badges takes the photo into the appropriate area in the Develop module.

- **Rating stars:** Five small dots appear at the bottom of the frame. These five dots are used to apply star ratings to a photo by clicking on it. (I clicked on the second dot to give this one two stars.)

When you hover over a thumbnail some other icons (not visible in Figure 6.4) appear:

- **Pick Flag:** Click this icon to turn on rating flags that indicate whether a photo is a pick, a reject, or neither. You click on it to change the rating.

- **Rotational arrows:** Click on the left arrow to rotate the photo counterclockwise and click on the right arrow to rotate the photo clockwise.

- **Quick Collection Markers:** This icon is the gray circle at the top right of the thumbnail. When this icon is clicked the photo is added to the Quick Collection, shown in the Catalog panel.

All of these icons are useful, but you may not need all of them. For example, I don't use Quick Collections, so I don't like having the Quick Collection button on the thumbnail because it gets clicked accidentally way too often. Fortunately, I can remove it from the Thumbnail in the View Options.

Viewing options

Figure 6.5 shows the Library View Options dialog box. To open it, choose View ➪ View Options, or press Command+J (Ctrl+J). This dialog box is divided into two tabs: Grid View and Loupe View. The settings in each of these tabs allow you to modify the way information is displayed in those views.

To rid yourself of the Quick Collection marker, click the Grid View tab and deselect the Quick Collection Markers option in the Cell Icons area. I recommend that you leave everything else at the default settings for now, but feel free to explore these settings so that you know what some of the possibilities are. When you finish this chapter come back to see if you want to change anything.

The settings in the Loupe View tab allow you to set up two different overlay scenarios that display information on top of the image (in the top-left corner) when you're in Loupe view. Choose which overlay to use by selecting from the pop-up menu at the top. Use the other pop-up menus to change the information that's displayed. To have an overlay show for only a moment, select the Show briefly when photo changes option. Be sure to select the Show Info Overlay option to activate your settings.

NOTE The Develop module has its own viewing options in the View menu. The settings are the same as those in the Loupe view of the Library View Options dialog box.

TIP You can hide the badges and Quick Collection markers that appear on the thumbnails in the Filmstrip. Go to the Interface section of the main preferences and deselect the Show badges in filmstrip option.

FIGURE 6.5

The Library View Options dialog box allows you to customize the information displayed in the Grid and Loupe views. Deselect anything you don't want to see, or change the information that's displayed using the pop-up menus.

 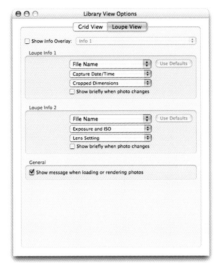

Keywording and Metadata in Action

The idea behind keywords is quite simple. Anytime you want to find photos that have a particular keyword all you have to do is search for that keyword. Every photo in the catalog that matches the keyword you search for is instantly displayed in Grid view and Filmstrip. You look at how those searches are done in a moment. First, let's look at how keyword tags are added and removed.

Adding and removing keywords

Figure 6.6 shows my Keywording panel with the keywords that were applied to the selected photo during import (highlighted in blue). There are a couple of ways to add or remove keyword tags using this panel. You can click in the main window where the keywords are shown and begin typing new keywords. You just have to be sure to separate them with a comma so that they are seen as individual keywords. To delete any of those keywords, highlight them and press Delete. You can also add keywords by clicking in the box below labeled Click here to add keywords and typing the new keyword.

TIP   If you type an existing keyword, be sure to spell it exactly the same. Otherwise, you end up with multiple keywords that are used for the same thing, which becomes confusing. Lightroom tries to help with this by offering suggestions of matching keywords as you type.

The Keywording panel offers two other ways to add keywords. The first is the section labeled Keyword Suggestions. This is a new feature in Lightroom 2. It's designed to speed up keywording by suggesting keywords that you've already used based on keywords that are applied to the selected image, as well as keywords that are applied to other images that were captured at about the same time. For example, if I have several photos that have the keywords Mt. Hood and Waterfall assigned to them, when I add the keyword Mt. Hood to a new image the Waterfall keyword is added to the Keyword Suggestions list, making it available for quick access.

FIGURE 6.6

The main window of the Keywording panel shows the keyword tags that are currently applied to the selected photo(s).

> **TIP** You can select multiple photos to add or remove keywords from all of them at once. When multiple photos are selected and a keyword is applied to some of them, but not all, an asterisk shows beside the keyword.

Another way to add keywords is to use the list of the nine most recent keywords that are displayed in the Keyword Set section. You can quickly add any of these keywords to the selected photo by clicking on it. The keyword tags shown in light type are the keywords that are currently applied to the selected photo. If you want to remove one of these keywords from the selected image, click on the keyword. This list is populated with the keywords you use as you use them. The more popular keywords move to the top of the list. Another way to make this list work for you is to modify it for your specific needs so that you don't have to wait for it to populate.

Figure 6.7 shows the pop-up menu that's accessed by clicking in the box next to Keyword Set. This menu allows you to create *keyword presets,* which are sets of customized keyword sets that are appropriate for specific uses, such as weddings and portrait photography. You can choose one of the default presets or create your own. You can even modify one of the existing presets to suit your needs. This is a huge timesaver when you tend to shoot the same kinds of subject matter.

FIGURE 6.7

Keyword presets are an efficient way to group keywords into sets that are used for specific uses. You can create, modify, and delete these presets with ease using this pop-up menu.

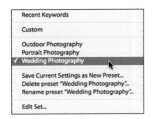

Organizing keywords

All of the keywords that are created are stored in the Keyword List panel, shown in Figure 6.8. As you can imagine, this panel can become an unmanageable mess if steps aren't taken to organize it.

FIGURE 6.8

The Keyword List panel keeps track of all of the keywords in use. This list can get very long so it's important to keep these keywords organized.

The first thing you notice when you look at Figure 6.8 is that some keywords are nested inside of other keywords. This hierarchical organizational structure is very similar to the filing cabinet structure you created with your folders in Chapter 3. In this case, all of the keywords spelled with all uppercase letters are main keyword categories that contain other sub keywords. A keyword that contains other keywords is called a *containing keyword*. Using all capital letters helps to distinguish between top level containing keywords and regular keywords, which makes it easier to understand the organization.

Keywords that contain other tags, containing keywords, have a light-colored twirly next to them. Unused keywords are grayed out.

The keyword tags that have check marks beside them, Karyn and Robby, are keywords that are applied to the currently active photo(s). The keyword tag that has a hyphen (-) beside it, DOGS, indicates that a keyword inside of the DOGS keyword is also applied. That happens to be the Lily keyword.

You may notice that there's a problem with these keywords. The Robby and Karyn keywords I added to the photos during import were new keywords—they weren't already being used in my system. Because of that, they appear at the top level with my main keywords. They really should be inside of the PEOPLE keyword. Fortunately, this is easy to fix. Keywords are moved just like files and folders. Click and drag them to the desired location. In this case, I can individually drag and drop the Robby and Karyn keywords onto the PEOPLE keyword.

The Karyn and Robby keyword tags are children of the PEOPLE keyword tag. This relationship is often called a parent/child relationship.

Moving these keywords inside of the PEOPLE keyword helps, but now the list of names inside of PEOPLE is growing. This section can be organized a bit more by adding two sub-keywords named Family and Friends. Though these keywords are containing keywords, they aren't spelled with all uppercase letters because they're not at the top of the hierarchy. Follow these steps to add keywords to the Keyword List panel:

1. Click on the plus sign (+) on the header of the Keyword List panel. The Create Keyword Tag dialog box appears, as shown in Figure 6.9. (The minus sign is used to delete keywords.)

2. Type Friends in the Keyword Tag box. Select the Put inside "PEOPLE" option. If this box is left deselected, the new keyword would be placed at the top level with all of the main keywords.

FIGURE 6.9

The Create Keyword Tag dialog box appears when you click the + symbol on the header of the Keyword Tags panel.

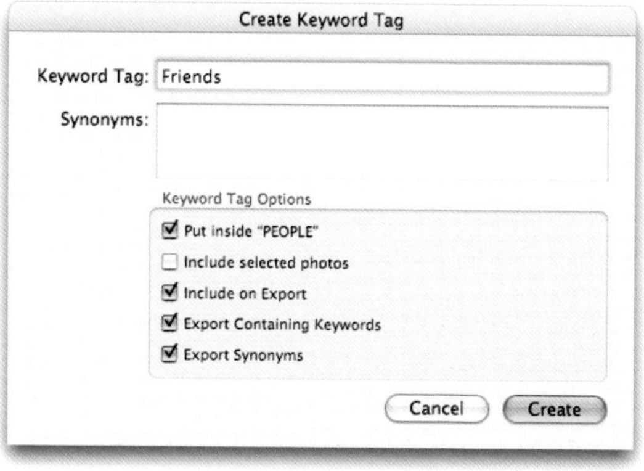

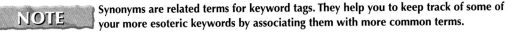
3. Click and drag all keywords for friends into this new container.

4. Repeat the process with a new keyword called Family so that you have a keyword group for family members inside of the PEOPLE keyword.

> **NOTE**   Synonyms are related terms for keyword tags. They help you to keep track of some of your more esoteric keywords by associating them with more common terms.

Sorting with keywords

After you get all of your keywords in place it becomes incredibly easy to find what you want. Here are some different ways the PEOPLE keyword can be used to find photos in this catalog:

■ Hovering over the PEOPLE keywords in the Keyword List panel causes an arrow icon to appear to the right of the keyword, as shown in Figure 6.10. When this arrow is clicked all 288 photos with that keyword are displayed in the image display area and the Filmstrip.

FIGURE 6.10 _____

When you hover over a keyword an arrow appears to the right. Click on this arrow to sort for that keyword and any keywords it contains.

■ Clicking the arrow on the Friends keyword displays only the 41 photos that have the Friends keyword applied to them.

■ Clicking the arrow on one person's name displays only the photos that have that individual keyword applied.

> **TIP**   Another way to manage keywords is to right-click on the keyword. When you do, a contextual menu opens with many of the main keywording options.

If you shoot a lot, it doesn't take long for the Keyword List to become lengthy and complex. When you need to find a specific keyword it's much faster to type it into the Filter Keywords box at the top of the Keyword List panel and press Enter. This instantly hides all keywords that don't match the words you typed.

The Keyword List panel is used to create new keywords and manage existing keywords. It also allows you to filter your catalog for specific keywords. You'll learn an even better way to filter in a moment. But first, take a look at the Metadata panel.

Using the Metadata panel

The Metadata panel, shown in Figure 6.11, is located directly below the Keyword List panel. This panel displays a wide variety of information about selected photo. Some of this information, such as exposure information, is metadata that was created when the image was initially captured. You add other information, such as ratings and labels, during the editing process.

Here are some of the things you can do with this panel.

FIGURE 6.11

The Metadata panel allows you to view information about the selected file(s). Different sets of information are displayed by choosing from the pop-up menu on the header. Here it's set to display all metadata.

- Choose from the Preset pop-up to change or apply a different metadata preset. (Metadata presets are discussed in Chapter 5.)

- The information fields displayed in this panel can be changed by choosing from the pop-up on the panel's header. When it is set to ALL it displays every metadata field. When it's set to Default the list is shortened to contain only the most common metadata fields.

- To rename a single selected file, click in the File Name box and type a new one. To rename a group of selected files, click the Batch Rename button to the right of the file name. This displays the Rename Photos dialog box, which is the same as the File Naming section of the Import dialog box.

- Use the Go to buttons to the right of any field to sort your catalog for that particular field. For example, if you click the Show button next to File Type in Figure 6.11, all raw files in the catalog are displayed. Scroll farther down and click the Go to button next to a particular camera model, and all photos shot with that particular camera are displayed.

Doing broad sorts with the Keyword List and Metadata panels is incredibly useful when managing large numbers of photos. But this is just the beginning of what's possible with Lightroom.

Using Labels, Stars, and Flags

At this point in the workflow photos are imported and keywords are applied to them. Now it's time to sort the winners and the losers from the rest of the photos. The easiest way to accomplish this is to use a system to identify each category of photos. Lightroom provides three systems: colored labels, rating stars, and flags. The following sections give a quick look at each rating system and how to use them to design a multilevel rating system for every photo in your catalog.

Adding colored labels

Colored labels are my favorite rating tool. I guess it's because I'm a visual person so I notice the colors — or maybe I just like looking at them. I use colored labels to identify photos with different qualities. I use a red label to identify photos I want to delete, and I use a green label to identify my better-than-average photos, as shown in Figure 6.12. If a photo falls in between those two extremes, it doesn't get a label. This quick sort comes early in the workflow because it allows me to focus on the most important images when I'm ready to move into the Develop module. There are several ways to label a file. Following are three of them:

FIGURE 6.12

Photos to be deleted are marked with red labels, green labels denote better-than-average photos, and neutral photos have no label. Notice that labels show in the Grid view and the Filmstrip.

NOTE A photo can only have one colored label at a time.

- **Menu command:** Choose Photo ➪ Set Color Label and select from the pop-up menu shown in the first frame of Figure 6.13. (You can also get to this menu by right-clicking a thumbnail.) Click a color to place its label on all selected photos. In the sample here, Red is already applied to the selected photo. If you choose it now, the label is removed from the photo.

FIGURE 6.13

The Photo menu allows you to set colored labels, rating stars, and flags. You can also get to these menus by right-clicking a thumbnail.

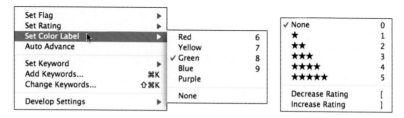

- **Keyboard shortcut:** The first image in Figure 6.13 shows my favorite method for adding colored labels — the numbers adjacent to the label names. Purple is the only color that doesn't have a shortcut (nor does None), because there are not enough numbers. Using the number keys is much faster than navigating to a menu. When you use a number, Lightroom lets you know that you're adding or removing a label by showing a brief message. The shortcut keys act in a toggle manner. Pressing a key once applies the label; pressing it a second time removes the label.

TIP Hold down the Shift key when applying a label or star with a number key to automatically advance to the next thumbnail.

- **Color Label tool:** If you look at the toolbar in Figure 6.12 you see five colored boxes just to the left of the Thumbnails slider. (If this tool isn't displayed on your toolbar, click the triangular icon on the right side of the toolbar and select it from the Toolbar menu.) Clicking one of these colored boxes adds or removes that label to the selected photo(s). (If you use the shortcut keys you don't need this on your toolbar.)

Adding rating stars

Rating stars work in much the same way as labels. They range from one star to five stars. Just like labels, these stars can have any meaning you want to give them. Most people tend to use a scale of importance where a one-star rating is somewhat important, a rating of two stars is a little more important, and so on. I use them to add a second layer of ratings to my photos with green labels. (You learn how to do that in a bit.) Here's the meaning I give them:

- **No stars:** Nothing of importance.
- **1 star:** Moderately important.
- **2 stars:** Important.
- **3 Stars:** Very important.
- **4 stars:** The best photos I've shot; portfolio material.
- **5 stars:** I don't use five stars in my system.

Many of the photos in my catalog don't have any stars. Of the photos with stars, most of them are one-star ratings, with very few having four stars. Noted photographer and author Peter Krogh, in his excellent book, *The DAM Book,* suggests that you visualize these star ratings as a pyramid. The large number of photos with no stars forms the base of the pyramid and the few photos with four stars are at the narrow peak, with the other star rating forming the middle tiers of the pyramid. Visualizing this pyramid while you apply rating stars helps to ensure that only the most important photos get the higher ratings.

NOTE   Something else Krogh recommends is that you refrain from using a five-star rating. He suggests that you leave it in reserve so that you have room to grow as your skills increase over time. When you begin to create true five-star images, you'll have a rating star for them.

Stars are added in the same ways as labels. You can choose Photo ➪ Set Rating, or you can use keyboard shortcuts noted in the second frame of Figure 6.13. You can also add a Rating tool to the toolbar, although there's little need for it if you remember the intuitive keyboard shortcuts. You can also add stars by clicking the rating stars buttons on a thumbnail in Grid view. These are the five small dots that show underneath each thumbnail.

TIP   Turn on Auto Advance (Photo ➪ Auto Advance) to automatically move to the next photo after labeling or rating. This is especially nice when you're in Loupe view.

Adding flags

Flags work much like labels and stars. A pick flag (P) indicates a photo is of interest — my green label. A rejected flag (X) indicates that a photo is a reject and will be deleted — my red label. And an unflagged flag (U) indicates a photo is neither a pick nor a reject — my no label. (All photos are automatically unflagged, just as they are unlabeled, too.) To be honest with you, I don't use flags much. But they're there in case you want a third way to rate your photos.

Thinking globally

To get the most from labels, stars, and flags you need to think *globally* when using them. What this means is that a particular color label or star rating should mean the same thing everywhere in your catalog. In my system, a green label always means that the photo is a pick. Every photo that has three stars is considered very important. This kind of consistency is incredibly valuable. If you set rules like these and follow them, then you know that when you filter your entire catalog for photos with four stars, only your very best photos are displayed.

Making the Labeling Process More Efficient

One of the keys to an efficient workflow is the ability to apply the same information and settings to similar files in an efficient manner. Lightroom has two systems for sharing information and settings: the Sync Metadata button and the Painter tool. The major difference between these tools is that Sync Metadata copies the current file information and applies it to selected files, while the Paint tool lets you select from a range of settings in two interactive pop-up menus.

Using the Sync Metadata button

The Sync Metadata button allows you to synchronize the metadata fields of several photos at once. It's located below the right-side panel group. This button is only active when more than one file is selected. The file that's most selected is the file whose settings are shared with the other selected files when the button is clicked. Figure 6.14 shows the Synchronize Metadata dialog box.

Notice that this is similar to the metadata preset created in Chapter 5 except that it also shows the star rating and the color label of the photo. To apply these settings to other files you have to check the appropriate boxes on the right side, or click the Check Filled button at the bottom of the screen to automatically check all boxes where a field contains information.

NOTE The Sync Setting button is used to share Quick Develop settings. Quick Develop settings are covered in Chapter 7.

Using the Painter tool

The Sync Metadata button is okay for sharing information, but it's not exactly user friendly. A much more efficient way to apply similar information to groups of files is to use the Painter tool, which is located on the toolbar. If you don't see it on your toolbar, select it from the toolbar's pop-up menu.

Click the Painter tool to activate it. When you do, two new pop-up menus appear on the toolbar to the right of the tool's button, as shown in Figure 6.15. The first menu is used to select the type of information you want to apply to photos, such as Keywords, Label, Flag, and so on. The second menu allows you to fine-tune that information. This tool is used just like a can of spray paint. Fill the can with information by choosing settings from the two pop-up menus. Then just click and paint the thumbnails you want to change — they don't even have to be selected. You can spray one thumbnail or rows of them.

In Figure 6.15, Rotation is selected in the first menu, and Rotate Right (CW) is selected in the second menu. Now any thumbnails painted with the Painter tool rotate 90 degrees clockwise. If you spray them again, they rotate again. If you want to add keywords, click Keywords in the first pop-up menu and type a new or existing keyword into the second menu. When you finish painting click back in the circular well where the tool is stored to disable it, or click Done on the right side of the toolbar.

FIGURE 6.14

The Synchronize Metadata dialog box allows you to share various metadata from the most selected file with other selected files. Use the check boxes to select which metadata fields you want to share.

FIGURE 6.15

The Painter tool is activated by clicking its button on the toolbar. When it's active the two menus shown appear next to it. Use these menus to control the information applied by the tool.

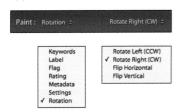

NOTE Choosing Settings from the first menu allows you to apply presets from the Develop module. (We discuss develop presets in Chapter 7.)

The Painter tool is one of the fastest and most efficient ways of applying the same setting to similar files because they don't have to be selected in advance. Just remember that once you activate it, every thumbnail you click is affected until you deactivate the tool.

Filtering and Searching with the Library Filter Bar

Adding colored labels, stars, and flags is cool, but to truly make them useful you need the ability to quickly locate photos that you marked with them. Lightroom 2 gives you a couple of different ways to sort and filter. The easiest and most powerful is the new Library Filter Bar which is, in my opinion, the second-coolest new feature in Lightroom 2. (You'll see the coolest feature in Chapter 7.)

The Library Filter Bar is only visible in the Grid view. It's near the top of the screen between the Module Picker and the image display area. If you don't see it choose View ➪ Show Filter Bar, or just use the keyboard shortcut key \ (backslash), to toggle the Library Filter Bar off and on. The Library Filter Bar allows you to search and filter folders, collections, or the entire catalog in three different ways: Text, Attribute, and Metadata. Click one of these selections on the bar to open it. Let's take a look at each of these filtering methods.

Text

When Text is chosen the Library Filter Bar formats for text searches, as shown in the first frame of Figure 6.14. Though this layout looks simple, it's actually quite powerful because it searches the entire catalog. Here's how you use it:

1. Use the first menu field to determine which metadata you want to filter for. If you're looking for a specific filename, choose Filename from the menu, shown in the second frame of Figure 6.16. By default this field is set to Any Searchable Field. You can leave it set at this when searching for a filename, but when your catalog is large, the quality of your searches improves when you're specific here.

2. The second menu field is used to refine how the text you filter for is used during the search. By default this is set to Contains, which means that if the text you're searching for appears in any form in the field you're searching, the photo will be shown with the returns.

3. Type the text you want to search for into the text field on the right. The filter begins searching as you type. Any files that match your search parameters appear in the Grid view below.

Attribute

The Attribute category is similar to the Filter Bar in Lightroom 1. It's used to filter the selected folder for flags, rating stars, and colored labels.

Using this section of the Library Filter Bar is fairly straightforward. Select a folder and choose the item you want to filter for. For instance, if you want to filter for all green labels, you highlight the label by clicking on the green swatch. To turn the green filter off, you click on it again. You can even choose more than one filtering parameter. For example, if I want to filter a folder for all green labels with two stars, I choose both of those attributes by clicking them. To turn one of the filter attributes off, click it again to deselect it.

FIGURE 6.16

In this figure the Library Filter Bar is formatted for searching your catalog for specific words. The search is refined by selecting from the first two menus.

TIP You can filter for more than one color label by clicking each label you want to use.

The Copy Status section on the far right of the Attribute bar allows you to filter for master photos or virtual copies. (Master photos and virtual copies are discussed in Chapter 7.)

NEW FEATURE It's now possible to filter for photos that don't have a label by selecting the dark-gray box (No Label) in the Color section of Filter view. I can't tell you how many times photographers asked me how to do this in Lightroom 1. To the best of my knowledge, it wasn't possible. Now it's easy.

This category can be combined with the text category by selecting both of them from the bar's header. Doing so allows you to filter for specific textual parameters as well as specific attributes at the same time, such as a specific filename with a rating of two stars. Just keep in mind that when Attribute is selected, only the selected folder is filtered. If you want to filter all photos, choose All Photographs from the Catalog panel before filtering.

TIP You can select multiple folders in the Folder panel using the Shift or Command/Ctrl keys to filter all of them together.

When you filter for stars you have the option of choosing three options by clicking the button to the right of rating. By default it displays a greater than or equal symbol. This means that if you filter for two stars any returned images must have two stars or more. Click on the symbol to change it to Rating is less than or equal to, or Rating is equal to. When stars are selected for filtering, they are deselected by clicking on them a second time. For example, if you're filtering for two stars, clicking in the second star turns the star filter off.

 It's easy to forget to turn these filters off before collapsing or hiding the Library Filter Bar. This can lead to confusion when you can't find some of your photos. Always remember to turn each attribute off when you're finished with it. The fastest way to do this is to choose None from the bar's header.

Metadata Browser

The Metadata feature, also called the Metadata Browser, allows you to perform powerful searches of the selected folder based on a wide range of metadata. With this view, you can sort your photos by keyword, camera, lens, color label, and more. Figure 6.17 shows the Metadata Browser for all photos on my system. (I chose All Photographs from the Catalog panel.) Using this feature is easy. If I want to see all photos shot with my Canon EOS 5D, all I have to do is click the camera name in the Camera Column. I can refine my search by choosing a specific lens from the Lens column. This is much faster than using the Metadata panel on the right side of the workspace. It's also more powerful because I can filter for more than one metadata criteria.

The Metadata Browser is extremely flexible. Each of the columns shown in Figure 6.17 can be changed to filter for a different metadata field by clicking its name and selecting from the pop-up menu. For example, if you want to filter for a specific date, click on the name of one of the columns and choose Date from the pop-up menu. The column will then be populated with every date that applies to the photos in your catalog. Additional columns are added by clicking the button on the right side of any column's header and selecting from the pop-up menu. (This button shows when you hover over the column.) Columns are also removed by choosing from this menu.

FIGURE 6.17

The Metadata Browser allows you to perform powerful searches of a selected folder or the entire catalog.

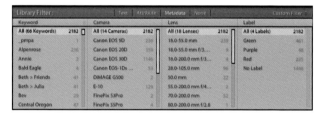

 The Attribute and Metadata categories can be used together by choosing each, just like the Text and Attribute categories.

Custom Filters

Before you move on, I want to point out one more thing on the Library Filter Bar. On the far right side of the bar's header is a button named Custom Filters. (If you have the Attribute category selected the default setting is Default Columns.) Figure 6.16 shows the pop-up menu you get when you click Custom Filters. Here's what each of these setting does:

- **Default:** Sets the chosen category to its default.

- **Filters Off:** Turns all filters off.

- **Flagged:** Displays photos with any flag in the selected folder or collection.

- **Location Columns:** Opens the Metadata Browser with the columns labeled with: Country, State or Province, City, and Location.

- **Rated:** Displays all rated photos in the selected folder of collection. That means that any photo with a star on it is displayed.

- **Unrated:** Only photos without a rating are displayed.

- **Save Current Settings as New Preset:** Allows you to create your custom filtering schemes and save them to the Custom Filters menu.

- **Delete Preset:** Use this to delete one of your custom presets when you don't need it anymore. This option isn't shown in Figure 6.18 because it only appears when a custom filter is in use. (The preset must be chosen first in order to delete it.)

- **Update Preset:** Use this to modify a preset to reflect the current settings.

Custom Filters are very powerful because they allow you to create filtering scenarios that fit your needs. If you take the time to create some custom filters, you can work quickly and efficiently when performing common filtering tasks with the Library Filter Bar.

FIGURE 6.18

The Custom Filters menu allows you to quickly change the focus of the Library Filter Bar and to save filtering presets that fit your workflow.

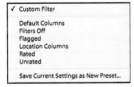

Filmstrip Source Filter Bar

One of the problems with the Library Filter Bar is that it can only be used while in Grid view in the Library module. That means that if you're in the Develop module and you need to filter a folder, you have to go to the Library module to perform the filtering task. This doesn't lend itself to a smooth workflow. This problem is solved with the placement of a secondary filter bar on the Filmstrip called the Source Filter Bar, shown in Figure 6.19. The Source Filter Bar is a replica of the Attribute category of the Library Filter Bar. Because the Filmstrip is visible in all modules, this bar allows you to perform the most common filter functions that are used in other modules, which are flags, stars, and colored labels without returning to the Library module.

FIGURE 6.19

The Filmstrip Source Filter Bar allows you to use filters in all modules. Though this set of filters doesn't have as many features as the Library Filter Bar, it contains the main filters you're likely to need on other modules.

Notice that this bar also features the Custom Filters menu. This gives you access to your custom filters while you're in a different module than the Library module. Keep in mind that if you select a custom filter that uses the Metadata Browser, such as Location Columns, while in a module other than the Library module, the columns won't be visible — or useable.

On the far right side of this bar is a switch button that looks like a light switch. This turns the filters off and on. When the switch is up, the filter is on. When the switch is down, the filter is off. The cool thing about this switch is that you can turn off a filter without resetting it. When you turn the filter back on, the settings you last used are reinstated.

Putting the Workflow into Action

You just spent some time exploring the nuts and bolts of labeling and filtering. It seems like there are lots of moving parts here. However, when you see how all of the pieces come together, you realize that the organizational phase of the Production Workflow is comprised of three main tasks: keywording, applying labels and stars, and sorting and filtering. To see how I use the Library module to quickly accomplish those tasks with the images I imported in Chapter 5, follow these steps:

1. I begin by viewing the photos in Grid view with a thumbnail size that allows me to get a good look at individual photos — while still fitting as many thumbnails as possible on the screen. This is a good time to use the Tab key (or Shift+Tab) to hide the side panels, which maximizes the Grid view area.

   The objective here is to get a quick overview of all imported photos. If I see any obvious rejects — for example, when the flash didn't fire and the frame is black, or I have a picture of my foot because I accidentally hit the shutter release — I delete them on the spot. (I discuss Delete versus Remove later in the chapter.)

TIP It's a good idea at this step to be careful about selecting files for deletion. Hard drives keep getting cheaper and it doesn't take a lot of room to store a digital file. If you think you'll ever be able to use the image — or even part of it in the Creative Workflow — don't delete it. Instead, leave it unlabeled.

   During this step I'm also looking for groups of photos and individual photos that need additional keywording. When you work with a large quantity or variety of image content, say from a vacation, this step can take a while. If you're short on time, try to keep this phase as general as possible. Save *deep-keywording* for later. By this I mean very specific keywording that may only affect small numbers of photos. Just be sure to get the keywording done when you have time later.

2. At this point I have a good overview of the imported photos. Now it's time to begin sorting through them, picking my favorites and any other rejects. I move from Grid view to Loupe view (Fit view) so I can get a better look at each photo, zooming in when necessary. I use green labels (8) to identify the picks and red labels (6) to identify rejects to be deleted later. If I have several similar photos, I use Compare view to compare them and select the best shots. Everything that falls in between a pick and a reject remains unlabeled. I make sure Auto Advance is turned on (Photo ➪ Auto Advance) so that I automatically advance to the next thumbnail when I add a label.

    The objective is to identify as many good photos as possible during this step. That way, I can make a second pass with rating stars to select my favorites from these picks. If this is a job for a client, I choose everything I want to present to him or her now. Then we select the favorites together when I show them the photos.

CROSS-REF For more information on presentations, see Chapter 8.

3. After all photos are evaluated and labeled, I switch back to Grid view (G) and open the Attribute category of the Library Filter Bar. (I could also use the Source Filter Bar on the Filmstrip.) I click the red label to filter for photos with red thumbnails only. I take one last look at these images. (If I change my mind on one, I press the 6 key to remove the red label. When I do, the thumbnail is removed from the view because it's no longer being picked up by the filter.) When I'm satisfied with the photos with red labels I select all photos by choosing Edit ➪ Select All, or press Cmd+A (Ctrl+A) and press Delete. When the Delete dialog box opens, I click Delete from Disk.

4. I turn off the red filter and turn on the green filter, allowing me to concentrate on my picks. I make a new pass through these images looking for standouts. When I see them, I give them a one-star rating.

    If I'm working with a client, I save higher ratings for the client to apply. When we go through the green-labeled photos together I point out the one-star images, saying that they're my favorites from the picks. We use two stars to indicate photos the client is interested in and three stars for photos the client orders.

    If this is a personal project, I add higher ratings to images that stand out from the others. Otherwise, I wait until the green-labeled favorites are processed in the Develop module before looking at them for photos that deserve a higher rating.

The photos are now ready for their trip to the Develop module. Something that facilitates that trip is to save all of the green-labeled photos as a collection, which makes them easier to locate and manage as a group. I don't always do this, but it can be quite handy, especially when working with a client, so let's look at how collections work.

Using Collections

Collections are virtual groups of images. When you create a collection, the photos aren't placed inside the collection. Instead a shortcut to them is created and placed inside the collection. That's why one photo can be in more than one collection. Collections can be intended to be permanent, as in one named Portfolio, or they can be temporary like the one created here for the Smith family. The only difference between the two is that the temporary collection is deleted when its purpose is served.

Creating a collection

Creating collections is easy. Follow these steps:

1. For the project I'm working on here I choose the Smith Family folder and filter for green labels so that only my picks appear. Then I select all photos (Cmd/Ctrl+A).

2. I click on the plus (+) sign on the Collections panel to open the Collections menu, shown in Figure 6.20. I choose Create Collection and the Create Collection dialog box opens.

FIGURE 6.20

When Create Collection is selected from the Collections menu the Create Collection dialog box opens.

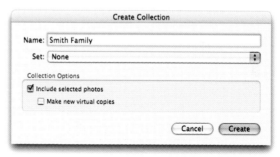

3. I name the collection and select the Include selected photos option. The Make new virtual copies is not selected.

CROSS-REF Virtual copies are discussed in more detail in Chapter 7.

The Set menu is used to add a collection to a collection set. For example, I can place all collections created for clients into a set named Clients. These sets are useful when you generate lots of collections. To create a Collection Set, choose Create Collection Set from the Collections menu.

4. Click Create.

That's all there is to it. Anytime I want to see my picks from the Smith Family shoot, I click on the collection. If I want to remove a photo from the collection, I select it and press Delete while the collection is being displayed in the Grid view. The reference to the photo is removed from the collection without affecting the original. If I want to add photos, I select them in the Grid view and click and drag them onto the collection. A few months from now after the Smiths have viewed and selected images for printing I can delete this collection so that the list doesn't get cluttered. If I ever need it again, I can re-create it using the previous steps.

NOTE Deleting a collection does not affect the original photos.

Quick Collection

The Quick Collection is the most temporary of collections. Photos are added by clicking the thumbnail's Quick Collection Marker or by pressing B. You can also click and drag photos onto Quick Collection in the Catalog panel. One way to use a Quick Collection is to quickly gather photos that are later moved into a normal collection. You can also create a new collection from a Quick Collection by choosing File ➪ Save Quick Collection (Alt+Command/Ctrl+B). To remove all photos from the Quick Collection choose File ➪ Clear Quick Collection (Shift+Command/Ctrl+B).

A new feature in Lightroom 2 is the ability to designate any collection as the target collection so that when you add photos to the Quick Collection they go into the target collection rather than the Quick Collection. This allows you to skip the step of moving photos from the Quick Collection into a more permanent collection. To designate a collection as the target collection, choose Edit ➪ Set as Target Collection. When you do, a small plus sign shows next to the designated collection.

Smart Collections

Another new feature in Lightroom 2 is Smart Collections. The Collections panel, shown in Figure 6.21, shows the default Smart Collections that come with Lightroom 2. You can see that these Smart Collections are filtering my entire catalog to find matches for their specific criteria. This is nice, but when you have thousands of images in your catalog, these Smart Collections aren't as useful. Fortunately, you can create your own Smart Collections. Here's how:

FIGURE 6.21

Smart Collections intelligently filter your catalog for specific criteria.

1. Click the plus sign on the Collections panel to open the Collections menu.

2. Choose Create Smart Collection. When the Create Smart Collection dialog box opens use the menus to design the type of Smart Collection you desire. Click the plus sign to add other filter options to the collection.

3. Click Create (not shown in Figure 6.21).

In Figure 6.22 you can see that I created a new Smart Collection that tracks of all of my photos that have a green label and a two-star rating.

FIGURE 6.22

Create your own smart collections using the Create Smart Collection dialog box.

Managing Missing Files and Folders

Before you finish this chapter, I want to discuss a couple of file management issues. This is different from the file organization discussed in Chapter 3. What is discussed here is the relationship between the photos in your catalog and the files that exist on the hard drive.

Earlier, the analogy of the card catalog at the library and how it relates to the Lightroom catalog was discussed. If a book is moved in the library to another shelf or completely removed from the library, someone needs to update the card catalog. Otherwise it keeps directing people to the wrong place. Lightroom is like the card catalog, and your hard drive is like the shelves where the books are stored. Fortunately, Lightroom is much smarter than the average library card catalog at keeping track of the photos in its catalog.

Working with missing photos

Lightroom does an amazing job of tracking the things you import into it. It even notices when a file or folder is moved or renamed outside of it — using the computer's operating system. These changes are updated as soon as Lightroom sees them. When folders and files are deleted or moved offline to an external hard drive that is later disconnected from the system, Lightroom doesn't have access to them. It still displays the thumbnails because they're part of the catalog, but the actual files aren't available.

One of the most common reasons for missing folders is when photos are stored offline. When a photo is offline you can still add metadata and run filters on it in the Grid view. (If you're on the road with your laptop, this is a great way to catch up on keywording your photos.) But when you try to zoom in closer than the Fill magnification preset, a warning is displayed stating the file is offline or missing (unless you created 1:1 previews). Because of this you are not able to use any of the Develop module's tools (or Quick Develop) on the photo. When photos are missing, Lightroom reports the problem in a couple of ways.

Missing folders

When a folder is missing, its name in the Folders panel is grayed out and a question mark icon appears on top of the folder icon, as shown in Figure 6.23. This is meant as a warning. If you know the files were permanently moved outside of Lightroom, it's okay to delete the folder from the Folders panel now. If you know where the folder was moved to, or the hard drive is back online, you can inform Lightroom. Right-click on the folder name and choose Find Missing Folder. When the Select New Location dialog box appears, use it to guide Lightroom to the new folder location.

FIGURE 6.23

When my portable hard drive is disconnected, the folder containing my photos from Hawaii is offline. Lightroom indicates this by displaying a question mark icon on the folder name.

Missing photos

 When a file is missing a Missing Photo icon appears in the right corner on the thumbnail. If the whole folder is missing, this icon appears on all of its thumbnails. (Sometimes the icon doesn't appear until the thumbnail is selected.) If you know where the file is you can click on this icon and use the dialog box in Figure 6.24 to locate it.

 To display all missing files, click Missing Files in the Catalog panel.

FIGURE 6.24

To locate a missing file, click the Missing Photo button on its thumbnail and use the Missing Photo dialog box that appears to relocate it by clicking Locate.

Deleting and removing unwanted files and folders

The easiest way to avoid missing folders and files is to keep Lightroom informed by always using it, instead of using your operating system, to move or delete photos. When you decide to delete a file in Lightroom you have two choices: You can remove it from the catalog or you can delete it from the hard drive (which also removes it from the catalog). Removing a photo deletes its entry from the catalog without affecting the original file. Figure 6.25 shows the dialog box that appears when you press the Delete key, or you can choose Photos ➪ Delete Photo.

You have two choices when deleting a folder. You can select it and click on the minus symbol (-) on the header of the Folders panel or you can select it and press the Delete key. The only difference is that when you use the Delete key you are presented with a dialog box similar to Figure 6.25, allowing you to choose to remove the folder from the catalog or delete it from the hard drive. When you use the minus symbol icon a dialog appears informing you that if you proceed the photos will be removed from the catalog, but not from the hard drive. It doesn't give you the option of deleting the files from the drive.

FIGURE 6.25

When you choose to delete a file or folder from the hard drive, Lightroom checks with you to see if you really want to delete it, or if you just want to remove it from the catalog.

Summary

The primary purpose of the Library module is to organize your photos. The first level of this organization is applying keywords. If you take the time to do this properly, you'll be able to find any file you want when you need it. Keyword searches can be carried out on the entire catalog or within a single folder. The key to using keywords is to organize them in the Keyword List panel. The more organized this panel is, the more powerful it will be when you need to find something.

The next level of organization is using labels and stars (as well as flags) to place identifiers onto thumbnails. The most common way to use labels is to identify the winners and losers. In my system, I use green labels to identify my picks and red labels to identify rejects. I then use star ratings to rate the quality of all green labels. The important thing to remember about using labels and stars is to make your rating system global so that a particular label or star has the same meaning no matter where it appears in your catalog.

The Library Filter Bar allows you to browse and filter an individual folder, a collection, or the entire catalog in a number of ways. The main divisions of this view are Text, Attribute, and Metadata The real power of keyword tags and labels becomes apparent when these filters come into play. After photos are filtered they can be placed in temporary or permanent collections.

Be careful about moving photos and their folders outside of Lightroom. Otherwise, you may begin to get error messages about missing files. If you know where the missing files are located, you can use these messages to relink them to Lightroom's catalog.

Now that you know how to identify your favorite images, you can see what happens to them in the next phase of the workflow as they move from the Library module to the Develop module.

Chapter 7

Processing Photos with the Develop Module

By now you should have a good feel for the organizational capabilities of the Library module. Lightroom truly makes digital asset management easy to understand and implement. It's one of the main reasons to begin using Lightroom in the first place. However, it isn't the only really great thing about Lightroom. In my view, the Develop module is just as important because it creates a clear path for the editing phase of the Production Workflow.

In this chapter, you take that pathway as you explore the editing tools in the Develop module. To facilitate that exploration, you practice on a sample file so you can see exactly how some of these tools are used. By the end of this chapter you'll know exactly how to enhance the quality of your photos quickly and efficiently so that they're ready to share with other people, or to be moved into Photoshop for advanced editing.

Understanding Image Basics

Before you begin learning to use the editing tools, there are some fundamental concepts you need to cover. They deal with the way a digital photo file's tonality and color are interpreted and managed in Lightroom and Photoshop. You begin with one of my favorite subjects: color.

Working with color

Understanding color is critical in digital photography. That's because there are so many things you can do to influence it and manage the way it's used in the workflow. This section explains color theory and how three separate color channels combine to create all of the colors in a digital photo. Let's begin by looking at monitor calibration and how it helps you to feel confident when making important color decisions.

Calibrating your monitor

You've seen banks of televisions in electronics stores where every TV displays the same channel in different colors. When you buy a TV, you don't really worry about those differences. You simply want a TV that looks good when you get it home. No one will be comparing your TV to his and wondering why they don't look the same.

You run into the same phenomenon when dealing with digital images: Not all computer monitors display tonal information and color the same. Unlike TV sets, this can be problematic. What's the use of tweaking an image in Photoshop if the color is going to look different as soon as it's viewed somewhere else?

Back in the days of film, you didn't run into this problem as much. If a photographer was shooting slide film, the colors in the slide became the true colors — the reference point to which everything else was compared. Any reproductions strived to match the original. Everything's different with digital files because they're viewed on a wide range of equipment. Predicting what an image will look like when someone else sees it in his particular viewing environment can be difficult.

If you send a sample of an edited file to someone in New York, how do you know he's seeing the same thing you see when he opens the file? If you send a file out for printing, how can you feel confident that the photolab and you are on the same page when it comes to color? Even though you can't control the variables in all these scenarios, you can control the biggest variable — your own computer monitor. That's why monitor calibration is the first step to color management.

The idea behind monitor calibration is to establish some standards and get everyone to use them. These standards refer to the color temperature, brightness, and contrast the monitor displays. The standards are shared when you use devices to measure and calibrate your monitor. This way, you can create custom *profiles* that describe the changes necessary to make a particular monitor work within the standardized environment.

NOTE   Think of a profile as a language interpreter — just like an interpreter at the United Nations. In the case of the color profile, color is the language that's being interpreted. Profiles allow all the devices in a digital workflow to interpret and understand color. Cameras, monitors, and printers all have color profiles.

A number of monitor calibration devices are available on the market. I have experience with the ColorVision Spyder2 Pro and the Gretag Macbeth Eye-One Display 2, as shown in Figure 7.1. Each of these devices currently retails for about $250. Either does a decent job. (A newer version of the Spyder, called the Spyder3 Pro, is available, but I haven't used it.)

Although these devices work a little differently from one another, for the most part they can be used by following these steps:

1. Install the software that comes with the calibration device.
2. Plug the device into a USB port on your system — preferably a port on the back of your machine, not a USB hub.
3. Launch the software, and tell it to calibrate and profile your system.

Calibration allows you to adjust your system so that your display is ready to profile. Profiling creates a snapshot of your display that describes it to other devices.

4. The software takes you through some preliminaries and asks you a couple of questions.

   Pay special attention to the questions about color space and gamma. Choose 6500k for color temperature and 2.2 for gamma as your starting points to be consistent with most of the rest of the world.

FIGURE 7.1

The Gretag Macbeth Eye-One Display 2 monitor calibration device in position for calibration

CAUTION Many Mac users believe they're supposed to choose 1.8 as their gamma because 1.8 is known as a Mac setting. In the very early days, 1.8 was a gamma setting for Macs. It was created so that those displays would match the limitations of an early Apple dot-matrix printer. Today, 2.2 is the standard gamma setting for computer displays. The 1.8 setting is no longer necessary and can actually cause problems if used.

5. When the calibration software is finished, it prompts you to save the newly created profile and make it your default.

6. The profiling software also reminds you to recalibrate at certain intervals so that your viewing environment stays consistent.

   This interval is set in the preferences. All my systems are set to remind me every two weeks. I don't always recalibrate every two weeks, but I do try to do it every month with my main systems.

TIP If you plan to move from a CRT monitor to an LCD monitor (as many people are doing) and you have an older calibration device, think about upgrading to the newer generation of devices. When I moved from CRT to LCD, my older device didn't do a very good job on the LCDs. When I bought a newer model, all my systems came into balance.

Don't go crazy over calibration and profiling. You can reach a point of diminishing returns when striving for perfect color, especially when dealing with outside printing sources. Make an effort to get calibrated, but don't worry if you are not getting a perfect match to your prints. Lots of variables can affect printing. Some of them are discussed in Chapter 12.

Exploring color theory

One of the first things to understand about color is that it's personal. Everyone has his own preferences for what he likes. When I worked in a professional photolab, we had a lab standard for skin-tone colors. However, there were certain customers who wanted the skin tones in their prints to have a particular tint. Even though we didn't like the color the customer liked, we did everything in our power to make them happy.

Some of this bias relates to personal taste, and some of it is more related to actual color perception. Not everyone sees color the same. In fact, your own color perception can shift as blood sugar levels go up and down. Some people are deficient in seeing color on a red-green axis; others are deficient on a blue-yellow axis. However, few people are completely color blind.

Even though our experience of color can be highly subjective, the physics behind color theory is rock solid. The main distinction you need to make when talking about color is whether you are talking about *additive* color or *subtractive* color.

- **Additive color** describes the way light waves combine to create color. This is the way you see things, and it's how most color adjustment happens in Lightroom and Photoshop. It's called additive because equal amounts of pure red, green, and blue light added together create white.

- **Subtractive color** describes the way pigments work together. If you add equal amounts of red, green, and blue paint together, you get something pretty far from white — more of a muddy gray. In order to get white with pigments in subtractive color, you subtract colors (no color = a white canvas).

  Inkjet printers use pigment inks to print on white paper. When you print an image with pure white in it, the white is the color of the paper because it doesn't have any ink on it. Even though inkjet printers use subtractive dyes and inks, you still use additive color in Photoshop to prepare files for printing on them. The printer drivers take care of any conversion necessary.

The discussion here is going to center around additive color and the six colors that are used when managing color in digital photography: red and its opposite — or *complementary color* — cyan; green and its complement, magenta; and blue and its complement, yellow. Figure 7.2 shows these colors and where they meet. When you have equal amounts of complementary colors, you end up with gray — in other words, they cancel each other out color-wise.

FIGURE 7.2

Six colors are used to create color in Photoshop: red, cyan, green, magenta, blue, and yellow. Notice the colors that are created where any two colors overlap.

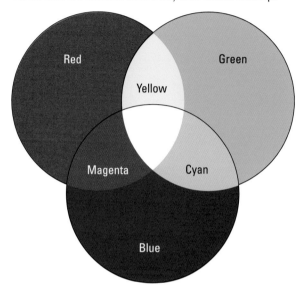

I'm talking about only three *primary colors* here: red, green, and blue (RGB). These three colors combine in countless ways to form all the colors that a human eye is capable of seeing. It's just easier to work with and combine these colors if you have a way of expressing their opposites or complements: cyan, magenta, and yellow.

NOTE **Color is a science with, theoretically, many ways to model colors and their relationships. RGB (red, green, and blue) is just one of these *color models*. Others are CMYK (cyan, magenta, yellow, and black) and HSV (hue, saturation, and value).**

The relationship among these colors gets even more interesting because each of these six colors is composed of two component colors. The two components of any color are two of the other five colors.

Here's how the colors break down into components:

- Red is composed of magenta and yellow.
- Green is composed of cyan and yellow.
- Blue is composed of cyan and magenta.
- Cyan is composed of green and blue.
- Magenta is composed of red and blue.
- Yellow is composed of red and green.

113

This may seem confusing at first, like an endless shell game — especially if you're used to thinking about the way pigments such as paint combine. But Figure 7.3 shows an easy way to remember these relationships: The primary colors — red, green, and blue — are directly above their complementary colors (the ones that cancel them out) — cyan, magenta, and yellow. Here's the trick to understanding this: The two component colors of any color are the two colors that are not directly across from it. For example, red is composed of magenta and yellow. Cyan can't be a component of red because it's the opposite of red.

FIGURE 7.3

Component colors of any one color are the two colors that are not directly across from it on this chart. Complementary colors can't be components of their complement because they are opposites.

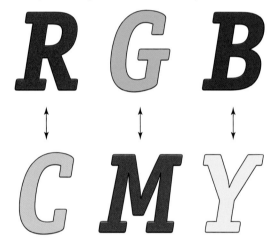

When I discovered this many years ago, it completely changed the way I thought about colors and their components. All I have to do now is visualize this simple chart, and I know how all the colors relate to one another — which colors are complements and which are components.

Understanding color channels

Because you're working with an RGB color model, your images are composed of three separate color channels. One channel represents the red content of the image, the second channel represents the green content of the image, and the third channel represents the blue content of the image. When those three channels are combined they create the overall color of the photo just like the red, green, and blue wavelengths of light do. If one color channel's tonal values are higher than the two other channels, that channel's color is dominant in the photo.

> **NOTE** When the values of all three channels are the same the color is called *neutral*. This means the color doesn't have any bias toward a particular color channel — it's gray.

Here's the weird part: Each of these channels is composed of *grayscale* data — all the tones are gray. Figure 7.4 shows a color image with each of its three channels — Red, Green, and Blue. Notice that the red flowers are light in the Red channel (a higher tonal value), but dark in the Blue channel (low tonal value), but the fence in the middle looks the same in both channels (neutral value).

You can measure the intensity of each channel in a color photo to determine the tonal values of each channel. It works a little different in Lightroom than it does in Photoshop. Lightroom uses a tonal scale of 0–100 percent, with 0 percent representing pure black and 100 percent representing pure white. Photoshop uses an older system. Tones are measured on a scale of 0–255 (0 = black and 255 = white). The main reason it's done differently is because the older system used in Photoshop is not sufficient for describing the large amount of information in a raw file.

You look at what this means in Lightroom in just a moment. For now, the main thing to get from this discussion is that when you're working in an RGB color model, every digital image is composed of three individual channels, one for each primary color. The brighter that color is on its channel, the more predominant it is in the overall color mix.

Understanding histograms

The primary tool that's used to evaluate the tones in a digital photo is the *histogram*. A histogram is a graphical representation of the distribution of the tones in an image. It consists of a graph that ranges from pure black on the left to pure white on the right. All of the tonal values that combine to make all colors in the photo are represented in between.

Figure 7.5 shows two histograms. The first one is the Histogram palette from Photoshop CS3. This display is in a special mode that shows the histograms for each of the three channels: Red, Green, and Blue. The black histogram at the top represents all three color channels combined.

> **NOTE** The histogram of a raw file often looks different in Lightroom than it does in Photoshop. That's because unprocessed data is graphed in Lightroom, which isn't possible in Photoshop. This is also why a histogram sometimes looks different on your camera's display than it does in Lightroom's Histogram panel. The camera displays the histogram of the raw file's embedded JPEG rather than the actual data.

The second image in Figure 7.5 shows the histogram display in Lightroom. All of the information from the first image is combined into a composite. This graph not only shows the histograms for different color channels, it also shows where those channels overlap. For example, the cyan-colored area in the center of the graph, just above the dip in the middle of the gray graph, is cyan because it's where the Green and Blue channels overlap (green + blue = cyan). When all six colors overlap, the color of the graph is gray. This is a much more efficient and informative way of displaying histogram information than the usual view of Photoshop's Histogram palette.

FIGURE 7.4

The images show a color photo with each of its three channels. When a color is predominant in a channel, it appears light in tone — such as the reds in the Red channel. When a color is the complement of the channel, it appears dark in tone — like the yellow in the Blue channel.

Red

Green

Blue

CROSS-REF Chapter 14 provides a hands-on channel exercise that uses the image shown in Figure 7.4.

FIGURE 7.5

The first image shows the color All Channels view of the Histogram palette in Photoshop CS3. The top graph displays the combined channels. The lower graphs display individual channels. The second image shows the Histogram panel from Lightroom. It displays the same information composited into a single graph.

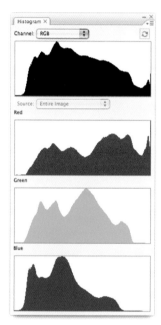

TIP If you want Photoshop CS3's histogram to display composite information, choose Colors from the Histogram palette's Channel menu.

A histogram works like this: Imagine side-by-side vertical columns, one for each of the individual tonal values that a histogram represents. The columns start with black on the left and end with white on the right. In between, there are other columns representing all the shades of gray between black and white. The height of a column is governed by the number of pixels in the image having that particular tonal value. If the image includes lots of middle gray tones, then the columns around the middle of the histogram are taller. Because these columns are standing right next to each other, they form a graph when viewed as a group.

The shape of the histogram's middle region doesn't matter as much as what's going on with its endpoints. If an image has full tonal range with detail in the shadows and highlights, the graph covers most of the space between black on the left and white on the right, as shown in the first set of images in Figure 7.6. Each end comes to a stop before hitting the edge of the graph. If an image is underexposed, then all tones move to the left. When that happens all tones that used to describe the darkest shadows are *clipped* off the end of the histogram, forcing them to pure black (0), as shown in the second set of images in Figure 7.6. If an image is overexposed, the opposite happens. The histogram moves to the right. All the tones describing bright highlights get clipped and become pure white (100 percent), losing all detail, as shown in the third set of images in Figure 7.6.

When you shoot with your digital SLR camera you need to pay attention to histograms. Many dSLR cameras have a feature that you can turn on to display a histogram every time you take a photo. This can be a great way to evaluate an exposure as soon as you shoot it. You don't even need to see the image preview to know whether your exposure is good. All you need to see is the histogram — which is great on a bright day when it's hard to see the image preview on the camera.

TIP   If only one channel in a raw file is unclipped — especially in the highlights — you may be able to recover detail from the clipped area.

One more thing to consider when evaluating a histogram is the tonal key of the image. When an image is a bright scene (high-key) or a dark scene (low-key), the histogram can fool you. Figure 7.7 shows two photos and their accompanying histograms. At first glance, the histogram for the top image appears normal, and the histogram for the darker, bottom image appears to be underexposed. The first clue to indicate this isn't the case is that you don't see any shadow clipping in the histogram in the second histogram.

In fact, both of these images were made with exactly the same exposure. The difference in the histograms is from the differences in subject matter. The second portrait contains more dark tones while the first portrait contains mostly medium tones.

Even with the best exposure, the scene may not contain the darkest and brightest tones you want to see. In these cases, it becomes necessary to adjust the histogram of the image. You see how this happens in just a moment, but first you get an overview of the Develop module.

FIGURE 7.6

When evaluating exposure, always pay attention to the endpoints of the histogram. A normal exposure provides a full range of midtones, as shown in the first set of images. An underexposure shifts the histogram to the left, clipping shadows, as shown in the second set of images. An overexposure shifts the histogram to the right, clipping highlights, as shown in the last set of images.

Photos by Denyce Weiler

FIGURE 7.7

When evaluating a histogram, consider the tonal content of the image. These images were exposed exactly the same. (The exposure information is visible at the bottom of the Histogram panel.)

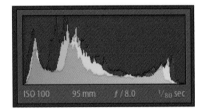

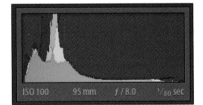

Photos by Denyce Weiler

Surveying the Develop Module Panels

The first thing you notice when you look at the Develop module, shown in Figure 7.8, is that it looks a lot like the Library module. All of the main components are here: central viewing area, side panels, Toolbar, and Filmstrip. The main difference is that the contents of the panels and Toolbar are different.

FIGURE 7.8

The Develop module looks very similar to the Library module. The main differences are in the contents of the panels and the tools on the Toolbar.

Photos by Natalia Tsvetkov

TIP   There are several ways to move an image from the Library module to the Develop module. Here are three: click on Develop in the Module Picker, use the keyboard shortcut (D), or click a thumbnail's Develop badge from the Grid view if it has previously been edited in Develop.

Lightroom's Develop module panels are grouped into two sets. The panels on the left allow you to apply presets and manage the file's history, while the panels on the right contain all of the image-editing tools. Begin with the panels on the left. You already know about the Navigator panel, so begin with Presets.

Presets panel

Lightroom is loaded with presets. The Presets panel is one of the main places to find them. This panel is in all of the modules, except for the Library module. The Presets panel is divided into two categories: Lightroom Presets and User Presets. Lightroom Presets contains default presets that come with Lightroom. Some of these presets, such as B&W High Contrast, are creative while others, such as Auto Tone, are more production oriented. To preview a preset, hover the cursor over it. If you like a preset and want to apply it, click it.

The idea behind presets like these isn't new. But the way they are presented clearly is. When used properly to carry out repetitive tasks, presets increase the efficiency of the workflow dramatically. Lightroom's default presets are nice, but I rarely use them because they don't fit my needs. I prefer to create my own, which is quite easy. When I create those presets, they're stored in the User Presets folder. You look more closely at presets later in this chapter and the next chapter.

Snapshots panel

Snapshots have been part of Photoshop's History palette for many years. They have always been one of my favorite features. Snapshots allow you to take a snapshot of a photo to preserve its current editing state. One way to use them is to save different versions of the same file. Say you're experimenting with some radical cropping ideas. You can try one crop, make a snapshot of it, and then undo that crop and try a different crop, and make another snapshot of it. When you're through experimenting you can click on each of the snapshots to find the one you like most and use it.

One of the problems with Snapshots in Photoshop is that they, like the rest of the history, are *volatile*. When the file is closed, its history, including any Snapshots, is permanently deleted. Because all editing carried out in Lightroom is recorded as metadata, snapshots and history are not volatile. They'll always be there unless you choose to remove them.

History panel

The History panel is like a chronological timeline. It keeps track of every edit that's done in the Develop module (as well as the Quick Develop panel in the Library module). It's similar to the History palette in Photoshop, except that new history states are added to the top of the list. The very first setting, called Import, is always on the bottom. Another thing that's different is that the number of steps available in Photoshop's History is limited. The number of history steps in Lightroom is virtually unlimited. That, combined with the permanent nature of the history, means that you can always revisit every editing step.

Click on a previous history state to go back in time. Hovering over history states shows a preview of that state in the Navigator palette. If you don't like the editing path you took, you can back up as many steps as you want and try something different. Just be advised that as soon as you do something new, all of the old future history states disappear. Also, history states cannot be rearranged within the panel, nor can they be deleted individually.

Processing panels

You take a close look at each of the panels on the right side later in this chapter. Here's a quick introduction to give you an overview of all of them.

- **Histogram:** Displays the selected photo's histogram with clipping indicators.

- **Tool Strip:** This is a new feature in Lightroom 2. All of the editing tools that used to be on the Toolbar in Lightroom 1 have been moved here. Also some new tools have been added. Selecting a tool opens a contextual panel with options for that tool.

- **Basic:** The Basic panel provides all of the basic color and tonal adjustment sliders that represent the meat and potatoes of the Develop module.

- **Tone Curve:** Advanced tonal adjustment is accomplished with the Tone Curve panel. The controls here are quite similar to the Curves command in Photoshop — although much easier to understand and use.

- **HSL/Color/Grayscale:** This panel contains sliders for performing advanced color adjustment and custom black-and-white conversions. If you're used to doing these things in Photoshop, be prepared to be blown away by how much more advanced this panel is.

- **Split Toning:** The Split Toning panel allows you to tone the highlights and shadows of an image, each with a different predominant color. Some interesting effects can be accomplished with it, but I generally use it for one thing: toning black-and-white images to give them a warm tone. (You learn how to do that later.)

- **Detail:** This is where you reduce noise and enhance the basic sharpness (capture sharpening) of the photo.

- **Vignettes:** This is another new panel for Lightroom 2. Vignetting was moved from the Lens Corrections panel in Lightroom 1 into this new panel. A cool new feature called Post-Crop was also added.

- **Camera Calibration:** This panel is used to fine-tune the color your camera produces. If your camera is always off in color by the same amount, you can compensate for it using the color sliders in the Camera Calibration panel. A new feature allows you to choose from an assortment of preexisting camera profiles to fine-tune how color is rendered from of your dSLR's chip.

123

Adjusting Tonality and Color

The editing workflow in the Develop module is very straightforward. Tonal and color adjustment are carried out with the panels on the right beginning with the Basic panel and working down from there. The main editing tools on the Tool Strip — such as the Spot Removal tool and Crop Overlay tool — are occasionally used to make necessary adjustments.

Using the Basic panel

The controls in the Basic panel, shown in Figure 7.9, allow you to adjust the basic qualities of the image. This panel is divided into three main areas: White Balance, Tone, and Presence. The Treatment section at the top is used to change the photo to black and white by clicking Grayscale. To change it back to color, click Color.

FIGURE 7.9

The Basic panel is where most of the action takes place in the Develop module. This is where a photo's overall tonality and color balance are established.

Adjusting white balance

Human eyes do some things much better than cameras do. One of those things is to adjust the color of the light. If I look at a piece of paper outside on a sunny day it looks white to me. If I later look at that same piece of paper under incandescent light in my office, it still looks white even though the color of the light is much redder. Cameras only see color the way you tell them to see it. If you photograph that same piece of paper outside with your camera's white balance set to Daylight, and then take the paper inside and photograph it under incandescent light with the white balance still set to Daylight, the second photo will be much redder because the light source's *color temperature* was warmer.

Color temperature refers to the color of various wavelengths of light. Light is measured in degrees of Kelvin. The lower temperatures represent the warmer colors, and higher temperatures equal cooler colors. Table 7.1 lists Kelvin temperatures and how they translate to the colors of various light sources.

TABLE 7.1

The White Balance of Common Light Sources

Color Temperature in Kelvin Degrees	Light Source
1000–2000 K	Candlelight
2500–3500 K	Tungsten bulb — household variety -Incandescent
3000–4000 K	Sunrise/Sunset — clear sky
4000–5000 K	Fluorescent lamps
5000–5500 K	Electronic flash
5000–6500 K	Daylight — clear sky, sun overhead
6500–8000 K	Daylight — moderately overcast sky
9000–10000 K	Daylight — shade or heavily overcast sky

In a sense, white balance is how this variation of light source is managed. When white balance is set correctly, neutral subjects stay neutral in color (all three color channels are the same) no matter what color light they're photographed under because the setting compensates for the light. Film photographers solve this problem by buying film that matches the light source they will be using. If the light source changes, they have to switch film. Fortunately, dSLR users don't have to change the chip in their camera when the color of the light source changes. They select the appropriate white balance setting for the shooting environment. They can even choose Auto to let the camera make the decision on the fly, which is very useful when shooting with mixed light sources although it can't be completely trusted. Shooting raw solves this problem because white balance isn't assigned to the file until it's processed by ACR or exported from Lightroom.

NOTE Some digital photographers create a *custom white balance* before they begin shooting. They point their camera at a special neutral target and set the white balance to the exact color of the light. This is one of the best ways of establishing an exact white balance before shooting.

Lightroom allows you to modify the white balance of a photo if you don't like the way the camera captures it. This is the first step in the basic editing portion of the Production Workflow.

The best way to explain the editing process is for you to take a photo through the workflow so each panel can be explained as it's encountered. So, as they say, let's take it from the top:

1. Open the practice file titled `garden_girl.dng` from the downloadable practice files on the Web site. Notice that the white balance setting next to WB: says As Shot. This means the white balance values shown are the values the image was captured with.

> **NOTE** All of the practice files used in the hands-on exercises can be downloaded from the Web site at **www.wiley.com/go/workflow**.

2. Click As Shot to open a pop-up menu, as shown in Figure 7.10. Because this is a raw file, all of the standard camera white balance presets are available. That's because white balance is unassigned on a raw file. If this were a TIFF or JPEG file, the list would only have three choices: Auto, As Shot, and Custom.

FIGURE 7.10
_____

The White Balance menu on the Basic panel offers two options. The first set shows all of the standard white balance presets found on most dSLR cameras. This full list is only available for raw files because white balance is unassigned in raw files. All other files are limited to the three choices shown in the second image.

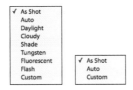

Click on the various presets so you can see how they're designed to compensate for color variations. Notice how the Temp and Tint values change when you change presets. Also notice what a poor job the Auto white balance preset does with this image. That's because Auto attempts to average out the all of the colors in the image. It has a hard time doing so when there's a predominant color like the green here.

> **TIP** Hide the panels on the left when working with the editing panels to maximize the image display area.

3. These presets offer a very general way to adjust white balance. A more flexible system is to use the Temp and Tint sliders. The Temp slider controls the blue/yellow color axis, while the Tint slider controls the green/magenta color axis. Moving either slider to the left adds cooler color tones, while moving the sliders to the right adds warmer tones.

   Experiment with the sliders to see how they affect the color. Notice that small movements can cause noticeable changes. Whenever you want to undo all adjustments and return the color to your starting place simply change the white balance preset back to As Shot.

> **NOTE** You may have noticed that there is no red/cyan axis here. If you recall how colors are mixed, you realize that such a slider isn't necessary. To add red, move both of the Temp and Tint sliders to the right, adding yellow and magenta, which equals red. If you want to add cyan, move them to the left to add blue and green. Even though there are only two sliders, all six colors can be addressed.

4. This system gives you much more control over the exact white balance. It only requires a bit of trial and error. However, there's a much better way to quickly find an accurate white balance. When shooting raw it's possible to create an accurate custom white balance after the fact. All you need in something in the image that you know is neutral.

    Notice that as you move the cursor over the image, red, green, and blue readings appear in the Toolbar's Info box. (If the Info box is not visible on your Toolbar, open the Toolbar Options menu and select it.) Also notice that a preview of the new color balance is shown in the Navigator panel if it's visible.

    Move your cursor so it's over the darkest tones on the model's shirt. This shirt is supposed to be black, but when I hover over it on the left side I see that it has more blue in it than red or green. When I look at the flesh tones on that side of her face I can see the blue. You can try moving the Temp slider to add yellow, but you'd have to come back and remeasure until you get it right. There's a faster method.

5. Click the White Balance Selector (W). It's the button at the top of the Basic panel that looks like an eyedropper. This tool is used to neutralize a colorcast. If you recall, when the white balance is set correctly when shooting, a white object appears white when photographed. When the white balance is incorrect, there's a color shift. The White Balance Selector neutralizes the values of the three color channels wherever you click. For it to work correctly, you have to click on something that's supposed to have a neutral color — like true black, white, or gray.

    When you hover over the black shirt with the White Balance Selector a grid appears showing the pixels under the cursor. This is called a Loupe grid (not to be confused with Loupe view). The readout at the bottom of the dialog box shows the color values for the pixel in the center of the grid. When you click, all three numbers are brought to the same value.

    In Figure 7.11, the cursor is over her hair so that you can see all the variations in color. If you click here, the hair becomes grayer as all of the three color channels are neutralized, which is not exactly what you want here.

    Another feature of the Loupe grid is that it helps you get a closer look at each pixel underneath the White Balance Selector. This way, you can see if you're about to click a stray pixel that's different from the majority of surrounding pixels. If you don't want to see the Loupe grid, deselect the Show Loupe option on the Toolbar.

6. Use the White Balance Selector to click on the young woman's black shirt. When you do the color gets warmer as the Blue channel reading is brought into line with the other channels. This is called *click-balancing*. When you do it the white balance preset changes to Custom because you're creating a custom white balance. Click on different parts of the shirt with the White Balance Selector until you like the overall color. I found that the shirt of the right side gave me the most pleasing color, but I had to click several times before I found it because there's so much variation in color.

FIGURE 7.11

Use the White Balance Adjuster's Loupe grid to monitor the color of the pixels under the tool. To adjust this tool's options, select from the tool options shown on the Toolbar.

> **TIP** Deselect the Auto Dismiss option to make it easier to click on different areas. When you get the color you want, click Done, or click the well where the White Balance Selector is normally stored to return it to the well.

There's a lot a variation in this black shirt, which causes a bit of a problem when looking for a neutral. The left side of it is cooler because blue light is reflecting off of some blue flowers in front of her. You can see the blue tint to the skin in her face. Because this side has more blue, it causes the White Balance Selector to overcorrect by adding too much yellow.

Another problem here is that clothing is famously unreliable when used as a neutral target. That's because optical brighteners are added to fabric, especially whites. Laundry detergents also contain optical brighteners. Therefore, clothing that looks white or black, or even gray, may not reflect light in the normal way. (Try click-balancing on a white wedding dress and you'll see what I mean! They are designed to be very white.) Standard office paper also has optical brighteners added to it so it's not reliable as a neutral target. It's best to use something that's designed for the purpose.

It would have been difficult to use the White Balance Selector if the model hadn't been wearing a black shirt because noting else in the image is supposed to be neutral. Even with the black shirt, the White Balance Selector provides erratic results. That's why many professional photographers place a neutral target with known values into the image so they can click-balance on it with the White Balance Selector. Figure 7.12 shows the target I used when I photographed the Smiths. You

128

may have noticed it earlier. This fold-up target, from a company called PhotoVision (`www.photo visionvideo.com`) gives me three neutrals to work with, though I usually use the gray to be consistent. (It also has a reflector on the back.) This all sounds great except there's still one problem: I can't place my neutral target in every image.

NOTE Some photographers create an in-camera custom white balance, using products like ExpoDisc (`www.expodisc.com`), before they begin shooting. If you're shooting JPEG, then I strongly recommend this practice because you don't have as much flexibility with white balance during postproduction. Also, even if you are shooting raw, sometimes it isn't possible to place a white balance target in a scene.

FIGURE 7.12

Many professional photographers make one exposure with a white balance target in it before they begin shooting. That way they can record the color of the light and use the target to custom white balance their raw files with the White Balance Selector.

Synchronizing Develop settings with multiple photos

One of the best things about Lightroom is that it's easy to share settings with multiple photos. (You saw this in Chapter 6 when you worked with Synchronize Metadata.) When I use the target in Figure 7.12 to adjust the white balance I'm able to share that setting with all images that were photographed in the same light. Here's how it works:

1. Select all photos you want to adjust. (You can do this in the Grid view before moving into the Develop module, or you can use the Filmstrip if you're already in the Develop module.) Make sure that the photo with the exposure target is the photo that's displayed in the image display area (it's the most selected photo).

2. Use the White Balance Selector to click-balance on the exposure target, setting a custom white balance for that image.

TIP If I had shot additional photos of these people in another light source, say indoors with incandescent light, I would have shot a second exposure target indoors to use for custom white balancing all photos shot with that light source.

Sync... **3.** Click Synchronize to synchronize your white balance setting. (This button only appears when multiple photos are selected.) The dialog box shown in Figure 7.13 appears. Because nothing other than white balance has been changed, you can go ahead and click Sync (Synchronize). However, if other changes have been made to the source photo or the other photos, click Check None and then individually select White Balance before clicking Synchronize.

FIGURE 7.13

When you synchronize Develop module settings using the Synchronize button you have the choice of synchronizing all settings or selecting specific settings to share.

Auto Sync You can speed things up when multiple photos are selected and you already plan to synchronize them. Hold down the Command (Ctrl) key and the Synchronize button changes to Auto Sync. Click it to activate Auto Synchronize. Now all changes to the source image are automatically applied to selected images. Click the button again to turn it off.

NOTE The Copy and Paste buttons are used in a similar way. When you click Copy a dialog box similar to Figure 7.13 opens. Choose the setting you want to copy. To paste these settings to other photos, select the photos and click Paste. If you're in a real hurry you can click Previous Button to apply the previous settings to a selected image without using the Copy and Paste buttons. The Sync button becomes the Previous button when the Shift key is depressed.

That's all it takes to synchronize the color for all images or any other setting you want to share, including spot removal and cropping...but we're getting ahead of ourselves. File this away for the moment as the fastest way to adjust multiple similar images.

Adjusting image brightness and contrast

After you get the overall color balance looking good with the white balance controls, move down to the Basic panel's tonal sliders (refer to Figure 7.9). This section of the panel contains the primary controls for adjusting the brightness and contrast of the photos. (When the terms "brightness" and "contrast" are used in this way it refers to the tonal qualities of the image, rather than the Brightness and Contrast sliders.) These controls are:

- **Auto:** The Auto button allows Lightroom to analyze the image and make some basic adjustments to it. I've never been a big fan of teaching automatic color or tonal adjustments because I want you to know how to make informed decisions. However, in the Production Workflow there are times when quick ballpark adjustments are useful.

NEW FEATURE The auto tone feature has been overhauled and vastly improved in Lightroom 2.

- **Exposure:** This slider adjusts overall brightness, though it has the greatest effect on highlights causing the lightest tones to slide off the right side of the histogram and become pure white with no detail. It's used to control highlight clipping. Higher values result in increased highlight clipping. These values are in increments of f-stops. A value of +1.00 is similar to increasing exposure by 1 stop. A value of -1.00 is similar to decreasing exposure by 1 stop.

- **Recovery:** The Recovery slider is used to tone down extreme highlights. It should only be used when difficult highlights present themselves because of its tendency to reduce overall contrast.

- **Fill Light:** This slider is used to lighten, or open up, difficult shadow areas to reveal detail that's being lost. This slider should only be used when problem shadows are present because of its tendency to reduce overall contrast and reveal shadow noise.

- **Blacks:** The Blacks slider is used to control shadow clipping. Higher values result in greater shadow clipping, causing the darkest tones to slide off the end of the histogram and become pure black with no detail.

NOTE When you hover over these first four sliders, the matching tonal regions on the histogram are highlighted.

- **Brightness:** This slider is used to adjust brightness of the midtones after the previous sliders have been set. Higher values result in an increase in brightness, while lower values reduce it.

- **Contrast:** The Contrast slider is used to adjust midtone contrast. Higher values increase contrast, while lower values decrease contrast. With that said, I have to say that I rarely use this slider. Quite often it isn't necessary, and when it is, I prefer the results of using the Tone Curve panel.

Now that you have the overall color where you want it on the practice photo, it's time to adjust its basic tonal qualities. Follow these steps:

1. Go back to where you were with the practice photo in Step 3 of the last example. Look at the histogram for this photo, as shown in Figure 7.14. It's easy to see that the highlights and shadows are being clipped because both ends of the histogram touch the edge. There's another way to tell that clipping is occurring. The two small triangles at each end of the top of the panel are illuminated, which indicates clipping. The highlight clipping indicator on the right is white, indicating all channels are clipping. The shadow clipping indicator on the left shows that only the darkest magentas are being clipped — the Red and Blue channels.

The histogram for the practice image shows that some clipping is occurring. Clipping previews are activated by clicking on the small triangles at the top of the panel. Shadow clipping is shown in blue and highlight clipping is displayed in bright red. (It is exaggerated here for clarity.)

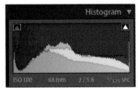

2. Clipping information is useful, especially when put into the context of the image. To preview it, click each of the clipping indicators to turn them on. All highlights that are clipping are displayed in red, and all shadows clipping is displayed in blue. (You can press J to toggle the preview off and on, or you can simply hover over one of the triangles when they're in the off position to display its clipping only.)

TIP In an image like the one in Figure 7.14 it's hard to see the red color of the highlight clipping because of the red flowers. Fortunately, you can use a different way of previewing this information that's been in Photoshop for years. Hold down the Alt key while moving the Exposure, Recovery, and Blacks sliders. The problem with this method is that is doesn't work with any of the other sliders such as the Brightness slider.

3. Slide the Exposure slider to the left until most of the clipping is gone from the preview. If you remove all of the clipping, the image looks very dark and the highlights don't look rich. Allow some clipping on the shoulders and hair. I use a value of -0.60. These are difficult highlights because they're so much brighter than most of the other image content.

4. Slide the Recovery slider to the right to increase the amount of highlight recovery. Move it to the right until the clipping in the highlights is reduced. I moved it all the way up to 100. Be aware that this slider has a much greater impact on raw files than it does on other file types because of the ability of raw files to capture a greater amount of highlight information.

5. Now that the highlights are under control, you can move to the shadows. The blue clipping indicator shows that very little clipping is occurring in the shadows; it's mostly in the deepest areas of the black shirt. Increase the value of the Blacks slider so that you can see the effect. Turn off the clipping preview so you can see what happens to the image as this value is increased.

> **TIP** Sometimes it's hard to fine-tune a value using a slider because the numbers move in large increments. To use smaller values, hover over the number next to the slider. Click and drag right or left when the hand icon appears. (These are called *Scrubby Sliders*.) To type a specific value, click on the number to highlight it and then type a value. When a value is highlighted you can use the up and down cursor arrows on your keyboard to make single value changes. Double-click any slider to quickly return it to its default setting.

Try lowering the value. If you take it all of the way down to 0 the clipping goes away, but the image contrast looks flat because there aren't any true blacks in the photo. It's often better to let insignificant shadows go black because it helps the image look better when a rich black tone is present. I leave the value at 6. If these were problem shadows — occurring in areas where detail is important on the main subject — I would use the Fill Light slider to lighten them.

6. Okay, now that the lightest and darkest tones are set, the overall contrast of the image is established. All you have to do is adjust the midtone brightness with the Brightness slider. Slide it to the right to lighten the image and slide it to the left to darken it. (When the photo is lightened, the highlight clipping on the shoulder reappears.) I set this value to +96.

From a workflow point of view the idea is to move quickly here. Try not to spend too much time getting caught up in the tonal intricacies of an image at this point. Anything you do can be modified or undone later on.

> **TIP** If you decide you want to begin again with the sliders on a panel, there's a quick way to reset all of them at once. Hold down the Alt key and all of the Develop panels and subpanels display a reset option on their headers. Click the one you want to reset. This works for almost all of these panels on the right side of the Develop module. This keyboard modifier also works with dialog box settings in Photoshop.

Using the Presence controls

The Presence controls, as shown in Figure 7.15, allow you to do two things: increase midtone contrast and adjust color saturation.

FIGURE 7.15

The Presence section of the Basic panel allows you to adjust midtone contrast and color saturation.

The Clarity slider

The Clarity slider is designed to increase *local contrast* — contrast along edges of detail. This adjustment slider was developed to mimic a technique with Photoshop's Unsharp Mask filter that uses a low value for Amount and a high value for Radius, which is the opposite of the way the Unsharp Mask is generally used.

CROSS-REF Chapter 21 discusses the Unsharp Mask filter in more detail.

The overall effect of the Clarity slider is greater contrast that adds depth to the image. I love the effect on scenes where contrast is already low, such as on a foggy day or when shooting through glass. It also looks great on most landscape images. However, it can have a negative impact on a person's skin by accentuating the imperfections. Therefore, I tend to be careful when using this control on portraits, especially if I'm planning to take them into Photoshop for advanced editing.

It's best to zoom to 1:1 when using this control, otherwise it's difficult to see the effect. Also, be advised that high values may affect highlight clipping so you might have to revisit some tonal settings after adjusting clarity.

Adjusting overall saturation

A color's saturation is the overall intensity of the color. It's the difference between a color photo and a black and white. (The colors in the black-and-white photo are de-saturated.) Lightroom has two sliders for adjusting the overall color saturation of a photo: Vibrance and Saturation. The main difference between these two settings is that Vibrance is a smarter version of Saturation.

The Saturation slider affects all colors the same as values are increased or decreased. A value of -100 equals a monotone, and a value of +100 equals double saturation. The Vibrance slider balances saturation by affecting colors with low saturation more than highly saturated colors. It also protects skin tones by preventing them from becoming oversaturated. Try using these two sliders on your practice photo so you can compare and contrast them. You'll probably find that you prefer the Vibrance slider. Just be careful not to overdo it, otherwise the color will look fake.

Fine-tuning tonality with the Tone Curve panel

The tonal controls in the Basic panel allow you to establish the overall tonal scale of a photo. Sometimes, though, you want to adjust specific tonal ranges of that scale without affecting the others too much. That's when you move down to the Tone Curve panel.

The Tone Curve panel is similar to the Curves command in Photoshop. Both are shown in Figure 7.16. These tonal adjustment tools work on the same principles, but the Tone Curve in Lightroom is much more sophisticated and easy to use. I go into the theory of the idea behind curves in Chapter 13 when I discuss the Curves command in Photoshop CS3. Here, I focus on using this tool to quickly achieve the results you're looking for. However, I do need to discuss the basic ideas behind curves.

FIGURE 7.16

The Tone Curve panel in Lightroom (left) is a much more intuitive interface than the Curves dialog box (right) in Photoshop CS3.

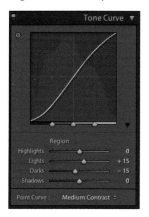
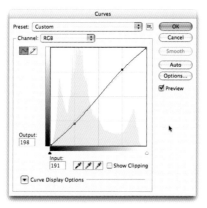

The diagonal line on the graph represents the tonal range of the photo. The lower-left corner of the line represents pure black (0 percent), while the upper-right corner represents pure white (100 percent). The length of the diagonal line linking them represents all of the tones in between. In Lightroom, the two endpoints of the line cannot be moved. However, any point between these two endpoints can be adjusted by moving it up or down. The traditional way to adjust curves in Photoshop is to click and drag a point on the diagonal line up or down to lighten or darken that region of tones. When a point is moved the shape of the line changes as nearby tones are also affected. But because of the way the line curves, it becomes apparent that tones that are farther away from the point that was adjusted are affected less than the nearby tones.

The Tone Curve sliders allow you to change four different tonal regions. Each of these regions is marked in the graph by a vertical line. When the cursor is moved over the curve line of any of the four sliders, the region of the curve that will be affected is illuminated on the graph. This area is highlighted with a bubble indicating the maximum amount of adjustment available in that region. You can change the size of the bubble by using the three sliders below the graph.

This may seem complicated, but the good part is that you don't have to understand how curves work to use the Tone Curve panel. Just follow these steps:

1. Go back to the practice file you used in the last example. Click and drag the Lights slider to the right, stopping at +5. Click and drag the Darks slider to the left, stopping at a value of -5. Notice the impact of these small changes.

   You just lightened the lighter midtones and darkened the darker midtones. The result of this is to expand the tonal range of the midtone region. This expansion adds contrast to the midtones without affecting the darkest and lightest tones. The resulting curve has a gentle S-curve. This is generally the way tone curves are used. Keep in mind that the Tone curve is intended for tweaking, so begin with small adjustments.

2. In Figure 7.17 you can see three small triangles at the bottom of the histogram. These sliders are called *split controls* because they affect the range of tonal adjustment on specific regions. When you drag them sideways they change the way tonal regions are split by the Region sliders. These changes are reflected in the bubble highlight along the diagonal line.

   To modify the range of tones affected by a slider, move the split control sliders below the graph. The default setting for the sliders is 25 percent, 50 percent, and 75 percent. When these sliders are moved they affect the range of tones inside the adjustment bubble. In the first image in Figure 7.17 the two outside sliders are at the default settings of 25 percent and 75 percent. In the second image they are repositioned to 12 percent and 88 percent. That means that the Shadows slider affects the range between 0 percent and 12 percent now, instead of 0 percent–25 percent. The highlight tones that are represented by the Highlights slider in the first image are now in the range of 88 percent–100 percent, instead of 75 percent–100 percent. Practice with this technique until you get a feel for how these changes affect the action of the sliders.

FIGURE 7.17

The tonal regions affected by the Tone Curve sliders are modified by adjusting the Highlight split and Shadow split sliders directly below the graph. When these sliders are moved outward they reduce the size of the shadow and highlight adjustment bubbles.

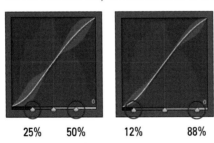

      25%   50%   12%   88%

3. Now that you understand how the Tone Curve panel works, I want to show you something really cool. Click on the target icon on the top left of the panel. This activates the Targeted Adjustment tool. Notice that as you drag it across details in the photo, the corresponding tones are displayed on the graph in the Tone Curves panel. Here's the cool part. Hover over the model's forehead. Try to find an area that is close to 50 percent on the graph. Click on the spot and drag the mouse upward to increase the values for the area. Click and drag downward to darken the tones.

CAUTION If you're using a mouse that has a zoom feature, you may have trouble getting this to work. Try pressing the Spacebar to reveal the adjustment icon.

This Targeted Adjustment tool takes the guesswork out of using the Tone Curve controls. Instead of guessing if a tone you want to adjust is in the Lights or Darks, you can simply click and drag it to adjust it, letting the sliders take care of themselves. Click the target again to deactivate the tool, or click Done on the Toolbar. (You can also press Esc to cancel any tool.)

NOTE The two numbers in the upper-left corner of the Tone Curve graph indicate the before adjustment and after adjustment tonal percentages. The number in the lower-right corner indicates the actual adjustment that's been applied to that region.

4. Go back to where the image was before Step 2. Go to the History panel on the left and scroll downward. When you find the lowest history state that says Dark Tones - 5 click on it to take the image back to the end of Step 1. You can also back up in time by using the Undo command (Command/Ctrl+Z). Each time you press it you back up one step. To move a step forward (Redo), press Shift+Command (Ctrl)+Z.

CAUTION Command (Ctrl) +Z works differently in Photoshop. It's more of a toggle. The first time you use it the result is Undo. When you use it again the result is Redo. This allows you to quickly go back and forth to evaluate a particular adjustment.

The Tone Curve controls are designed as a supplement to the Basic panel's controls. Use them to make minor tweaks when necessary. If you don't see a need for the Tone Curve controls, it's okay to skip this panel completely.

Fine-tuning color with the HSL and Color panels

The HSL/Color/Grayscale panel combines three panels into one. The HSL and Color panels give you incredible control over the colors in a photo, while the Grayscale panel allows you to fine-tune how those colors are represented by grayscale tones in a black-and-white conversion. The HSL and Color both allow you to modify the Hue, Saturation, and Luminance of eight colors.

People sometimes get the terms hue, saturation, and luminance confused. Here's what they mean:

- **Hue:** Describes the color itself — red as opposed to orange
- **Saturation:** Describes the purity of the colors in the color range — bright colors as opposed to dull colors
- **Luminance:** Describes the brightness of the color range — light colors as opposed to dark colors

Both the Color and HSL panels work in much the same way; they just present the same controls in different layouts. There is, however, one huge difference. The HSL panel, shown in Figure 7.18, has your friend the Targeted Adjustment tool.

FIGURE 7.18

The HSL panel allows you to address the three main qualities of color: hue, saturation, and luminance. To see all controls at once, click All.

NOTE When working with color in Lightroom two more colors are added to this mix. They are orange and purple. Orange is a combination of red and yellow. It's useful for this color to be added because it covers most of the color range of Caucasian skin color. Purple is a combination of blue and magenta. Also, cyan is referred to as aqua.

Let's take the HSL panel for a spin so that you can see how easy it is to gain control over specific colors in an image. When you finish this exercise you'll never think about color the same way again.

1. With the practice file still open, click Hue at the top of the HSL panel. Click and drag the Red slider to the right until the value is +100. The red flowers in the background are now orange, yet most other colors stay the same.

2. Click and drag the Green slider to the left to make all the greens more yellow.

3. These changes make the purple flowers in the upper left more obvious. Adjusting the values of the Purple and Magenta sliders don't help to make the color blend in, but there is a way to adjust the flowers. Click Saturation to activate the Saturation sliders. Click and drag the Purple slider all the way to the left (-100) to remove all color from this range. Click Luminance to display the Luminance sliders. Click and drag the Purple slider all the way to the right to lighten the area. Now this section of purple flowers isn't as obvious as it was.

4. Compare the new version with the old. Click the Before and After views button on the left side of the Toolbar, next to the Loupe button. The view is divided into two panels, as shown in Figure 7.19. The view on the left is of the photo before any develop settings were applied. The view on the right is the photo with the current adjustments. To change the way these views display, click the triangle next to the icon to display a pop-up menu. Choose Before/After Left/Right Split. This splits the photo down the middle with before on the left and after on the right. (You can also click the button itself to cycle through the four settings.)

TIP Every adjustment panel has a small on and off button at the far left of its header. (It looks like a light switch.) Click it to turn off the adjustment. Click it again to turn it back on. This is a great way to hide only one adjustment instead of all adjustments with Before and After views.

FIGURE 7.19

Before and After views allow you to compare your current editing state to the original photo. You can zoom in and pan both images at once. Choose from the menu beside the button to change the way the two images display. This one is Before/After Left/Right Split. The other option buttons allow you to copy or swap settings between the two images.

> **TIP**
>
> Remember that you can add tools to the Toolbar by clicking the triangle button on the right of the bar and choosing from the Toolbar menu.

5. Zoom in to get a closer look, and use the Hand tool to drag and reposition the image. As you hover over the image, two sets of color values are displayed on the Tool bar. The first number is the before color value and the second number is the current value. When you zoom in on the face it's clear to see that the global change in color had a negative impact on skin-tone colors, especially around the nose. The lips are also completely desaturated because they contain some of the same tones we were modifying in the purple flowers.

6. Click on the Loupe view button to return to a single image display. Make these adjustments with the Targeted Adjustment tool. First, return the HSL values to their defaults. Click All to display all three setting groups. Press and hold the Alt key. The word Reset appears next to the names of each section. Click each of these headings to reset the values in them.

7. Zoom out so you can see the red flowers. Click Hue and then click the Targeted Adjustment tool to activate it. Click on a red flower and drag the mouse upward. Notice that the Red and Orange sliders both move. That's because the Targeted Adjustment tool sees orange in the flower, too. Try working with this tool in the Saturation and Luminance sections too by choosing them from the header. You can also change what's being affected with the Targeted Adjustment tool by choosing from the contextual menu on the Toolbar. When you finish experimenting, click Done or press Esc to cancel.

> **CAUTION**
>
> When the Targeted Adjustment tool is activated, it stays active until you; click Done, cancel, or click on the tool's button again.

As you can see, Lightroom gives you an amazing amount of control over the color ranges in an image. This control is especially useful when converting color photos to black and white.

Creating custom black-and-white photos

Black-and-white images are called grayscale because the tones they use are neutral — different shades of gray. True grayscale images in Photoshop use a color model with only one channel, rather than the three channels used by the RGB color model. That means that, in essence, when you convert a color photo to black and white you combine the three grayscale color channels (refer to Figure 7.4) into a single grayscale channel. The Grayscale panel enables you to manage that conversion by choosing how the tones of the original colors are emphasized.

This concept is much easier to understand when you see it in action. Just follow these steps:

1. Go back to the practice image. If you made any radical changes in the HSL panel, undo them now. Click Grayscale, next to HSL and Color, to open the Grayscale panel, as shown in Figure 7.20.

FIGURE 7.20

The Grayscale panel allows you to adjust the grayscale brightness of specific colors.

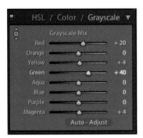

2. Increasing a color's value makes its grayscale value lighter. Lowering the value darkens the corresponding tones. Click and drag the Red slider to the left. As you do, the tones in the red flowers in the background get darker. Stop when you get close to -20.

3. Click and drag the Green slider to the right to increase the brightness of all green tones, stopping when the value is close to +40.

TIP Click the Auto button to let Photoshop automatically convert the tones in the image. This works quite well and is often a good starting place for further experimentation.

4. To see the effect of your changes, click the on/off switch button on the left of the panel's header. This switch turns off the grayscale mix, while leaving the image in Grayscale mode. Turn the switch back on when you're ready to continue.

5. Use the Targeted Adjustment tool to click on the plants in the background to lighten them more. As you do, notice that the Yellow slider is moving with the Green slider. That's because the plants have yellow in them as well as green. Continue working with the grayscale mix until you like your results.

> **TIP** Sometimes you need to revisit the Basic panel to fine-tune the image's brightness and contrast after doing a grayscale conversion. If you know you're planning to make a black and white from the start, change it to grayscale in the Basic panel before adjusting tonality. You can also press V to convert the photo to grayscale. Press V again to switch it back to color.

The Grayscale panel works much like the HSL and Color panels. It gives you the ability to custom mix the way specific colors are interpreted during the grayscale conversion process. It's perfect for darkening blue skies or lightening flesh tones without affecting other tones in the photo.

Applying a brown tone with the Split Toning panel

Split toning is a process where a colorcast is added to the highlights and a second colorcast is added to the shadows. The colors used for these two tones can be similar or completely different. When they're applied to a color photo the results can look quite unusual. I know many photographers who use split toning on color photos for special effects, but most use it for adding a color tone to black-and-white images. This color is usually a warm brown tone (sometimes called sepia) though any color can be used.

> **NOTE** Before Photoshop and digital photography, shooting color negative film and processing it in slide film chemistry — or vice versa — was called *cross-processing*. That's why you often hear people call split-toned color images cross-processed.

Figure 7.21, shows the Split Toning panel. You can use it to give your black-and-white practice photo a warm tone. Follow these steps:

1. Pick up where you left off with Step 5 in the last exercise. Go to the Split Toning panel, directly below the HSL, Color, Grayscale panel. In the Highlights section adjust the Hue setting to 35. Adjust the Saturation slider to 15. As you move the sliders, the color swatch next to Highlights shows a preview of the color that's created by the combination of the sliders. The photo now has a slight tone that's mostly visible in the highlights.

> **NEW FEATURE** You can also click on a color swatch and use the new color picker in Lightroom 2 to visually select a specific color. This new feature is discussed in Chapter 8.

2. Go to the Shadow section. Click and drag the slides to duplicate the settings from the Highlights sliders. Now that the shadows are toned, the overall toning is much easier to see. Experiment with different color combinations until you get a nice warm brown tone. (Some people prefer a cooler, more chocolaty brown.)

In Steps 1 and 2, you used the same color for toning the highlights and shadows. I usually do this when toning a grayscale image. However, in a true split-toned image the two colors are different. If you decide you want to use different colors for your toning, you can use the Balance slider to shift the overall color preference toward the shadow tone or the highlight tone.

FIGURE 7.21

The Split Toning panel is ideal for quickly toning grayscale photos. The sliders on the top are used to adjust the highlight toning, and the sliders on the bottom are used to adjust shadow toning. The small color patches preview the color mix for each set of sliders.

After you find the split-toning mix you like, it's a good idea to save it so that you don't have to remember it or experiment every time you want to apply it to a photo. Fortunately, that's easy to do in Lightroom.

Saving time with presets

Lightroom is loaded with presets. That's because it's intended to be a true Production Workflow tool, and presets are one of the most efficient ways of editing images quickly. These presets come in two varieties: presets that come with Lightroom and user-created presets.

The Develop presets function much like Actions in Photoshop, though they're much easier to create and use. (Photoshop Actions are discussed in Chapter 18.) The idea behind both Presets and Actions is to create a shortcut that records editing steps so they can be applied to other images with the click of a button.

 Layout presets in the Slideshow, Print, and Web modules are called templates.

To create a Develop preset for your brown tone mixture in the Split Toning panel, follow these steps:

1. Click on the plus sign (+) on the header of the Presets panel. The New Develop Preset dialog box appears (see Figure 7.22), which enables you to choose the settings needed to create the effect.

FIGURE 7.22

The New Develop Preset dialog box. When creating a Develop preset in the New Develop Preset dialog box you need to be sure to include only the steps that are necessary to complete the desired result.

2. Because this preset will be used on all sorts of images, be sure that only the necessary steps are included in the new preset. For example, the Basic Tone settings on your practice file are unique to it. You don't want to apply those settings to other photos when they're toned. Click Check None to clear the check boxes.

3. Select the Split Toning and the Treatment (Grayscale) options only. Now when the preset is applied to a color photo, the photo changes to grayscale and the current split toning recipe is applied. (Select the Auto Grayscale Mix option if you want Lightroom to automatically mix the grayscale tones before toning.)

4. Type a name in the Preset Name box and click Create. The new preset is added to the User Presets in the Presets panel. Any color image can now be converted to grayscale and toned by selecting it and clicking the preset.

Learning to use presets is extremely powerful. It's the most efficient way to apply quick creative touches during the production phase of the workflow. It's much better to spend a bit of time creating these presets than it is to work with every file on a custom basis. If you find yourself using the same techniques on different photos, look for a way to automate the process with a preset. In Chapter 5, you learn that Develop presets can be used during the import process. This is where those presets are created and managed.

If you begin to accumulate lots of Develop presets, you can organize them into folders. To create a new folder, right-click on a preset and choose New Folder. After you create the folder, presets are dragged into it in the usual way. To modify an existing preset, make the desired changes to the photo and right-click on the preset. Choose Update with Current Settings. To delete a preset, right-click it and choose Delete or use the minus sign (-) on the panel's header.

Creating multiple versions of the same photo

Sometimes it's a good idea to save a version of a photo before making changes to it. This is especially useful when you need different versions for output such as a color photo and a black and white. The fastest and least complicated way to save the current editing state of a photo is to take a snapshot of it with the Snapshots panel.

Taking snapshots

The Snapshots panel is easy to use. To create a new snapshot of a photo, click the plus sign (+) on the panel's header and type a new name for the snapshot. To make three snapshots of your practice file, follow these steps:

1. Go back to your favorite sepia version of the practice file. Click the plus sign (+) on the Snapshots panel header. When the new snapshot is added, name it Brown Tone.

TIP   To create a snapshot of a history state, right-click on the state and choose Create Snapshot.

2. Go to the Split Toning panel and click the on/off button on the panel's header. This deactivates the Split Toning adjustments and returns the photo to black and white.

3. Go to the Snapshots panel and create a new snapshot called Black & White.

4. Click on HSL on the HSL/Color/Grayscale panel to return the photo to color (or press V).

5. Go to the Snapshots panel and create a new snapshot called Color.

Now you have three different snapshots of this particular photo. The photo can be instantly returned to those settings by clicking on the appropriate snapshot. Snapshots are a great way to create different versions of a photo that stay with the originating file. I use them mostly when I'm not sure about how I want to solve a particular problem. I try a couple of solutions and take snapshots of them. Then I can compare them to see which one is the solution I'll use.

Creating virtual copies

One of the problems with snapshots is that they can only be accessed in the Develop module, which can be clumsy when you're showing photos to someone else. A different way to create another version of a photo is to make a *virtual copy* of it. A virtual copy is like a duplicate of the photo, but it's virtual because no second file is really created. Instead, metadata describing the second version is stored in the catalog. These copies only become real files when they're exported or edited in external software such as Photoshop. The best thing about virtual copies is that they're like real copies of the photo that can be edited and managed independently. Follow these steps to make a virtual copy of your practice file:

1. The practice file should be in color right now (see Step 5 earlier). There are several ways to create a virtual copy. The formal way is to choose Photo ➪ Create Virtual Copy (Command/Ctrl+'). The easiest is with a right-click. To create one now, right-click on the main image display (or the thumbnail in the Filmstrip) and choose Create Virtual Copy from the contextual menu. A second thumbnail is added to the Filmstrip and it becomes the selected thumbnail, meaning any new editing is applied to the copy.

   The original thumbnail has a 2 in the upper-left corner signifying that there are two copies of it. When the mouse is hovered, the original 1 of 2 displays, indicating that it's the *master photo*. The new thumbnail displays 2 of 2 when the mouse is hovered over it, indicating that it is the second of two copies.

   The new thumbnail also has a page-turn icon in its lower-left corner. This tells you that it's a virtual copy. Double-clicking this icon selects the original thumbnail that the virtual copy is linked to.

> **TIP** Virtual copies can be created in all modules, though there is no menu command for it in the Slideshow, Print, and Web modules.

2. Go to the Grid view of the Library module (G). The original and its copy are joined in the middle, as shown in Figure 7.23. This lets you know that the thumbnails share the same original. If you don't want to see both copies, click one of the vertical bars in front of the first thumbnail or to the right of the second thumbnail. This places them into a stack with the original file on top. Click one of the buttons again to reveal both copies.

3. Go back to the Develop module (D) and apply your new Brown Tone preset to the virtual copy. Now you have two independent versions of the same photo that can be used in any of Lightroom's modules.

> **TIP** You can use the Copy Status section of the Attribute section of the Library Filter Bar to locate all virtual copies in the selected folder.

Virtual copies are extremely useful, but I've seen several photographers get buried under too many. If you're experimenting, use snapshots to track various versions. When you really need a second file, create a virtual copy. Make your life easier by stacking virtual copies when you're not using them.

FIGURE 7.23

When a virtual copy is next to its original in the Grid view the vertical line between them is eliminated, indicating that they're related. To stack them, click one of the vertical lines at either side (circled). Notice that both files have the same name. Copies are identified in the Copy Name field of the Metadata panel.

Improving the Finer Points with the Detail Panel

The Detail panel, shown in Figure 7.24, combines sliders for two of those things photographers hear a lot about, but often don't understand: noise removal and sharpening. In Lightroom 2 another section labeled Chromatic Aberration has been relocated to the Detail panel. This section controls one of the more esoteric things you run into when different colored rays of light are not all focused on the same plane. Let's explore these concepts as we look at their respective sliders.

Removing noise

Noise in a digital photo manifests as tiny *artifacts* — distortions introduced by the digital process — that look much like the grain in film. In the early days of digital photography, noise was an issue in nearly every photo. Fortunately, digital cameras have improved in leaps and bounds over the last ten years. Today, the chips in most dSLR cameras do a very good job of minimizing noise. However, under certain conditions even those cameras produce noisy images.

Noise comes in two basic types: luminance noise (often called grayscale noise) and color noise. Luminance noise is all the same color of gray. It's usually found in the darker tones of underexposed photos (especially when lightening them) and photos shot at higher ISO settings. Color noise is speckled with different colors. I don't see it as often, but when I do it's usually in photos shot at night with longer exposures. (The long exposure makes the camera's chip heat up, which causes the noise.)

FIGURE 7.24

The Detail preview window in the Detail panel is a new feature in Lightroom 2. It always displays a 1:1 preview of the photo. Use the Target button to change the contents of the preview window by clicking on the main image display.

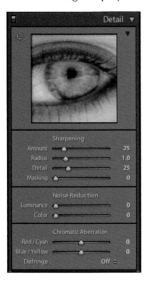

 To effectively remove noise it's necessary to zoom to 1:1 magnification; otherwise it's hard to see it. That's why the preview window in the Detail panel always displays 1:1.

Both of the Noise Reduction sliders work the same way. Use Luminance if you see grayscale noise and use Color if you see color speckles in the noise. (It's not uncommon to see color noise after the luminance noise is removed.) The Detail panel in Lightroom 2 has a new Preview widow that provides a 1:1 preview of the photo. To view a different part of the image in this preview, click the Target button and hover over the main image display area. Click when you find the spot you want to choose.

Figure 7.25 shows an image that has luminance noise visible in the dark background behind the young woman. To remove this noise, the level of the Luminance slider is increased to 75. You can see that the noise is reduced considerably in the After image. However, her facial features are also softer (not as sharp) due to the blurring effect of the filter. Because of this, a bit of sharpening often needs to be applied to counter the softening effect.

FIGURE 7.25

Noise is visible in the background of this photo. When it's removed with the Luminance Noise Reduction slider the overall sharpness of the image is reduced.

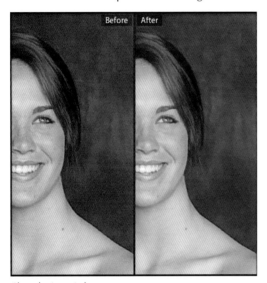

Photo by Jerry Auker

Understanding sharpening

I work with lots of photographers, most of them professionals. One of the first questions I ask is how they handle sharpening in their workflow. That's because sharpening is one of the most misunderstood aspects of the postproduction workflow. When it's done incorrectly during the production phase of the workflow it has a detrimental effect on the final images. If someone is making this mistake I want him or her to know before we move on to other things.

Three kinds of sharpening

At first thought, sharpening seems like a no-brainer. Who wouldn't want their photos to be sharp? However, the subject is much more complicated. The main reason is that there are three different kinds of sharpening. Each of these types of sharpening needs to be applied at the appropriate time:

- **Capture sharpening:** This sharpening isn't really about fixing blurry exposures, though it can help a bit. It's about bringing digitally captured images into line. By their very nature, digital image files need to have some sharpening applied. This sharpening pass is considered baseline sharpening.

- **Creative sharpening:** This is done during the creative phase of the workflow. It's used to fine-tune an image creatively by selectively sharpening — or blurring — areas of the image. (When the term "sharpening" is used here, it also refers to its opposite, *blurring*, which is the lack of sharpness.)

- **Output sharpening:** When a photo file is prepared for output such as printing or onscreen viewing it usually needs a final sharpening pass. One of the things to understand here is that size matters. A file that's being prepared for printing as a 5-x-7-inch print requires a completely different sharpening scenario than the same file being prepared as a 16 x 20. The 5 x 7 would look great, but the 16 x 20 would not be sharp enough. Sharpening scenarios also differ for different kinds of output such as onscreen viewing and printing press output. Output sharpening is usually applied in Photoshop at the end of the Creative Workflow.

CROSS-REF Output sharpening in Lightroom is discussed in Chapter 8. Creative and output sharpening with Photoshop are discussed in Chapter 21.

The reason sharpening is divided into these three areas is because oversharpening degrades the quality of a photo by introducing unwanted artifacts. Oversharpening occurs when output sharpening settings, which are stronger, are used for capture sharpening. Later when the image is sized and prepared for output it's necessary to sharpen again because the resizing affects the first sharpening pass. When the second sharpening pass is carried out on a previously oversharpened file it can adversely affect the quality of the image. The thing to remember is that while a file is in Lightroom all sharpening settings can be undone. However, after the file leaves Lightroom for advanced editing in Photoshop, you'll have to live with any capture sharpening applied during the production phase of the workflow.

CAUTION Most cameras have a sharpening setting that allows you to apply different sharpening presets to your photos as you capture them. If you're shooting raw, this setting has no permanent effect on the image. However, if you shoot JPEG, it does have a permanent effect. I always recommend turning off all in-camera sharpening when shooting JPEG because it's easy to add sharpening later but impossible to remove it after the fact.

Capture sharpening with the Detail panel

Digital photo sharpening is nothing more than enhanced edge contrast. Lightroom and Photoshop trick you into thinking a photo looks sharper by isolating edge detail and enhancing contrast along those edges. One side of the edge is lightened while the other side is darkened. The enhanced edge contrast is often referred to as *haloing* because of the effect it causes along the edge. Each of the Sharpening sliders in the Detail panel affects edges in different ways.

There is no magic formula for capture sharpening because the amount of sharpening often depends on the content of the image. Images with lots of edge detail, like the bowl of silver rings in Figure 7.26, can handle more sharpening than images with fewer hard edges, such as photos of people.

FIGURE 7.26

This bowl of silver rings has a high frequency of edge detail, which means it needs more sharpening than a photo with less edge detail. The second image shows the Sharpening preview when pressing the Alt key in conjunction with the Radius slider.

Photo by Jordan Sleeth

There are four sliders in the Sharpening section. Each is designed to affect a different aspect of the process. Here's a brief description of each of them:

- **Amount** is just that — the amount of sharpening. Higher values equal more edge contrast, which equals more edge detail. The red color on the right side of this slider is a reminder to be careful about going to high on this value. For general capture sharpening try to stay below 50.

- **Radius** determines how many surrounding pixels are considered when the Smart Sharpen filter finds an edge. Higher values expand the size of the sharpening halo. Extreme values create noticeable halos that detract from the image. Notice that a value of 3.0 is the maximum value. You can go much higher in Photoshop. Adobe did this because they understand the need for low levels of sharpening at this phase of the workflow.

- **Detail** is used to modify the degree of sharpening applied by the Amount and Radius sliders. Lower values restrict sharpening to edges with higher contrast, which reduces overall haloing. Higher values increase haloing and apply sharpening effects to most of the image. When working with photos that have a high frequency of image detail, use higher settings. When editing images with a low frequency of detail, use lower settings.

- **Masking** is also used to control the effects of the Amount and Radius sliders by creating an edge mask that attempts to isolate higher-contrast edges that benefit the most from sharpening. Low values allow sharpening to be applied to a greater range of detail. High values restrict sharpening to edges with the strongest contrast.

> **NOTE** When you edit raw files you notice that a small amount of sharpening is applied in the Detail panel by default. This default sharpening is used to get these unprocessed files into the ballpark. It's up to you to determine if this baseline level of sharpening is adequate for the image(s) in question.

These four sliders may seem confusing at first because they all affect one another. My recommendation is to focus on using the Amount and Radius sliders. When working with images with a high degree of detail, use the Detail slider to manage how sharpening is applied. When editing a photo with a mixture of high and low detail frequency, use the Masking slider.

> **TIP** Hold down the Alt key to preview the halos in the Detail preview window while adjusting the Radius and Detail sliders. Using the Alt key with the Mask slider previews the mask. Affected areas appear as white while protected areas appear as black.

Let's use the Detail panel to address the capture sharpening of your practice file. Follow these steps:

1. Zoom to 1:1. The overall focus of the image is a bit soft so this photo needs a little more sharpening than if it was in perfect focus. Keep in mind, though, that poorly focused photos can't be helped much by sharpening.

   Experiment with the Sharpening sliders while viewing the woman's face in the main display area. Notice that her skin becomes hard and crunchy, as opposed to soft and smooth, as the Amount, Radius, and Detail values increase because contrast is added to small details in her skin. Any crunchiness at this stage will be amplified by future output sharpening, so keep it at a minimum now.

2. Use the Masking slider to tone down the effects of the other sliders. The final settings I use for this photo are Amount = 35, Radius = 1.3, Detail = 7, Masking = 35.

Sharpening is a necessary part of any digital workflow. Learn to use these sliders, but don't make yourself crazy agonizing over the countless variations possible. Try to move quickly so that you don't spend too much time here. The most important thing to remember about sharpening during this stage of the workflow is to be careful about overdoing it. In fact, it's better to leave photos at their default settings than it is to oversharpen them.

Removing chromatic aberration

Chromatic aberration is caused by different wavelengths of light not being focused in the same spot. When it appears in your photo it looks like colored fringing — usually magenta or cyan — around details in the image. Low-quality lenses can cause chromatic aberration, and it can also appear when a subject has strong backlighting. When these two conditions combine, expect to see chromatic aberration. When you do, use the Chromatic Aberration sliders in the Detail panel to remove it.

Like noise reduction, chromatic aberration is best evaluated when zoomed to 1:1. Figure 7.27 shows a detail of a tree branch with strong backlighting. In the first frame, the magenta fringing is very obvious. The second frame shows the branch after adjusting the Chromatic Aberration Red/Cyan slider to a value of +50. The adjustment removed the fringing without affecting the overall color.

151

The Defringe menu is used to control the edges that are affected. Choose All Edges to correct fringing on all edges. This can cause unwanted gray lines to show up where colors make a strong transition. If this happens, choose Highlight Edges so that the only edges affected are in areas where fringing is likely to occur. Choosing Off deactivates defringing.

FIGURE 7.27

Strong backlighting caused colored fringing around these tree branches (left). The fringing was removed (right) by adjusting the Red/Cyan slider under Chromatic Aberration.

Using Lightroom's Vignetting Tools

In Lightroom 1, there was only one way to change the tonal ranges of a photo's corners to adjust vignetting. There are three methods in Lightroom 2. Two of those methods, Lens Correction and Post-Crop, are in the new Vignettes panel, shown in Figure 7.28.

FIGURE 7.28

The new Vignettes panel in Lightroom allows you to control the tonality of the edges of a photo.

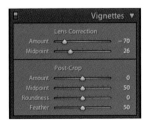

Adjusting lens vignetting

In-camera lens vignetting is often caused by a lens defect that causes the outer edges of the photo to be darker than the rest of the photo. It occurs with lower-quality lenses and lenses with ill-fitting lens hoods where the edge of the hood is seen by the lens.

This problem is easily solved with the Lens Correction slider in the Vignettes panel. Increase the Amount value to lighten the corners. Adjust the Midpoint slider to change the size of the area affected by the Amount slider. Higher values restrict the tonal changes to the edges. Lower values increase the size of the affected area by moving them closer to the center.

Many people use this slider in the opposite way. When the Amount slider is lowered the corners of a photo can be darkened, giving it a more finished look. The first image in Figure 7.29 has this effect.

FIGURE 7.29

The first frame here has its corners darkened by using a negative value with the Lens Correction slider. The Post-Crop slider works the same way on cropped photos. Here a positive value was used to create a light vignette.

Adjusting vignetting in cropped photos

One problem with the Lens Correction tool is that it only affects the original corners of the image. If cropping is applied, the darkened corners are cropped out. This problem is solved with the addition of a new vignetting tool in Lightroom 2 called Post-Crop. All darkening/lightening is contained within the boundaries of the cropping overlay. If the crop is changed, the adjustments are modified to stay inside the cropping boundaries. (Cropping is covered in just a moment.)

Post-Crop works in much the same way as Lens Correction. The only difference is that there are two additional sliders: Roundness and Feather. Here's what they do:

- **Roundness:** This slider adjusts the shape of the vignette. Positive values make the shape rounder. Negative values cause the shape to become more square.

- **Feather:** This slider softens the inner transitional boundary of the vignette. Positive values soften the transition, and lower values create a harder transition.

Both the Lens Correction and Post-Crop sliders can be used to quickly add a finished look to all photos from a shoot by applying the settings to one photo and synchronizing them with the rest of the photos. If one of those photos is going to be moved into Photoshop for advanced editing, these settings should be turned off so more sophisticated techniques can be used for edge darkening.

Using the New Tool Strip

In Lightroom all of the main editing tools have been relocated from the Toolbar to the new Tool Strip. When a tool is selected a contextual panel opens below the Tool Strip to reveal settings specific to that tool. I applaud the engineers at Adobe for coming up with such an elegant solution for making it easier to use these tools.

Three of these tools were on the Toolbar in Lightroom 1: Crop Overlay, Spot Removal, and Red Eye Correction. Two new tools have been added, the Graduated Filter and Adjustment Brush. Of all of these tools, the Adjustment Brush is the most exciting so let's begin with it.

Using the Adjustment Brush tool

 Click the Adjustment Bursh tool button on the Tool Strip to activate it. When you do, the a panel opens with all of the Adjustment Brush options shown in Figure 7.30. (To hide the panel, click the tool a second time.) At first, this tool looks complicated, but when you take a closer look it's easy to see that there are two main sections: Effect and Brush.

Painting in effects

The way this tool works is simple. You choose an effect from the Effect section and then you use a brush to paint in the effect wherever you want it. It creates something called a *mask* that allows the effect to only show where you want it. For example, you could use a negative Brightness value to darken the edges of the photo to customize the shape of your vignetting instead of using the Vignettes panel. You can even paint different effects into different regions of the photo.

The new Tool Strip has five tool buttons on its header. When one of these tools is chosen a panel opens to reveal options for that tool. This view shows the comprehensive Adjustment Brush options. (Notice that the on/off button is at the lower left instead of upper left.)

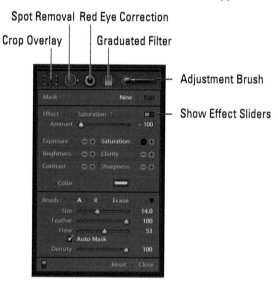

CROSS-REF **Chapter 16 covers masking in detail.**

Try this tool on the practice photo. Follow these steps:

1. Open the practice file titled garden_girl.dng from the downloadable practice files on the Web site. If you've been using in the previous examples, make sure it's being displayed in color (V). Click the Adjustment Brush tool to activate it (K). Choose Saturation from the Effect pop-up menu or by choosing it from the presets below the Amount slider, and lower the value to -100, which removes all color saturation. (You can also specify minus saturation by clicking the minus sign next to Saturation.)

   Make sure that Auto Mask in the Brush section is unselected and that the Feather value is set to 0.

2. Begin painting the model to desaturate her, while leaving the background intact. When you begin painting, a circular pin appears where you first applied the stroke. The pin is like a push pin that marks a correction area. Additional strokes are applied to that selected correction area. Use the scroll wheel on your mouse to reduce the size of the brush when you get close to an edge. When you do, notice that the Size slider in the Brush section changes accordingly.

TIP **To create a new adjustment area click New in the Mask section. When you begin to paint, a new pin marks the spot. To edit a preexisting mask, click its pin to make it active. The active pin is the one with the black inner circle. Use H to hide/reveal all pins.**

3. Zoom in when you get near the edges so you can see them better (Command/Ctrl++). Use Command/Ctrl+- to zoom back out. If you need to pan the zoomed image, hold down the Shift key to temporarily access the Hand tool. (These shortcuts also work in Photoshop.)

4. If you notice a place where the background was accidentally desaturated, choose Erase from the Brush section. To go back to painting click one of the brush presets: A or B. (You can also hold down Alt to temporarily switch the tool to its opposite function.) When you finish, your photo should look something like Figure 7.31.

TIP **You can click on a pin and drag to the right to increase the current value or drag to the left to decrease it.**

FIGURE 7.31

The Adjustment Brush tool is used here to paint out the color by creating a mask. When you hover over the area after painting, a pin appears, allowing you to reselect the mask.

5. After a mask is in place, you can change it in a number of ways. Go to the Amount slider in the Effect section and increase the value to -70. Notice that some of the saturation comes back into the photo. This slider allows you to modify the mask after you paint it.

   Choose Brightness from the Effect presets. When you do the mask becomes a brightness mask instead of a saturation mask. Increasing the value lightens the model and decreasing it darkens her.

6. If you were through with the image you would click Done at the footer of the panel to collapse the panel and accept the changes. Click Close to cancel the changes and remove all painting.

7. Below the Amount slider is a set of the same six adjustments that are in the effect pop-up menu: Exposure, Brightness, Contrast, and Clarity have the same effects as the same sliders in the Basic panel. Sharpness adds or removes sharpness. Positive values increase sharpness, and negative values decrease it. You can use the plus and minus buttons to adjust these settings, but it's easier to control them by choosing an Effect preset and using the Amount slider.

   Click the Show Effect Sliders button to the right of the Effect presets. (It looks like an on/off switch on its side.) This changes all of the plus/minus buttons to sliders, making them more useful because each has its own amount slider. But it does something else too.

8. Press Reset at the footer of the panel to remove all painting. Change the Saturation value to -100 and the Brightness value to 25. Now when you paint you'll be modifying color saturation and tonal brightness. You can even do this to a preexisting mask by selecting it first. That means you can paint the mask and then work with these six sliders to get just the effect you're looking for. This has to be the coolest improvement to Lightroom 2!

The Color control is used to paint with a color tint overlay. For example, you can use a warm color to tint the sky to enhance it for a late afternoon shot. Choose the color using the Color swatch at the bottom of the Effect section. Use the Effect Amount slider to modify the color's translucency.

Working with brushes

To get the most from the Adjustment Brush you need to understand a few basics about working with brushes. The lower section of the panel is used to modify several brush characteristics. These are:

- **Brush Presets:** The Adjustment Brush has three presets; A, B, and Erase. Each of these presets is *sticky*; when a preset is active and you use the sliders below it, those setting remain in effect for that preset. If you choose the A preset and change the Size value to 2.5, then if you switch to B and then back to A, the size setting will be where you left it. This allows you to store two brushes and an erasing brush.

- **Size:** This is the size of the brush. Higher values increase the size of the brush, which is reflected in the size of the cursor. You can also use the bracket keys [ ] to change the size of the brush. The left key decreases the size and the right] key increases it. (This is also a Photoshop shortcut.)

- **Feather**: The feather setting affects the hardness/softness of the edge of the brush. When you paint along hard edges use lower settings. When painting along softer edges, use a higher setting to hide your strokes.

- **Flow:** This setting allows you to control the amount of paint going to the brush. Lower values restrict the flow. This causes the brush to work more like an airbrush or spray can. The more you apply it in one place, the greater the buildup of paint.

- **Auto Mask:** Sometimes it's hard to paint along an edge. You probably noticed it while working on the practice file. Auto Mask helps by looking at the colors you're painting and restricting the brush to those colors. Turning this on for the last exercise would have made it much easier to paint the edges of the girl. Be sure to turn it off when painting areas with lots of colors.

- **Density:** This affects the intensity of the brush strokes. Higher values create more effect and lower values reduce it.

 Brush settings cannot be modified after painting as the Effect settings can be.

Getting creative

Because of this new tool there are a number of common things that can now be accomplished in Lightroom 2 that couldn't be done in Lightroom 1. The main one is local toning, also known as burning and dodging. Local toning allows you to even out the tones in the image by lightening things that are too dark and darkening things that are too light.

Another thing you can do is creative sharpening. For example, you can use negative sharpness settings to paint the background behind the girl to soften the focus. When you do this, the subject tends to stand out from the background better. Then you can increase the sharpness to a low positive value and paint the girl's eyes to sharpen them a bit.

A third technique is to use negative values with the Clarity slider to soften skin to get a beauty retouching effect. Just paint any skin that you want to soften. Be sure to turn on Auto Mask when you work around the eyes or other important details so they are unaffected.

CROSS-REF Each of the three preceding techniques is covered in detail in the Photoshop chapters of the book. However, this is a good place to become familiar with them.

TIP Remember that you can save some of your favorite settings as presets in the Presets panel. If you accumulate several Adjustment Brush presets, consider organizing them into their own folder.

Using the Graduated Filter tool

 The Graduated Filter tool works in much the same way as the Painting tool. Instead of using a brush, though, a linear gradient is used to modify image properties. A gradient applies more of an effect to one part of the photo than it does to another. The effect fades along the length of the gradient. Follow these steps to learn how it's done:

CROSS-REF To learn more about how gradients are used with masks in Photoshop, see Chapter 16.

1. Activate the Graduated Filter tool. If you still have the practice image garden_girl.dng open, click Reset on the Adjustment Brush tool panel to undo any work you did with that tool.

2. Choose Brightness from the presets and lower the amount to -100. Click in the top-right corner and drag across the image toward the lower-right corner, as shown in Figure 7.32. When you do, a gradient is applied along the length of the line you draw. The tones at the beginning of the line are darker than the tones at the end. Change the value of the Amount slider to see how different settings affect the image.

3. When you use the Graduated Filter three lines appear perpendicular to the gradient line you draw. These lines represent the tonal range of the gradient. The first line up in the corner represents the darkest tones, the middle line with the pin on it represents the mid-tones, and the line in the lower left (with the hand on it in Figure 7.32) represents the lightest tones of the gradient.

   Click and drag the middle line to the right and notice how it compresses the darker tones toward the upper right. Now drag the line toward the lower left and notice how it spreads the darker tones toward the middle.

FIGURE 7.32

After choosing Brightness and lowering the value to -100, a gradient is drawn from the top right to the lower left. Use the pin to select the gradient if other gradients are present. Click and drag a line to modify the transitions between it and the next line.

4. Click in another corner and draw another gradient. You can't do this with the Gradient tool in Photoshop. With that tool all new gradients replace the old. In Lightroom, not only can you create multiple gradients, you can also mix the gradient actions. For example, you can create a gradient that darkens and another that desaturates.

Ideal scenarios for this tool are when straight edges are involved. Say you have a photo of the ocean. You can use this tool to darken and saturate the blues in the sky without changing the beach because of the gradient effect. You could even use the Color setting to add more blue to the upper portion of the sky.

Retouching in Lightroom

Lightroom isn't really intended for serious retouching. However, it has a couple of tools that are used to quickly clean-up problems during the production phase of the workflow. They are the Spot Removal and Red-Eye Correction tools. Both tools are borrowed from Photoshop.

Removing spots

 When you choose the Spot Removal tool (N) your have two tool options: Clone and Heal. The idea behind both is similar to the way the Clone Stamp and Healing Brush tools are used in Photoshop. Information from one part of the photo is sampled and applied to another part of the photo. This is usually done to hide spots and other annoyances. The Clone tool makes a literal copy of sampled information, and the Healing tool intelligently blends the sampled information into the target area. I use the more powerful Healing tool whenever possible because it is so forgiving.

CROSS-REF See Chapter 17 for a detailed discussion on how the Clone Stamp and Healing Brush tools work in Photoshop.

Both the Clone and Heal options are used in the same way. The Size slider is used to adjust the size of the brush and Opacity is used to change the intensity of the effect. The Opacity slider is a welcome addition to Lightroom 2 because it allows you to tone down retouching if it's too strong.

When using the Spot Removal tool it's best to begin with a brush size just a bit larger than the targeted area (the thing to be removed). When you click on the spot to be retouched two circles appear. The first circle shows the spot where you clicked. Drag the other circle (the Sample circle) to any area you want to sample. As the Sample circle moves, the information inside it previews inside the Spot circle. An arrow that appears, as shown in Figure 7.33, points from the Sample circle to the Spot circle. Press H to hide the circles. Hold the H key down to temporarily hide them. Repeat the process on other spots as needed.

There are several things you can do after you apply this tool. You can change the circle size by clicking its edge and dragging inward or outward. You can change the opacity to blend retouching. You can change the position of either circle by clicking and dragging it. And you can change the action from Heal to Clone after the fact to see if you prefer one option to the other.

NOTE Because Lightroom is nondestructive, all retouching can be undone at any time by clicking the Remove Spots tool's Reset button.

If you're used to Photoshop's versions of these tools, you'll find these severely lacking. When you think about it, that's the way it should be. Lightroom is intended for doing things fast. Time–consuming, complicated projects need the power of Photoshop. However, there's something you can do in Lightroom that you can't do in Photoshop. You can remove something in one photo and then share that retouching with other photos. (This can be done to raw files in ACR.) At first this doesn't sound very useful. For example, if I had taken several photos of the German shepherd in Figure 7.30, the trash would be in all of them. But it wouldn't be in exactly the same place unless I was using a tripod and I didn't change my zoom setting. As you know, that's rarely the case. If the spot moves around in the frame, it's hard to synchronize the spot removal. But there is a time when a problem area is in exactly the same spot in every photo — it's called sensor dust.

FIGURE 7.33

Removing spots — large or small — is a snap with the Remove Spots tool. Here the Heal option (no pun intended) is used to remove a piece of trash. Click on the trash and drag the brighter circle to the right until you find a suitable area to sample. Notice how the dark line in the pavement is lined up.

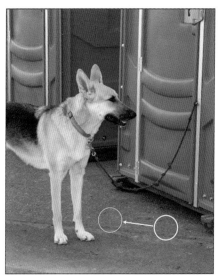

Just after Lightroom 1 was released a photographer came to me with a problem. She had photographed 150 pieces of jewelry for a client's Web site. All photos were shot against a white background. When she took a close look at the photos she noticed a large dark spot caused by sensor dust in the same place on the background in every photo. She called me in a panic because she needed to deliver the project and didn't have time to retouch 150 JPEG photos with Photoshop. I imported all of the images into Lightroom, used Remove Spots on one of them, and then shared the retouching settings with all 150 photos. Then I quickly went though all of the photos and moved the Sample circle on a few images where detail was being sampled by it instead of the white background. The whole project, including import, took about 15 minutes.

Removing red eye

Red eye is caused by light reflecting off the retina and bouncing back into the lens of the camera. It usually appears when a camera's flash is on the same plane as the lens. The effect is more pronounced in subjects who have gray or blue eyes, as well as children. It's a snap to remove in Lightroom with the Red Eye tool.

Click the tool to activate it. Then click in the center of the red area and drag outward until all of the red is covered by the cursor. When you release the mouse button the red is shaded with gray and two new sliders appear on the Toolbar: Pupil Size and Darken. Pupil Size is used to adjust the size of the cursor and Darken is used to darken or lighten the resulting tones. Click the Loupe (L) button when you finish with the tool or press Return. Use the tool's Reset button to undo changes.

161

Cropping Photos

There is one more tool in the Tool Strip, and it's probably the most important: the Crop Overlay tool. The coolest thing about the Crop Overlay tool is that — unlike Photoshop's Crop tool — it can be modified or undone after the fact.

The Crop Overlay, shown in Figure 7.34, has two important options. The first one looks like a small padlock. It's used to lock or unlock the cropping *aspect ratio* — the ratio of the cropping height to the width. The second setting is to the left of the lock. It's called Aspect. This is where specific aspect sizes are selected. Keep in mind that these are aspect ratios rather than actual sizes. For example, there is no difference between the 8 x 10 aspect ratio and the 4 x 5 aspect ratio because they have the same ratio of height to width. Sizing isn't applied until the file is output, exported, or opened in Photoshop. To use this tool, follow these steps:

FIGURE 7.34

The Crop Overlay tool is used to control all aspects of cropping. Click Reset to undo cropping at any time, or click Close to accept cropping changes.

1. Open the practice file one more time. Click the Crop Overlay tool (R) to activate it. Select 4x5 from the Aspect menu. Adjust the size of the crop by clicking and dragging one of its corners. The aspect ratio stays the same. Click on the image and drag it to reposition it inside the crop overlay. (This is the opposite of the way a crop is repositioned in Photoshop so it might take some getting used to.)

2. Click Reset to undo any cropping. This time select the Crop Frame tool to the left of Aspect. Use it to draw the crop you want by clicking and dragging across the image. The crop proportions are still locked to 4x5.

3. Changing a crop from horizontal to vertical, or vice versa, is a bit tricky. Click and drag one of the lower corners to the right or left until the cropping orientation flips. Drag it back to change it back to the original orientation. This takes a bit of practice but will become natural to you in no time.

4. Click the lock icon to unlock the aspect ratio. Now you can change the cropping on either of the sides, making the crop wider without changing its height.

5. The crop is rotated in three ways. When the cursor is moved outside the crop overlay the cursor changes to a curved arrow. Click and drag up or down to rotate the crop. You can also use the Straighten Slider on the Toolbar. A third option is to use the Straighten tool to draw a line on any line in the photo that you want to be vertical or horizontal.

TIP You can display a grid while cropping. Choose View ⇨ Crop Guide Overlay and choose from the menu. Or press O to cycle through the different overlay styles. To have the grid show only when you click on the crop overlay, choose View ⇨ Tool Overlay ⇨ Auto Show. To turn the grid off completely, select Never Show.

6. When you're satisfied with your crop, click Close on the Tool Strip or press Enter. The image is now displayed in its cropped state in the Filmstrip and Grid view. If you decide to change the cropping later all you have to do is click the Crop Overlay tool again.

Like every other setting in Lightroom, cropping can be shared with other images with the Synchronize button. This is especially powerful when several images all need to be cropped to the same aspect ratio. You might have to tweak a few of them, but it's much faster than cropping them one at a time.

Putting the Workflow into Action

Whew! You covered a lot of ground as you uncovered the details of the Develop module. Now it's a good idea to step back and get the big picture of how these details combine to create this phase of the production workflow. Even though there are lots of moving parts here, it's important to remember that efficiency is the main goal at this point of the workflow. Don't get me wrong; creativity is important, and it should be emphasized whenever it can be done efficiently, especially if the images will never be making the trip into Photoshop for advanced editing.

At the end of the last chapter the selected photos of the Smith family were labeled, filtered, and ready for the Develop module. Follow these steps to see how they make the trip through the Develop module:

1. The first thing to do in the Develop module is select the photo where the people are holding the calibration target (refer to Figure 7.12). The White Balance Selector is used to click-balance on the target's gray panel to custom white balance the photo. I then select all photos and use the Synchronize button to apply the custom white balance to them. I don't need this target photo anymore, so I press 8 to remove its green label, which removes it from the filtered view.

   If there were other poses in this portrait session that were shot under different light, I would make individual adjustments to the groups of photos in those groups. If those photos were from something like a vacation, and there were lots of them, I wouldn't be too picky about white balance unless I saw obvious problems.

TIP If you aren't using the panels on the left, maximize the viewing area by hiding them.

2. I select the first frame and adjust the Exposure, Blacks, and Brightness sliders with the clipping previews turned on in the Histogram panel. I allow some of the deep shadows in the shrubbery to clip, but I'm very careful about preventing any highlight clipping. I don't adjust the Recovery or Fill Light values because I don't have problem highlights or shadows in these images. I don't apply any Clarity adjustment to the photo because it accentuates the people's wrinkles. I move down to the Tone Curve panel and change the Lights value to +2 and the Darks value to -2 to add a touch of midtone contrast. Before I move on, I synchronize all of these values with all images.

> **TIP** When selecting groups of photos it's often faster to use the Filmstrip than it is to go back to Grid view.

3. The color looks good so I skip the HSL panel. I also skip the Split Toning panel. (In fact, I leave them collapsed unless I need them.) When I get to the Detail panel I zoom the image to 1:1 magnification. I first inspect the selected photo for noise, looking mostly in the darker tones. I don't see any so I move to the faces and begin evaluating the image for sharpness. I'm happy with the default settings, but I look at a few images to make sure they all look the same. If I had noticed any chromatic aberration during this step I would go directly to the Lens Correction panel.

> **TIP** You can save yourself a bit of time by using Auto Sync when working with groups of photos.

4. Now I take a moment to quickly survey each photo. I notice that several frames from the closer pose are suffering a bit of highlight clipping. I select one of those photos, adjust the Exposure setting, and then share that setting with the rest of the photos in that pose. During this step I look for any quick retouching that needs to be taken care of and any images that need cropping. I notice several where a light stand is showing on the right so I select one of those frames and crop it using the Original aspect ratio. I synchronize that setting with the other similar photos. I also use the Adjustment Brush tool set to Lighten Midtones to lighten the man's hair in some of the photos where it's blending into the dark background.

5. I move to the Vignettes panel and use Post-Crop to gently darken the corners of the selected photo. I then share that effect with the rest of the photos.

6. These photos are ready to show to my friends. However, I want to give them some options so I filter for my favorite picks that I labeled with one star in Chapter 6. I select some of these picks and make virtual copies of them. I use presets to change some of them to black and white and some of them to brown tone. That way they can decide which look they like when I present the photos to them.

This photo shoot took only a few minutes to process in the Develop module. The fact that the images are quite consistent helped to speed the process along. If the photos weren't as consistent, I'd still move fast here, saving my editing time for the photos the Smiths select for printing.

Using the Library Module's Quick Develop Panel

Now that you know something about the Develop module tools, you can go back to the Library module and learn about the Quick Develop panel.

The improved Quick Develop panel in Lightroom 2, as shown in Figure 7.35, provides the ability to make quick tonal and color adjustments while in the Library module. Any changes applied in this panel are recorded in the Develop module's history. Also, the corresponding sliders in the Basic panel are adjusted appropriately. The Quick Develop panel is divided into three areas. Each area can be collapsed individually by clicking the dark twirly to its right.

FIGURE 7.35

The Library module's Quick Develop panel gives you easy access to basic white balance and tonal adjustments. To expand the subpanels, click the gray twirlys on the right.

- The top section provides access to a variety of presets. Develop presets are applied with the Saved Preset menu, Cropping presets are applied with the Crop Ratio menu, and the Treatment menu allows you to select Grayscale or Color.

- The second section contains color controls. These are the same controls found in the White Balance section of the Develop module's Basic panel. The difference is that these controls use buttons to change settings instead of sliders. These buttons change values in increments. The buttons with the single arrow use small increments and the buttons with double arrows make changes in larger increments. For example, the single arrow button on Brightness changes brightness by 1/3 or a stop. The double-arrow button makes changes in full-stop increments.

165

■ The third section provides all of the tonal controls, as well as Clarity and Vibrance. When the Alt (Option) key is pressed, these buttons switch to Sharpness and Saturation, respectively. There is no clipping preview here so you have to use the Histogram panel to monitor the ends of the histogram.

NOTE The Auto Tone button is used to automatically adjust settings for Exposure, Blacks, Brightness, and Contrast. Because these settings are heavily influenced by the tonal qualities of the photo's subject matter, the results are often uneven.

Though the buttons in the Quick Develop module make rough adjustments, the panel is still quite useful for quickly making adjustments during the organizational phase of the production workflow. Remember to use the Sync Settings button when you need to share settings with a group of photos.

Summary

This chapter began by looking at color theory and how it applies to digital photos. Then you explored how that information is interpreted with a histogram. The most important thing to remember about histograms it that you have to pay attention to the ends of the histogram when making tonal and color adjustments. If data begins to slip off the end of the histogram tonal clipping will occur.

The three panels on the left side of the Develop module have various functions. The Presets panel is all about efficiency. Whenever you find that you do the same thing over and over, create a preset to do it for you. The History panel provides access to every develop modification made to the photo. To jump to any moment in a file's history, click on the appropriate History state. The Snapshots panel is used to make a snapshot of any History state.

The panels on the right of the Develop module are where all of the magic happens. They allow you to adjust tone and color in just about any imaginable way. Some of these panels, such as the White Balance and Basic panels, are used on every image. Others such as Split Toning and HSL are only used for special purposes.

The Tool Strip is where the main editing tools in the Develop module are stored. The Cropping tool is used to create any desired cropping. The Spot Removal tool has two settings: Clone and Heal. I prefer Heal because it does a much better job of blending the spot removal. The new Adjustment Brush tool provides a whole new level of tonal and color adjustment because it allows you to paint desired corrections into local areas of the photo. The Graduated Filter tool works like the Adjustment Brush, except that it uses a gradient instead of a brush to apply changes. As you learn to use this handful of tools, you'll be amazed at the things you'll be able to accomplish with them.

The secret to using all of these tools and panels in the workflow is to only use the ones you need for the job you're doing. Also, it's important to select representative images so that you can synchronize their settings with other photos. Whenever possible, save the detail work on special images for Photoshop and the Creative Workflow.

Chapter 8

Sharing Photos with Others

This chapter explores the third main function of Lightroom — presenting and outputting files so that you can share them with others. For professional photographers, this is where they get to show their work to clients and prospective clients — it's where the rubber meets the road. For nonprofessionals, this is where they get to enjoy and share the fruits of their labor with friends and family.

Lightroom gives digital photographers many options when it comes to sharing their work. That's because it devotes three of its five modules — Slideshow, Print, and Web — to creating different types of output. This section takes a step-by-step approach as you explore those output modules and learn how they're used to design your own slide shows, prints, and Web galleries.

The reason the Slideshow, Print, and Web modules are covered together is because these modules have much in common. They not only share the same goal of creating output but they also share many of the same layout and design elements such as text overlays. However, the way these design elements are implemented in each of these three modules varies depending on the form of the output. For the most part, though, these differences are minor.

Your exploration of Lightroom's output modules begins with a close look at the Slideshow module. After you understand this module, the other two will be intuitive and easy to understand.

IN THIS CHAPTER

Improving your presentations to clients

Quickly creating custom slide shows to showcase your work

Using Lightroom's Print module to print and save JPEGs of print layouts

Sharing your work online with easy-to-design Web galleries

Creating Slide Shows

When I was a child we had a great-uncle named Uncle Tex. He was a chemistry professor and avid photographer who lived in Terre Haute, Indiana. When Uncle Tex and Aunt Louise came to visit us the entire family gathered in the evening to see his latest photos. The kids would lie on the floor and watch each photo as it was projected with an old Kodak carousel slide projector onto a portable, rollup screen. We sat for hours listening to Uncle Tex's voiceover while the hot, noisy slide projector chugged along, loading and ejecting slide after slide. Though I credit these marathon sessions with kindling my early interest in photography, as a child I had a hard time sitting through Uncle Tex's slideshows because they were so boring to watch.

I'm happy to say that slideshows have come of age and they'll never be the same. Now any computer can serve as a slide projector and a screen, and slideshow layouts have a visual impact that was never possible with an old-fashioned slideshow. What's even better is that these modern slideshows are easy to create in Lightroom. I wish Uncle Tex were here to see it.

Surveying the Slideshow module

All three of the output modules look very similar to the Slideshow module, shown in Figure 8.1. Each module contains the Preview, Template Browser, and the Collections panels on the left side. The right-side panels in each module contain all of the design and layout panels used for that particular form of output. Each module also has the usual Toolbar, though the tools on it are minimal.

The Preview panel is much like the Navigator panel except that it has no function other than showing a preview of the templates in the Template Browser. There are no magnification presets. Let's look at the rest of the panels.

Template Browser panel

The Template Browser panel is much like the Presets panel in the Develop module. The Template Browser panel is the most important panel in any of the output modules because it allows you to save layouts after you create them. Once you have the layouts you use most often stored here, you'll find that you rarely need to use the design panels on the right.

The Template Browser panel contains two groups of templates: Lightroom Templates and User Templates. Hover the cursor over any of the templates to preview them in the Preview panel. After one of these templates is selected its design can be modified with the design and layout panels on the right. Keep in mind that modifications made to a template with the design and layout panels do not change the template. Only the current layout is modified. However, you can save your new design as a user template, and you can update that template later if you change the design.

Collections panel

The Collections panel that you saw in the Library module has been added to all of the output modules in Lightroom 2. This is very useful because it keeps you from needing to go back to the Library module to select the collection you want to work with.

FIGURE 8.1

The layout of the Slideshow module is similar to the two other output modules. The Preview, Template Browser, and Collections panels are on the left. All design and layout panels are on the right.

Something that's different about the Collections panel in the output modules is that it allows you to easily create output-specific collections. For example, sometimes you want to create a slideshow of all photos in a collection with the Slideshow module, but you want to print only a few of them in the Print module. This is easy to do by using the main collection to create two output-specific collections in each module. Here's how I do it for the Smith family:

1. Right-click on the Smith Family collection and choose Create Slideshow from the pop-up menu. The Create Slideshow dialog box opens, as shown in Figure 8.2.

2. Lightroom suggests naming the collection Smith Family Slideshow, so I don't even have to type a name. Click Include all filmstrip photos so that they're automatically added.

3. Click Create, and the new collection is added to the list in the Collections panel.

4. To create a collection for printing, move to the Print module and follow the same steps (except that I choose the photos for the printing collection manually because I only want a few).

This new feature is a welcome addition to Lightroom 2 because of the flexibility it adds to managing collections for specific output scenarios.

FIGURE 8.2

A new feature in Lightroom 2 is the ability to create output specific collections. Here I'm creating one that will be used to hold all of the images in the Smith Family slideshow.

Slideshow design panels

The design and layout panels on the right allow you to create just the kind of slide show you want. With them you control every aspect of the look and feel of the slide show, as well as sound when music is added. Rather than discussing them here, the following sections look at how they're used in the creation process by creating your own slide show.

Designing slide shows

It is best to use some of your own images for this exercise so that you can follow along. Take a moment to find a small group you want to work with. They can be edited images or photos you just uploaded from your camera. Follow these steps:

1. In the Library module, select the images you want to use. You can create a main collection now, or just create a slideshow collection in the Slideshow module.

2. Go to the Slideshow module by clicking on it in the Module Picker. Follow the steps in the previous example to create a slideshow collection. You can add all of the images, or select a few. If you want to make any changes to the order of the photos, click and drag their thumbnails to the appropriate spot on the Filmstrip.

3. Go to the Lightroom Templates in the Template Browser, shown in Figure 8.3, and click on each of the templates. Notice how each has a different emphasis in presentation. Some focus on displaying the image, while others add relevant information. Also notice that when you click on a template to select it, the settings in the design and layout panels change to the settings that were used to create the template.

4. When you finish experimenting, click the Caption and Rating template so you can use it for your starting point.

    One of the main features of this template is that the current star rating is displayed at the upper left of the image area and a caption appears below. The information for the caption is drawn from the caption field in the Metadata panel. If you don't have any information in that field, the empty quotes are displayed. I show you how to fix this in a moment.

FIGURE 8.3

The Template Browser contains some default templates that are in a folder named Lightroom Templates. Each of these is designed to accentuate a specific presentation feature.

5. Hide the panels on the left and make sure the panels on the right are visible. Right-click on the header of one of the design and layout panels. When the contextual menu opens, choose Show All unless it's grayed out. This uncollapses all panels in the set.

6. Begin with the Options panel, as shown in Figure 8.4. Select Stroke Border to add a border around the photos. Change the stroke Width value to 4 px to make the line around the image thicker. Click the color swatch to change the color of the stroke. The new Color Picker, shown in the second image in Figure 8.4, appears. This new feature provides an intuitive and easy way to make color selections.

FIGURE 8.4

The Options panel allows you to control some basic settings. When you click on the Stroke Border color swatch (or any color swatch in the output modules), Lightroom's new Color Picker opens.

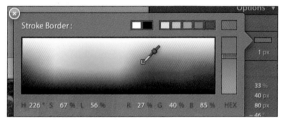

This new feature provides an intuitive way to work with color. Use the eyedropper to select a color and use the vertical slider on the right to increase or decrease saturation. Use the gray and the black-and-white swatches at the top to quickly select neutral tones. The two swatches directly above the saturation slider compare the before color with the current choice. The readouts below display the currently selected color with HSL values on the left and percentages of color on the right.

If you don't see a color spectrum, use the vertical slider on the right to increase saturation. Click anywhere on the spectrum to change the current color pick. For the Smith Family project, I select the light gray swatch, second from the left in the gray row of swatches. When you like the color of your stroke, click the X at the top-left corner of the dialog box to close it.

CAUTION   If you select the Zoom to Fill Frame option at the top, all vertical images are cropped to fit the horizontal orientation — much like the Fill zoom preset in the Library and Develop modules.

7. Because you're using a light background, you can see the shadow that's being cast behind the frame of the photo. Experiment with the Opacity, Offset, and Radius sliders in the Shadow options to see if you want to change their settings. They function as follows:

   ▓ **Opacity:** Controls the lightness or darkness of the shadow

   ▓ **Offset:** Controls the shadow's distance from the image

   ▓ **Radius:** Controls the hardness or softness of the shadow's edge

   ▓ **Angle:** Controls the direction of the shadow

   You can also change the angle of the shadow by using the adjustment knob next to it. Click and drag it in a circular motion. The small dot indicates the direction toward which the shadow is being cast.

   I plan to use a black background for the Smith Family slideshow so these settings become moot for me because a shadow won't be visible against black.

8. Go to the Layout panel, as shown in Figure 8.5, and click and drag one of the sliders to the right. All four sliders should move together as the image boundary is enlarged. (If only one slider moves, select the Link All option to link all sliders together.) Move the sliders to a value of 40 px (40 pixels).

9. Deselect the Link All option to unlink the sliders. Click and drag the bottom slider to a value of 75 to create more space below the image area. (To change two sliders at the same time, select the check boxes next to the individual sliders.) Deselect the Show Guides option and hide the guidelines.

10. Go to the Overlays panel, as shown in Figure 8.6. Select the Identity Plate option. If you created an identity plate earlier, it is displayed in a text box in the upper-left corner of the slide. This is a great way for a professional photographer to brand a slide show with his or her identity. Click on any corner of the text box to change its size. Click inside the box and drag it to reposition it. Notice that the box automatically anchors itself to the corners and sides of the image frame as it's dragged. Double-click on the text to open the Identity Plate Editor if you want to quickly change its text or to create a custom Identity Plate for this slideshow.

FIGURE 8.5

The sliders in the Layout panel are used to adjust the size and placement of the area used to display photos. It restricts how close horizontal and vertical photos come to the edges of the frame.

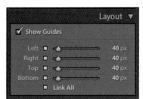

FIGURE 8.6

The Overlays panel provides all sorts of options for adding text adornments to your slides. You can also use it to add rating stars to your slides so you can keep track of favorites.

You can also modify the contents of this text box without changing the main identity plate by using the Identity Plate area of the Overlays panel. Select the Override Color option and click on the swatch to change the color of the type. Decrease the value of the Opacity slider to make the text more transparent. Click on the Identity Plate preview area to open a menu that allows you to create a custom identity plate by choosing Edit. In my case, I don't want an identity plate in my slide show. I want a nice, clean presentation so I deselect the Identity Plate option.

11. One of the things I like about this layout is that the photo's rating stars are displayed in the upper left of the image area. My stars are light colored, so they stand out from the dark background in this set of images. You can change the color if you need to by clicking on the color swatch. Use the Opacity and Scale sliders to change the way the stars look. I changed my Scale value to 40 percent.

12. Go to the Backdrop panel, as shown in Figure 8.7. The background you're currently using is a gradient from the color of the Background Color to the Color Wash color. To change these colors, click on their respective swatches. The direction of this gradient is controlled with the Angle slider. Experiment with the angle slider so you can see how it affects the direction of the wash gradient. I usually change it to -25 so that the dark area is at the bottom right of the slider.

FIGURE 8.7

The Backdrop panel controls the background that appears around the slides. Deselect the Color Wash option to create a single-color background. Deselect the Background Color option to create a black background.

If you want a solid color, deselect the Color Wash option and use the Background Color swatch to select the color. I want a black background. To quickly create it, I deselect the Color Wash and Background Color options so that no color is used for the background.

NOTE   **Use Background Image to place an image behind all slides.**

13. A new panel has been added to the Slideshow module in Lightroom called Titles, as shown in Figure 8.8. This new panel is a needed addition because it allows you to create an introductory slide and an ending slide. You can use Intro Screen to add a title to your slideshow with the Identity Plate editor, (the same way you used it in Step 11), or you can choose a solid colored background. The Ending Screen area is used in the same way. Add credits, or simply provide a final screen with a neutral color so viewers know the slideshow is over.

NOTE   These two slides are the only slides that can have a different design from the other slides in the slideshow.

FIGURE 8.8

Use the new Titles panel in Lightroom 2 to create an introductory screen and/or an ending screen.

14. Go to the Playback panel, shown in Figure 8.9. If you have some music on your system, select the Soundtrack option to add music. This works a little differently for Mac and Windows. The following looks at each procedure:

   - **Mac:** Use iTunes to create a playlist of the songs you want to play during the slide show. Arrange them in the order in which you want them to play. Choose that playlist from the Library pop-up menu in the Slideshow's Playback panel.

   - **Windows:** Prepare your music by gathering MP3s of the songs into a special folder. Rename the songs if necessary so that they are in the order in which you want them to play. Select the Soundtrack option and use the Browse for Folder dialog box to navigate to your special folder and select it.

   Unfortunately, you can't select individual songs with either of these systems, which is a severe limitation. Also, music can only be played when the slide show is being presented in Lightroom.

CAUTION   Music is only played when a slide show is show in Lightroom. Music, as well as fade transitions, is removed when a slide show is exported as a PDF file.

FIGURE 8.9

Use the Playback panel to add music and timed transitions to your slideshow.

15. Make sure the Slide Duration option is selected. Use the slider to adjust the length of time each slide is displayed. Use the Fades slider to control the length of fades from one image to the next. (Unfortunately, fade is the only transition effect, which is another limitation of this module.) If you want to manually control the slide show with the right and left arrows on your keyboard, deselect the Slide Duration option.

16. You're almost ready. You just have to do something about the empty quotes at the bottom of the screen. When captions are added to the metadata of each file, they can be cool. But that's not how I want to use them here.

    Make sure the Toolbar is visible (T). Click on the quotes to make the text box active. Notice that options for the text box appear on the Toolbar called Custom Settings. Click on the Custom settings menu and choose from the list of metadata in the pop-up menu. The options are Custom Text, Date, Equipment, Exposure, Filename, Sequence, and Edit. I choose Filename for the Smith Family slideshow.

    Use the Text Overlays section of the Overlays panel to change any characteristics of this text, such as color or font. (I changed mine to dark gray.) Move down to the Shadow section directly below and deselect Shadow to remove the shadow because it makes type this small look blurry.

17. Make any further adjustments to the text box. I made mine smaller by dragging a corner inward and then I dragged the box to the right so that it appears just below the right corner of the image. Do the same to yours. Notice that a small anchor box indicates where the text is anchored relative to the edges of the slide, as shown in Figure 8.10. Now, if you adjust the image size in the Layout panel, the filename will stay anchored in the same spot on the slide.

18. I want to add a slideshow title under the middle of each image in my slideshow. Click the Add Text button on the Toolbar. Type a name for your slide show into the textbox on the Toolbar. I typed "The Smith Family". When you press Enter a new text box appears on the lower left of the slide. Move it into position and use the Text Overlay section of the Overlays panel to modify any characteristics of this type.

FIGURE 8.10

When a text box is active the white boxes on the sides and corners indicate a text box is active. Click and drag a corner to scale the size of the text. The yellow box indicates where the box is anchored. Contents are changed by selecting from the Custom Settings menu or by typing text in the text box on the toolbar.

NOTE   The Text Overlay controls affect the currently active text box. Click on a text box to make it the active text box so that modifications to the Overlay panel affect it.

19. Save these settings as a template. Click the Create New Preset button, the plus symbol, on the header of the Presets panel and choose a name for the template. I name mine "Title and File name." You can use these settings as a starting point for future projects where you want the title and filename to be part of the slide show.

Playing your slide shows

You can preview a slide show in the main viewing area using the slide show controls on the Toolbar or by clicking the Preview button beneath the panels on the right. I prefer to preview it exactly as it will be shown. To do that, click the Play button to its right. You can also start a slide show by simply pressing Enter. To stop a slide show press Esc.

TIP   If you're using music with a slide show, make sure your media player is open so that the music begins when the slide show starts.

You can pause the automatic timing of a slide show by pressing the Spacebar. Use the right arrow key to manually advance forward and use the left arrow key to back up. One of the coolest things about a slide show is that you can add and remove ratings during the slide show using the keyboard shortcuts. That way if you're showing a slide show to a client you can add ratings along the way.

TIP   If you decide to change the order of some of the photos, cancel the slide show and rearrange them in the Filmstrip by dragging and dropping.

Slide shows are also a great way to browse through new images just after importing them. Because of that, there's a quick way to launch an instant slide show from the Library module (as well as the other four modules) by choosing Window ➪ Impromptu Slideshow (Command/Ctrl+Enter). This immediately launches a slide show of the selected photos. The current settings in the Slideshow module are used as settings for the Impromptu Slideshow.

Exporting your slide shows

In my opinion, this is one of the weakest areas of Lightroom. That's because slide shows can only be exported as PDF presentations or JPEG files. PDF files are very limited in what they can do. They can only be viewed in Adobe Acrobat or Adobe Reader; music cannot be included unless it's added later on using the full version of Adobe Acrobat; if you randomized the images with the Random Order button, the randomization is eliminated; any duration settings you apply are also eliminated. This is a far cry from most other slide show packages on the market. For that reason, I rarely export slide shows as PDFs. I prefer to show them on my system. However, take a look at the export procedure in case you want to give it a try.

To export a slide show, click Export on the right side. When the Export Slideshow to PDF dialog box appears, as shown in Figure 8.11, choose a name for the slide show and select a folder to save it to. I create a new folder titled "Slideshow" inside the original images folder. (This is the way I always save slide shows so I know where to find them later.) Use the other settings as follows:

- Choose from the Common sizes menu to select a specific size. The larger the size, the larger the overall size of the PDF file. The Screen setting is the size that your monitor is currently set to.

- The Quality setting is used to adjust the JPEG compression for each image. Higher quality settings result in larger files. Lower quality settings produce smaller file sizes. If you're planning to e-mail the slide show to someone, choose a setting below 50.

Figure 8.12 shows the completed slide show.

FIGURE 8.11

When you export your Lightroom slide shows, the Export Slideshow to PDF dialog box appears. The settings in this dialog box are used to control the size and quality of the slide show.

FIGURE 8.12

I choose a simple presentation for my slide show. Rating stars are displayed in the upper-left corner and the filename is displayed in the lower-right corner.

> **TIP** If you send one of these presentations to someone, be sure to tell him or her to open it with one of the Acrobat products. Otherwise the slide show effect, as minimal as it may be, may not be visible.

As you can see, custom slide shows are easy to create and show in Lightroom. They offer a great way to share photos with friends or to present them to perspective clients. The biggest problem with them is that when the slide show is exported as a PDF most of the multimedia elements are stripped out of the presentation.

> **NEW FEATURE** Adobe addressed the PDF limitations by adding a new feature to Lightroom 2 that allows you to export each slide as a JPEG file by clicking the Export JPEG button. This feature is useful for someone who wants to design the slides in Lightroom but use different slide show software for creating the final multimedia slide show. This adds another layer to the workflow, but it helps people who have more advanced slide show programs at their disposal.

Printing with Lightroom

The Lightroom Print module is used to design all sorts of printing layouts — from fine art and contact sheets to specialized package prints. The way it's used is very similar to the Slideshow module. Design and layout panels are used to make the prints fit the page the way you want them to fit. Special layouts are saved as templates. Then the designs are output with a printer, such as an inkjet printer. If you don't want to do your own printing, a new feature allows you to export print layouts as JPEG files so that they can be printed at a photo lab.

Surveying the Print module

The Print module, shown in Figure 8.13, looks a lot like the Slideshow module. On the left is the Template Browser panel with a folder for Lightroom's default templates and a folder for user-created templates. Below this panel (not shown in Figure 8.10) is the Collections panel. It's exactly the same as the Collections panel in the Slideshow module, except that print collections are created when a new selection is created. Above the Template Browser is the Preview module. This preview works a bit differently than the Preview module in the Slideshow module. It displays the various templates when the mouse hovers over them, as shown in Figure 8.13; however, no image content is shown in the preview window.

The panels on the right serve a similar function to the design and layout panels in the Slideshow module. They just control the design and layout process in terms that relate to printing, rather than creating slide shows.

FIGURE 8.13

The Print module is very similar to the Slideshow module. When the cursor is hovered over a template the template's layout is shown in the Preview panel. (The Collections panel, below the Template Browser, is not visible in this figure. The Windows version combines the Page Setup and Print Settings buttons into a single button.)

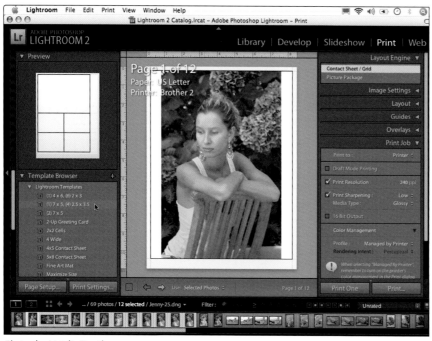

Photos by Natalia Tsvetkov

Laying out and printing photos

The Print module offers lots of design options. You can create a layout for a single image, a contact sheet, or a picture package. Sometimes all you need to do is select some photos and choose a preset. But for you to get the most of this module, you need to know how the various design controls are used. This section explains the basic layout process to help you with that understanding. Follow these steps:

1. Choose some photos that have already been through the editing process in the Develop module. You can use a collection, a filter, or select some individual photos.

    You probably see the Info Overlay that appears on top of the image with page, paper, and printer. The info is useful, but I don't like looking at it all of the time. Turn it off for now. Choose View ➪ Hide Info Overlay (I). Press the I key again when you want to see the Info Overlay.

2. Select at least four photos in the Filmstrip, with at least one of them in landscape, or horizontal, orientation. Select 2x2 Cells from the Template Browser. The page in the central viewing area is divided into four individual cells — two across and two down. Each of the first four selected images is added to the cells.

    Any landscape orientation photos don't fill the cell because it's a portrait orientation, or vertical. To fix this go to the Image Settings panel and select the Auto-Rotate to fit option. While you're there, select the Zoom to Fill Frame option to maximize the size of each cell. Notice that some cropping may occur on the ends of the photos, much like the same setting in the Slideshow module.

    Your layout should look something like Figure 8.14. Select the Stroke Border option in the Image Settings panel and change the Width value to 5.0 pt (points). Click on the color swatch to change the color if you want to. I left it black.

> **TIP** If you want to see the same photo in every cell, select the **Repeat One Photo per Page** option. This is a good way to print several small copies of the some photo.

3. Use the Layout panel, as shown in Figure 8.15, to change the way these cells are oriented. Select the Keep Square option, which is a little more than halfway down the panel. When you do, the four cells become square and any rotated images rotate back to their original orientation. Because Zoom to Fill Frame is selected in the Image Settings panel, each photo looks like it's being cropped to fit the square aspect ratio. However, they aren't being cropped; parts of them are being hidden. Click and drag individual photos to move them inside the cell. Go ahead and move any that need to be moved.

FIGURE 8.14

This layout is often referred to as a four-up. When Auto-Rotate to fit is selected in the Image Settings panel the photos are automatically rotated to fit their cells if necessary. When Repeat One Photo per Page is selected every cell on the page is filled with the same image.

Photos by Natalia Tsvetkov

FIGURE 8.15

The Print module Layout panel is very similar to the Layout panel in the Slideshow module. These sliders are used to design any grid style layout you desire.

4. Go to the Margins area of the Layout panel and change the Top margin to 0.75 inches and the Bottom margin to 1.25 inches. This gives you more room at the top and bottom of the page by moving the top and bottom rows of images closer together. Changing the Left and Right values affects the size of the cells.

> **TIP** You can click a number to manually change it without using the slider.

5. The Page Grid sliders are used to add more cells to the grid. Right now you're using a 2x2 layout. That means you have two columns and two rows. When additional cells are needed these values are changed. For example, the 4x5 Contact Sheet template uses four columns and five rows.

   Cell Spacing is used to modify the distance between cells. Give your photos a bit of breathing room. Change the Horizontal Cell Spacing value to 0.50 inches. Notice that the Vertical slider also moves to maintain the square aspect ratio.

   You may have noticed that the Cell Size sliders move at the same time as the Cell Spacing sliders. These two sets of sliders are tied together because when you change one, the other has to change. Think of them as different ways to lay out the page. One way is focused on the distance between cells, while the other is oriented to the actual cell size. If one of those measurements is more important than the other, you can use the appropriate slider to fine-tune it.

> **TIP** To use a different scale of measurement like centimeters or points, choose from the Ruler Units menu at the top of the panel. (You can also right-click on the ruler and select from the contextual menu to change units. This also works in Photoshop.) To hide or show Rulers press Command/(Ctrl)+R.

6. Click on the Guides panel to control which guides appear on the image preview. Keep in mind that these guides are for layout only. They do not show on the final print. This panel allows you to show or hide different guides and grids. Use it to hide anything you don't need to see. Show Guides is deselected to hide them all. Select the Image Print Sizes option to display the size of each cell.

7. Go to the Overlays panel, shown in Figure 8.16. This panel provides access to the different types of information you can add to the photos in the layout. The Identity Plate section is almost the same here as in the Overlays panel in the Slideshow module. The only difference is that you can select the Render on every image option to have the identity plate appear on every photo on the page. This is a great way to add your name or logo to every image. If you do this, think about lowering the Opacity value so that the image shows through the type.

   If your identity plate is rotated in the wrong direction, you can use the pop-up menu at the top of the panel to change its rotation. To activate the menu, click the Rotate Identity Plate button at the top of the panel. In Figure 8.16 it shows 0 degrees of rotation.

   The Page Options section allows you to turn on various page options. Add crop marks when you plan to cut the photos apart after printing. Leave this unchecked if you plan to keep all of the photos on one sheet. When you select the Page Info option, the same information that appeared in the Info Overlay is added to the bottom of the page.

The Identity Plate section of the Overlays panel allows you to place your identity plate on every image. To change the rotation of the identity plate use the Rotation menu, circled.

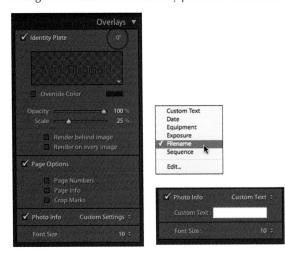

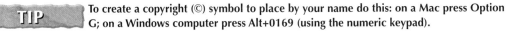

8. Remember how you added the filename to each slide in the slide show? Do it here, too. Go to the bottom of the Overlays panel and select the Photo Info option. Click Custom Settings to the right and select Filename from the pop-up menu. Now the photos are labeled with their filenames. Use the Font Size menu to change the size of the type. If you want to add a copyright notice to every photo instead, choose Custom Text and type your notice into the Custom Text field that appears.

> **TIP** To create a copyright (©) symbol to place by your name do this: on a Mac press Option G; on a Windows computer press Alt+0169 (using the numeric keypad).

9. I want to show you one more thing here. Open the Photo Info menu again and select Edit. The Text Template Editor, shown in Figure 8.17, appears. You may have already noticed one of these editors in other parts of Lightroom. It allows you to create an information template that displays exactly the information you want to show.

   Use the menus to select the information you want to include and click Insert to add a token for it to the text template, as shown in the Example window. Click and drag these token in the Example window to change the order in which they're displayed.

   Add the filename after the copyright information. Click Insert next to Filename. A token titled Filename is added to the preview window. Click and drag this token so that it comes before the Custom Text token. Then click the Preset menu at the top and save this template. I called mine Filename + Copyright. This choice is now available in the Photo Info pop-up menu shown in Figure 8.16.

FIGURE 8.17

The Text Template Editor allows you to choose from all sorts of information when applying a text overlay to your images.

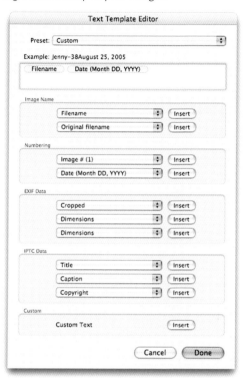

10. Print this page. Click the Print Settings button at the bottom of the left side panels. Use the Print dialog box to choose your printer and set it up. Use the Page Setup button beside it if you need to change the paper size or orientation.

NOTE The Windows version combines the Print Setting and Page Setup buttons into a single Page Setup button.

CAUTION If you have more than four images selected on the Filmstrip, more than one page prints because Lightroom thinks you want to print all of the selected photos.

11. Go to the Print Job module. If you know what resolution you need for your printer, change the Print Resolution to that value by clicking on the current value and typing your setting. If you don't know, change it to 300.

NOTE   Draft Mode Printing creates low-quality prints that you can use to check layout and placement, saving your ink for more important jobs. When this option is checked, the Print Job options below it are deactivated.

Lightroom 1 had a remedial sharpening feature in the Print Job panel. With Lightroom 2 this feature has been improved with new algorithms. Now when you choose one of the sharpening presets you can specify the type of media you'll be printing on to fine-tune the sharpening results. I recommend beginning with the Medium setting. After you see the prints you can determine if you prefer a higher or lower setting for your printer and paper type.

CROSS-REF   For more information on output sharpening, see Chapter 7.

12. Go to the Color Management section. You can try making a print with the setting at Managed by Printer, but I rarely see printers that do a good job of this. It's usually better to use a special profile that is designed for your printer and the paper you are using. To do this, click on the Profile menu and choose Other and select the profile for the paper you're using. If you don't have profiles, choose Managed by Printer.

    When a printer profile is selected the Rendering Intent menu becomes active. Perceptual is the best all-purpose rendering intent. Go ahead and leave Rendering Intent set to Perceptual.

CROSS-REF   Printer profiles and inkjet printer driver settings are discussed in detail in Chapter 21.

13. As soon as you change the Profile a message appears at the bottom of the panel, as shown in Figure 8.18. This message reminds you to turn off any color management in the printer driver. If you don't, Lightroom and the printer both try to color manage the job, resulting in unpredictable color. To turn off your printer's color management click the Print Settings button. This opens the Print dialog box for your printer. These dialog boxes vary from printer to printer. Find the color management area of your printer driver and disable any color management. Now the printer will accept the data sent to it by Lightroom without trying to manage it.

14. Click Print to open the Print dialog box so that you can make any necessary modifications to the driver settings. If you already took care of that in Step 10, you can click Print One to bypass the Print dialog box and go straight to printing.

    If you don't have printer profiles, select Managed by Printer. Make sure to enable ICM Method for Image Color Management (Windows), or select ColorSync in the Color Management settings (Mac OS) in the printer driver.

FIGURE 8.18

FIGURE 8.18

The Print Job panel in the first image is used to prepare a print job for printing to an inkjet printer. Be sure to select the correct printer profile from the Profile menu if you have profiles for your printer. The second image shows the Print Job panel when JPEG File is chosen from the Print to menu.

Now that you know how to use the Print dialog box for printing I have to be honest and say that I rarely used the Print module in Lightroom 1 because I don't do much inkjet printing. Most of the printing I do is done by photo labs. When I do make inkjet prints, it's for special fine-art prints that are printed from Photoshop using its more advanced printing dialog box. In Lightroom 1, it wasn't possible to use these templates for output by a photo lab. That's all changed in Lightroom 2.

Creating JPEG files from your layouts

A new feature in Lightroom 2 allows you to create files from your layouts so you can take them to a photolab for printing. This is a nice feature for people who want to create and use templates for designing photo books and albums. Here's how easy it is to create files in the Print module instead of prints. Follow these steps:

1. You may have noticed a field at the top of the Print Job panel called Print to. Click the menu beside it and select JPEG File. Now the option settings in the Print Job panel change to options used to create JPEG files, as shown in the second frame of Figure 8.18.

2. Use the JPEG Quality slider to adjust the file compression. If you're sending this file to a lab, leave it at 100 for the highest quality. Apply standard print sharpening and specify the media.

3. Use the Profile menu to select the correct color space. Most labs prefer sRGB. However, some labs provide photographers with the profile they use. If you have one of these,

select it. Leave Rendering Intent set to Perceptual. Use Custom File Dimensions if you need to specify a particular dimension.

4. Click Print to File to select where the files are saved. I usually place them in a folder on my desktop named For Printing.

CROSS-REF   **Color spaces are discussed in detail in Chapter 12.**

This new feature opens a whole new door for Lightroom output. Now it's possible to create templates for photo book layouts that are printed by a lab. Or if you want to quickly create a set of contact sheets from a job, you can use one of your saved templates and output files instead of having to mess with the inkjet printer. I guarantee that you'll be using the Print Module with much greater regularity.

Using the New Picture Package feature

A really cool new feature in the Lightroom 2 Print module is the Picture Package layout style. This panel allows you to create picture packages of a single photo. This new feature, combined with the ability to output the layouts as JPEG files for printing at a lab, is a great feature for portrait photographers.

To see this new feature, choose Picture Package from the Layout Engine at the top of the right side panels. The first thing you notice when you select it is that the content of the Image Settings panel changes and some features from other panels are combined into a new panel named Rulers, Grid & Guides. These panels are fairly self-explanatory. Let's focus on the most important new panel here, the Cells panel.

Figure 8.19 shows the new Cells panel, along with the new Rulers, Grid, & Guides panels. Here's how you use the Cells panel to create your own picture package:

1. Click Clear Layout to clear the current layout and display a blank page.

2. Click the 5x7 button to add a 5x7 to the layout. Notice that you can click the downward pointing arrow to open a pop-up menu of common sizes. Choosing one of these changes the button preset to that size and adds a cell to the layout. Select Edit if you want to create a custom size. Click the 5x7 button again to add a second 5x7 to the layout. If your photos are being cropped you can press the Command/(Ctrl) key and click and drag them inside the box to reposition them.

TIP   **After you add a cell its size can be adjusted by selecting it and dragging the handles that appear around its boundary. You can also use the Adjust Selected Cell area to change the size of a cell. To delete a cell, hover over it and click the X that appears or right-click and choose Delete Cell.**

3. Click the 4x6 button to add a 4x6. Notice that it is created on a second page because there isn't enough room on the first page. Right-click on the 4x6 cell and choose Rotate Cell. After the cell rotates click and drag it to the left of the page. Click the 4x6 button again to add another cell. Notice that the new cell is rotated to match the existing 4x6 cell as it's added.

FIGURE 8.19

The new Cells panel allows you to build your own custom picture packages.

4. Click the 2.5x3.5 button twice to add two wallets to the layout. Now it should look something like Figure 8.20. Now you can either print this package on an inkjet printer or print it to a JPEG file that can be printed at a photo lab. To use this package with another image, select the image from the Filmstrip.

FIGURE 8.20

The new Picture Package feature in Lightroom 2 allows you to create custom picture packages. When there isn't enough space to hold all of the sizes, new pages are created to hold additional cells. You can include up to six pages in a layout.

The Auto Layout button automatically creates an efficient layout that's easy to cut apart and trim. However, this isn't always the most efficient use of paper. If you click it, the two 4x6s rotate to the horizontal position. This creates a third page to hold the wallets because there isn't room for them on the second page.

> **TIP** When multiple photos are selected from the Filmstrip a picture package is created for each of them.

When creating picture packages you can use one of the three Lightroom default template presets in the Template Browser panel (the first three presets that use parentheses), or you can build your own. When you create your own picture packages, be sure to save the layout as a preset in case you want to use it again.

Creating Photo Galleries for the Internet

One of the best things about digital photography is the ability to instantly share your photos with people across the globe by putting them on the Internet. It's been possible to do this with Photoshop for many years, but Lightroom makes the process intuitive and easy by allowing you to create Web photo galleries. Think of these galleries as online slide shows — although in many cases they offer a cooler multimedia experience than the slide shows in the Slideshow module.

> **NOTE** To get the most advantage from this module you need a Web site or some sort of online presence to upload your galleries to.

The Web module works just like the Slideshow and Print modules. Selected images are brought into the module or chosen from the Content panel, a template is used to create a general layout for the images, and then the design and layout panels are used to fine-tune the layout. When it's ready, the new design is saved as a template (if necessary), and the photos are output (uploaded in this case). This module has something special in common with the Print module. Some of the content of the design and layout panels on the right change depending on the type of template that's being used. Take a closer look in the following sections.

Choosing a Web style

When it comes to designing Web sites, two types of programming languages predominate: HTML (HyperText Markup Language) and Flash.

HTML

HTML is the basic, universal language of Web design. It's used in just about every Web site you see. This language is not only basic; it's also very powerful and flexible.

Flash

Flash is a Web programming language that's mainly focused on creating a multimedia experience. A company called Macromedia, which is now owned by Adobe, developed it. This programming language allows a Web developer to make the most of situations that require movies or any kind of animation. That animation ability, combined with the clean-looking layouts created in Flash, makes it perfect for online slide shows and presentations, which are called Web galleries.

Surveying the Web module

The Web module, as shown in Figure 8.21, has the same familiar layout as the other output modules: Preview, Template Browser, and Collections panels on the left, and design and layout panels on the right. Like the Print module, the Preview panel displays a preview of a template when the cursor is hovered over a template in the Template Browser, much like the Print Module. However, there's something else in this panel that you need to take a closer look at.

Template panel

The Template panel has a wide array of predesigned templates. These templates come in two varieties: HTML and Flash. You can tell which is which when you preview a template in the Preview panel by the stylized "f" symbol that displays in the lower-left corner. You can see it in Figure 8.21. HTML templates display "HTML" in the corner of the Preview window.

When you select one of these templates the main display area switches to that layout and populates it with the images in the Filmstrip. Take a moment to try each of these templates so you can see what they look like with images in them. If you're short on space, hide the panels on the right so that you can see all of the display area. Use the navigational buttons on each sample so you can see how they work. Many are similar layouts that use different color sets in the designs.

CAUTION **If you're working with a large folder or collection of photos it can take a while to see them in the main display area. (You can monitor this by watching the Status Bar that replaces the Identity Plate when Lightroom is working.) Use a small collection while you explore the various templates so you don't have to wait for each template to populate with photos.**

After you spend a few minutes trying the different templates you'll see that the Flash templates look much more dynamic than the HTML templates. About the only time I would consider using the HTML templates is if I were creating new content for an old Web site — for example, when adding a new photo album to a section with existing albums already created with HTML. I might be able to modify one of the HTML templates so that it fits into the existing HTML design. Another reason I might choose an HTML template is when I plan to tinker with the code that Lightroom creates when the Web site is exported. Most of the time, however, neither of these situations applies, so I use the Flash templates.

FIGURE 8.21

The Web module provides everything you need for designing Web galleries. Here you can see that part of the gallery is hidden by the panels on the right. To reveal the rest of it, collapse the panels on the left when you don't need them.

Engine panel

The Engine panel indicates if a selected template is HTML or Flash. (*Engine* refers to the programming behind how galleries are created with HTML or Flash.) Clicking on either of these settings selects the default template for that Web style and configures the panels below for that style of Web gallery. Three other Web styles are also listed: Airtight AutoViewer, Airtight PostcardViewer, and Airtight SimpleViewer. All three of these Flash viewers were created by Airtight Interactive (www.airtightinteractive.com). Each is a testament to what's possible in Flash. I don't go into these viewers here, but feel free to come back and explore them and their setting when you're through with this section.

Web design panels

As I mentioned a moment ago, the contents of some of the design and layout panels change depending on whether an HTML or a Flash template is used. Much of this is due to the fact that many design elements for one style of Web site don't apply to the other. Another reason is that some elements are implemented differently depending on the Web style. For example, to use your identity plate on a Flash design you need to use the Appearance panel. To do the same thing with an HTML Web site, you use the Site Info panel.

CAUTION Be aware that these settings are not sticky between the two Web styles. If you begin designing an HTML Web gallery and switch to a Flash template, your settings from the HTML panels don't always stick. What's worse is that when you go back to the HTML template your settings revert to their defaults.

Designing a Web gallery

I have some photos of bicycle racing at Alpenrose Dairy in Portland, Oregon (www.alpenrose. com). This family-owned dairy in the heart of southwest Portland provides resources for all sorts of events; from bar mitzvahs to the Little League World Series. It's truly an asset to the community. One of the many activities it supports is bicycle racing in various forms. (The only velodrome in Oregon is at Alpenrose.) These photos were shot during a women's *cyclocross* event — a type of race popular in Europe that combines on-road racing with off-road racing. I want to show these photos on my Web site so everyone involved can enjoy them. Here's how I do it:

1. I select the photos I want to use in the Library module and save them as a collection. After the photos are in a collection I can move them around to change their order if I need to.

2. I move to the Web module and, if necessary, select the new collection from the Collections panel.

3. I like the cool factor of the Flash presentations, so I select Flash in the Gallery panel's menu. (This is the same as selecting the Flash gallery (default) template from the Template Browser panel.)

4. I move to the Site Info panel. This panel allows me to provide information for Web site visitors. This information includes descriptive and contact information. Here are the changes I make, as shown in Figure 8.22.

   ▨ **Site Title:** I plan to use my identity plate to identify the site, so I don't need this. I highlight the type in its text box and delete it. When I press Enter, the words "Site Title" are removed from the preview in the main display area.

   ▨ **Collection Title:** I type Cyclocross Racing at Alpenrose Dairy into this box.

   ▨ **Collection Description:** This is the text that's displayed when the person viewing the Web site clicks on the View menu — just below the site title/identity plate — and clicks About these Photos. Use this to add any special information you want visitors to see. I don't need it here so I remove it by highlighting and deleting the text in the box, leaving it empty.

FIGURE 8.22

The Site Info panel has the same function as the Overlays panel in the Slideshow and Print modules. Use it to add information to your Web gallery.

- **Contact Info:** This allows me to add a contact link so visitors have a way to send e-mail to me. It can also be used to add a link that goes to another Web page. I want to use it for e-mail here, so I type Email Mark into the text box. If I were trying to sell photos of the event I would change this to Order Prints and link it to a print ordering section of my Web site.

- **Web or Mail Link:** This is where I supply the link for the contact name I typed into Contact Info. I type my e-mail address: `mailto:books@ddroom.com`. Be sure to include the mailto portion so the Web browsers know what to do with the link.

5. If this was an HTML template, I would add my identity plate while I was in the Site Info panel. Because it's Flash, however, I have to move down to the Appearance panel, as shown in Figure 8.23. I select the Identity Plate option. (Remember that you can click on the preview of the identity plate in the Appearance panel to change it.)

FIGURE 8.23

Use the Appearance panel to add your identity plate to a Web site. To change the basic layout of the gallery, select from the Layout menu at the top of the panel.

6. The two sections labeled Large Images and Thumbnail Images are used to adjust the size of the large images and the thumbnails. I leave both set to Large.

7. The most important part of the Appearance panel is easy to miss. It's the Layout menu at the top of the panel. This menu provides four Flash layout options. When one of these is selected you can quickly preview its layout in the Preview panel. Here's how each affects the layout:

   ◍ **Scrolling:** Displays a scrollable row of image thumbnails beneath a larger version of the images in your Web photo gallery.

   ◍ **Paginated:** Displays a page of image thumbnails to the left of the larger version of the photos. Navigation controls are available for moving to different image thumbnail pages.

   ◍ **Left:** Displays a scrollable column of image thumbnails to the left of a larger version of the photos in your Web photo gallery. (This is the default setting.)

   ◍ **Slideshow Only:** Displays a large version of the images one at a time in your Web photo gallery with navigation buttons below.

   I want visitors to my Web site to have control over the images, so I know I don't want to use Slideshow Only. Of the three other choices I think Left displays these images the best so I leave this setting on Left.

8. Now all I need to do to finish this design is to modify some of the colors. To do so, I move up to the Color Palette panel, shown in Figure 8.24. All of the colors in these photos show up nicely against the dark background, but the black is just a bit too dark. I change the background color to a dark gray. Then I change the border color to a lighter shade of gray. I then change the Controls Background to black and the Controls Foreground to white to make all of the navigational controls white on a black background.

9. Now is a good time to save my template. I Click the Add button on the left and name the new template Flash - Neutral Color. That way I know that it's a Flash layout with neutral colors. If I decide to make further changes to this design, I can save them by right-clicking on the template name and choosing Update with Current Settings.

FIGURE 8.24

The Color Palette module provides control over the colors used in the design. Use it to fine-tune the look of a Web gallery.

195

10. I click Preview in Browser below the left panel group to view my Web gallery in my actual browser. Be aware that this may take a few minutes — especially if you have lots of photos in the slide show — because Lightroom has to create all thumbnail and gallery photos, as well as the code for the gallery. The status bar at the top of the screen keeps you informed.

11. I like what I see in my browser, so I close it and return to Lightroom to add some information to each slide. I go to the Image Info panel, shown in Figure 8.25. The two menus here allow me to add metadata or custom information below each large photo as it's displayed. I open the Title menu and choose Filename so that the filename of each image is displayed. If I want to add custom text, such as the name of the race, I select Custom Text from the menu and then type my text into the Custom Text box. I deselect the Caption option because I don't need additional information below the filename.

FIGURE 8.25

Use the Image Info module to add title and caption information to your photos. Select from the pop-up menus on the right to choose the contents of those fields. When Custom Text is selected a text box appears, allowing you to type the text into the box.

12. A couple of finishing touches and I'll be ready to upload this gallery. I go to the Output Settings panel, as shown in Figure 8.26. This panel allows me to do three important things. First, I can control the level of JPEG compression that's applied to the large versions of my photos when the Web site is uploaded or exported. Lower values allow the photos to load faster, but they also affect the quality when values are low. The main preview area provides a preview of how these settings affect quality. However, be advised that you might need to hide some panels so you can view the larger photos at the actual size at which they display. I choose a Quality value of 60.

The second thing this panel allows me to do is control which metadata is attached to the files created for the Web gallery and to add a copyright overlay to those images. The Metadata section of this panel allows you to limit the metadata that's embedded in the JPG files that are created for the Web site. Choosing Copyright Only removes all other metadata, such as keyword tags, from the files. This is useful if you have information in a file's metadata that you don't really want to share with the world.

TIP   Remember to use the Color Palette panel to change the color of this text.

FIGURE 8.26

The Output Settings panel allows you to control three things. The Quality setting manages the file size and quality of the large image JPEG files. The Metadata menu is used to limit the metadata that's embedded in the large photos. Select the Add Copyright Watermark option to add an overlay of the information in the copyright field of each photo's metadata.

When Add Copyright Watermark is selected the information in the Copyright section of a file's metadata is displayed in the lower-left corner of the large image. I select this option so that my copyright information serves as a reminder that the images on this site are owned by me.

The final feature of this panel is that it allows me to apply sharpening to the Web photos as they're created for the gallery. This new feature in Lightroom 2 is welcome because sharpening Web gallery photos was could not be done automatically in Lightroom 1. I leave it set to Standard, which gives me great results. Figure 8.27 shows what the design of my Web gallery looks like.

FIGURE 8.27

The design of my Web gallery is complete and it's ready to be uploaded it to my Web site.

13. Now it's time to upload this gallery to my Web site. There are two ways to do this. The first is to use Lightroom's *File Transfer Protocol* (FTP) capabilities by clicking the Upload button. FTP is the common system that's used to transfer files (upload) from your computer to a server on the Internet.

The other way to upload files is to click Export, which tells Lightroom to create all of the necessary folders and files for the Web gallery and store them in a location of your choosing. This is a good option when you plan to use other FTP software to upload your site, or you plan to show it to people offline — on your computer rather than on the Web.

I'm going to use Lightroom to upload my gallery, but I need to provide Lightroom with some information about the server that stores my Web site. I go to the Upload Settings panel and click on the FTP server menu and select Edit. The Configure FTP File Transfer dialog box appears, as shown in Figure 8.28.

FIGURE 8.28

When you choose Custom Settings from the Upload Settings Panel, the Configure FTP File Transfer dialog box appears. This dialog box allows you to create a preset for uploading Web galleries to your Web site. If you have multiple Web sites, create a preset for each one.

This is where I type all of the server information for the server that's *hosting* my Web site — the computer where my Web site is stored online. If fill in the information, and then I select the Put in Subfolder option and name the folder Alpenrose. This creates a special folder on my Web site to contain this gallery, making it easier to manage or remove the gallery from my Web site later on. After all of the server information is filled in I name the preset to save this information so that I won't have to fill it out again.

I select the Store password in preset option so that I don't have to remember my password every time I use this preset. If I were concerned about security, I would leave this unchecked.

TIP   Upload presets are great for people who manage multiple Web sites. After they are created they're added to the FTP server menu.

When all of the information is complete I click OK to create the preset. Then I click the Upload button to upload this new gallery to my Web site.

The design and layout I just created is one of many possibilities. No matter which you choose, the path you take will be similar. Begin with a template, add any overlay information you want the viewer to see, enhance the visual experience by experimenting with layouts and colors, choose output settings, and then upload the new gallery. The process will go even faster after you accumulate some of your own templates because you won't have to do much work to prepare a new gallery.

Presenting for Professionals

For professional photographers, this is the point in the workflow where they're either presenting their picks to the client, or they're delivering finished output — files, prints, and so on. For those who are presenting to clients this is their opportunity to make a sale.

Not very long ago the options for presenting were fairly limited. Most photographers who shot negative film used contact sheets and small proof prints to present their work to their clients. This system worked for a long time, but there were a couple of problems with it. First, the quality of these proofs was quite low. Everyone understood that they were merely facsimiles of what was possible when a skilled printer printed the negative.

The second problem was that it's hard for the average person to visualize what a large print will look like when holding a small one in his or her hand. An 11 x 14 seems big when you're holding a 4 x 5, but once it's hung on the wall it seems small. Also, because it's hard to see details in small prints, clients didn't make an emotional connection with them. Because of these problems, I recommend that you use proof prints as a last resort when presenting to clients.

Presenting with the Library module

One of the easiest ways to present photos to a client is to use the Library module in Lightroom. After you become comfortable with it you'll be able to quickly put together professional presentations.

NOTE Even if you're not a professional, you'll find these techniques useful.

Preparing Lightroom

The viewing environment in Lightroom is incredibly flexible. If you take the time to learn a few keyboard commands you'll be ready to present like a pro. Here are the main things you should know to set up the workspace for presenting:

- **Maximize real estate.** Hide the Toolbar (T), hide the Library Filter Bar (\), make the Filmstrip smaller, hide the Module Picker, hide the side panels (Tab), and go to full screen (F).
- **Enhance the experience.** Turn down the lights (L) and consider hiding the Filmstrip.
- **Know all necessary keyboard shortcuts.** Loupe (E), Grid (G), Compare view (C), Survey view (N). Also know all shortcuts for the flags, labels, and stars you use.

It's a good idea to render 1:1 previews before you present if you'll be zooming in on them. Choose Library ⇨ Previews ⇨ Render 1:1 Previews. This keeps the client from having to wait while previews are rendered during the presentation.

During the presentation

When you're ready to present, keep the following tips in mind:

- **Go through all images once without stopping.** (Think about using a slide show to add a multimedia dimension.) Then go back to the beginning and place stars on the photos the client likes most.

- **Help clients make difficult decisions between similar images by using Compare view or Survey view.** Zoom in close to check expressions, as shown in Figure 8.29.

- **When all picks are made, filter for the picks only so the clients only see the images they order.**

- **Use the Presets in the Quick Develop module to quickly apply a Develop preset in case the client wants to see black and white, brown tone, or any other special effects you offer.**

FIGURE 8.29

It's easy to see that the pose on the left is superior when these two photos (selected in the Filmstrip) are compared in Compare view at 1:1 magnification. Use this view and the Survey view to help clients make difficult choices.

Familiarize yourself with these techniques so that they become second nature. That way, when you work with clients your attention will be on them instead of your computer.

Using a projector

Show big to sell big has been a common adage in the photography business for a long time. It usually refers to showing clients large samples of your work to interest them in purchasing a large print from their photo session. Now that digital projectors have become affordable it's easy to present large previews to a client. These larger previews give the client the opportunity to see details and imagine what a large print will look like. It also allows them to form an emotional attachment to a large image.

NOTE A projector is just like a big monitor. It shows whatever is on the computer's display.

Some professional photographers use specialized presentation software. My favorite is ProSelect by Time Exposure (http://timeexposure.com). This software is amazing flexible and easy to learn. If you use a projector, it allows you to calibrate the size of your projector's display so that you can project to size. That means you can show a client exactly what a 16 x 20 looks like. Lightroom is also excellent presentation software when the previous techniques are combined with a projector.

If you are a professional photographer, especially a portrait photographer, you have to consider that a projector is just as important as your camera. Every professional I know who switched from presenting on an average computer monitor to a digital projector increased sales immediately. Many of them doubled print sales because they began to sell more big prints, which have a higher profit margin.

The key to getting the most from a projector is to create a viewing environment designed for projecting. Do it in a room where you can turn off all of the lights because stray light diminishes a projected image. Also consider installing high-quality speakers that are easy to plug into your computer. Most important of all, give clients a comfortable place to sit where they can see the screen and you. That way you will be able to talk to them easily and you'll be able to see their expressions as they view the images.

Summary

This chapter was devoted to exploring Lightroom's export modules — the Slideshow, Print, and Web modules. These three modules were covered together because of the similarities in the way they're designed and used. No matter whether you're creating a slide show, prints, or a Web gallery, the process is the same:

- Select photos in the Library module first, or use the Collections panel or the Filmstrip in a specific output module to select photos.
- Select a template from the Template Browser.

- Make graphical modifications to the appearance of the project using the design and layout panels on the right.

- Add any textual overlays to convey any necessary information.

- Consider saving the modified template as a new template.

- Create the output.

- Share it with someone else.

Take some time to explore the three output modules. Find the things that you like about each one. Then, when you're ready to share your photos with others, you'll know exactly which module is best for your needs.

If you're a professional photographer you can use the various viewing options in the Library module to present your photos to your clients. Work with the keyboard shortcuts covered until you're comfortable giving presentations. Also, seriously consider purchasing a digital projector to enhance your sales presentations. Remember: show big to sell big.

Chapter 9

Creating Files to Use Outside of Lightroom

IN THIS CHAPTER

Exporting files from Lightroom

Making exporting a success

S o far, you've explored three major types of output options in Lightroom — slide shows, inkjet printing, and Web galleries. However, there's one important option that isn't in one of the three output modules. Quite often it's necessary to output a file for use outside of Lightroom after editing. For example, I mentioned in the last chapter that I have most printing done at a professional photolab. When I do, I'm not interested in creating layouts in the Print module and saving them as JPEGs. I just want prints from the files. That means that I need a way to create files a lab can use (TIFF or JPEG) from my adjusted files. Lightroom provides a simple way of creating these new files by exporting versions of the original files with their current Lightroom Develop settings.

Exporting Photo Files from Lightroom

To export files from Lightroom select the files in the Grid view, the Filmstrip, or choose a collection. Then click the Export button in the Library module below the left panel group. The Export dialog box can also be displayed from any of Lightroom's five modules by choosing File ➪ Export (Shift+Command/Ctrl+E). You can also right-click on an image in any module and select Export from the contextual menu. Right-clicking offers the added advantage of being able to choose an export preset directly from the menu.

If you need to edit a photo in Photoshop you can open it directly from Lightroom without exporting a file first. I show you how in Chapter 11.

When any of these actions are taken, the Export dialog box appears, as shown in Figure 9.1. The settings in this dialog control all of the attributes of files created during the export process. These attributes vary, depending on the file type being created.

FIGURE 9.1

The Export dialog box is used to tell Lightroom what kind of file you want to create. When a preset is selected from the pane on the left, the appropriate settings are applied in the panes on the right. In this case, the Burn Full-Sized JPEGs preset is selected.

Using export presets

The default Lightroom presets in the left-hand pane are designed for specific, common output scenarios. These presets work just like the presets in the Template Browsers in the three output modules. When you select a preset, the fields in the panes on the right are filled in with the appropriate information for that task. Take a moment to click on each of these presets and notice how they affect those settings.

> **TIP** The For E-Mail preset is a fast way to prepare files for e-mailing. If the settings aren't exactly what you want for your E-mail files, change the settings and save your own preset.

The pane at the top of the dialog box is similar to the Presets pane. When you click on it you are offered two choices: Files on Disk, which writes the new files to the hard drive, and Files on CD/DVD, which burns the files to CD or DVD. The main difference between these two settings is that the Post Processing pane at the bottom of the stack is not visible when Files on CD/DVD is chosen.

If your have any export *plug-ins*, they will also be available here. Plug-ins are third-party applications that provide added functionality to the Export dialog box. Some of these are designed to export and upload files to online stock agencies, such as iStockphoto, and Web galleries such as Flickr.

Choosing an export location

The Export Location pane is used to tell Lightroom where to store the exported photos. Click Choose to select a location and select the Put in Subfolder option to create a new folder during the export process — which is always a good idea. If you plan to keep the files, refer to the organizational guidelines in Chapter 3 when creating the new folder. If you're creating a couple of quick files to e-mail to someone and you don't plan to keep them long term, send them to a temporary folder on your Desktop so you remember to dispose of them when they're no longer needed.

There are a couple of significant upgrades to the Export Location section in Lightroom 2. The first is the Export To menu. When I export full-sized JPEGs for printing at a lab I want to save them and organize them in a subfolder inside of the main project folder. This new menu allows me to find that folder quickly by choosing Same folder as original photo. With Lightroom 1 it was necessary to navigate to the folder by clicking Choose.

> **NEW FEATURE** Added functionality to the Export Location pane allows you to add exported photos to the catalog as they're exported.

The other new addition is much more important. It's the Add to this Catalog option. In Lightroom 1, exported photos were not part of the catalog. Photographers who wanted to import exported files had to go through the extra step of using the Import dialog box to do so after exporting. (It was possible to add exported photos to the catalog during export, but the process was so esoteric that few people knew how to do it.) Now, by simply selecting this check box, the exported folder and all of its photos are added to the Catalog automatically.

The additional Stack with Original option creates an extra thumbnail for the new file that's stacked with the original. This option is grayed out when Put in Subfolder is selected, which avoids the confusion of stacking images together that are stored in different subfolders.

Naming exported files

Quite often it's necessary to rename files as they're exported. Sometimes it's necessary to completely change the name, while in other cases additional information is added to the end of the filename. I'm a strong advocate for keeping the root of a derivative file's name the same as the original file's name. (This is one of the reasons for establishing a base name early in the process — during import preferably.)

The File Naming section of the Export dialog box provides the usual naming options. When you open the Template menu you can choose to keep the file's name the same by selecting Filename. Be careful if you select this option because it can lead to confusion when different versions of a photo have the same name. You can completely change the name by choosing Custom Text, which can also lead to confusion if you ever need to match the exported file with its original. Or you can modify the file's name by adding information to it. For example, when I export full-sized JPEGs I add "-FSJ", (Full-Sized JPG), to the end of the file's name. That means that a file named photo123.jpg becomes photo123-FSJ.jpg. Let's look at how that's done.

Figure 9.2 shows the Filename Template Editor that's accessed by choosing Edit from the File Naming Template menu. (This dialog box is also found in the File Naming section of the Import dialog box.) Click Insert next to Custom Text to add a token representing custom text to the main window. (Remember that tokens can be rearranged by clicking and dragging them to the correct position.) When you click Done, the text box in the File Naming section is activated so that the custom text can be added.

> **TIP**   If you use a particular style of renaming, such as the one used earlier, save it as a preset in the Filename Template Editor's presets so it will be available as a user preset in the File Naming Template menu in the future.

The Filename Template Editor works much like the Text Template Editor we saw in Chapter 8. Use the menus to select information to be used in the filename and click Insert to add a token for the information to the preview window. Click and drag tokens to change their order in the name.

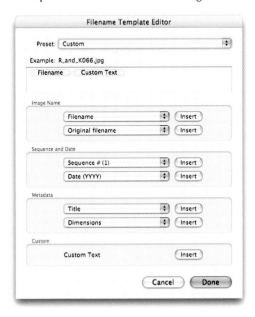

Choosing file settings

The File Settings section of the Export dialog box is where you tell Lightroom what file type you want to create from the exported files. The options are JPEG, PSD, TIFF, DNG, and Original. Original is used to make a copy of the original file with the current settings.

When one of these file types is selected, any file saving options that are available for it appear in the File Settings area. The JPEG and TIFF file types have options for file compression. The DNG file type has the same options as the Import DNG options in Lightroom's main preferences. (There are no additional settings for the Original option.)

After the file format is selected, fundamental properties for that file can be fine-tuned in the File Settings pane. raw files don't have attributes like color space or resolution assigned to them. Because of that, you need to make some decisions about those file characteristics when exporting a raw file to a JPEG, PSD, or TIFF. Figure 9.3 shows the File Settings pane when TIFF is selected in the Format menu. Let's look at those settings:

FIGURE 9.3

After you select a file type from the Format menu, various settings are used to apply the necessary characteristics to the file so that it suits its intended use.

■ **Color Space:** This setting is used to select the appropriate color space for the file. The options are sRGB, Adobe RGB (1998), and ProPhoto RGB. Color space is discussed in detail in Chapter 12, but the bottom line here is to select sRGB for files going to a lab, online, or directly to a client unless the lab or client specifies otherwise. Stay away from ProPhoto RGB unless you are creating a 16-bit file for a printer designed to print 16-bit files. If you have a profile from the lab you intend to use to print these files, you can select it by choosing Other from the Color Space menu.

 When DNG or Original is selected the Image Settings area is grayed out.

■ **Bit Depth:** The choices here are 8-bits/component and 16-bits/compont. This option is only available for PSD and TIFF file types. Bit depth is another file characteristic that isn't assigned to a raw file until it is exported or converted to another file type. A 16-bit file has a great deal more information than an 8-bit file made from the same raw file, but most often that extra information isn't necessary. Use 8-bit unless you have a good reason for doing otherwise. High-bit files are discussed in detail in Chapter 13.

■ **Compression:** This is used to compress the file size. With the TIFF file format the options are None, LZW, and ZIP. When the JPEG file type is selected this becomes a slider ranging from 0 to 100. If you're exporting files for a lab, leave it at 100. If you're exporting for e-mail, use a value of 50 or lower.

Sizing the photos

The Image Sizing pane gives you access to everything you need to make sure the exported files are the correct size. The last thing you want to have to do is open them and resize them after export. Here are the settings found in the Image Resizing pane:

■ **Resize to Fit:** This menu allows you to choose from four different options for the dimensions you want to specify: Width & Height, Dimensions, Long Edge, and Short Edge. You can choose to use pixels, inches, or centimeters as your unit of measurement.

TIP **If you're exporting full-sized JPEGs, deselect Resize to fit to disable all resizing.**

Use Width & Height to specify exact values for those measurements. However, be aware that when landscape (horizontal) and portrait (vertical) photos are combined during export the exported photos will have different dimensions. For instance, if I type a value of 4 inches for width, all of the horizontal photos will be 4 inches wide and all of the vertical photos will be 4 inches wide. When you need to size vertical and horizontal photos together, choose the Dimensions settings and put the longest dimension into each field. This way, long and short dimensions are adjusted correctly no matter what their orientation. If I set them to a value of 6 inches, then my horizontals will be 6 inches wide and the verticals will be 6 inches tall. The other dimension in each case will fall into line. Here it becomes 4 inches.

When images are enlarged, especially when they're small to begin with, quality can be adversely affected. The Don't Enlarge option is used to ensure that no small files are accidentally enlarged. It's a good idea to select this if you think small files are mixed with larger ones.

■ **Resolution:** This setting is used to make sure the file's resolution fits the intended use. If you're exporting files for a lab, set this to 300 pixels per inch (ppi). If you're exporting files for e-mail or the Web, set this to 72 ppi. If you're not sure how the file will be used, 300 ppi is always a safe choice. Resolution is discussed in detail in Chapter 21.

Controlling metadata

The Metadata section is used to limit and control any metadata attached to exported files. When the Minimize Embedded Metadata option is selected only copyright metadata is exported with the file. (This option isn't available when DNG or Original file formats are selected in the File Settings area.) Selecting this option is useful when you're creating files for someone else and you don't want to share all of the metadata with him or her. Say you're a fashion photographer, and you use metadata to track the people involved with each shoot — models, stylists, assistants, and so on. This metadata is proprietary information that needs to be stripped out of exported files that are leaving the studio.

When the Write Keywords as Lightroom Hierarchy option is selected only the lowest level of keywords is shown in the Keywording panel, as shown in the first frame of Figure 9.4. For example, when I imported the photos of the Smith Family in Chapter 5 I applied some keywords to them. They were Robby, Karyn, and Lily. If you recall, the people's names are subkeywords held in the Friends container keyword, which is held in the PEOPLE container keyword. The dog's name, Lily, is a subkeyword of the DOGS keyword. (This is the same as saying the DOGS is a parent keyword and Lily is a child of that parent.)

What this means is that as long as the exported file is used with the current Lightroom catalog, the hierarchy of all keyword tags is understood. When the catalog sees Lily, it knows the Lily keyword is a child of the DOGS keyword tag. However, if this file is cataloged on a different system that doesn't recognize the hierarchy, then only the lowest-level keywords, as shown in the first frame of Figure 9.4, are cataloged.

FIGURE 9.4

When the Write Keywords as Lightroom Hierarchy option is selected in the Metadata section of the Export dialog box, only the lowest-level keywords are attached to the exported files. When none of the check boxes in the Metadata pane are selected, all keywords — parents and children — are exported with the file. Here they're listed in alphabetical order. (These figures are from the Library module's Keywording panel.)

When neither of these check boxes is selected, all keyword metadata appears in the Keywording panel, including container (parent) keywords, as shown in the second frame of Figure 9.4. All keyword tags — parent and child — are exported as a flattened list (no parent/child relationships). This is the best way to preserve all keywords, but their hierarchy is no longer in place.

When Add Copyright Watermark is selected the information in the copyright field of the metadata is overlaid on the lower-left corner of the image. This is a very basic overlay. The type cannot be moved, nor can its characteristics be modified.

Applying post-processing steps

The Post-Processing After Export menu, shown in Figure 9.5, is used to do something extra with the files after they're exported. Select Show in Finder (Explorer) to open the exported photos folder in the Mac Finder or Windows Explorer. Selecting the Open in Photoshop option opens each of the exported images in Photoshop so you can add finishing touches that can only be done in Photoshop. If you prefer to use other software for post-export editing, select the Open in Other Application option and choose that application with the Application menu below the After Export menu.

FIGURE 9.5

Use the After Export menu in the Post-Processing pane to use external software to add processing to the photos as they're exported.

The Go to Export Actions Folder Now option allows you to use Photoshop Actions with Lightroom. If you have a special action that applies a funky border to the finished image, for example, you can use it here to apply that border to all of the images during export.

CROSS-REF I show you how to create an action and use it for post-processing during export in Chapter 18.

Putting the Workflow into Action

As you can see, there are many options here. Five different file types can be created with the Export dialog box. Some of those file types allow for a great deal of variation. Because of that, it's difficult to lay out an exact workflow. However, I want to point out some highlights that will help you get the most from this dialog box:

- **Presets are your friend.** The Presets pane has lots of room to display your user presets. Take advantage of that by creating presets for every type of file you export.

- **Sometimes exported files are intended to be permanent,** and other times they're disposable. When files are permanent, store them in a subfolder that's inside the source folder and add them to the catalog during export.

  When you create temporary files — such as files for e-mail — store them in a temporary folder on your desktop and don't add them to the catalog.

- **Keep the root filename the same whenever possible.** Use the Filename Template Editor to add additional information after the root name.

- **Choose the appropriate file type with the Format menu.** Remember, you can export DNG versions of your raw files and copies of original files by selecting those options here.

- **Use the Image Settings pane to create exactly the kind of file you need.** If you're exporting files to use as proofs, consider adding your copyright information.

- **If you have proprietary or personal information in a file's metadata,** select the Minimize Embedded Metadata option to remove it from the exported file.

- **Use the After Export menu to move exported files** to the next step in the workflow — such as Photoshop — whenever possible.

TIP To quickly export a photo(s) with the previous settings choose File ⇨ Export with Previous. You can also choose this option from the Export section of the right-click contextual menu you get in the Grid and Loupe views. This saves time by bypassing the Export dialog box.

Summary

For many photographers the Export dialog box is the main way to create output of the photos in their Lightroom Catalog. That's because they need files ready for printing at a lab or delivering to clients more than they need slide shows, inkjet prints, and Web galleries. In Chapter 8, you saw that it's possible to output JPEG files from layouts in the Print module. But when all you need is a file, the Export dialog box is the way to go.

The Export dialog box allows you to define all sorts of file attributes when exporting photos. When raw files are concerned, this is the first time attributes such as color space and resolution have been assigned to the photo — albeit, a version of the photo. If you need different versions of a photo, say one for printing and one for a Web site, you can export the photo twice with the appropriate settings for each use.

There's a lot going on in the Export dialog box. At first it may seem overwhelming, but after you use it a couple of times you'll see how easy it is to export files. Just start at the top and work your way down the menus — or better yet, use a preset designed exactly for the kind of file you plan to export.

Chapter 10

Putting the Production Workflow into Action

In the last six chapters, you explored how Lightroom is used to accomplish the goals of the Production Workflow, as shown in Figure 10.1. In each of those chapters, you looked at the workflow implications for the subject of that chapter, but you haven't put all of the parts together to create the entire Production Workflow — from import to output.

This chapter outlines the basic steps of the Lightroom workflow so you can see all of the major steps in one place. Then I show you how a wildlife photographer uses Lightroom to manage his demanding Production Workflow while photographing polar bears in the Arctic. At the end of this chapter, you'll be ready to leave Lightroom behind and begin exploring Photoshop CS3 and the Creative Workflow.

Surveying the Production Workflow

Review the first figure in this book, as shown in Figure 10.1, which represents the main goals of the Production Workflow. This list probably looks a little different now that you have a firm understanding of Lightroom. Let's review how it's used to accomplish all of these goals quickly and efficiently.

FIGURE 10.1

Here's the Production Workflow schematic you looked at in Chapter 1. Remember that some of these steps can take place concurrently. For example, Steps 1, 2, and 3 are addressed during Import.

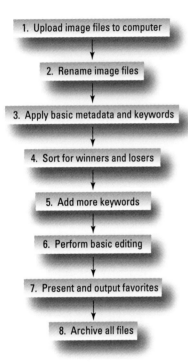

The Production Workflow

1. Upload image files to computer

2. Rename image files

3. Apply basic metadata and keywords

4. Sort for winners and losers

5. Add more keywords

6. Perform basic editing

7. Present and output favorites

8. Archive all files

Importing new photos

The first step in the Production Workflow is to use Lightroom's Import dialog box to transfer photos to your computer. Follow these steps to ensure that you get the most from the importing process:

1. Decide if you want to convert to DNG during import.

2. Place the photos into a unique folder that fits your overall organizational system.

3. Use the Backup to feature to make a backup of the originals. Send the files to a backup hard drive or place them into a temporary Burn folder.

4. Take the opportunity to give the photos a meaningful name that will be used for all derivative files. If in doubt, use the same name as the folder in Step 2 with a sequence number.

5. Apply a metadata preset to add your copyright information to each file's metadata.

6. Add general keyword tags now. Specific keyword tags that don't apply to all images are added later.

7. Determine the type of previews you need and select them from the Initial Previews menu. If you plan to take a close look at every image later, select 1:1. The import process will take longer, but you won't have to wait for images to render when you zoom in on them.

Getting organized in the Library module

After the files become part of the Lightroom catalog, it's time to get them organized. Follow these steps to help you identify the most important images quickly:

8. Begin by viewing the photos in Grid view. The objective here is to get a quick overview of all imported photos. Delete any obvious rejects. Identify groups of photos and individual photos that need additional keywording. Try to move quickly through this first look at the photos. Additional, deep keywording can be done later if necessary.

9. Switch to Loupe view (or Impromptu Slideshow), and begin taking a closer look at the photos. Use keyboard shortcuts to identify picks and rejects. (I used green for picks and red for rejects.) Use Auto Advance to make the process flow more efficiently.

10. Go back to Grid view and use the Library Filter to filter for red and find all files to be deleted. Take one more quick look at them before selecting all and deleting.

11. Turn off the red filter and turn on the green filter. Now only the picks are displayed. Go through the photos again. Compare similar photos and eliminate weaker candidates by removing their colored labels. Use rating stars to identify standouts.

12. Create a collection of all picks — green labels in my case.

Processing photos in the Develop module

After the important photos are identified, it time to move them into the Develop module for processing. The goal is to move quickly while applying basic corrections. Continue where you left off with Step 12 and follow these steps:

13. If you plan to use a specific crop on all photos go ahead and apply it to one of them now. Then select all photos and synchronize the crop with the first one. You can make cropping adjustments as you move through the editing process later if you need to.

> **TIP** **Work with groups of similar images whenever possible.**

14. When the color of the light used to capture the photos was consistent (for example, daylight or fluorescent) you can adjust the white balance of one photo with the White Balance Selector and synchronize it with the rest of them. (Remember, this works best with raw files.) You can also work with groups of photos created with similar light. If you

photographed a neutral calibration target in any photos, click-balance on it to establish a custom white balance and share that white balance with similar photos.

15. Select the first frame and use the other settings in the Basic panel to adjust the brightness and contrast of the tonal scale. Be sure to use the histogram's clipping previews to make sure you aren't losing any important shadow or highlight detail. Synchronize these settings with all similar images.

> **TIP** **Use Develop presets to save time whenever possible.**

16. Continue moving down the Develop panels, using any that are appropriate for the groups of images you're working with. Add any creative touches you want, such as vignetting or skin softening. Just remember that the goal at this point is to move quickly.

Creating output and archiving

The next stage is the workflow is to create output and archive your work. Pick up where you left off in Step 16 and follow these steps:

17. Use the Slideshow, Print, and Web modules to create specific types of output for printing or presentation. Save presets of your favorite layouts so you won't have to re-create them.

18. Use the Export dialog box to export derivative files for printing or distribution. If you plan to keep these files, add them to the Lightroom catalog during Import.

19. Protect your work by backing up all files, as well as the Lightroom catalog. If the photos are important, make two backups and store them in separate locations.

Something to remember is that this workflow is like a piece of music. It's open to interpretation by every person who performs it. A good example is our national anthem. Whenever you hear someone sing it before a sporting event it always sounds different because each singer fits the song to his or her personal style.

The Lightroom workflow is the same. Different types of photographers emphasize different things. A wedding photographer might focus on using presets to quickly apply creative effects, while a stock photographer may be more focused on the organizational aspects of applying meaningful keywords and metadata. With that in mind, I want to finish this section by showing you how one photographer has adapted Lightroom to meet his demanding Production Workflow needs.

Putting the Workflow into Action

Photographer Mark Wilson photographs a wide variety of nature and wildlife all over the globe. Recently he returned for a trip to Cape Churchill in Manitoba, Canada, where he spent ten days photographing migrating polar bears. The polar bears were making the annual trek to their winter hunting grounds on the sea ice. Figure 10.2 shows an amazing photo from the trip.

FIGURE 10.2

These polar bear photos were shot in one of the harshest environments on earth. These conditions, combined with the large number of exposures necessary to capture these unpredictable animals, require an extremely efficient workflow.

Photos by Mark Wilson

The conditions Wilson was shooting under were about as extreme as they get. Besides the fact that the temperature was minus 35 degrees Centigrade with high wind, the animals themselves were very unpredictable. An additional factor was the angle of light because the sun was low on the horizon all day. All of this unpredictability added up to shooting a large quantity of similar frames — up to 2000 a day.

While shooting, Wilson closely monitored his exposures to be sure that the histograms on his raw files showed no clipping. He also monitored the camera's white balance to be sure that his custom settings were adjusted for the often-changing light conditions. Taking this step helped to limit the amount of editing in the Develop module adjusting white balance. It also helped because he couldn't place a white balance target in the scene while he was shooting. During lulls in the action, he browsed his photos on the camera's display and deleted substandard images on the spot.

Uploading and importing

Back at the lodge after a day of shooting, Wilson would upload the day's images to his laptop with Lightroom's Import dialog box. Figure 10.3 shows how he configures it. Look at some of these settings to see why Wilson prefers them.

FIGURE 10.3

When Mark Wilson uploads new photos he converts them to DNG and organizes the folders by date. He also uses a custom file-naming template that allows him to insert a meaningful piece of text after the date at the beginning of the filename.

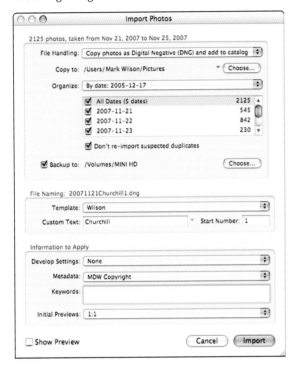

File handling

Wilson is a big believer in DNG because it offers the most secure form of metadata storage. All metadata — even the original raw file if you desire — is stored as part of the DNG file. As Wilson puts it, "The metadata and the image cannot be separated, corrupted, or lost during data transfer or due to some electronic calamity."

Folder organization

All photos are uploaded to the Pictures folder on the laptop. (They'll be transferred to a permanent location upon returning home.) Wilson uses a combination of date and descriptive words in his folder-naming strategy. He feels this system suits the type of photography he does because he covers a broad scope of subject matter. When he needs to find something he uses keywords to find it quickly, rather than searching for a specific folder.

Creating backups

Wilson brings two portable hard drives as backup storage drives. During the Import process all files are backed up to one of these drives. The Lightroom catalog is also backed up onto one of them.

File naming

Wilson uses a custom file-naming template, as shown in Figure 10.4, that allows him to easily mimic his folder-naming strategy and to give him more flexibility with file naming during import. (Choose Edit from the File Naming Template to open this dialog box.)

FIGURE 10.4

The Filename Template Editor is used to create a file-naming scheme that's similar to the folder-naming scheme.

Image previews

Photography in these extreme conditions lends itself to creating multiple images that have similar exposures and compositions. Wilson knows that he'll need to evaluate each similar image at 100 percent magnification in order to determine which is best, so he saves time later by choosing to create 1:1 initial previews during import.

Selecting "the Good, the Bad, and the Ugly"

Wilson uses colored labels and rating stars to rate his photos in two different ways. He does it a little differently than I do, so I want so show you his system. When he evaluates his photos he looks for three criteria — composition, sharpness, and exposure. Colored labels are used to indicate how individual image matches these criteria: Yellow is used to tag interesting images that are acceptable in only one or two of the evaluation criteria, but not all three; and red is used to tag rejects. Purple is used to tag any images that need the advanced editing in Photoshop. Rating stars are used to rate images on quality. Two stars are used to rate an image as excellent. One star is used for really good images, and neutral images remain unrated.

The goal is to identify what Wilson calls "the Good, the Bad, and the Ugly." Good images are all of the one- and two-star picks. They stay in the Lightroom catalog. The Bad images are the unrated images that are not edited in the Develop module. They're removed from the catalog, but remain on the system's hard drive. The Ugly images are just that. They're removed from the catalog and deleted from the hard drive.

> **TIP** Wilson uses stacks to group similar photos. This helps to make a big job feel more manageable.

All side panels are closed and Grid view is used to identify clusters of similar images that can be evaluated as groups. When those groups are identified, the view is changed to Loupe for a closer examination. Each image is evaluated for composition and exposure in the Fit zoom magnification preset, and then zoomed to the 1:1 zoom preset to check focus. During this process the appropriate labels and stars are added to images with the keyboard shortcut keys.

> **TIP** Wilson uses the Z key (or the spacebar) to alternate between the two most recent zoom presets in the Library module.

The Survey viewing mode is used to compare large groups of similar images. After the best two or three images are identified the viewing mode is switched to Compare, as shown in Figure 10.5, so that similar images can be compared at 1:1 magnification.

FIGURE 10.5

Similar images are evaluated in the Compare or Survey modes for composition, exposure, and focus. The image on the left got a one-star rating.

Photos by Mark Wilson

This process is often carried out in more than one pass. Groups of images that are easily evaluated are done on the first pass. More complicated evaluations are saved for later. As Wilson says, "Burnout can be a problem when evaluating a thousand images at once, so it's nice to be able to group the images into manageably sized sets."

Adding keywords

When such a large number of images needs to be evaluated, it pays to be organized. Wilson creates the expected keyword tags before the trip so that he doesn't have to worry about creating them in the field. If other keyword tags are needed, they're created during the editing process.

General keyword tags — such as Arctic, Canada, and Churchill — are added during the import process. Additional keywords are added to groups of images selected from the Grid view. Keywords are added using the Recent Keyword list in the Keywording panel when possible. When a needed keyword isn't in the recent keyword list, the group of images to be keyworded is dragged and dropped onto the appropriate keyword in the Keywording panel. After all large groups have been keyworded, another pass is made to apply individual keyword tags to single photos.

Processing in the Develop module

Basic spot removal and cropping is often done in the field, but advanced tonal and color adjustment is saved until the images can be evaluated on a calibrated monitor. This happens when Wilson returns home from the trip. He transfers the images to his main system and the main Lightroom catalog. After the photos are on the system, their order is rearranged, if necessary, and they're renamed to preserve this order.

TIP Wilson edits his photos in chronological order so that it's easy for him to keep track of which files are already edited and which ones need editing.

Wilson does what he calls "editing by the numbers." He starts with Basic panel and moves down the panels on the right side, using the controls that are appropriate for the images being edited. Most necessary exposure and color adjustments are done with the Basic panel — starting at the top and working down the panel. Further tonal modifications are made with the Tone Curve panel and HSL panel when necessary. Any additional rough cropping and spot removal are also taken care of at this time. Again, groups of images are adjusted first, and then specific images that require individual adjustment are addressed.

Final steps

Besides the occasional slide show, Wilson rarely uses Lightroom's output modules. Most of his output is in the form of files for e-mail, publication, and printing at a pro lab. These files are created as needed using the Export dialog box. When files are prepared for the lab, he uses the Color Space section of the Export dialog box's File Settings to apply a profile supplied by the lab.

When all editing is complete, Wilson makes multiple backup copies of the images and the Lightroom catalog and stores them in separate locations.

> **NOTE**   **View more of Mark Wilson's photography on the Web at `www.hakunamatata photography.com`.**

Summary

Before Lightroom was officially introduced in 2007, nearly everything covered in Part II was possible in Photoshop, with the help of Bridge and Adobe Camera Raw (for raw photos). The problem was that not many people understood the process, or how to create an efficient system from it. Most struggled through the production portion of their workflows without a clue as to what they were missing. Lightroom removes those problems because it makes the workflow process transparent and easy to understand.

Different types of photographers have different needs when it comes to their Production Workflows. In this chapter, you saw how a wildlife photographer uses Lightroom to handle his demanding workflow. Something you may have noticed is that the primary focus of his workflow is centered on evaluating large numbers of images and applying relevant metadata to them. Other photographers, such as wedding photographers, appreciate the additional power of using Develop presets to quickly apply their special creative touches and the output modules for creating a wide variety of output. The beauty of Lightroom is that it's flexible enough to handle these diverse needs equally well without any major differences in the way it's used.

This chapter completes the portion on the Production Workflow, as well as Part II of this book. You're ready now to leave Lightroom behind and move into the powerful world of Photoshop CS3 and explore how it's used to accomplish the goals of the Creative Workflow. You come back to Lightroom later when you see how it relates to Photoshop, but for the most part we're through discussing it. Be sure to revisit the ideas and techniques presented in these chapters as you learn to manage your own Production Workflow with Lightroom.

Part III

Understanding Basic Photoshop Concepts

Part III marks the transition from Lightroom to Photoshop — from the Production Workflow to the Creative Workflow. One of the things you're going to notice as you move forward is that there's an awful lot going on in Photoshop CS3. That's because Photoshop is one of the most powerful image-editing applications available. This kind of power leads to a complexity that can be intimidating for new users. However, once you understand some of the basics, the way Photoshop works makes lots of sense.

The chapters in this part focus on those basic concepts. We begin with the most fundamental concept — opening files — and work our way up to creating complex selections. By the end of Part III you'll be ready to move into some of the more advanced techniques in Parts IV and V that make Photoshop the perfect tool for your Creative Workflow.

Chapter 11

Opening Files in Photoshop

You have some choices when it's time to take a special image into Photoshop for advanced editing. If you're working in Lightroom you can open a file into Photoshop directly from Lightroom. If you're already in Photoshop and you know which file you want, you can choose File ➪ Open. A third way is to use Photoshop CS3's file browser, Adobe Bridge, to visually browse through files to find the one you want.

When raw files are opened from Photoshop or Bridge they need to go through Adobe Camera Raw (ACR) to be converted into a file type that Photoshop uses. (Remember, raw files cannot be edited directly in Photoshop.) This process is similar to making adjustments to a photo in Lightroom's Develop module and then opening the file into Photoshop from Lightroom.

Because you're using Lightroom to handle all of your Production Workflow, you may find it easiest to open files into Photoshop directly from Lightroom. However, there are times when you may want to use Bridge and ACR instead. That's why you should have a basic understanding of how these two pieces of software are used and when they might be more desirable than Lightroom for opening Lightroom files into Photoshop.

IN THIS CHAPTER

Using Lightroom to open files in Photoshop

Using Adobe Bridge to open files outside of Lightroom

Converting raw files with Adobe Camera Raw using Lightroom's Develop module settings

Ensuring that Lightroom and Bridge/ACR communicate about metadata changes

Opening Files from Lightroom

When a file is opened into Photoshop from Lightroom all of the current settings can be applied. To open a file directly from Lightroom, choose Photo ➪ Edit In ➪ Edit in Adobe Photoshop CS3 (Command/Ctrl+E). You can also right-click on a photo in any of the five modules and choose this command from the contextual menu.

When you open a raw file into Photoshop from Lightroom the file opens with all of your settings. The type of file that opens is determined by the External Editing preferences you looked at in Chapter 3. These settings control the file format, the color space, bit depth, and resolution of the file that opens in Photoshop.

When you select a JPEG, TIFF, or PSF file to open into Photoshop the dialog box shown in Figure 11.1 gives you control over the type of file that's opened. Because these file types already have attributes such as color space and bit depth assigned to them, they are not subject to the settings in the External Editing preferences. (When you use this method you have the additional options if multiple photos are selected.)

FIGURE 11.1

Lightroom needs to know what kind of file you want to use for editing in Photoshop. When a raw file is selected, the two bottom options are grayed out. Use the down arrow to expand the Copy File Options.

The Edit Photo with Adobe Photoshop CS3 dialog box provides three options for the type of file that opens in Photoshop when you click Edit:

- **Edit a Copy with Lightroom Adjustments.** This is what you'll want to use 99 percent of the time so that you can take advantage of any editing in Lightroom's Develop module.

- **Edit a Copy.** This allows you to edit a copy of a TIFF, JPEG, or PSD file without Lightroom adjustments.

- **Edit Original.** This allows you to edit the original TIFF, JPEG, or PSD file without Lightroom adjustments.

One of the things I don't like about using Lightroom to open files into Photoshop is that a new thumbnail version of the photo appears in the Lightroom catalog right beside the original, even if the new file is saved somewhere else.

When I edit a file I usually save the edited version and the final version inside of special subfolders (see Chapter 3). When those folders and files are automatically imported into Lightroom the photo thumbnails appear in the correct place in Lightroom, but a duplicate thumbnail is also placed in the originating folder next to the original thumbnail. This adds a level of confusion that I don't like. I want all thumbnails to be in their appropriate places. This type of confusion is the reason I use folders in the first place. I don't like seeing multiple versions of the same photo in the same place. I would rather see them only in the folders I saved them to.

One option is to select the Stack with original option at the bottom of the dialog box. This automatically stacks the new thumbnail with the original thumbnail. Stacking helps to make these various versions more manageable, but if you want to use one of those versions you'll still have to sort through the stack to find the one you want. This is one of the main reasons I prefer to open files into Photoshop from Bridge. When I finish editing them I can synchronize the folder in Lightroom to update any additional files I create if I want them to be part of the catalog.

Using Adobe Bridge CS3

Early versions of Photoshop had no file browser. If users wanted the ability to visually browse through folders and files, they had to purchase a separate file browser from someone other than Adobe. When Adobe released Photoshop 7, it finally included a very useful file browser that was part of Photoshop. With the release of Photoshop CS2, the file browser was retooled and separated from Photoshop. The file browser became Adobe Bridge, stand-alone software that could be used even if Photoshop wasn't running. When Photoshop CS3 was launched, an updated version of Bridge was launched, too — Adobe Bridge CS3, as shown in Figure 11.2.

NOTE The biggest difference between Bridge and Lightroom is that Bridge is a true file browser — it shows you everything in the folder you point it at. It isn't necessary to import photos into it as it is with Lightroom.

NOTE Bridge comes with Photoshop CS3. When you install Photoshop, Bridge also is installed. You can launch it independently of Photoshop, if you want, by clicking its icon in your Applications folder (Mac) or by clicking its icon in the All Programs menu, in the Start menu (Windows).

Bridge is a very powerful file browser. It would be easy to write an entire book about it. However, because you're using Lightroom to accomplish many of the things Bridge is used for, you won't need to go too deep into it. I just want to show you some basic things about Bridge so that you'll feel comfortable using it to open files into Photoshop. If you want to know more about it, you can read a more detailed discussion in one of my other books, *Photoshop CS3 Restoration and Retouching Bible* (Wiley).

 To open Bridge from Photoshop, choose File ➪ Browse. You also can launch Bridge by clicking the Go to Bridge button at the top right of the Photoshop CS3 workspace. When Bridge is already running, this is a quick way to jump to it from Photoshop.

FIGURE 11.2

Adobe Bridge CS3 default view shares many similarities with Lightroom's Library module. The gray icon in the upper right-hand corner of the selected thumbnail indicates that its settings have been modified in ACR.

Surveying Adobe Bridge

Before you can use Bridge, you need a basic understanding of the Bridge Workspace. This workspace is composed of seven panels. Some of them are similar to the panels in Lightroom's Library module. Here's what they do:

- **Favorites panel:** This panel is used to store favorite locations so they can be accessed quickly. To add a new favorite, locate the folder in the Content panel and drag it into the Favorites panel. New items are also added using the General preferences in Bridge.

- **Folders panel:** This is hidden behind the Favorites panel in Figure 11.2. This panel displays a folder tree just like the Folders panel in Lightroom.

- **Filter panel:** This panel populates with information from the selected folder. Every variation among the various files is listed. For example, only the label colors being used in the folder are shown. Click on any item here to filter for that item. Use the Sort menu to change sorting order.

■ **Content panel:** This panel displays thumbnails of the contents of the folder or location selected in the Folders or Favorites panels. The size of these thumbnails is adjusted with the Thumbnails slider located at the bottom right of the window. The information displayed below the thumbnails can be modified in Bridge's Thumbnails preferences.

■ **Preview panel:** The Preview panel shows a preview of the selected photo. When more than one photo is selected (up to nine), all are displayed. Click on an image in the Preview panel with the magnifier icon to open Bridge's version of the Loupe tool.

■ **Metadata panel:** This is much like the Metadata panel in Lightroom's Library module except that it cannot be used for sorting. The metadata fields with a pencil icon beside them are the only ones that are editable by clicking on them.

■ **Keywords panel:** Like the Keywords panel in Lightroom, though not nearly as user friendly.

Many of these features are obsolete for Lightroom users because they're intended for Digital Asset Management (DAM), which is accomplished much more easily in Lightroom. For those users, Bridge is more of a gateway into Photoshop than DAM software. However, there is one way that Bridge is more flexible than Lightroom: With Bridge, each of the panels can be removed or relocated to different locations — with the exception of the Content area. This allows users to configure the Bridge workspace for specific purposes. To remove a panel or to add a new one, choose Window and then choose from the list in Figure 11.3.

FIGURE 11.3

Bridge CS3 comes with six workspaces installed. To create a custom workspace, organize the work area the way you want it and click Save Workspace. As you can see, I saved two custom workspaces: Mark's Default and Large Previews.

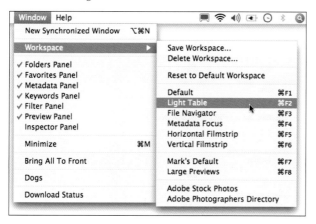

To move a panel, click its title and drag it to a new location. A blue box, or in some cases a blue line, indicates the location of where the panel will be placed when you release the mouse button. This flexibility allows you to arrange elements in Bridge just the way you want them. The height and width of panels is changed by clicking and dragging the lines between them. Explore some of these differences by selecting from the different workspace presets shown in Figure 11.3. If you create your own workspace, save it by choosing Save Workspace. I use two custom workspaces. One is a modified version of the default workspace. The other one is designed to maximize the size of the Preview panel and minimize the size of the Content panel. I call this one Large Previews. (I have to admit that I don't use this second custom workspace much since I began using Lightroom.)

Setting Bridge preferences

To open Bridge's preferences, as shown in Figure 11.4, choose Bridge CS3 ➪ Preferences (Edit ➪ Preferences). Select from the menus on the left to choose which preference set to modify. Only a few of these preference sets are of interest here. Let's look at them:

FIGURE 11.4

The Bridge Preferences dialog box allows you to change many aspects of Bridge. Choose from the menus on the left to select the preference set to modify.

- **General:** Because you're using Lightroom for uploading new files, deselect the When a Camera is Connected, Launch Adobe Photo Downloads option so that Bridge stays out of the way during Lightroom importing sessions. To remove items from the Favorites list, deselect them here.

- **Thumbnails:** The Details section of this preference set allows you to choose which information is shown below each thumbnail. In Figure 11.3 you can see that I have file size and bit depth displayed. (Because these are raw files the bit depth shows as 16, even though a raw file has no bit depth.)
- **Labels:** Be sure that the names of the labels are the same as the color, that is, Red, Yellow, and so on. Some people change these labels to different words like To Print or To Delete. When you use custom names like these your Lightroom labels may not display properly in Bridge.

Opening files with Bridge

As I said earlier, much of what is done in Lightroom's Library module can be accomplished with Bridge. Rating stars and labels can be applied, files can be sorted, and metadata and keywords can be edited. However, after you spend time doing these things in Bridge you'll come to appreciate the simplicity of Lightroom's well-thought-out design.

> **NOTE** If you're working with a non-raw file, some of your Lightroom adjustments may not be visible in Bridge. However, when the file opens in Photoshop all adjustments will be in place.

You can open a single selected file from Bridge or you can open a selection of files. To select more than one file press Shift as you select contiguous thumbnails, and press Ctrl (Command) to select noncontiguous files — the same as selecting files in Lightroom. After files are selected, double-click one of them. If the files are non-raw, they open directly into Photoshop (unless you set Photoshop preferences to open JPEG and TIFF files in ACR, which I show you how to do in a moment). If the files are raw files, they have to make a trip through Adobe Camera Raw to be converted before opening in Photoshop.

Converting Raw Files with Adobe Camera Raw

Before a raw file can be opened in Photoshop it needs to be converted to a file format that's editable in Photoshop. When a raw file has been modified in Lightroom, and Bridge has access to the metadata, then all Lightroom changes are visible in Bridge. (I discuss metadata synchronization in a moment.) This is useful if you want to check your settings or to fine-tune them before opening the file. I always do this when I'm working on an important image — for example, an image for publication or large print.

> **CAUTION** When opening raw files modified in Lightroom 2 you need to use at least Camera Raw 4.5 because earlier versions can't use all of Lightroom's Develop module settings. (The version number is displayed at the top of the dialog box.) To update, choose Help ➪ Updates while in Bridge or Photoshop. Even with the updated raw converter there are still three adjustments that are not available in ACR: the Local Adjustment Brush, the Gradient Filter, and Post Crop Vignette.

Surveying Adobe Camera Raw

When you open a raw file from Bridge the Adobe Camera Raw converter opens, as shown in Figure 11.5. In this case, multiple files are selected in Bridge so they're displayed in a filmstrip that runs up and down the left side.

ACR is very similar to Lightroom's Develop module. Most of the tools and controls in the Develop processing panels are located somewhere in ACR. Let's take a closer look to compare and contrast ACR with the Develop module:

FIGURE 11.5

The Adobe Camera Raw converter is very similar to the Develop module in Lightroom. It allows you to process a raw file before you open it in Photoshop CS3. Notice that the Basic panel, on the right, has all the same adjustment sliders as the Basic panel in Lightroom's Develop module.

Toolbar   Panel selectors   Camera Raw Settings

Filmstrip   Zoom presets   Workflow Options

■ **Toolbar:** The Toolbar in ACR is at the top left of the dialog box. It has most of the same tools on Lightroom's Develop module Toolbar, with the exception of the Adjustment Brush and the Graduated Filter tools. One tool that isn't in Lightroom is the Color Sampler tool, fourth from the left. This tool is used to place a color sample point anywhere on the image so you can monitor how your adjustments affect tone and color. (You take a closer look at this tool in the context of Photoshop in Chapter 13.)

TIP Click and hold on the Crop tool to reveal the various cropping aspect ratios.

■ **Filmstrip:** All thumbnails selected in Bridge prior to opening ACR are displayed in the Filmstrip. It's used just like the Filmstrip in Lightroom, where multiple files can be selected and the most selected file is shown in the main display area. When groups of thumbnails are selected, all editing is applied to them at the same time (just like Auto Sync in Lightroom's Develop module). You can also edit one file and then select similar files before clicking the Synchronize button at the top (like Sync in Lightroom).

■ **Panels:** The panels are the same except that there is no Vignettes panel in ACR. The biggest difference is that the panels are laid on top of one another — including the Presets panel. Click a panel's icon to make it active. Only one panel can be visible at a time. One big difference in the panels is that the Presets panel doesn't have the same Develop presets that are in Lightroom. If you apply a preset in Lightroom, you may not be able to remove it in ACR.

■ **Action Buttons:** The Save Image button on the bottom of the screen opens a dialog box much like the Export dialog box in Lightroom's Library module, though it has much less functionality. Click Done to apply any settings (update XMP metadata) to the original file without opening it in Photoshop. Open is used to open the file(s) in Photoshop.

■ **Workflow Options:** At the bottom center of the window is a blue link for opening the Workflow Options dialog box, as shown in Figure 11.6. The options in it are very similar to Lightroom's External Editing preferences, discussed earlier.

FIGURE 11.6

The Workflow Options dialog box is used to determine file type and settings for the file being opened into Photoshop. The Size menu allows you to select from presets to increase or decrease the file's pixel dimensions when it's opened. Sizes with a minus symbol are smaller than the original, and sizes with a plus symbol are larger.

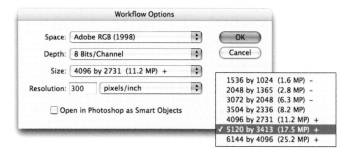

There are some important differences between these two dialog boxes. One difference is the ACR dialog box doesn't allow you to select a file format. That's assigned to the file when it's saved in Photoshop.

Another difference is that the Size menu in the ACR dialog box can be used to increase or decrease the file's pixel dimensions when it's opened in Photoshop. Sizes with a minus symbol beside them are smaller than the original and sizes with a plus symbol are larger. This is a quick way to change file size when the file is opened. Lightroom only opens files at their original pixel dimensions. The Resolution setting is used to put the file size into perspective. (Resolution and image sizing are discussed in detail in Chapter 21.)

> **TIP**   Hold down the Shift key while double-clicking a file to bypass ACR and open the file directly into Photoshop with the most recent ACR workflow settings. (This is much like Export with Previous in Lightroom.)

 ■ Camera Raw Settings: Clicking on the icon at the top right of the panel header opens the Camera Raw Settings menu. This menu provides access to a number of things, such as loading and saving settings, and changing or resetting the default settings.

Setting ACR preferences

You probably noticed the Camera Raw preferences earlier because they're located next to the Bridge preferences. To open them, choose Bridge CS3 ➪ Camera Raw Preferences (Edit ➪ Camera Raw Preferences). Let's look at the important settings in these preferences, as shown in Figure 11.7.

FIGURE 11.7

The Camera Raw Preferences dialog box allows you to change some important settings in ACR.

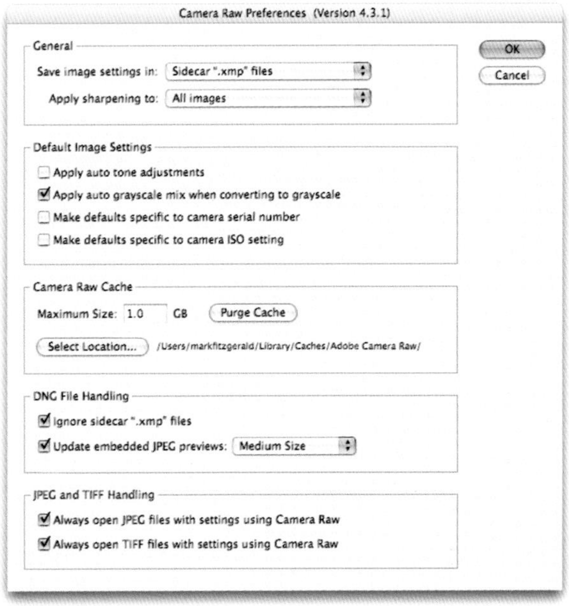

There are two settings in the General section that you need to pay attention to:

■ **Save image settings in:** The options here are Camera Raw database, which is a central location for all images, and sidecar ".xmp" files. You want to select sidecar ".xmp" files so that all adjustments stay with the original raw file. Otherwise, Lightroom won't have access to adjustments made in ACR.

CROSS-REF See Chapter 3 for a more detailed discussion of XMP files.

■ **Apply sharpening to:** There are two choices here. The first is to apply sharpening to Preview images only. This setting is used to prevent sharpening from being applied to files as they're opened in Photoshop. The second setting is All images. Because you're using Lightroom to do a bit of capture sharpening it's necessary to leave this set to All images so that the Lightroom sharpening is applied during file conversion.

Other settings of note are:

■ **DNG File Handling:** Select the Ignore sidecar ".xmp" files option so that all modifications are stored in the DNG files themselves. Otherwise ACR will create XMP files for DNG files, which isn't necessary. Selecting the Update embedded JPEG previews option ensures that DNG previews are updated, which is useful if the files will be viewed outside of Lightroom or Bridge.

■ **JPEG and TIFF Handling:** This is supposed to allow for JPEG and TIFF files to open in ACR so you can use the controls there to edit the file before opening it in Photoshop. To make it work you have to go into the Thumbnails section of the Bridge preferences and select the Prefer Adobe Camera Raw for JPEG and TIFF files option. (This can also be activated in the File Handling section of Photoshop's preferences.) The advantage to doing this is that you can open JPEG and TIFF files with the same develop settings you applied in Lightroom because those settings are interpreted by ACR. In order for this interplay to take place you have to select Include Develop settings in metadata inside JPEG, TIFF, and PSD files in the Metadata section of Lightroom's Catalog preferences.

After ACR is set up the way you want it you need to take a couple of extra steps to ensure that when you look at the same file in Lightroom and Bridge (as well as ACR) you see the same thing. In order for this to happen, all metadata needs to be synchronized between the two programs.

Synchronizing Metadata between Lightroom and Bridge

One of the tricks to using Lightroom and Bridge together is in ensuring that any metadata generated in Lightroom is available in Bridge, and vice versa. This metadata includes keywords, labels, and any modifications done in the Develop module or ACR. This is especially true with raw files because of the way their metadata is stored. When I view a file in Bridge that was previously modified in Lightroom, I need to be able to see the changes that were made. Likewise, when I change a label in Bridge or edit a file in ACR, I need to be able to see those changes in Lightroom. Without this interplay, it becomes very difficult to use Lightroom, Bridge, and ACR together.

Saving Lightroom metadata

Lightroom has a way of letting you know changes were made to a file. When metadata has been changed in Lightroom, but hasn't been saved, a small icon with three dots appears at the top right of the photos thumbnail in Grid view. This icon informs you that Lightroom hasn't written any changes to the metadata yet. It usually takes care of this by itself, but you can click on it to manually save the metadata. When you do, the dialog box shown in Figure 11.8 opens. You can also save metadata for selected files by choosing Metadata ⇨ Save Metadata to File (Command/Ctrl+S).

FIGURE 11.8

When you choose to save metadata in Lightroom, the first dialog box appears as a reminder. If any problems are encountered during the saving process after you click Save, the second dialog box appears.

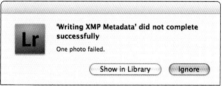

When there's a problem with saving metadata, the second dialog box shown in Figure 11.8 appears. This dialog box is usually an indication that you don't have permission to write to the location where the file is located. Checking the folder properties with your operating system to be certain you have read/write permission for the file usually solves this. (I see this happen occasionally when folders are imported from CDs or DVDs that come from someone else's computer.) The best way to handle metadata in Lightroom is to set it up so that all metadata is saved automatically by Lightroom.

- **For raw files:** Select the Automatically write changes into XMP option in the Metadata section of Lightroom's Catalog Settings.

- **For non-raw files:** Select the Include Develop settings in metadata inside JPEG, TIFF, and PSD files option in the same preferences dialog box.

When both of these options are selected, changes made in Lightroom are understood in Bridge and ACR, and vice versa. However, sometimes it's necessary for you to facilitate the conversation.

Reading Bridge and ACR metadata in Lightroom

Sometimes changes are made to a file in Bridge and/or ACR and the changes don't appear in Lightroom. There are a couple of ways to deal with this.

 When changes have been made to a file outside of Lightroom (Bridge or ACR) it alerts you by placing a button on the top-right corner of the affected thumbnail(s). When you click on this button, the dialog box shown in Figure 11.9 opens. Choose Import Settings from Disk to update Lightroom with the changes made with other programs, or choose Overwrite Settings to change them to the current Lightroom settings.

 The Save image settings in sidecar ".xmp" files must be selected in the ACR preferences for Lightroom to have access to any changes made in ACR.

 Another scenario that can occur is when changes are made in Bridge/ACR and Lightroom without updating the metadata. When that happens, a button with an exclamation mark appears on the thumbnail. When you click on this button the second dialog box shown in Figure 11.9 appears. The options are the same as when the changes were only made in the external software — Import Settings from Disk or Overwrite Settings.

FIGURE 11.9

When metadata is changed outside of Lightroom you are given the option to import that metadata or overwrite it with Lightroom's settings. You have the same options when metadata is changed in Lightroom and another application.

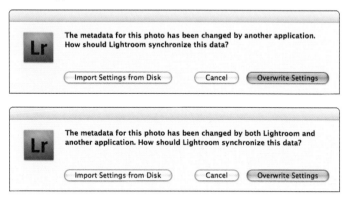

Reading metadata

Occasionally it takes a while for Lightroom to notice that changes have been made outside of it. When you know that you changed a file in ACR, but those changes aren't visible, you can manually read them. To read metadata updates to a file select the file in the Library module and choose Metadata ➪ Read Metadata from File. The dialog box shown in Figure 11.10 opens to warn you that this is a permanent change that cannot be undone in Lightroom.

FIGURE 11.10

When you choose Read Metadata Lightroom warns you that the Lightroom metadata will be overwritten and that the operation cannot be undone. When you choose Synchronize Folder the dialog box allows you to choose exactly what you want to accomplish during synchronization.

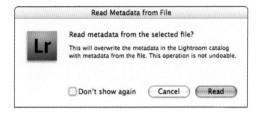

Synchronizing folders

Sometimes it's faster to update a folder of images instead of reading the metadata for individual images. Doing this is easy in Lightroom. Select the folder to be synchronized and choose Library ⇨ Synchronize Folder. Lightroom compares its catalog to the actual files and makes the necessary modifications to the catalog so that it reflects reality. (You can also right-click on a folder and choose this option from the contextual menu.) When the Synchronize Folder dialog box appears, as shown in Figure 11.10, you have a few options. Here's what they do:

■ **Import new photos:** You can import any new files to the catalog. If you want to see the files before importing, select Show import dialog before importing.

■ **Remove missing photos from the catalog:** If photos were deleted from the system outside of Lightroom, they can be removed from the catalog by selecting this. This is usually a good idea.

■ **Scan for metadata updates:** This checks for changes and lets you know if there are conflicts with changes made outside of Lightroom.

When you know lots of changes have been made outside of Lightroom, use Synchronize Folder to get Lightroom's catalog up to speed.

You can also right-click on a Folder and choose Save Metadata. This saves the metadata for all files in the folder. If Lightroom notices that a file's metadata has been changed outside of Lightroom, a warning dialog box appears.

This is the easiest way to get Lightroom's catalog updated with files opened and created outside of it.

Summary

At some point, your special Lightroom files need to be opened in Photoshop for the advanced editing the rest of this book focuses on. Those files can be opened directly from Lightroom, or they can be opened from Bridge. The main advantage to using Bridge is that new thumbnails aren't generated in the Lightroom catalog like they are when the file is opened from Lightroom.

When raw files are opened from Bridge, they need to go through Adobe Camera Raw. This gives you the opportunity to make any final adjustments to the raw file before a version of it is opened in Photoshop for editing. You can also open JPEG and TIFF files in ACR, which is a good idea when you want to modify any Develop settings made in Lightroom.

The interplay between Lightroom and Bridge/ACR works best when file metadata is synchronized with the file. Lightroom allows you to set up preferences so this happens automatically. However, sometimes you need to facilitate the interplay, especially in the case of raw files. This is a necessity if you plan to use Bridge to open files edited in Lightroom.

Chapter 12

Understanding the Photoshop Workspace

Photoshop is incredibly powerful. Almost any image modification that can be imagined can be carried out with its impressive set of tools. However, this power leads to a great deal of complexity, which doesn't lend itself to an intuitive workspace design. Compared to the elegant design of Lightroom's workspace, the Photoshop workspace is far from being easy to understand. However, if you're familiar with the logic behind how the workspace is configured, you can rearrange many of the workspace elements so that the tools you use most are easily available.

Photoshop's preferences are similar to Lightroom's in many ways. Obviously, the options are different for parts of each program, but the general idea is the same. However, when it comes to color-management settings, things are very different. That's because Lightroom doesn't worry about color management until files are being output or exported. Photoshop, on the other hand, begins managing a file's color as soon as the file is opened. For that reason, it's important to set up Photoshop's color settings early in the process. This section explores the color-management issue. By the end of this chapter, you'll not only know which color space is best for your Photoshop editing, you'll also know which color space to use when exporting Lightroom files.

Getting a Bird's-Eye View

It may not seem like it, but Photoshop does have many similarities to Lightroom. It uses menus, palettes (instead of panels), and a tool area. Let's compare and contrast these elements, shown in Figure 12.1, to the similar elements in Lightroom:

FIGURE 12.1

This is the default Photoshop workspace. The Tools palette on the left is in single-column mode. Two palette docks are visible on the right. The one on the left is collapsed. I never use the Color, Swatches, Styles palette group so I remove this group and replace it with the History, Actions palette group.

- **Menu Bar:** The menus across the top of the screen contain much of Photoshop's power. You may have noticed that while you worked in Lightroom, you rarely visited the menus. That's because so many things are done with panel controls and buttons. In Photoshop, menu commands are a mainstay. There are more than 400 commands buried in these menus so it's sometimes hard to remember where they are. Try to use the menu names as clues. For example, if you're doing something with a layer, then you probably want the Layer menu.

- **Palettes:** Photoshop's palettes are similar to the panels in Lightroom. Each is designed with a specific purpose in mind. These palettes are different from Lightroom because they can be moved to any location within the workspace, individually or in groups. (We take a closer look at some of the fine points of using palettes in a moment.)

- **Tools palette:** Photoshop's crowded Tools palette, on the left of the workspace, makes the Tool Strip in Lightroom seem anemic. That's because it contains almost 60 tools. Similar tools are stacked in groups with only the top tool visible. To reposition the Tools palette, click and drag it by its title tab.

A new feature introduce in Photoshop CS3 is the ability to use the Tools palette as a single column instead of the traditional double-column. Click the double-arrow icon at the top of the Tools palette to alternate between single- and double-column layout. Throughout this book I refer to the single-column arrangement, so it would be best for you to use it, too.

■ **Tool Options bar:** The Tool Options bar, just below the Menu bar, is used to modify the actions of the currently active tool. When a different tool is selected, the contextual content of this bar changes to the options available for that tool. This is very much like the contextual panel that opens when a tool is selected from Lightroom's Tool Strip.

■ **Workspace menu:** Because the workspace layout in Photoshop is extremely flexible, it's useful to be able to save different workspace layouts for different purposes. You can use the Workspace menu (at the top right next to the Go to Bridge button) to quickly change your workspace layout. For example, someone working with photos might prefer one layout, while someone focused on animation might prefer a completely different palette layout. Because of this, it's necessary for users to be able to store specialized workspaces that are designed for specific purposes. Choose from the included workspace presets or create your own presets.

 ■ Palette menus: Each palette has its own menu. It's accessed by clicking the icon at the top-right of the palette just below the "X." The commands in this menu allow you to modify the palette and get quick access to many commands used with that palette.

■ **Document window:** The central viewing area is where all of the work is done. Every time a photo is opened, it's displayed in a separate window in this area. There are a number of viewing options that are used to change the way these images display. We look at some of them in a moment.

Working with Palettes

Photoshop's palettes have been part of the program from the earliest days. However, the way they're used changed significantly with the release of Photoshop CS3. Let's look at some of the main characteristics of working with palettes:

■ **Palette groups:** Palettes are typically grouped together. The first frame of Figure 12.2 shows six palette groups. Click a palette's title tab to bring it to the front. Individual palettes are rearranged within the group by clicking and dragging them by their tabs.

■ **Palette docks:** A dock is a collection of palette groups that are displayed together in a vertical orientation, as shown in Figure 12.2. Individual palettes can be moved out of the dock by clicking the palette's title tab and dragging it out of the dock. When this is done, the palette becomes a *free-floating* palette that can be placed anywhere in the workspace. It can also be added to another dock. When a free-floating palette is dragged over a dock, a blue line or box indicates the drop zone where the palette will be placed when the mouse button is released. A group of palettes can be relocated in the same way by dragging it by its title bar. The group can become free-floating, be added to another dock, or be repositioned up or down in the same dock.

FIGURE 12.2

In the first frame here both palette docks are expanded, revealing all palette groups within the two docks. In the second frame both docks are collapsed to save room. Notice how the palettes in each group stay together when they are collapsed. Click on any palette to open it individually.

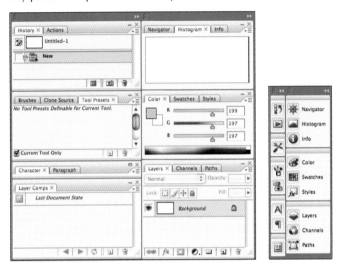

- **Adding and removing palettes:** To remove a palette, click the Close button (the X beside its name). To remove a group of palettes, click the Close button on its title bar. Palettes are added by using the Window command.

- **Hiding palette docks:** A new feature in Photoshop CS3 is the ability to maximize the viewing area by collapsing docks. The second frame in Figure 12.2 shows both palette docks collapsed. Click the arrow icons at the top right of the panel to collapse it. Click the icon again to uncollapse the dock. To open an individual collapsed palette, click its icon.

 TIP To temporarily hide all palettes, press Tab. Press it again to unhide them.

Use this flexibility to create a workspace that suits the way you work. For example, I don't use the Color, Swatches, and Styles palettes, so I remove this group. I always want to see the History palette, so I add the History/Actions palette group to replace the removed group. Then I save my workspace by choosing Window ⇨ Workspace ⇨ Save Workspace. That way, if anything gets changed I can instantly reset it with my saved workspace preset.

Viewing Photos in Different Ways

Photoshop, like Lightroom, provides a number of ways of viewing your files. When multiple files are open they stack on top of each other. This stacking arrangement can be changed by choosing Window ➪ Arrange. Let's look at some of the other ways you can change the way files are viewed:

- **Screen modes:** When a file opens in Photoshop it opens in its own window in the main document viewing area. There are four different ways of viewing this file called screen modes. To change the screen mode choose View ➪ Screen Mode and choose from the four options: Standard Screen Mode, Maximized Screen Mode, Full Screen Mode With Menu Bar, and Full Screen Mode. A faster way is to use the F key to cycle through the four settings.

  When I'm really focused on a project, I like to use one of the two full-screen modes to eliminate much of the visual clutter around the image.

- **Changing magnification:** There are a few ways to change magnification. If you use the Navigator palette, you can use the Magnification slider at the bottom or type a value directly into the box. My favorite way to change magnification is to use keyboard short-cuts to access Photoshop's zoom presets. Press Command/++ (Control++) to zoom in, and Command/+- (Control+-) to zoom out. Every time you use one of these key combinations the zoom moves to the next zoom preset — either up or down.

- **Panning:** When an image is zoomed in (or in Full Screen mode) you can use the Hand tool (H) to reposition the image within the viewing window. Simply click and drag the image.

> **TIP** Hold down the spacebar for quick access to the Hand tool. This way you don't have to change tools in the Tools palette.

Take the time to explore these three methods of changing the way an image is viewed. Learning to move seamlessly between them with keyboard shortcuts will help to make your workflow efficient.

Setting up Preferences

I don't have space to cover all of Photoshop's preferences so I want to focus on setting the most important preferences right now. To open Photoshop's preferences, as shown in Figure 12.3, choose Photoshop ➪ Preferences (Edit ➪ Preferences) and choose a preference set from the menu.

FIGURE 12.3

The Preferences dialog box gives you access to most of Photoshop's preferences. Choose from the menu of preference groups on the left to contextually change the contents of the panes on the right.

Main preferences

The main preferences are where most of Photoshop's preferences are addressed. These three areas contain the most important main preferences:

- **General preferences:** This section allows you to adjust some basic settings. I like to select the Automatically Launch Bridge option because I usually want Bridge open when I use Photoshop. I also like to select the Zoom with Scroll Wheel option so that I can use the scroll wheel to quickly zoom in and out. (This method doesn't use presets, which allows me to make smaller zoom adjustments.)

- **File Handling:** The most important section of the File Handling preferences is the File Compatibility section. I like to select the Ask Before Saving Layered TIFF Files option and select Always for Maximize PSD and PSB File Compatibility. (I discuss why these settings are chosen in later chapters.)

- **Performance:** If you don't have much memory (RAM) in your system, but you do have multiple hard drives, you can use the Scratch Disks area of these preferences to tell Photoshop to create virtual memory on a scratch disk if it runs out of RAM. This is one of the easiest ways to improve Photoshop's performance. In Figure 12.4, you can see where I selected a hard drive called Storage. You can select more than one drive, but be sure not to select the system drive because your operating system is already using it for its own version of virtual RAM.

FIGURE 12.4

If you don't have much RAM, but you do have an additional internal hard drive, you can tell Photoshop to use the extra hard drive as virtual RAM whenever it runs out of real RAM.

CAUTION Only use internal drives for scratch disks. The data pipeline to external drives is too slow to efficiently handle the data transfer.

TIP RAM has become very cheap in the past couple of years. More RAM is always a better alternative than using a scratch disk.

There are other preferences of importance here, but I'd rather wait to discuss them later on when you can see them in context. Feel free to explore them on your own now if you want to.

Setting color preferences

In many ways, the decision about which color space to use is more important than any of the preferences discussed previously. In order to make that choice intelligently, you have to know something about how computers and Photoshop use color.

Comparing color spaces

Red, green, and blue are the colors of a *color model* called RGB. A color model is an abstract way of mathematically describing colors. A common vocabulary is needed when discussing specific RGB colors within that model. Otherwise, when I say "red," how do I know you're thinking about the same color that I'm thinking about?

Colors are further classified into *color spaces*. A color space, among other things, defines the *gamut* of color that a device is capable of capturing or reproducing. For example, my monitor is capable of displaying only a certain palette of colors. Many of the colors I can see in nature can't be displayed on my monitor. However, my monitor can display colors that can't be printed on my inkjet printer. The monitor's gamut isn't as large as the spectrum that a human eye can see, but in some cases it's larger than the gamut of the printer. These kinds of color spaces — monitor and printer — are called *device-dependent* color spaces. A device-dependent color space describes the range of colors that a particular device can see and/or reproduce.

NOTE Devices can be subcategorized into input and output devices. A digital camera is an input device, and a printer is an output device.

The second type of color space is *device-independent* color space. These color spaces are used to describe the range of colors in color *editing spaces*. An editing space describes the total palette, or *gamut*, of colors available when editing a photo in Photoshop. A device-independent color space is not limited by the gamut of any particular device. The two most common editing spaces in Photoshop CS3 are Adobe RGB (1998) and sRGB:

- **Adobe RGB (1998)** is a large color space that is more applicable to high-end printing and reproduction.
- **sRGB** is a limited color space that is intended to be common to a wide range of devices.

The main difference between these two editing spaces is that Adobe RGB (1998) is larger than sRGB. It has a wider range of colors and more extreme colors in some cases.

Think about it this way: Imagine that I have two boxes of crayons. One box has 24 colors, and the other box has 120 colors. Suppose we both want to do a drawing of the same scene outside. If I gave you the 120-count box and kept the 24-count box, the results of our drawings would be quite different. The greens and browns in my trees would be more limited than yours because I don't have the same range of greens and browns to work with as you do.

This is sort of the way it works in Photoshop. When you edit digital files, you need to standardize the way color is managed in your Photoshop workflow. You can choose to work in a smaller color space like sRGB, or you can work in a larger color space like Adobe RGB (1998). The graphics in Figures 12.5 and 12.6 were created in ColorThink software, a product of Chromix in Seattle, and depict the color gamuts of Adobe RGB (1998) and sRGB.

NOTE When a photo file comes in contact with a color-managed device, the color space of that device is attached to the file with something called a *profile*. This profile is like a translator that interprets the colors in the file.

NOTE A third editing space is gaining popularity in the digital photography world. It's called ProPhoto RGB. Its color gamut is even larger than Adobe (1998). Currently, few output devices support such a large gamut, but that will change as technology moves forward. In the meantime, it's better to stay away from ProPhoto because converting images for output on some devices results in unpredictable color shifts — especially when working with 8-bit files.

At first it seems like a no-brainer to choose to work in a larger color space so that you're working with more colors, but that's not always the case. When you consider working spaces, you also must think about device color spaces — devices such as printers. Even though a working space may be device-independent, the files you edit will eventually come into contact with some kind of device. Usually that device's limited gamut is much smaller than the working space, which means that some of the colors you see on your monitor are not printable, leading to disappointments at printing time.

The real key to deciding which color space to use as your main Photoshop working space is how you plan to output your files. If you're using a commercial photo lab, ask what color space the lab prefers. Most will tell you that their equipment works in the sRGB color space. If you plan to do most of your printing at this lab, use sRGB as your working space. Some labs do work in the Adobe RGB (1998) color space. If your lab is one of them, take advantage of the larger color space.

FIGURE 12.5

This graph compares the color gamuts of Adobe RGB (1998) (the wireframed shape) and sRGB (the solid shape). Notice that the Adobe RGB (1998) gamut is much larger in some areas, like the yellows.

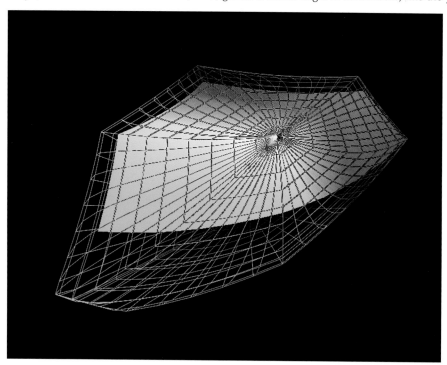

This is even more important when preparing photos for the Web. The sRGB color space is ideal for the Web. In fact, it was created with the Internet in mind. Back in the mid-1990s, Microsoft and Hewlett-Packard proposed a new standard color space that was best suited to the limited gamuts of cameras, printer, and monitors. With a common color space, users could have more confidence that when they placed photos on the Web, people who viewed the images would see them the way they were intended to be seen. (Naturally, monitor calibration, discussed in Chapter 7, comes into play here.)

> **TIP** Some labs provide a profile that describes their particular printer. Having one of these allows you to preview your image onscreen with the colors that the lab's printer is capable of reproducing. Printer profiles are discussed in Chapter 21.

Many people prefer to use inkjet printers for their output. Most inkjet printers work with a limited gamut of color. However, this can be misleading because the gamut isn't limited in every color of the spectrum. Figure 12.6 shows the color profile of an inkjet printer (the solid shape) compared with the sRGB and Adobe RGB (1998) color spaces (the wireframe shape). In the first image of Figure 12.6, you can see that the printer is capable of printing yellows that are well outside the limits of sRGB. In the second image, you can see that Adobe RGB (1998) contains most of the yellows that the printer can print, although it's capable of printing some extreme yellows that are outside the gamut of Adobe RGB (1998). If I were photographing a yellow Corvette and planning to print it on this printer, I would edit it in the larger Adobe RGB (1998) space.

FIGURE 12.6

The first image compares the inkjet (solid) to the sRGB working space (wireframe). The second image shows that the Adobe RGB (1998) working space (wireframe) comes closer to the gamut of the printer.

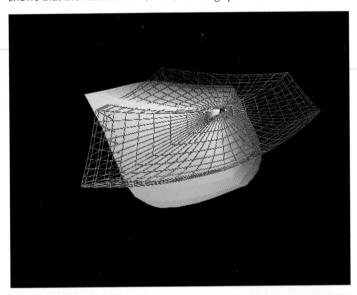

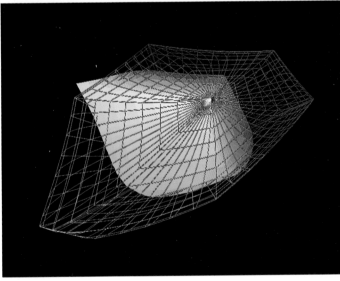

You must think about these sorts of things as you consider which working space to use in Photoshop. When the file opens in Photoshop a profile for the chosen color space is attached to it. Your working space choice really does depend on what you plan to do with files in the future. With that in mind, here's the bottom line:

- **Use sRGB** when you know that all of your workflow is oriented to producing images for the Web or for photo labs with printing equipment that is limited to sRGB. Doing this helps you to better predict what your color will look like when it's time to view photos online or in print.

- **Use Adobe RGB (1998)** when you're dealing with a lab that uses the larger color space, when outputting to an inkjet printer, or when you just aren't sure what you're going to do and you want to keep your options open.

> **TIP** You can change a photo's color profile after it's open in Photoshop by choosing Edit ⇨ Covert to Profile. This is best used for moving a photo to a smaller color space or assigning a special output profile supplied by your lab.

When you tell Photoshop which working space to use, you can set preferences so that Photoshop allows you to make the decision on the fly as you open files. That way, you can decide on a file-by-file basis.

Choosing your color working space

Now that you know about color spaces, you need to tell Photoshop how you want it to handle color: which color space to use and what to do when the color space of a file you're opening doesn't match your working space. Do that by following these steps:

1. Open the Color Settings dialog box, and choose Edit ⇨ Color Settings.

2. Click the pull-down menu in the Settings box, and select North America Prepress 2. This configures the color settings with the best starting points, as shown in Figure 12.7.

3. If you plan to use Adobe RGB (1998) as your working space, you're finished. Click OK. If you plan to use sRGB, click the pull-down menu in the RGB slot under Working Spaces. Select sRGB IEC61966-2.1, and click OK.

We don't really care about the other working spaces (CMYK, Gray, and Spot) right now, so leave them as they are.

I encourage people to configure the Color Settings dialog box by selecting North American Prepress 2 because this setting selects all the options under Profile Mismatches and Missing Profiles. When these check boxes are selected and Photoshop finds a discrepancy between the color space you're using and the color space of a file you're opening, it refers to the Color Management Policies boxes to resolve the *profile mismatch*, as shown in Figure 12.8.

FIGURE 12.7

In the Color Settings dialog box in Photoshop CS3, click North American Prepress 2 and then decide which RGB working space you want to have as your main working space.

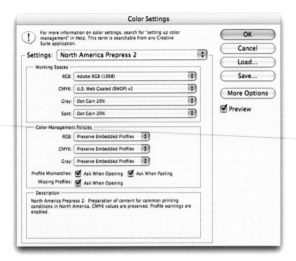

FIGURE 12.8

Photoshop's Color Management Policies in the Color Settings dialog box allow you to set up Photoshop CS3 to inform you of color profile mismatches and missing profiles.

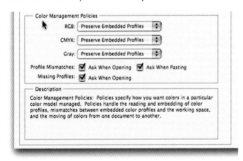

If you open a file with a color space that doesn't match your working space, Photoshop prompts you to make a decision about how you want to handle the issue, as shown in Figure 12.9. These are your choices:

- **Use the embedded profile (instead of the working space).** This opens the image in its own color space.

- **Convert document's colors to the working space.** Moves the file into your working space by mapping its colors to the appropriate equivalents in your color space.

■ **Discard the embedded profile (don't color manage).** This strips the image of any color profile. This usually isn't a good idea—although I have used it when experimenting.

FIGURE 12.9

The Embedded Profile Mismatch dialog box allows you to manage on the fly the color space conversion of files that don't match.

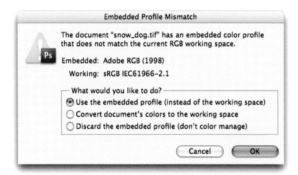

Don't bother trying to convert a file that's in the smaller sRGB color space into the larger working space of Adobe RGB (1998). When you begin with a small gamut, you pretty much have to live with it. The range of the original colors doesn't expand and change when the image is converted to a larger color space.

However, if you're opening a file with Adobe RGB (1998) into a working space of sRGB and you know that you need a smaller color space for output, converting an Adobe RGB (1998) file to sRGB before editing it is a good plan; that way, you'll see only colors that are reproducible.

TIP If you're using a digital SLR camera, you can set your camera's preferences to tell it which color space to use for capturing images. (If you're shooting raw, this setting doesn't have an effect because color space is unassigned.) I recommend that you set this preference on Adobe RGB (1998). This way, you can decide to work on photos in a smaller space or leave them their larger native color space when you open them in Photoshop.

After you get a handle on what's happening with profile mismatches and you get tired of being asked the same question every time you open a file, you can uncheck the question box in the Color Settings dialog box. I generally recommend against this, but I know that you may have reasons to make this choice.

Every once in a while, you get a file that doesn't have a profile—you don't know what color space it was created in. When this happens in Photoshop CS3 and you have the Color Settings set up the way I suggested earlier, you get a Missing Profile Warning dialog box, as shown in Figure 12.10. You have no way of knowing in what color space the file was created, so you have to make assumptions about how Photoshop should handle the remapping process. This would be the same as a representative from a new nation showing up at the United Nations without an interpreter. You might be able to make some guesses about what this person is saying, but if you aren't careful, some of those guesses could get you into trouble.

FIGURE 12.10

When a file is missing the color profile, you can assign the profile of your choice in the Missing Profile dialog box.

The best way to handle a missing profile is to make an educated guess about the lineage of the file. If you think it began as an Adobe RGB (1998) file, then you can convert it to that color space. If you're already working in Adobe RGB (1998), select Assign working RGB in the Missing Profile dialog box. If you aren't already working in Adobe RGB (1998), select Assign profile and select Adobe RGB (1998) from the selection box. Also select the check box next to "and then convert document to working RGB," as shown in Figure 12.10. If sRGB suits your needs better, choose it as your color space instead.

NOTE Digital SLR cameras always assign a profile to the photos they create. Usually, you encounter files without profiles only when they're coming from a scanner that hasn't been set up to *tag* the files it creates with color profiles.

When you use Lightroom or ACR to bring files into Photoshop, it's best to export or open them with the intended working color space. For example, if I'm using Adobe RGB (1998) for my Photoshop working space, then I should make sure that my Lightroom preferences are set up to open files into Photoshop with Adobe RGB (1998) attached by Lightroom. If I were to open the file from Lightroom with the smaller sRGB color space attached and then convert it to the larger Photoshop working space of Adobe RGB (1998), I would run the risk of limiting the image's color range.

Summary

Though it may not seem like it at first, there are many similarities between Lightroom and Photoshop. Both programs use panels/palettes, a Tool panel/palette, a menu bar, and a main viewing area. The main difference with Photoshop is that the layout of the workspace is very flexible, allowing you to create and save just about any workspace layout you want.

Most of Photoshop's preferences are grouped together in the main Preferences dialog box. Select from the menu of preference sets on the left to work with specific groups of preferences. You looked at the General, File Handling, and Performance preferences in this chapter. You come back to some of the others in later chapters.

The Color settings in Photoshop are one of the most important preferences, yet one of the least understood. In this section, I discussed the concept of color spaces while comparing and contrasting the two most important color spaces used in digital photography — sRGB and Adobe RGB (1998). The choice between these two spaces often comes down to the intended output use for your photo files.

Chapter 13

Adjusting Tonality and Color

With the workflow presented in this book, much of a photo's basic tonal and color corrections will have been made in Lightroom and/or ACR before it's opened in Photoshop. However, when important images are brought into Photoshop, it's always a good idea to reevaluate those decisions. Knowing how to use the tools presented in this chapter will help you to do that. Additionally, these tools are used with advanced selection and masking techniques to make precise localized tonal and color corrections that aren't possible in Lightroom. Those techniques are covered in upcoming chapters. For now, the focus is on how these tools are used to make general adjustments.

As you move through this chapter you'll notice that the tonal and color adjustment tools in Photoshop are very similar to the adjustment tools in Lightroom's Develop module. That's because they address the same set of fundamental image qualities: brightness, contrast, and color.

Adjusting Brightness and Contrast

When you explored tonal adjustments in Lightroom you used the sliders in the Basic panel to target the brightest whites and darkest darks in the image. These modifications set the overall contrast of the image. You used the histogram and its clipping previews to monitor your progress. The tonal adjustment process in Photoshop is very similar whether the adjustment is done with the Levels or Curves commands.

Using Levels

The first thing you notice about the Levels command is that it uses the histogram to display information about the image, as shown in Figure 13.1. The small triangles below the histogram at each end allow you to control where the ends of the histogram stop. The numbers below the sliders tell you exactly which tones are being affected. These triangles are called *input sliders*. When you click and drag them inward, you modify the histogram by moving the endpoint. Be sure the Histogram palette is visible if you want to see a real-time display that shows changes to the histogram as you use the tonal adjustment tools (Window ➪ Histogram). Use the Histogram palette menu to change the way information displays in it.

FIGURE 13.1

The Levels command allows you to modify the histogram by clicking and dragging the Input sliders.

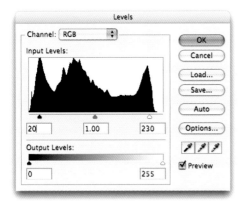

> **CAUTION**   The Levels window includes another set of sliders at the bottom. These sliders are called *output sliders* because they're used to limit the tones in an image for specific printing scenarios (output). You normally don't use them for image adjustment at this point.

When the black and the white Input sliders are moved, they have a similar effect on their respective endpoints. The black slider controls what the darkest tone in the image is — a value of 0, or pure black. It functions much like the Blacks slider in Lightroom's Develop module. The white slider works much like the Exposure slider in Lightroom. It controls what the lightest tone in the image is — a value of 255, or pure white. This means that whatever values these sliders are set on become the new blackest black (the black point) and the whitest white (the white point).

In Figure 13.2, the black and the white Input sliders have both been moved inward. The black slider is set at 26, and the white slider is set at 232. If you click OK at this point, the current tone of 26 becomes 0 and the current tone of 232 becomes 255. This can be verified by looking at the display in the Histogram palette that shows what the resulting histogram is going to look like.

FIGURE 13.2

The Histogram palette displays an updated histogram as the Levels Input sliders are moved. The new histogram is the gray one in the background.

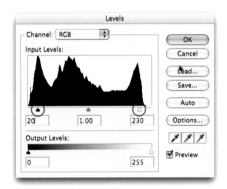
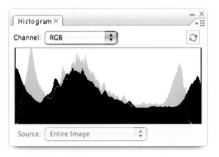

TIP   If you see a small exclamation icon in the Histogram palette it means that the currently displayed histogram is being created with cached information — not the latest info. When you click the icon the histogram updates so it's using the most current information.

If you look at the resulting image, you see that it looks more contrastier — the darkest tones are too dark, and the lightest tones are blown out, losing all detail. This is because you clipped the ends of the histogram and removed tonal information from the extreme shadows and highlights in the image by moving the sliders too far inward. This is similar to over-adjusting the Exposure and Black sliders in Lightroom.

Take the Levels command for a spin so you can get a feel for the three main sliders. Follow these steps:

1. Open the practice file titled `snow_dog.tif` from the downloadable practice files on the Web site.

NOTE   All of the practice files used in the hands-on exercises can be downloaded from the Web site.

2. Choose Image ➪ Adjustments ➪ Levels. You also can access the Levels dialog box by pressing Command/Ctrl+L.

    The histogram for `snow_dog` clearly shows that the image includes no deep black or bright white; the histogram data does not extend all the way to either end. This is born out in the image. Its contrast is flat, and the overall brightness is a little dark.

    If the Histogram palette isn't displayed on your Desktop, choose Windows ➪ Histogram.

3. Click and drag the black Input slider until the value is 23.

4. Click and drag the white Input slider until the value is 226.

Notice how much richer the image looks. The blacks have been punched up, and the whites look much cleaner.

5. Now click and drag the black slider to 45 and the white slider to 200.

Notice how the image's contrast goes too far. The darkest tones and the lightest tones lose detail because tonal information is being clipped.

6. Click Cancel.

When you work with Levels, be careful about clipping shadows and highlights when moving the endpoints. It's not only important to know when clipping is happening, it's also important to know where it's happening in the image.

Try adjusting snow_dog again. This time you learn a way to target the clipping in your image. Follow these steps to clip the image in just the right places:

1. Open snow_dog. If it's already open, be sure that no previous Levels adjustments have been applied.

NOTE If this file had already been adjusted in Lightroom, these overall adjustments might not be necessary.

2. This time, hold down the Alt key before clicking and dragging the black slider. The first thing you notice is that the image goes completely white. Keep dragging the slider until you see some detail appear in the image, as shown in the first frame of Figure 13.3.

This isn't as elegant as the clipping previews in Lightroom and ACR, but it still provides important information. The areas that begin to appear are what will become the darkest tones in the image if you stop as soon as you see them. If these pure black tones are in an important part of the image, you want to stop just before you see them so that you know that the darkest tones still have some detail.

3. Move the black slider back to the left until the preview becomes completely white. Release the mouse button.

4. Do the same thing with the whites. Hold the Alt key, and drag the white slider inward. Notice that the screen goes black. Keep dragging until some detail appears in the image, as shown in the second frame of Figure 13.3.

The areas that begin to appear are the brightest tones in the image. If they are showing in the preview, then you know you're beginning to blow out the highlights.

5. Move the white slider back to the right until the preview becomes completely black. Release the mouse button.

Now you can be confident that the image has a full range of tones from almost pure white to almost pure black.

6. Deselect the Preview option on the Levels window so that you can compare before and after. Be sure to recheck the box before clicking OK later.

FIGURE 13.3

Preview clipping by holding down the Alt key when adjusting the black and white Input sliders in Levels. The top image shows the clipping preview when adjusting shadows. The bottom image shows the highlight preview.

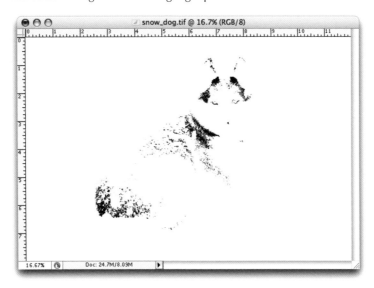

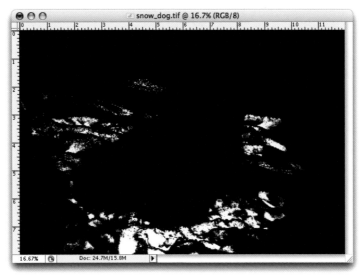

TIP Brains get used to what's in front of them pretty fast. The Preview option in most Photoshop dialog boxes helps you to "remember" what an image looked like before any changes were made. This is a great way to see whether you're on the right track with your adjustments.

7. The contrast of the image looks good, but the overall brightness is still a bit too dark. Click the middle Input slider. It's between the white Input slider and the black Input slider. This slider's function is much like the Brightness slider in Lightroom's Basic panel. Just below it is a readout displaying 1.00. Slide it to the left to lighten the image; and slide it to the right to darken.

   Holding down the Alt key here has no effect. Just move the slider until you like what you see.

8. Click OK.

Now the image has had its brightness and contrast fine-tuned. You know where the darkest and lightest parts of the image are, and you know that you're holding detail in them.

NOTE By the way, the terms "brightness" and "contrast" do not refer to the Brightness/Contrast command in Photoshop. Instead, they refer to the qualities of the image. Most Photoshop teachers will advise you to stay away from the Brightness/Contrast command and use the more powerful Levels command.

Sometimes, I let the shadows of an image clip if I think it makes the image look better by providing deeper blacks. I just make sure that those shadows are not in my main subject. In this example, any detail loss in the shadows is in the dog's fur — which would be unacceptable to me. If it were in a dark background, I might let it go if I thought it gave the image a little more snap. However, I'll almost never allow a highlight to blow out if I can prevent it. When a highlight is blown out and it gets printed, it becomes the color of the paper it's printed on.

So here's the lowdown on Levels. When adjusting an image with Levels, always start with either the black slider or the white slider. Do both ends, and get the black point and the white point set before adjusting the image's brightness with the gray slider in the middle. If you begin with the gray slider before working with the ends, you'll most likely have to revisit it later to readjust it.

Using Curves

If the Levels command is a chisel for refining an image's tonal range, then the Curves command is a scalpel. With Curves, you can target small ranges of an image's tonal qualities with much more control than the Levels command. Figure 13.4 shows the Curves dialog box. It's quite similar to the Tone Curve panel in Lightroom's Develop module, though not as elegant. It doesn't have sliders for the four tonal areas and it doesn't provide the preview bubbles that are in the Tone Curve panel. More importantly, the Curves dialog box doesn't have the Targeted Adjustment tool that's the coolest thing in the Tone Curve panel. Fortunately, in this case the lack of elegance doesn't equal a lack of power.

FIGURE 13.4

The updated Curves dialog box in Photoshop CS3 sports a number of improvements like Show Clipping and a histogram overlay. To see all the options, click Curve Display Options at the bottom left of the dialog box.

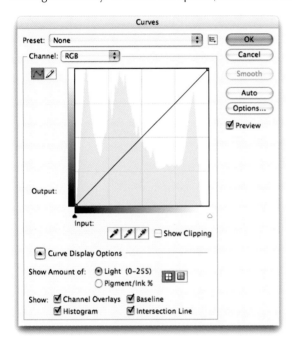

Curves works along the same lines as Levels. You set the black point and the white point and then adjust midtone values. The main difference with Curves is that you have much greater control when adjusting midtone values.

The interface can be intimidating, but after you understand what the various adjustments do, it begins to make sense. To give it a try, follow these steps:

1. Open the snow_dog sample file.

2. Open the Curves command by choosing Image ➪ Adjustments ➪ Curves. You also can access the Curves dialog box by pressing Command/Ctrl +M.

   Make sure that the Light (0-255) option is selected under Show Amount of: in the Curve Display Options. That way, the Curves dialog box is oriented as shown in Figure 13.4.

3. Grab the black Input slider on the left, and drag it horizontally toward the middle. The blacks get blacker just like the black slider in Levels.

4. Grab the white Input slider on the right, and slide it horizontally toward the middle. The whites get whiter just like the white slider in Levels.

5. Select the Show Clipping option to turn on the clipping preview.

NEW FEATURE In earlier versions of Photoshop, there was no way to preview clipping while using Curves. Because of that, in versions of Photoshop prior to CS3, it was best to set black and white points with Levels before moving to Curves to work on the midtones.

6. Slide the black and white sliders inward until you almost see clipping in the preview. (Remember that it can be okay to clip shadows a bit to get richer blacks, but you never want to clip highlights if you can help it.) After both sliders are set where you want them, deselect the Show Clipping option to return the image to its normal appearance. In my case, I ended up with a black value of 23 and a white value of 226, as shown in Figure 13.5.

FIGURE 13.5

Here are the black point and white point adjustments using Curves. Notice that the points are dragged straight to the side horizontally. To preview clipping in Curves, select the Show Clipping option.

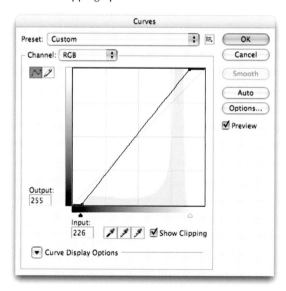

7. To lighten the image, click the middle of the diagonal line to place a point. Drag that point straight up. To darken, drag the point downward.

This point is like the gray slider in the Levels command. It represents the tones in the middle of the image. The big difference, however, is in the effect that adjustments have on this point as compared to the Levels command. When you move the gray slider in the Levels command, the effect on the tones around it is linear. With the Curves command, the effect of the adjustment is stronger on tones that are close to the point and weaker on tones that are farther away. That's why the command is called Curves, because the adjustment slopes away.

TIP If you want to nudge the settings on the black and white sliders, you can use the up and down arrows on the keyboard to move them one point at a time after you make them active by clicking them. This works with almost any slider in Photoshop, including Levels.

The diagonal line in the Curves dialog box is much steeper now that the endpoints are moved inward. Something to be aware of with the Curves command is that the steeper the diagonal line is, the more contrast the image has. Keep that in mind as you look at the midtones.

Now that the overall tonal range of the image has been established with the Input sliders, you want to unleash the real power of the Curves command. Whereas the Levels command has only two endpoint sliders and one grayscale slider in the middle, the Curves command allows up to 14 different adjustment points to be placed onto the curve line—although you rarely need more than a few.

To add an adjustment point to the diagonal line, simply click it. The higher up on the line you place the point, the lighter the tones that will be adjusted. To lighten the tones around the point, drag the point upward. To darken that region, drag the point downward.

Because the points represent tonal regions in your image, you want to be informed about the tones they represent before placing them. The best way to see how the tones of your image correspond to the points on the curve is to click the image while the Curves dialog box is open. When you do so, small circles temporarily appear on the Curves line to indicate where the tones you're clicking are located on the line. To place one of these preview points on the curve, Command+click (Ctrl+click) the tone in the image.

TIP To remove a point from the Curves line, click it and drag it out of the Curves window, or click it and press Delete.

Typically, the Curves command is used to increase midtone contrast. This is done by increasing the slope of the middle of the curve line where most of the midtone detail is located. A side effect of this is that you flatten out the curve on the toe (shadows) and the shoulder (highlights) and reduce contrast in those areas. The result of this type of adjustment is called an S-curve, as shown in the top set of images in Figure 13.6.

FIGURE 13.6

With a typical S-shaped curve, midtone contrast is increased while shadow and highlight contrast is slightly reduced, as shown in the top set of images. An inverted S-curve decreases midtone contrast, as shown in the bottom set of images.

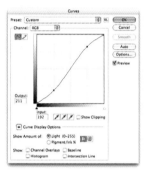

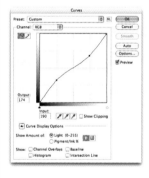

Follow these steps to clip the image using the Curves dialog box:

1. Open `snow_dog.tif` one more time. Open the Curves dialog box, and drag the black and white Input sliders inward until you almost see clipping.

    You may notice that the new input values are similar to the values you used for black and white input values with the Levels command (23 and 226, in my case).

2. Start clicking in the darker regions of the fur on the dog's hip. When you get an input value near 55, Command+click (Ctrl+click) to place a point on the line. This point represents the lower end of the darker regions that you want to adjust in the midtones.

3. Now click the side of the dog's face until you find an input value close to 150. When you do, Command+click (Ctrl+click) to set a point on the Curves line. This represents the upper end of the highlights that you want to adjust. You don't want to go much higher than 150 because you don't want to have too great of an effect on the snow, which is mostly in the range of 200 and above.

4. Carefully drag the upper point that represents 150 straight up until the value for the output is 160. Drag the lower point that represents 55 down until its output value is 40.

   The midtone contrast has increased slightly, just enough to add some snap to the midtones while the snow retains most of its detail. Try dragging the two points even farther. Notice how easy it is to go too far.

> **NOTE** The Output value in the Curves dialog box is what the Input becomes when you click OK. In this case, the dark region around 55 becomes 40 (darker), and the light region around 150 becomes 160 (lighter). If you make the darker regions of the midtones darker and the lighter regions lighter, then it makes sense that you're increasing midtone contrast because you're pulling the tones between 55 and 150 apart so that they now cover the area between 40 and 160.

I'm sure you've already figured this out by now: Just as an S-curve increases midtone contrast, an inverted S-curve decreases midtone contrast (refer to the bottom set of images in Figure 13.5), because it reduces the slope in the midtones.

Now that you've taken a good look at the Curves command, there's something you need to know: You can do most of your tonal adjustment with the Levels command. Quite often, you may not even need Curves. When you first start out with Photoshop, you should master the Levels command before going too deep into the Curves command.

When you begin to use the Curves command remember that it's like a scalpel when it comes to tonal adjustment. However, a scalpel in the hands of someone who doesn't know how to use it can make a real mess. The same is true for Curves. If you aren't careful, you can do more harm than good with the Curves command. So take it easy with Curves, and begin by making small adjustments until you become more comfortable and confident with this powerful tonal adjustment tool.

Balancing dynamic range with the Shadow/Highlights command

Sometimes, you can make your best exposure, but the *dynamic range* of the scene being photographed is too wide to get an exposure that looks good in the shadows and highlights. Dynamic range refers to the distance between the brightest tones and the lightest tones. You often run into this scenario when photographing a scene with bright backlighting where the main subject is in a shadow. Usually, the best way to solve this problem is to use a fill flash on your camera when you shoot the original scene so that you fill in the shadows with some light. Sometimes, though, a flash isn't an option, and you must deal with what you have.

When editing a file that suffers from this problem, making the image look its best with Levels or Curves can be difficult. That's why Adobe introduced a new command a few years ago in Photoshop CS called Shadows/Highlights. It's used to balance discrepancies between extreme shadows and highlights.

This command functions much like the Recovery and Fill Light sliders in the Basic panel of Lightroom's Develop module. Figure 13.7 shows the Shadows/Highlights dialog box. As you can see, this is one case where Photoshop's version of this tool gives you much more control over the tool's actions than the two sliders in Lightroom (although, the controls in Lightroom have the added advantage of working with the large amount of data contained in original raw files).

The Shadows/Highlights command with Photoshop's default settings. To see all the options shown, be sure to select the Show More Options option at the bottom left.

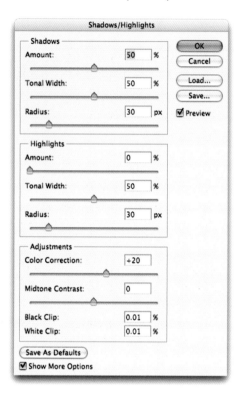

NOTE   It's better to handle this adjustment in Lightroom's Develop module when you're shooting raw. However, you should be familiar with this command in case you ever need it.

The first thing you notice in Figure 13.7 is that the Shadows/Highlights command allows you to work on the shadows and highlights independently via the two areas marked Shadows and Highlights. Each of these areas is controlled by three sliders labeled Amount, Tonal Width, and Radius. Look at the following list to see what each of these sliders is used for:

- **Amount:** Controls the amount of adjustment. Higher values in Shadows lighten the shadows more. Higher values in Highlights darken the highlights more.

- **Tonal Width:** Controls the range of tones that are affected by changes in amount. Higher settings in Shadows affect a larger range of shadow tones. Lower settings affect a narrower range. The opposite happens when adjusting Tonal Width in the Highlights; higher values affect larger ranges of highlight tones, and lower values affect smaller ranges of tones.

- **Radius:** Works like this: When the Shadows/Highlights command looks at an image, it decides whether a pixel is a shadow or a highlight by evaluating its surrounding pixels. The Radius slider allows you to fine-tune this decision making. Lower values restrict the area that is looked at when evaluations are made, and higher settings expand that range. Too large of a setting darkens or lightens the entire image rather than the area you are working on.

In addition to the Shadows and Highlights areas on the Shadows/Highlights command, there is an area labeled Adjustments. Here you have additional sliders that help to undo any unwanted shifts that might occur when the shadows and highlights are adjusted. You're most interested in these three:

- **Color Correction:** When tonal values are changed, colors can shift. For example, when shadows are lightened, a color that was dark before becomes lighter. The Color Correction slider allows you to control color *saturation* — the intensity of the color. Increasing the value of the Color Correction slider tends to increase saturation, and lowering it tends to decrease saturation. This command is available only when working on color images.

  Keep in mind that the Color Correction affects only portions of the image affected by the Shadows and Highlights sliders. When those adjustments are more extreme, the range of adjustment to Color Correction is greater.

- **Brightness:** This command is available only when working on grayscale images. It works something like the Color Correction slider. Moving the slider to the right lightens, and moving it to the left darkens the affected areas in the image.

- **Midtone Contrast:** Slider movement to the right increases midtone contrast, and movements to the left reduce it.

  In most cases, I'd rather change this with a Curves adjustment. However, if you're working quickly on some images, it may be faster to take care of it here.

To learn how all this works, follow these steps:

1. Open the practice file titled `bike_racing.tif`, as shown in Figure 13.8, from the downloadable practice files on the Web site.

   This exposure isn't bad, but it could be better. You want to lighten the faces of the riders and darken the track in the background.

2. Choose Image ➪ Adjustments ➪ Shadows/Highlights.

   When the dialog box opens, it most likely will have the default settings that you saw back in Figure 13.7. These tend to be way over the top, and you'll notice that the adjustment in the shadows is too strong. Also, the track is still too light.

FIGURE 13.8

Before and after using the Shadows/Highlights command. In the second image the highlights are darker and the shadows are lighter, completely changing the feel of the image.

TIP The default settings on the Shadows/Highlights command tend to be too strong in the shadows and too weak in the highlights. After you use the command a couple of times, you get a feel for the kinds of settings you like. When you do, open the command and dial in the settings you like. Click Save As Defaults on the lower left of the dialog box. The next time you open the Shadows/Highlights command, you can begin with more normal settings as a starting point.

3. Adjust the Shadows first. Start with the Radius slider. Move it to the right until you see the shadows begin to look more realistic. Moving it to the right limits the range of tones being affected. I moved it to 190px.

4. Now adjust the Amount in Shadows. I moved it down to 35 percent to back it off a bit.

5. Try experimenting with Tonal Width to see the effect this slider has on the image. I left it at 50 percent.

6. Now that the shadows are looking pretty good, address the highlights. Go down to the Highlights area, and move the Amount slider to the right until the track darkens. I stopped at 60 percent.

   If you notice any haloing around the riders, try adjusting the Radius slider in the Highlights area. If you decrease the Radius to 0px, the haloing goes away, but the image takes on a flat, fake look. Instead, try raising the Radius. I turned it up to 95px. There is still a slight haloing effect, but I like the way it looks, as shown in Figure 13.8.

7. Again, try experimenting with Tonal Width here. I left it at 50 percent.

8. Click the Preview check box a couple of times to toggle back and forth between before and after. If you want to fine-tune your adjustments, do so now.

9. Now look at the Color Correction slider. Try moving it to the left. As you do so, pay attention to the colors on the rider's jerseys. When you get close to a value of 0, the colors on the chests of riders 1 and 3 are *desaturated* — the colors lose some of their richness. Values of much less than 0 have little more effect. If you move the slider to the right, the colors on the chests of riders 1 and 3 get more saturated.

   Notice that the effect of saturating and desaturating with the Color Correction slider affects only the areas that were affected by adjustments in the Shadows portion of the Shadows/Highlights command.

10. When you like what you see, click OK.

CAUTION The Black Clip and White Clip boxes are used to clip shadow and highlight tones. Increasing these settings causes the image to become more contrasty. Generally, I prefer to use the Levels or Curves commands to better control clipping.

Be sure to look for two side effects when using the Shadows/Highlights command. The first is that your image can become flat in contrast if you overdo it. If this happens, try making a Levels or Curves adjustment to compensate for it. In fact, if you think you'll need to make a tonal adjustment with the Levels or Contrast commands, try to do it after using the Shadows/Highlights command.

The second side effect is that when you open shadows with any tonal adjustment tool, you reveal noise because noise tends to live in the shadows. If you watch for this as you adjust the Shadows sliders, you know when to take it easy on areas of extreme noise.

Working with 16-Bit Files

When you worked with the Levels and Curves commands you may have noticed something funny going on in the Histogram palette. When you adjusted the snow_dog.tif, some gaps appeared in the data area of the histogram. The image on the left in Figure 13.9 shows what mine looks like after I adjusted the file with Levels.

These gaps are called *combing* because they make the histogram look like a comb. Combing is caused by data that is thrown away when you make a Levels adjustment. If you think about it, this makes sense. When I adjusted Levels on snow_dog.tif, I moved the black Input slider to 23 and the white Input slider to 226. When I clicked OK, I told Photoshop to make level 23 the new 0 (pure black) and level 226 the new 255 (pure white). When that happens, the histogram is stretched from end to end. When you stretch the histogram, you pull the various tonal levels apart, creating gaps.

FIGURE 13.9

The first image indicates combing — data loss — in the histogram after adjusting Levels. To update the histogram after making a Levels adjustment, click the yellow exclamation icon shown in the second image.

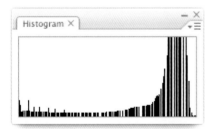
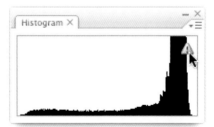
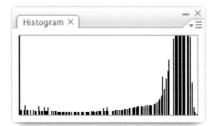

If you don't see combing after making a Levels adjustment, click the Exclamation icon in the Histogram palette, as shown in the second image in Figure 13.9.

The left side of the histogram in the first frame in Figure 13.9 shows some *spikes* in the shadow area. This is called just that — spiking. It's the result of tonal ranges being compressed during a Levels adjustment. It's happening here because the gray Input slider is moved to the left a bit to lighten the midtones. That compresses the shadow levels a bit.

If you decide to do another Levels adjustment on this image later, more data will be lost. Every time you make a Levels adjustment, you lose data. So cumulative adjustments result in increased data loss. The first image in Figure 13.10 shows what happens to the snow_dog.tif histogram after a few Levels adjustments. When you look at this histogram, you can see that the image is losing integrity in the highlights.

FIGURE 13.10

Cumulative adjustments result in severe data loss in 8-bit files, as shown in the frame on the left. When the same adjustments are done to a 16-bit version of the same file, data loss — combing and spiking — is non-existent, as shown on the right.

The second image in Figure 13.10 shows the histogram for a 16-bit version of the same snow_dog.tif image after the same set of Levels adjustments. Notice that the combing and spiking seen in the 8-bit version are nonexistent.

Sixteen-bit files are created from raw files during Export from Lightroom or during raw conversion in Adobe Camera Raw. They can also be created with a scanner.

The reason for this striking difference is that 16-bit files contain much more information than 8-bit files. That's because they devote more bits of information to describe each pixel. The difference between 8 and 16 may not seem like much, but consider this:

- An 8-bit file has 256 tonal values per channel. A 16-bit file contains over 65,000 tonal values per channel.

- An 8-bit file contains a possible 16.7 million colors. A 16-bit file contains more than 281 trillion colors.

> **NOTE** High-bit files usually are only 12-bit or 14-bit when they come out of a dSLR or a scanner. Photoshop treats any file larger than 8-bit as a 16-bit file. With this as a reality, the 16-bit files you bring into Photoshop don't actually have the full data range of a true16-bit file. However, as Figure 13.10 demonstrates, they contain much more information than an 8-bit file.

This may seem like overkill — and quite often it is. Humans can't even see 281 trillion individual colors. But if you're going to be making cumulative or massive adjustments in Photoshop, or if you're working with marginal original files, then having lots of extra editing headroom is good.

Here are a couple of things to remember about 16-bit files: Not all file formats support 16-bit. For example, saving a 16-bit file as a JPEG is impossible. If you try to do it, you won't see a JPEG option under Format in the Save As dialog box. If you need a JPEG, you can convert the file to 8-bit. Choose Image ➪ Mode ➪ 8 Bits/Channel. Now you can save it as JPEG, as well as all other common file formats.

> **NOTE** Most photolabs want only 8-bit files, so even if you're working with a lab that accepts TIFF files, you still need to convert them to 8-bit before sending them to the lab.

Sixteen-bit files contain much more information than 8-bit files, so they are larger in size. In fact, they're twice as big as 8-bit files. Because they're bigger, they consume more hard drive space and other computer resources like RAM. Also be aware that some commands in Photoshop CS3 don't work with 16-bit files. For example, the Variations command is grayed out when working with 16-bit files. Because of these issues it's best to save 16-bit files for difficult images that need massive adjustments or lots of retouching and other editing — what I call *heavy lifting*.

Measuring and Adjusting Color

There are many ways to adjust color in Photoshop. In this section, you investigate the four most common methods. Before exploring those methods, however, I want to show you how to measure the existing colors in an image.

Evaluating color with the Info palette and the Color Sampler tool

Photoshop provides two useful tools for evaluating color in your digital images: One is the Info palette, and the other is the Color Sampler tool. In combination, these two tools allow you to monitor and measure each color channel as you make adjustments to your image. Let's look at the Info palette first. Follow these steps:

1. Open the `spring_tulips.tif` file from the downloadable practice files on the Web site.
2. Click the Info palette; it's usually nested with the Navigator and Histogram palettes. If you don't see the Info palette, choose Window ➪ Info.

3. Move your cursor over the white horizontal fence section between the two vertical slats on the left. Look at the RGB readout on the Info palette while doing this. The three channels are very close in value — in the low 220s, as shown in Figure 13.11. That means the color of the fence in that spot is a very light shade of gray.

FIGURE 13.11

The Info palette provides lots of information about an image. Notice that the RGB readings change as you move the cursor because the sample below the cursor is continually updating. Even though this is an RGB image, you can still see the comparable CMYK values. Below these two readouts are fields for taking measurements and finding other general information.

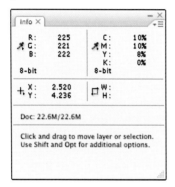

4. Move the cursor over some of the flowers. Notice that the red flowers at the top have high values in the Red channel and low values in the Green and Blue channels. The yellow flowers in the foreground have readings that are high in the Red and Green channels and low in the Blue channel.

5. Move the cursor over the middle vertical slat. Notice that it has a high Red value and a low Blue value. That's because it's reflecting the red and yellow flowers in the foreground.

> **TIP** Here's another way to put theory into action and see how various color channels combine to create the color we see in an image: Practice looking at a color and guessing its RGB values.

Having the ability to measure color is cool, but you can make this feature even cooler by adding the Color Sampler tool to the mix. The Color Sampler tool is stacked beneath the Eyedropper tool, near the bottom of the Toolbox, as shown in Figure 13.12. (Remember, the small arrow on Eyedropper tool's icon indicates that related tools are stacked beneath it.)

FIGURE 13.12

The Color Sampler tool is hidden beneath the Eyedropper tool. To reveal it, click and hold the Eyedropper tool until a side menu appears with all the tools stacked there. Hidden tools are indicated by a small triangle at the bottom right of the tool's icon. (Notice that the Toolbox is in the single-column mode, as discussed in the Preface.)

With the Color Sampler tool, you can place up to four sticky sample points anywhere in an image. A *sample point* can be used to monitor tonal adjustments while the adjustments are being made. After tonal adjustment is complete, the sample points can be permanently removed. This powerful feature is easy to use. Just follow these steps:

1. Select the Color Sampler tool from the Tools palette.

2. Before you use it, you need to configure it. Go to the options bar at the top of the screen and change the setting from point sample to at least 5 by 5, as shown in Figure 13.13.

FIGURE 13.13

Change the Sample Size on the options bar at the top of the screen. Choose at least 5 by 5 Average. To remove sample points from the image preview, click the Clear button.

This tells the tool to sample a grid of pixels that is 5 by 5 instead of a single point. This ensures that some renegade pixel that can't be seen isn't being sampled alone. When you choose 5 by 5, 25 pixels are measured and averaged.

NEW FEATURE In Photoshop CS2, the only options for Sample Size were point, 3 by 3, and 5 by 5. Photoshop CS3 has additional averaged sample sizes for sampling larger areas up to 101 by 101.

3. Open `spring_tulips.tif` again. Go back to the horizontal area you first measured in the preceding example. Find a spot that looks white, but where the three channels are not quite the same. This time, click instead of just hovering. When you do this, a measuring point is placed on the image with the number 1 beside it. Numbers that correspond to the RGB values at that point are added to the Info palette with #1 beside them.

4. Add another sample point to the same area you measured on the middle slat in Step 5 from the preceding exercise. Its values also are added to the Info palette.

> **TIP** After you place a point, you can move it somewhere else by clicking and dragging it. To delete it, click and drag it out of the image frame. To clear all sample points, click the Clear button on the options bar.

5. Choose Image ➭ Adjustments ➭ Levels to open the Levels command, or press Command+L (Ctrl+L). Grab the middle gray Input slider, and drag it to the left while watching the Info palette. Notice that a second row of numbers appears next to the sample values. These new numbers change as you move the gray slider.

   The Info palette is providing you with before and after information for your sample points, allowing you to see the effects a correction has on the color channels in an image.

6. Click OK. The second set of numbers disappears, but their values become the new sample points.

7. You use this image again in a moment. Press Command+Z (Ctrl+Z) to undo the Levels adjustment you just did. (This is the same as choosing Edit ➭ Undo.)

The ability to sample a particular area of the image and measure any changes can be very useful. This is especially the case when you know that something in the image should have a neutral color balance: All three color channels have the same value.

Now that you know how to evaluate color, look at what you can do to change it if you don't like it.

Adjusting color

After the brightness and contrast of an image are evaluated, you can look at the image's color. Color can be adjusted in Photoshop in several ways. In this section, you look at the main color correction tools and some methodologies for using them.

Removing a colorcast with Levels

While using the Levels command, you may have noticed that the command has its own set of three eyedroppers:

- **Black Point eyedropper:** This is used to assign a black point to the darkest part of the image. If you know where the darkest area of the image is, click it with this tool to set the black point and convert that spot to 0 Red, 0 Green, and 0 Blue (the default setting). Any tones that are darker than the tone you click on are clipped.

- **Gray Point eyedropper:** This is used for creating a neutral gray; the RGB values become the same anywhere you click.

■ **White Point eyedropper:** This works just like the Black Point eyedropper except that it's used to set the white point in the image. When you click the lightest part of the image, this tool sets it as the white point and converts that tone to 255 Red, 255 Green, and 255 Blue (the default settings). Any tones that are lighter than the tone you click on are clipped.

The tonal values that the Black Point eyedropper and the White Point eyedropper use for clipping points can be modified so that they don't clip to pure black (0) and pure white (255). For example, you can set them to clip at 15 and 240. This allows you to leave some room for printing processes that don't handle extreme shadows and highlights very well, such as newspaper. You can modify them by double-clicking the eyedroppers and setting the RGB values to the value you want to call pure white or black.

Although this sounds useful, I have never found much use for the Black Point and White Point eyedropper tools. The biggest problem with them is that you need to know where the lightest and darkest areas are in an image. I would rather handle clipping manually with clipping preview in Levels or Curves where I have more control, so I won't spend more time on the Black Point and White Point tools. Instead, let's focus on the middle tool here, the Gray Point eyedropper.

NOTE   The Gray Point eyedropper is designed for color correcting; therefore, it is available only when editing color images.

The Gray Point eyedropper functions much like the White Balance tool in Lightroom's Develop module. It's used to neutralize the color wherever you click it. It does this by setting the values to the Red, Green, and Blue channels to the same value. This new value is an average of the three original values unless a huge correction is being applied. It can be used any time you know that a certain area of an image should be neutral in color. Follow these steps:

1. Go back to the `spring_tulips.tif` practice image you used in the preceding example. If that image is not open, open it and repeat Steps 1 through 4 from the previous exercise.

2. Choose Image ➪ Adjustments ➪ Levels press Command+L (Ctrl+L) to open the Levels dialog box.

   When you use the Gray Point eyedropper, it affects any other Levels adjustments from that Levels session. Because of this, start with the Gray Point eyedropper if you plan to use it. Then do other Levels adjustments to finish fine-tuning the tones in the image.

3. Click the Options button, and be sure that the Enhance Per Channel Contrast is selected on the Auto Color Correction Options, as shown in Figure 13.14.

4. Click the Gray Point eyedropper to activate it. Now, anywhere you click in the image becomes neutral. Click sample point number 1 in the image. Notice that the readout in the Info palette shows that the numbers have been nudged into alignment.

   If they aren't exactly the same, it's probably because you didn't click in exactly the same spot as where the sample is placed. Not a problem — they don't have to be absolutely perfect.

FIGURE 13.14

When you click the Options button in Levels or Curves, the Auto Color Correction Options dialog box appears. For neutralizing color, be sure to select the Per Channel Contrast option.

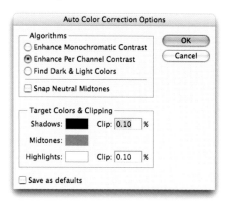

5. Every time you click the image, the gray point is reset. Click sample point 2. Notice that the whole image gets cooler.

   This is because that part of the white fence was reflecting all the red flowers. When you force the color to white, it removes the color being cast by the reflection, but the new color is unacceptable. The lesson learned here is that not all neutrals are created the same. When you use this tool, be sure that the color you click is actually supposed to be neutral.

6. Click sample point 1 to get the color back into alignment.

7. Now do your other Levels adjustments.

8. Click OK when you finish.

> **TIP** Curves has this same set of eyedroppers, which are used in the same way to set black point, white point, and neutral gray.

Sometimes, the image may not have anything that is supposed to be a neutral gray. Or maybe you use the Gray Point eyedropper, but you still want to do some further adjustment to get the colors to look just right. When that's the case, you're ready to move on to the main color adjustment tools in Photoshop CS3.

Learning color correction with the Variations command

The real trick to color correction is this: Identify the color that you don't like, and add its opposite until you don't see the offending color anymore. In order to pull this off, you must be able to see and identify the colors in an image. As you've seen, color is a science, but the perception of it is very personal.

I learned color theory when I began working in professional photolabs several years ago. Over the years, I color-corrected thousands of prints at those labs, so color correction became second nature to me. I sometimes have to remind myself just how difficult it was to learn color correction. With that in mind, I want to show you one of the best color-correction learning tools: the Variations command. Follow these steps to do some color correcting with the Variations command:

1. Open the `oregon_vineyard.tif` file from the downloadable practice files on the Web site. This image was captured late in the day. As you can see, the auto white balance on the camera overcompensated for the warm tones in the sky, which resulted in too cool of a white balance. Let's warm it up.

NOTE   The Variations command does not work on 16-bit files.

2. Choose Image ➪ Adjustments ➪ Variations; it's at the bottom. When the dialog box appears, you get what is called a color ring-around. The uncorrected image is in the center, and it's ringed by equal amounts of the individual six colors, as shown in Figure 13.15.

FIGURE 13.15

The Variations command displays a color ring-around of each of the six colors you use when making color adjustments. Click a color's thumbnail to add it. Use the Fine/Coarse slider to adjust the amount of color that will be used when color is added.

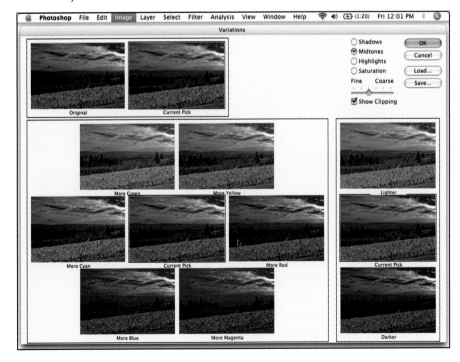

3. Add some red and possibly some yellow to warm up this image. Click the thumbnail just above where it says More Red. Notice that the current pick at the top of the screen changes to reflect the addition of red. Also notice that the whole ring-around has also been updated.

   A big chunk of red is added, but it may be too much. You need better control of this tool so you can be more discriminating with your color adjustment.

4. Click the Original thumbnail at the top left to reset the Current Pick thumbnail to its original setting.

5. Go to the Fine/Coarse slider at the top right of the window. Move the slider to the left so that it lines up with the first vertical mark on the left. Notice that the color value difference in the thumbnails is much lower now.

   Lowering the amount of color correction makes the Variations tool usable for color correction. Now you can make minor adjustments and build them up until you have added the appropriate amount of color.

6. Click the More Red thumbnail again. A small amount of red is added to the Current Pick preview. Continue to click the red thumbnail until you feel that you've added enough red. To back up and remove some red, click the More Cyan thumbnail. If you want to add some yellow, do it now.

> **TIP** You can adjust the shadows, midtones, and highlights in variations by clicking the appropriate buttons at the top right of the dialog box. If you have trouble with a color-cast that's only in the shadows, for example, you can try to address it without shifting the highlights as much.

7. When you're happy with the new color, click OK.

   This is the moment of truth. It can be hard to see your adjustments in the Variations window because everything is small. After you click OK, you really get a look at it. If you don't like it, press Command+Z (Ctrl+Z) to undo the Variations adjustment. Go back to Variations and try again with a different adjustment.

I encourage people who are new to color adjustment to begin with the Variations command because it can be a great tool for learning the differences among the six colors you use. Try sliding the Fine/Coarse slider all the way to the right. When you do, you see the color ring-around in its purest form with all the individual correction thumbnails completely saturated.

By looking at the color ring-around, you can train your eye to see the subtle differences in the colors; for example, you can learn to see the difference between red and magenta, or between green and cyan. As mentioned earlier, seeing these subtle differences is the trick to correcting color. After you can do that, your color-correcting experience will become much more powerful.

Using the Color Balance command

After you're comfortable with color and you've mastered the Variations command, you're ready to move up to a more flexible tool, the Color Balance command, as shown in Figure 13.16. The Color Balance command has most of the same adjustments as the Variations command, but it has some differences. One of the main differences is that you don't get thumbnails for visual comparison, but you do get a better preview because you see real-time adjustments in the image as you move the sliders.

The other big difference is that you can make color adjustments one color unit at a time by moving these sliders. With Variations, you don't really know how many units of color you're adding when you adjust the Fine/Coarse slider. Try adjusting a file with the Color Balance command. Follow these steps:

FIGURE 13.16

The Color Balance command has most of the same controls as the Variations command, including the ability to target shadows, midtones, and highlights separately.

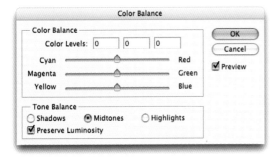

1. Open the oregon_vineyard.tif file again.

2. Choose Image ➪ Adjustments ➪ Color Balance, or press Command+B (Ctrl +B) to open the Color Balance dialog box.

   Make sure the Preserve Luminosity option is selected to prevent any color adjustment from affecting the tonal values in the image.

3. This time, instead of clicking the More Red thumbnail, move the Red/Cyan slider to the red side. As you do, notice that your image responds by getting redder.

   If the Color Balance dialog box blocks the image, grab the dialog's header where it says Color Balance and drag it to the side.

4. Adjust the red until it's almost where you want it, but stop short. Click the Highlights button to switch to highlight correction, and add more red to finish your correction.

   I use this technique of splitting my correction between midtones and highlights often, especially in portraits. I add about 75 percent of the color to the midtones and the remaining 25 percent to the highlights.

5. Add some yellow to the midtones and highlights. When you like the color, click Preview in the Color Balance window to turn off the Preview function. This shows you what the image looks like without the correction. Turn Preview on and off a few times to evaluate your correction.

TIP Our brains are really good at adapting to what's in front of our eyes, so we may lose track of what our adjustments are doing to the image. That's why the Preview function is so valuable. It's in almost every Photoshop CS3 dialog box. Use Preview to toggle any adjustment you're doing so that you'll know if you're on the right track.

6. When you like what you have, click OK. Figure 13.17 shows the image after color correcting with the Color Balance command. Now the colors in the sky look more like what you'd expect in late afternoon light.

FIGURE 13.17

The Color Balance command allows you to adjust the color of a photo's shadows, midtones, and highlights individually, allowing you to fine-tune an image's overall color. When you warmed up the color of this photo you split the color correction between the midtones and highlights.

Photo by John McAnulty

The Color Balance command gives you incredible control over the overall color of your images. When you understand color theory, you'll realize that it's the perfect tool for making global color adjustments to an image. I use it on just about everything.

Using the Hue/Saturation command

Even though the Color Balance command is my faithful companion, my favorite color adjustment tool is the Hue/Saturation command. With this amazing tool, you can work with color in a variety of ways that aren't possible with the Variations and Color Balance commands.

Figure 13.18 show the dialog box for the Hue/Saturation command. This command allows you to modify three aspects of a color: hue, saturation, and lightness. It works much like the HSL panel in Lightroom's Develop module. The main difference is that the sliders are arranged differently — more like the Color panel in Lightroom. Let's review the three color qualities addressed by these tools:

FIGURE 13.18

The Hue/Saturation command allows you to control three aspects of the color in an image: hue, saturation, and lightness.

- **Hue:** The color of a color — the difference in the red of an apple and the red of a strawberry is the hue. Use this slider to change the base color of a color.

- **Saturation:** The purity of a color — the difference between a black-and-white print and a color print. Use this slider to increase the saturation of a color with positive values or lower it with negative values.

- **Lightness:** Just what it sounds like — it's the lightness of a color. Positive values add white to the color, and negative values add black to the color.

These three sliders give you amazing control over the colors in an image. Follow these steps to learn some of the standard uses of the Hue/Saturation command:

1. Open the `high_desert_flower.tif` file from the downloadable practice files on the Web site.

2. Choose Image ⇨ Adjustments ⇨ Hue/Saturation, or press Command+U (Ctrl+U) to open the Hue/Saturation dialog box.

3. Move the Hue slider way to the left and right. Notice as you do that the bottom color bar shifts as you move the slider.

   The bottom color bar gives you a preview of how the relationships in the color spectrum change as you adjust. Look at a color on the upper color bar, and then look directly below it to see what the new color will be on the bottom color bar. Your image should be reflecting these changes.

4. Reset the Hue slider to 0.

5. Now adjust the Saturation slider all the way to the left. When you do, all color is removed from the image, and it takes on a black-and-white appearance. Adjust the slider all of the way to the right, and notice how all the colors become too saturated. Move the slider back to the left; stop at +15. Click the Preview check box a couple of times to look at the before and after versions.

6. You're going to skip the Lightness slider for the moment. It's more useful when specific colors are being targeted.

7. Leave the image open so you can use it in the next example.

When this command is used on all colors it functions much like the Saturation slider in the Basic panel of Lightroom's Develop module. It becomes most useful when it's used on specific colors. Follow these steps to learn how:

1. Open the `high_desert_flower.tif` file (if you didn't keep it open after the preceding steps). Adjust the Saturation slider to +15, and leave the Hue/Saturation dialog box open.

2. Your goal here is to change the color of the flower without changing the color of the rest of the image. To do that, you need to inform the Hue/Saturation command about the color range you want to adjust.

   Go to the top of the Hue/Saturation window, and click the drop-down list next to where it says Edit: Master. The interactive menu allows you to select the color range you want to work with: Reds, Yellows, Greens, Cyans, Blues, or Magentas.

3. The purple color of the flower is mostly magenta, but it also has some blue in it. Select Magentas, and move the Hue slider to +56. When you do this, you shift the magentas to more of a red hue.

The problem is that the colors in the flower that shifted were the magenta tones. The other tones weren't affected much. There's a better way to isolate the colors you want to adjust. Return the Magentas slider to 0.

You may notice that when you select the Magentas to edit, some eyedroppers light up on the Hue/Saturation dialog box, as shown in Figure 13.19. These eyedroppers are not available until you select a particular color to edit.

NOTE When you use the eyedropper, it isn't important which color you choose from the Edit box. After you click a color, Photoshop makes its own decision as to the color range and names it appropriately.

FIGURE 13.19

The Hue/Saturation dialog box shows the hue on only the Magentas after it has been changed. The eyedroppers allow you to fine-tune your selection of specific colors for adjustment by clicking on them in the image. They are not available for use until you select a color in the Edit box.

The eyedroppers have the following functions:

▨ **The first eyedropper allows you to click a specific color.** It's similar to selecting a color with the Targeted Adjustment tool in Lightroom's HSL panel, but changes are made by moving the sliders in the dialog.

  ▫ **The middle eyedropper allows you to add to the selection that was made with the first eyedropper.** Doing so increases the range of colors being affected.

  ▫ **The third eyedropper allows you to subtract colors from your selection.** Doing so decreases the range of colors being affected.

4. At this point, the first eyedropper should be active. Move your cursor over the image, and click the flower.

   You also can drag your cursor across the image while holding down the mouse button to sample different areas. Watch the two color bars at the bottom of the window to get an idea of the most representative area of the image to click.

5. Move the Hue slider back to 56. Notice how much cleaner the adjustment is around the outside fringes of the flower now that the affected color range is defined more accurately, as shown in Figure 13.20.

CAUTION Targeting specific colors with the Eyedropper tools affects all similar tones in the image.

6. If you still see some unevenness in the edges of the flower, try clicking and dragging across the flower to see if you can fine-tune your selection of colors that are being affected. If that doesn't work, try using the middle eyedropper to selectively add colors to be affected by your adjustment. Zoom in (press Command++/Ctrl++) and click colors to be added. If too many colors are being affected, use the third eyedropper to remove colors from the selection by clicking them.

7. Use the Lightness slider to tone down or lighten up the brightness of the colors you're adjusting. I didn't make any changes to Lightness, but you might want to.

   When you use the Lightness slider, you may notice that the colors become desaturated. That's because white is added when you lighten, and black is added when you darken. To compensate for this, increase the saturation.

8. When you're satisfied with the color, click OK. Press Command+Z (Ctrl+Z) repeatedly to undo the correction and reapply it so that you can compare before and after versions.

TIP Using the Undo/Redo (Command+Z/Ctrl+Z) command in Photoshop is a great way to check your work after you finish something. Consecutively pressing Command+Z (Ctrl+Z) cycles back and forth between Undo and Redo, allowing you to cycle the preview of your image between before and after states.

FIGURE 13.20

The top image was adjusted by selecting Magentas from the Edit box in Hue/Saturation. The bottom image was adjusted by clicking the colors in the image to be adjusted after selecting Magentas.

Summary

The Levels and Curves commands allow you to shape the histogram of an image so you take advantage of its tonal strengths. With these commands, you can accurately set the black and white points and adjust midtone brightness and contrast. Now in Photoshop CS3, you can preview clipping in either Levels or Curves, although these clipping previews are rudimentary compared to the clipping previews in Lightroom and ACR. The Curves command is very powerful. Like any powerful tool, it can be destructive in the untrained hand. Learn to master Levels before moving to Curves. When you do begin to use Curves, do so with a light hand.

The Shadow/Highlight command gives you a different approach for tonal adjustment. This command is perfectly suited to bringing deep shadows and bright highlights into parity. Its sliders function much like the Recovery and Fill Light sliders in Lightroom's Basic panel. Use the Shadow/Highlight command before using the Levels or Curves commands to get the most from it.

Sixteen-bit files contain a great deal of information. Sometimes that extra information is useful; other times it's a waste of space and processing power. Keep your workflow running smoothly by only using 16-bit files when you need the extra information.

Color can be a tricky issue due to the dichotomy between its subjective and objective natures. Color is a science, yet your experience of it can be quite personal. Before you can even address color in Photoshop CS3, you need to level the playing field by calibrating your monitor and setting up preferences in Photoshop to handle color the way you want it handled.

Color correction can be challenging to learn at first. That's why the Photoshop Variations command is very useful for the color-correction novice. It provides an interactive color ring-around to help the beginner learn the differences between colors.

After you gain a better understanding of color correction, you can use the Color Balance and Hue/Saturation commands to take control of the color in your digital images. Other tools in Photoshop also are available for working with color, but if you learn the tools in this chapter and become comfortable with them, you can handle 99 percent of your Photoshop color-correction needs.

Chapter 14

Working with Layers

T he use of layers is one of the most powerful concepts in Photoshop. Layers are so important that a comprehensive main menu and a full palette are dedicated to working with them. Even with all these controls, you must remember that working with layers is more than a set of commands and options: Using layers is a workflow methodology.

Layers in Photoshop allow you to build flexibility into your editing workflow so that you're able to keep your future options open. You do this by placing important image information on separate layers. Understanding how layers work in Photoshop will change the way you work with important images forever.

This chapter gets you up to speed with the whole concept of layers and how to work with them in Photoshop. It covers everything from creating layers in a variety of ways to different ways of merging multiple layers and flattening all layers. By the end of this chapter, you'll be ready to take advantage of some of the techniques shared in later chapters.

Because the use of layers is central to much of what you do later, this is one of the more important chapters in the Photoshop part of this book. Even if you already feel comfortable with layers, I suggest you review this chapter as a refresher. You may even pick up a new trick or two.

What Are Layers?

Think about music for a moment. When a band is in a recording studio putting together songs for a new CD, a sound engineer records each singer and instrument individually on separate sound tracks. In fact, vocals and instruments often are recorded at different times with different musicians in attendance. Sometimes, multiple recordings of the same vocalist or instrument are overlaid to create the sound the CD's producer wants. No one really knows what the song sounds like until all the pieces are blended together on a mixing board and played back as a single musical piece.

All these separate tracks give the producer a tremendous amount of creative control. If she doesn't like the way a particular instrument sounds, she can modify it — or even toss it out and re-create it — without affecting all the other pieces. If she had to work with a single track of all vocals and instruments recorded at the same time, massaging the sound would be very difficult. This is very similar to the concept of layers in Photoshop.

Photoshop has used layers since version 3.0. They allow you to isolate various elements of an image so one element can be managed separately from other elements. Just like the sound engineer in a recording studio, you control all the separate elements of an image. If you don't like the way all these pieces fit together, you can modify some of them or throw them away without compromising the whole image. This ability creates a huge amount of flexibility when editing an image. When you can potentially invest hours of work on an image in Photoshop, you don't want to have to go back to the beginning to fix something that should be a minor adjustment.

Layers, in their most basic sense, are layers of image information that sit on top of each other. The best way to see this is to do a little experimenting with these steps:

1. Create a new file by choosing File ➪ New (Command+N/Ctrl+N), and give it the following properties: width = 6, height = 4, resolution = 300, Color Mode = RGB Color, and Background Contents = White. These settings are shown in Figure 14.1. Be sure to choose inches from the drop-down list next to the Width and Height input boxes.

2. Select the Rectangular Marquee tool (M) from the Tools palette. It's the second tool from the top on the single-column Tools palette.

    If you don't see the Rectangular Marquee tool, it's hidden beneath another tool. Click and hold your mouse button on the tool that you see there to reveal other choices, as shown in Figure 14.2.

3. Use the Rectangular Marquee tool to draw a selection in the middle of the new file you created. Make it any size you want. You should see the "marching ants" that indicate something is selected.

NOTE Selections are discussed at length in Chapter 15. For now, just be aware that a selection isolates part of an image so that you can affect it by itself.

FIGURE 14.1

The New file dialog box allows you to create a new file that has no content. Think of it as a black canvas.

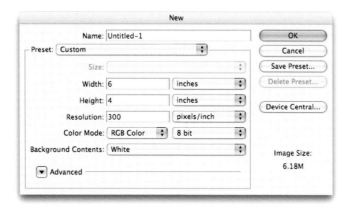

FIGURE 14.2

To save room in the Tools palette, many tools are stacked on top of each other. A small black triangle at the bottom right of a tool's button indicates that tools are stacked below.

4. Press D to set your color swatches to their default colors — black as the foreground color and white as the background color.

5. Select the Paint Bucket tool (G) from the Tools palette. It's the twelfth tool from the top on the single-column Tools palette. Click inside the selection to fill it with black paint.

   If you don't see the Paint Bucket in the Tools palette, it's hidden under the Gradient tool.

6. Deselect the rectangular selection by choosing Select ➪ Deselect (Command+D/Ctrl+D).

You just created a black box in the middle of your white image. Cool, huh? But what if you now decide to move the black box to a different part of the image? To do this you must go back to the preceding section and repeat Steps 3 through 6. If the file has been closed and reopened, which deletes the history states for the steps you just did, you need to go back to Step 1 and begin again with a new file. In this case, that's easy to do. But that isn't always true in Photoshop.

Try again. This time, use a separate layer for your black box. Follow these steps:

1. Repeat Steps 1 through 4 in the previous exercise.

2. Choose Layer ➪ New ➪ New Layer. Click OK when the New Layer dialog box appears.

   Look at the Layers palette. A new layer called Layer 1 appears above the Background layer.

3. Select the Paint Bucket tool from the Tools palette, and click inside the selection to fill it with black paint.

4. Choose Select ➪ Deselect (Command+D/Ctrl+D) to deactivate the selection around the black box you just created. Your Layers palette should look something like Figure 14.3. You get into the details of this palette in a moment.

FIGURE 14.3

The Layers palette in this example has two layers. Creating the black box on a separate layer allows it to be moved independently of the Background layer. To hide a layer's visibility, click the eyeball to the left of it.

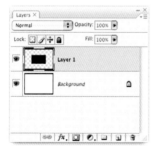

5. Select the Move tool at the top of the Tools palette (V). Click the black box, and drag it to a new position while holding down the mouse button. The Move tool allows you to move a layer, other than the Background layer, to any position you desire.

NOTE You don't have to actually click on the box itself to move it. You can click anywhere and drag because the entire layer is active.

By creating the black box on its own layer, you can isolate it to work with it independently, which is an immensely powerful tool to have in your arsenal.

6. Go to the Layers palette, and click the eyeball next to the thumbnail on Layer 1 to hide the layer. Click the eyeball again to make Layer 1 reappear.

7. Click the eyeball icon on the Background layer. Now the Background layer is hidden, so none of the white is visible. Click the eyeball again to make the Background layer visible again.

What's up with the checkerboard? When Layer 1 is the only layer visible, a gray and white checkerboard surrounds the black box. Photoshop uses this checkerboard to indicate *transparency*; in other words, the area has no image information. When part of a layer has no information, you can see right through it to the layer below.

As you move through the rest of this book, you'll see layers used to create lots of flexibility in your editing workflow. The goal with layers is to create a bulletproof workflow that keeps all options open so you can make future adjustments if you change your mind — or if you learn a new and improved technique.

Using Adjustment Layers

The first place to begin harnessing the power of layers is with adjustment layers. In Chapter 13, you learned that data is lost every time you make tonal adjustments to an image. This data loss appears as combing and spiking in an image's histogram. The solution in Chapter 13 was to work with a 16-bit file so you had plenty of extra data for cumulative adjustments. Sometimes though, you don't have a 16-bit file to work with, or you may not really need one. Even if you do, you still may want to do tonal and color adjustments in a *nondestructive* way. Photoshop solves this problem by allowing you to isolate tonal adjustments to individual layers. Those layers are called adjustment layers.

Revisit one of your projects from Chapter 13 and adjust its tonality again with an adjustment layer. Follow these steps:

1. Open snow_dog.tif practice file from the downloadable practice files on the Web site.

2. Choose Layer ➪ New Adjustment Layer ➪ Levels. (Before you click on Levels, look at the different kinds of adjustment layers that you can create, as shown in Figure 14.4.)

3. Click OK when the New Layer dialog box opens. When you do, the Levels dialog box appears. Adjust the image, checking for shadow and highlight clipping with the Alt key. When you finish making your tonal adjustments, click OK.

I don't usually bother naming adjustment layers unless I have more than one of the same kind of layer, such as Levels, Curves, Color Balance, and so on.

4. Look at the Layers palette. A new layer named Levels 1 is above the Background layer, as shown in Figure 14.5. Click the eyeball icon next to it. Now the image looks the way it did without the adjustment. Turn the layer's visibility back on.

5. Double-click the thumbnail that's directly to the right of the eyeball on Levels 1 to open the Levels dialog box. (On a Mac the thumbnail looks like a histogram. On a Windows machine it looks like a yin-yang symbol.) The settings you entered last time still appear because the adjustment layer remembers them.

FIGURE 14.4

When you choose New Adjustment Layer from the Layer menu you have the option of creating an adjustment layer for almost all tonal and color correction commands in the Image ⇨ Adjustments menu.

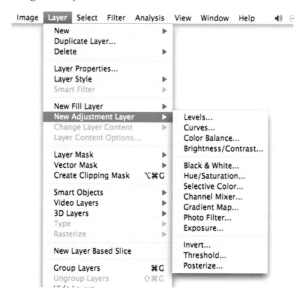

FIGURE 14.5

The new Levels adjustment layer appears above the most current layer. Click the eyeball button to hide the visibility of the layer's effects on the image.

If you make a straight Levels adjustment without an adjustment layer, the Levels dialog box re-opens with its default settings of 0, 1.00, and 255, without taking into consideration any changes that were made previously.

6. Try adjusting the color of the image with a Color Balance adjustment layer; choose Layer ➪ New Adjustment Layer ➪ Color Balance. Notice that it adds a third layer to the stack in the Layers palette.

An adjustment layer allows you to repeatedly change the settings of a particular tonal adjustment. Some loss of information inevitably occurs, but it happens only once when the layer is flattened.

TIP You can test this by making cumulative adjustments to the Levels 1 layer while monitoring the Histogram palette. Notice that data loss in the histogram stays about the same every time you make a new adjustment. That's because the histogram is tracking only the effects of the final outcome when the adjustment layer is flattened.

I don't use adjustment layers if I'm working quickly with an image, spending only a few minutes or even seconds with it. In those cases, I don't need the flexibility of an adjustment layer. However, when I spend lots of time editing an image, I'm sure to use adjustment layers to do all tonal and color adjustment. That way if I want to tweak an adjustment, I don't have to redo all of the work.

I want to tell you one more thing about adjustment layers: You can have more than one of a particular type. It's quite common to have one Levels adjustment layer for overall image adjustment and a second Levels adjustment layer that is used only for a particular printer. This way, the second Levels layer is used only to compensate for any variations with that printer. It's only turned on when you're ready to print. This is a very common use of Levels, Curves, and Color Balance adjustment layers.

This kind of flexibility is only the beginning of what you can do with adjustment layers. These special layers are covered in Chapter 16 when masking is discussed.

Working with the Layers Palette

In Photoshop, you can always find more than one way to do things. Often, one way is as good as another: It just depends on how you like to work. This is especially true with layers.

You've worked with Layers in two different places — the Layer menu at the top of the screen and the Layers palette. For the most part, you've used these two areas to do different things with the layers you were working on. You went to the Layer menu to create adjustment layers, and you used the Layers palette to work with them after they were in place. What if I told you that you can access almost every command in the Layer menu from somewhere on the Layers palette? Follow these steps to find out how:

1. Open snow_dog.tif again.

2. Click the Create a New Fill or Adjustment Layer button at the bottom of the Layers palette, near the center, as shown in Figure 14.6. This button is a shortcut for creating a new adjustment layer. Click Levels.

3. Notice that the New Layer dialog box doesn't open as it did when you used the Layer menu. Instead, the Levels Adjustment dialog box opens immediately, and an often unnecessary step is skipped.

FIGURE 14.6

Click the Create a New Fill or Adjustment Layer button at the bottom of the Layers palette to quickly create a new adjustment layer. Compare the options here to the options under New Adjustment Layer in the Layers command in Figure 14.4.

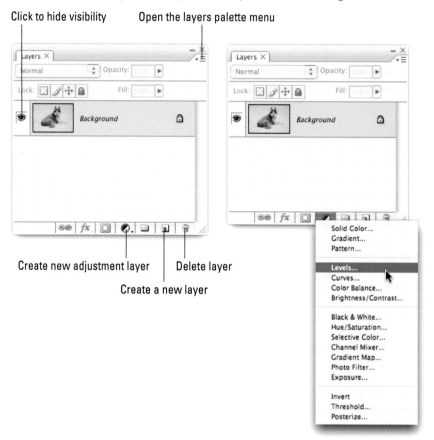

Using this button saves time, especially if you don't care about naming an adjustment layer. In fact, the whole process of using the button instead of digging through the Layer menu saves considerable time. During a long editing session this saved time can add up, making your workflow more efficient.

Another button at the bottom of the Layers palette that's useful is the Create a New Layer button, just to the left of the Delete Layer button (the trashcan). In the second exercise of this chapter, you created a new layer by choosing Layer ➪ New ➪ Layer. You then had to click through a New Layer dialog box. You can do this with a single click by using the Create a New Layer button. Much more efficient, don't you think?

The Delete Layer button is used to do just that. Either click a layer to make it active and then click the Delete Layer button, or click and drag any layer — other than the Background layer — onto the button to delete it. Try both by creating a new layer first.; You'll discover that dragging saves a step because you don't have to confirm the deletion. You can delete a layer in other ways, but this is the fastest and the most elegant.

Several commands and options that are quite useful are hidden from view in the Layers palette menu. This menu is revealed by clicking the Palette Menu button (the three horizontal lines just below the Close button at the top right of the palette). Figure 14.7 shows the list of commands and options that is revealed when clicking this button. The command I use here the most often is the Flatten Image command. I can get to it much faster here than by using the Layer menu.

FIGURE 14.7

The Layers Palette menu is accessed by clicking the button just below the Close button at the top right of the Layers palette. It gives you quick access to many of the same commands that are in the Layer menu.

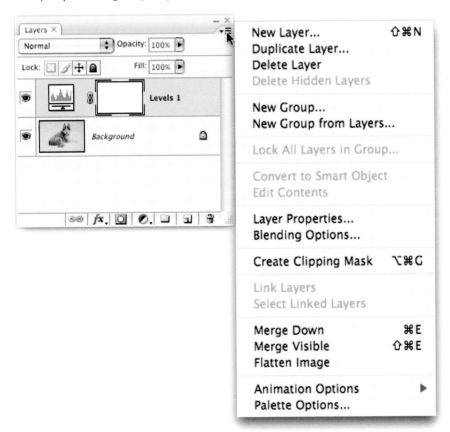

> **TIP**   Every palette is loaded with options. Hover your cursor over the icons to learn what
> they are and investigate the Palette options in the palette menu. Working with palettes
> like this saves time and makes your editing more efficient.

Understanding the Background Layer

Earlier, I said that you can't do certain things with a Background layer. You can't move a Background layer, or change its stacking order; it must always be on the bottom of the layer stack. That's because a Background layer has special properties. This special nature is indicated by a small lock icon that appears on the right side of the layer circled in Figure 14.8. This locking property is designed to keep you from making inadvertent changes to the Background layer. But what if you want to do something to a Background layer that's prohibited, such as move it?

FIGURE 14.8
_____

When a layer has the name Background, it is locked, as indicated by a lock icon on the layer (circled in this figure). When a layer is locked, a number of things can't be done to it, such as moving it, or changing its stacking order.

Follow these steps to re-create the first section of the second exercise in this chapter and then make changes to the Background layer:

1. Create a new file by choosing File ➪ New (Command+N/Ctrl+N), and give it the following properties: width = 6, height = 4, resolution = 300, Color Mode = RGB Color, and Background Contents = White.

   Be sure to choose inches from the drop-down menu next to the Width and Height input boxes before clicking OK.

2. Select the Rectangular Marquee tool (M) from the Tools palette.

3. Use the Rectangular Marquee tool to draw a selection in the middle of the new file you created. Make it any size you want. You should see the marching ants that indicate something is selected.

4. Press D to set your color swatches to their default colors — black as the foreground color and white as the background color.

5. Choose Layer ⇨ New ⇨ New Layer. When the New Layer dialog box appears, click OK (or click the Create a New Layer button on the bottom of the Layers palette).

6. Select the Paint Bucket tool from the Tools palette, and click inside the selection to fill it with black paint.

7. Choose Select ⇨ Deselect (Command+D/Ctrl+D) to deactivate the selection.

8. Select the Move tool (V) and use it to drag Layer 1 to the right or left. This is the same thing you did in an earlier exercise.

9. Click on the Background layer and try to move it with the Move tool. Notice that when you do, the error message shown in Figure 14.9 appears.

FIGURE 14.9

If you try to move the Background layer, you get this message. To move it, you must rename it by double-clicking its name. Anything other than Background will do for the name.

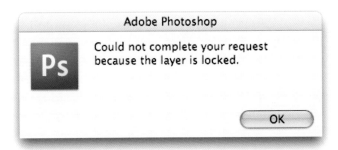

10. If you want to move the Background layer, unlock it by double-clicking the layer's name. The New Layer dialog box opens, and Layer 0 is suggested as a new name. You can type a different name or just click OK. As soon as you do, the lock icon disappears. Now you can reposition the layer with the Move tool. Give it a try by dragging it to the right or left.

> **NOTE** An image can only have one official Background layer. You can rename a second layer Background, but it won't automatically be locked like a true Background layer. If you want to convert an ordinary layer to a Background layer, select the layer and choose Layer ⇨ New ⇨ Background From Layer.

11. Undo the move of Layer 0 so that the bottom layer is back in position.

12. Now try something different. Click the thumbnail in Layer 1, and drag it so that it's below Layer 0. The two layers swap positions, and Layer 1 becomes hidden below Layer 0 because the white in Layer 0 fills the entire layer.

13. Go back to Step 9 before the Background layer was renamed by backing up three steps in the History palette. Try dragging Layer 1 below the Background layer. Now it won't work because a layer named Background has to be the bottom layer.

You need to be aware of the special nature of the Background layer only when you want to do something illegal to a Background layer, such as move it, transform it, or change its stacking order. When that need arises, just remember to rename the layer and you'll be in business.

Managing Layers

To take advantage of the flexibility that using layers provides, you must be comfortable working with the Layers palette. You need to know how to move layers up and down in the Layers palette's layer stack, individually and together; how to create a new layer by cutting something from an existing layer; how to merge two layers; and how to flatten all layers. Let's explore each of these ideas one at a time.

Moving layers

Follow these steps to get some practice moving layers in the layer stack:

1. Open the `layers_fun.psd` practice file from the downloadable practice files on the Web site. You should see something similar to Figure 14.10.

2. Select the Move tool (V) from the Tools palette. Make sure that the green triangle layer is active.

FIGURE 14.10

The `layers_fun.psd` file contains four separate layers: the white Background layer, the red square layer, the yellow circle layer, and the green triangle layer. The layer highlighted in blue — the green triangle layer — is the active layer.

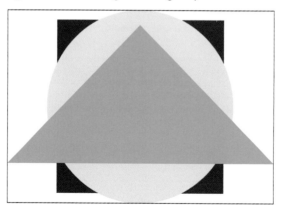
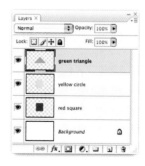

3. Click anywhere in the image and drag while holding down the mouse button. As you do, the green layer begins moving in the direction it's being dragged. Notice that only the green layer is moving.

4. Click the yellow circle layer in the Layers palette to make it active. Move it to a new position with the Move tool.

5. Click the red square layer in the Layers palette to make it active. Move it to a new position with the Move tool.

6. Click the yellow circle layer. Choose Image ⇨ Adjustment ⇨ Hue/Saturation (Command+U/Ctrl+U), and adjust the Hue on the Master channel to +143. Notice that only the yellow layer is affected by this change.

Something to take away from this exercise is that only the layer that's currently active is affected by a tool or command. That's almost always the case when you work with layers. When a layered image is being edited, adjustments usually must be performed on a layer-by-layer basis.

NOTE Adjustment layers are an exception to this rule. When you place an adjustment layer into an image, it affects all the layers that are below it. If you need to make the same color adjustment to all layers, do it with a Color Balance adjustment layer at the top of the stack; don't try to adjust every layer individually.

You can do some things to multiple layers at the same time. Repositioning with the Move tool is one of them. Here's how:

1. Open the `layer_fun.psd` file. If it is already open from the preceding exercise, return it to its opening state by clicking the image's icon at the top of the History palette.

2. This time, you want to move all layers — except the Background layer — at the same time. The green triangle layer should already be active. Hold down the Shift key and click the red square layer so that all three layers are active, as shown in Figure 14.11.

TIP To select *contiguous* layers — layers that are next to each other — click the first layer, and then Shift+click the last layer. To select noncontiguous layers, press Command (Ctrl) while clicking them individually. You also can use the Command (Ctrl) key to deselect a selected layer.

FIGURE 14.11

You can select multiple layers by using the Shift or Command/Ctrl keys as modifiers when clicking the layers. When multiple layers are selected, they can be moved with the Move tool as a group.

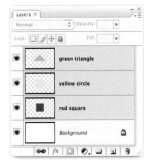

303

3. Use the Move tool to move all three layers at the same time. Experiment with different combinations of layers and the Move tool.

All the moving done here has been on an x-, y-axis — up and down, or side to side. As you saw in an earlier exercise, you can move layers forward and backward by changing their position in the layer stack in the Layers palette. Try this little exercise:

1. Open the `layer_fun.psd` file. If you already have it open from the preceding exercise, return it to its opening state by clicking the image's icon at the top of the Layers palette.

2. Click the red square layer in the Layers palette, and drag it upward while holding down the mouse button. Drag the layer up until it is between the green triangle layer and the yellow circle layer. When you see a black line appear between them, release the mouse button.

   Now the red square layer is above the yellow circle layer, as shown in Figure 14.12.

FIGUER 14.12

The red square layer was moved above the yellow circle layer by dragging it upward in the Layers palette. When a layer is moved up in the layer stack, it hides information on layers that are below it.

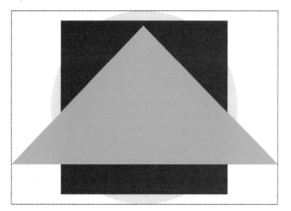
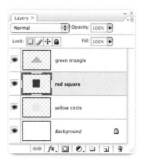

3. Select two contiguous layers with the Shift key, and move them up or down together in the Layers stack.

You can move layers together or by themselves. You can move them on an x-, y-axis and on a z-axis forward or backward in space by moving them up and down in the layer stack. Sometimes, though, you may want to move only part of a layer rather than the whole layer. To do this, you need to cut or copy sections of information from a layer before you can move it.

Creating a new layer by copying

Earlier you created new layers by using the New Layer command in the Layer menu and by using the Create a New Layer button at the bottom of the Layers palette. In both cases, the new layers you created were completely empty. Sometimes though, you want to create a new layer with information in it by copying all or part of an existing layer.

Duplicating an entire layer works very much like creating a new empty layer. You can do it in two ways:

- **You can duplicate a layer using the Layer menu.** To use this method, follow these steps:

    1. Make sure that the layer to be duplicated is currently active.

    2. Choose Layer ⇨ Duplicate Layer.

    3. When the New Layer dialog box appears, click OK.

- **You can duplicate a layer using the Layers palette.** To use this method, click the layer to be duplicated and drag it to the Create a New Layer button on the Layers palette.

The second method is faster because it's more direct and you don't have to go through the New Layer dialog box. Either way works just fine, so choose the method you prefer.

Creating a layer from part of another layer works a little differently. To do this, a selection tool is used to isolate the part of the image to be copied to the new layer. Selection tools haven't been discussed in detail yet, so I'll help you out on this one by supplying the selection. Follow these steps:

1. Open the `girls_vette.tif` practice file from the downloadable practice files on the Web site.

   The goal here is to copy this young woman and place the new layer beside her so that you get the effect of twins.

2. Choose Select ⇨ Load Selection to load the selection that is provided. The Load Selection dialog box appears with the selection already selected, so just click OK.

   After the selection is loaded, the marching ants start moving around the girl. This indicates that a selection is active, as shown in Figure 14.13. Only this area is affected in the next step.

3. Choose Layer ⇨ New ⇨ Layer via Copy (Command+J/Ctrl+J).

   The marching ants go away, and the image looks the same as it did before. The clue that something has changed is in the Layer menu. A new layer called Layer 1 has been created above the Background layer.

4. Go to the Layers palette, and turn off the visibility of the Background layer by clicking the eyeball. Now the new layer is more obvious because you can see all the transparency around it, as shown in Figure 14.14.

FIGURE 14.13

The marching ants surrounding the girl show that a selection has been created in the shape of her outline. When part of an image is selected, only that part of the image is affected by changes.

Photo by Jerry Auker

FIGURE 14.14

The girl has been copied to a new layer. When the visibility of the Background layer is turned off, you can see the new layer by itself. The checkerboard surrounding the girl indicates that no image information is available in that area.

5. Turn the visibility of Layer 1 back on. Select the Move tool (V). Click anywhere in the image, and drag the girl's "twin" to her new spot. I moved her to the front, as shown in Figure 14.15.

TIP Here's a great shortcut. When you need the Move tool, you can hold down the Command (Ctrl) key to temporarily access it. This saves switching tools just to move something.

FIGURE 14.15

The girl's "twin" has been positioned next to her. For this effect to look realistic, more work must be done to blend her into the background. However, this is a good start.

6. If you're up for more fun, duplicate Layer 1 to create another copy of the girl and move it somewhere else.

In reality, you probably won't be creating many images like this. However, copying information from one layer to another is a very common technique in restoration and retouching. Often, you may need to copy information from a layer and move it into another image — for example, when you're doing a head-swap, as you do in Chapter 20.

Merging and flattening layers

One of the main reasons for creating layers is to have flexibility in the future. Consider the previous exercise with the girl. As long as you keep Layer 1 around, you can continue to reposition the copy of the girl. When you go through the effort to create layers in an image, you usually intend to keep them intact.

Sometimes though, it is desirable to merge layers together. For example, when reconstructing someone's eye in a restoration job, you may need to copy information from a couple of different eyes and merge them together onto a single layer so that they can be worked on as one unit.

Also, not everyone is prepared to deal with layered files. Often, when sharing files with someone else, like a graphic designer, you should supply a flattened file — all layers merged into a single layer — to avoid confusion. If any modifications need to be made, they can be done on the saved layered file. Then a new flattened file can be sent to the designer.

When you take a file to a photo lab, it almost always has to be flattened. Very few labs will accept layered files because the file size is much larger. That's right: every layer adds to the overall file size. If a Background layer is duplicated, the file size instantly doubles. Smaller pieces copied to a layer add smaller amounts to the overall file size.

NOTE   To save layers when saving a file, choose PSD or TIFF as the file format. A JPEG file doesn't save individual layers. When you save a JPEG, all layers are automatically flattened in the JPEG file.

Follow these steps to get a quick look at how merging and flattening is done:

1. Open the `layer_fun.psd` file again. Make sure that the green triangle layer is active. Choose Layer ➪ Merge Down (Command+E/Ctrl+E).

CAUTION   If you do something to a layered file and you don't get the expected result, you're probably on the wrong layer. Whenever things don't go the way you expect them to, check the Layers palette first to see which layer is active.

    Notice that the green triangle layer and the yellow circle layer are now combined into one layer called yellow circle. The green triangle was merged with the yellow circle; they are no longer independent, as shown in Figure 14.16.

2. Select the Move tool (V), and move the new combination. Notice that they move together now. They have to because they are one.

3. Merge the newly combined layer with the red square layer below by choosing Layer ➪ Merge Down (Command+E/Ctrl+E).

    Now all three of the colored layers are combined into one layer called red square. Any movement with the Move tool affects all of the colored shapes because they are all part of the same layer.

4. Do it one more time. Merge the red square layer with the Background layer. Now try the Move tool. It won't work because all layers have been merged down to the Background layer, and by its very nature, the Background layer is locked.

FIGURE 14.16

When the green triangle layer is merged with the yellow circle layer, they become one layer called yellow circle. Any changes you make with the Move tool affect them both.

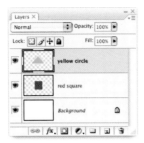

5. If the goal is to merge all layers into one, there's a faster way. Go back to the opening state of the image by clicking the thumbnail at the top of the History palette. This time, instead of merging one layer at a time, choose Layer ⇨ Flatten Image. (You also can access Flatten Image from the Layers palette options menu.)

6. Here's one more wrinkle that's quite useful. Suppose you want to merge all the layers except the Background layer. The fastest way to do this is to turn off the visibility of the Background layer and choose Layer ⇨ Merge Visible. Only the layers that are currently visible get merged. (Naturally, this command also can be accessed from the Layers palette options menu.)

So that's the scoop on merging and flattening layers. When you use layers to separate image elements, you have to know how to bring them back together when it's appropriate. You'll see some of those instances in better context later in the book.

Layer Opacity and Blending Modes

A big feature of layers is that you can control the way one layer blends with the layers below it. The most basic way to affect the interaction between two layers is to adjust the opacity of the upper layer. Here's how to do that:

1. Open the layer_fun.psd file again. If it's still open from the preceding exercise, return it to its opening state by clicking the thumbnail at the top of the History palette.

2. Select the yellow circle layer, and adjust its Opacity to 50 percent by typing a value of **50** into the box, by clicking the arrow next to the input box and using the slider as shown in Figure 14.17, or by using a *scrubby slider*.

> **TIP** Wherever a slider is available in Photoshop CS3, a scrubby slider also is available. A scrubby slider is a cool little shortcut that allows you to adjust a slider without clicking the arrow to activate it. To use a scrubby slider, move the cursor to the left of the input window. When a hand with double arrows appears, circled in Figure 14.17, click and drag to the right or left to raise or lower the value.

FIGURE 14.17

When the Opacity of the yellow circle layer is lowered to 50 percent, it's only 50 percent visible. Opacity can be changed by using the Opacity slider or by using a scrubby
slider (circled), next to the Opacity input area.

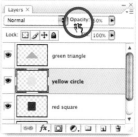

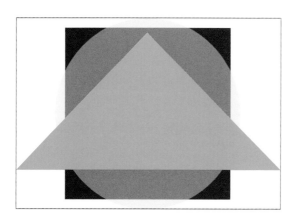

Another way to change how layers interact with one another is to change the *blending mode* of a
layer. A layer's blending mode affects the way it interacts with the layer directly below it. Blending
modes are used in a number of ways. You see them later in this book. For now, I want to introduce
the idea by showing you a cool way to deal with overexposed and underexposed images using a
method called *self-blending*. A self-blend is when a layer is duplicated and blended with itself using
a blending mode.

Sometimes, an overexposed image can be hard to deal with in Levels or Curves. If you're working
quickly and you don't feel like spending lots of time fixing an overexposure, you can use a fast
two-step process to make a huge improvement on the image:

1. Duplicate the layer.
2. Click where it says Normal to see the Blending Mode drop-down list. Change the duplicate layer's blending mode to Multiply. The Multiply blending mode is easy to remember
   because it's right below Darken, which is what you want to do.

Figure 14.18 shows an original image and the result of doing a self-blend with the Multiply blending mode. This adjustment took about 5 seconds.

FIGURE 14.18

Self-blending this photo with the Multiply blending mode is a quick way to bring its tonal range into line.

TIP
Sometimes, doing one self-blend isn't enough. When that happens, duplicate the new layer so you create a third layer. Because this is a duplicate of a blended layer, it already has the correct blending mode selected. If a self-blend is a bit too strong, simply reduce the layer's opacity until you like the overall effect.

To get a look under the hood of what's going on here, look at the histogram after doing a self-blend. Figure 14.19 shows the histogram I got when I blended the image in Figure 14.18.

FIGURE 14.19

Notice that when you use the Multiply blending mode, most of the adjustment is happening in the middle and lighter tones. The darker tones show a bit of spiking, but it's fairly minimal. The result is very similar to moving the gray slider in Levels to the right.

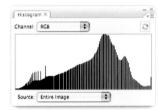

Fixing an underexposed image works in exactly the same way with one minor change. The blending mode on the self-blend is set to Screen instead of Multiply. Screen is easy to remember because it's just below Lighten, which is the end result you're looking for.

> **TIP** If you want to know more about the various blending modes and how they work, take a look at Photoshop CS3's help. Choose Help ⇨ Photoshop Help, and type list of blending modes in the search field. Number 1 in the search returns should be "list of blending modes"; click it to see a complete listing with explanations.

Summary

Working with layers in Photoshop opens the door to greater workflow flexibility and editing power. Layers are used extensively in later projects in this book, so you want to develop an understanding of how to work with them now.

An adjustment layer is one of the most basic types of layers. With these layers, you can make repeated nondestructive tonal adjustments to an image. Adjustment layers can be created from most of the options under the Image ⇨ Adjustments menu with the notable exception of Variations.

As with most things in Photoshop, you can work with layers in many ways. You can reach commands by going to the Layer menu at the top of the screen or by accessing the hidden commands on the Layers palette. Use whichever system is more comfortable for you.

Layers can be moved, duplicated, and copied. The stacking order also can be changed by dragging individual layers up and down in the Layers palette. Just remember that certain things can't be done to the Background layer because it's automatically locked. To unlock it, just change its name to something other than Background.

Layer blending modes provide another way of working with layers. By using blending modes, you can quickly fix overexposed and underexposed images. This is just the beginning of the usefulness of blending modes. You run into them again later in this book.

Part IV

Going Beyond the Basics

Now that you have a feel for some of Photoshop's fundamental concepts, it's time to explore some of the amazing tools in Photoshop CS3 and how they're used in the creative portion of the digital workflow. We start off with one of Photoshop's most recognizable toolsets: the selection tools. In this section you'll see how the various selection tools work, and how they can be combined to quickly create perfect selections.

Then you move one of the most important things you can learn in this part, working with layer masks. If you've never used layer masks, prepare to have your Photoshop world shift because once you learn to use them it will change your Creative Workflow forever. That's because layer masks are one of the keys to developing a flexible, nondestructive editing workflow in Photoshop.

A little farther along in this part, you explore Photoshop's primary retouching tools and how they're used to remove improve digital photos. The things you learn here prepare you for Part V, where you put these tools to work solving various retouching problems.

I complete Part IV by demonstrating a cool technique for using some of Photoshop's editing tools in Lightroom by creating automated editing packets called actions and droplets. You'll learn how to have Photoshop automatically place a copyright symbol on images as they're exported from Lightroom.

Chapter 15

Working with Selections

S elections have been touched on a few times in this book. I don't really like to mention something without explaining it. But I don't want to confuse you by trying to explain everything at once. Photoshop, or any other complicated system, is so powerful because of the interaction of several different concepts. Talking about one thing without mentioning another sometimes is difficult.

The reason I was able to get away with using selections without explaining them is that the concept of selections is one of the few that seems to be familiar to new users. By that I mean that most people have seen the "marching ants" that define a selection, and they understand that selections are usually created around objects in an image.

If that doesn't apply to you, fear not. By the end of this chapter, you'll not only know what a selection is, you'll also know when to use one selection tool rather than another and how to combine selection tools to create complex selections. You'll also know how to modify the edge of a selection with the new Refine Edge command and how to combine the new Smart Filters feature in Photoshop CS3 with your selections.

What Is a Selection?

Photoshop selections provide a system for isolating pixel information in an image so that adjustments are applied only to the selected area. This is very useful when it's necessary to darken something or adjust its color independently of the rest of the image. Selections also are useful for isolating part of an image that is duplicated and moved to another layer or image. You saw this in Chapter 14 when you copied the young lady in front of the Corvette to a different layer. In that example, the selection was provided for you. (In a little bit, you learn how that selection was created.)

Let's begin this exploration into selections by looking at one of the most basic selection toolsets, the Marquee tools.

Using Photoshop's Main Selection Tools

Like just about everything else in Photoshop, there's more than one way to create a selection in Photoshop. The primary selection tools are located in the Tools palette. They're called the Lasso tools, the Marquee tools, the Magic Wand tool, and the Quick Selection tool. As you look at these tools, notice how each is best suited to creating a particular type of selection.

The Marquee tools

You'll find the Marquee tools under the second icon from the top in the single-column Tools palette. The toolset consists of four tools that are stacked together, as shown in Figure 15.1:

FIGURE 15.1

The Marquee tools

- **Rectangular Marquee:** Used for making rectangular selections
- **Elliptical Marquee:** Used for making elliptical selections
- **Single Row Marquee:** Used for selecting a row that's only 1 pixel high
- **Single Column Marquee:** Used for selecting a column that's only 1 pixel wide

I don't think I've ever used the Single Row Marquee or Single Column Marquee. However, I use the Rectangular Marquee and Elliptical Marquee all the time. They both work in pretty much the same way, so you'll look at the Rectangular marquee here. Follow these steps:

1. Choose File ⇨ New to create a new file, and give it the following properties: Width = 6 inches, Height = 4 inches, Resolution = 300, Color Mode = RGB Color/8-bit, and Background = White.

2. Select the Rectangular Marquee tool (M) from the Tools palette. Go to the top-left area of the new file. Click and drag downward to the lower right. As you do, you'll see a rectangular shape outlined by the marching ants and anchored at the spot where you first clicked. When you let go of the mouse button, the selection floats on the image.

3. Try something else. Remove the selection by going to the Select menu and choosing Deselect (Command+D/Ctrl+D).

TIP You also can deselect by clicking outside the selected area with any of the other Marquee tools.

4. Being able to draw a rectangle is cool, but what if you really need a square? You can get a square in two ways. The first way is to hold down the Shift key while you draw the selection. Give it a try. Draw a new selection while holding down the Shift key. This time it's a square because the Shift key locks the aspect ratio to a square ratio.

NOTE When using the Elliptical Marquee tool, the Shift key modifier creates a perfect circle.

5. Deselect again. Now go to the options bar, click the drop-down list next to Style, and choose Fixed Aspect Ratio. Type a value of **1** in the Width and Height boxes. Draw another square selection.

   This feature is very useful when you need to draw a rectangular selection that has a fixed aspect ratio other than one-to-one. Using the Shift key is faster if you need a square.

NOTE The Fixed Size option in the Style drop-down list allows you to draw a rectangular selection that is an exact size.

6. Select the Brush tool (B) from the Tools palette. Set the brush's properties to any settings you want. Now use the Brush to draw a stroke across the entire image that begins and ends outside the boundaries of the selection. Notice that the stroke appears only within the selection, as shown in Figure 15.2.

FIGURE 15.2

When a selection is active, changes to the image occur only within the selection. When this brushstroke was drawn, only the pixels inside the selection were affected. The pixels outside the selection were protected from change.

This is what a selection is all about. When a selection is active, any action taken affects only pixels within the boundaries of the selection. All the pixels outside the selection are protected from any changes.

To change the color you're painting with, go to the two color swatches at the bottom of the single-column Tools palette. The top swatch — the one on the left — is the foreground color. The swatch on the right is the background color. When you use a tool like the Brush that paints with color, the foreground color is the one being used. Click the color to change it. When the Color Picker dialog box appears, select the color you want and click OK.

7. While you're here, try one more thing. Undo the paint stroke you just made, and then choose Select ⇨ Inverse (Shift+Command/Ctrl+I). This inverts the selection so that pixels outside the original box are now selected and the pixels inside the box are protected (unselected).

   The only change you'll notice is that the marching ants begin to march around the perimeter of the image. (If you can't see the edges of your image, zoom out.)

8. Draw another stroke across the image. This time the paint is applied only outside the box, as shown in Figure 15.3.

   The ability to invert any selection is very useful. It allows you to alternately isolate opposite areas of an image. It also allows you to make a difficult selection by selecting something easier and then inverting it.

FIGURE 15.3

You can invert a selection with the Select menu's Inverse command. This flips the selection so that pixels that were unselected become selected, and vice versa. When a selection is inverted, changes occur only outside the original selection. Pixels inside it become protected.

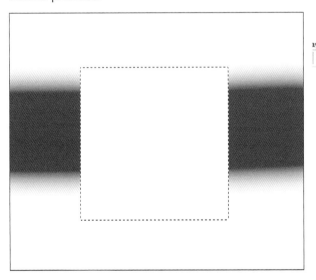

In the previous exercise, you visited the Select menu twice. That's because the Select menu is the main place to go to modify the properties of a selection after it's been created. Another way to access some of the commands in the Select menu is to right-click with your mouse anytime a selection is active and the Selection tool is chosen, as shown in Figure 15.4. Notice that this context-sensitive menu has some options that aren't in the Select menu in Figure 15.3. Also, be aware that if you right-click when no selection is active, you get a different context-sensitive menu.

The Elliptical Marquee tool works the same way. I use this tool often when I want to darken the corners of an image, as you see later. The Shift modifier key restricts the tool to drawing perfect circles.

The Marquee tools are wonderful when you need to select an ellipse or a rectangle. But quite often you need to make selections that are more organic, free-form shapes. There are a few tools in Photoshop that are perfect for those kinds of selections. The first set we'll look at are the Lasso tools.

FIGURE 15.4

Selection properties and other useful shortcuts can be accessed quickly by right-clicking when a selection is active. If you right-click when a selection isn't active, you get a different menu because the right-click options are sensitive to the context in which it's being used.

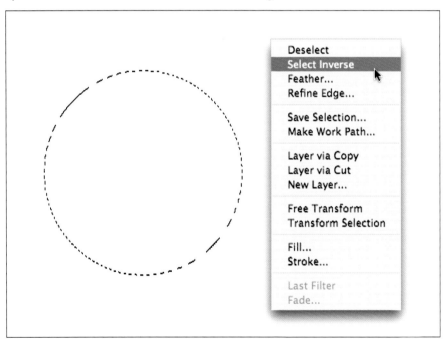

The Lasso tools

I've always liked the name Lasso for the set of tools discussed in this section. It implies that the tool is used to throw a selection around something to gain control of it. In this case, instead of a rope, you throw a line of marching ants.

NOTE The term *marching ants* describes the moving, dashed line that surrounds a selected area because the moving line looks like ants marching in unison.

The Lasso toolset is the third icon from the top on the single-column Tools palette. There are three Lasso tools stacked together, as shown in Figure 15.5:

FIGURE 15.5

The Lasso toolset

- **Lasso tool:** A true free-form tool. You can create a selection with just about any type of organic shape. This tool is not very well suited to creating selections with hard lines — selecting the side of a building, for example.

- **Polygonal Lasso tool:** Used to create selections with straight lines. Every time you click with this tool, a straight line is drawn between your current click and the most previous click. It works quite well for selecting areas with hard edges.

- **Magnetic Lasso tool:** A "smart" selection tool. It's designed to see the lines that divide regions of differing tonal contrast — the boundary around a silhouette against a bright sky, for example.

The Polygonal Lasso tool is useful when straight lines are needed, but I rarely use it. Most of the time, I need a selection that follows the contours unique to a specific situation in a specific image. For that reason, the focus here is on the two other Lasso tools: the Lasso and Magnetic Lasso tools.

Following are some exercises to compare and contrast these two tools:

1. Open the `snow_dog.tif` practice file from the downloadable practice files at `www.wiley.com/go/workflow`. Make a Levels adjustment (Command+L/Ctrl+L) similar to the one you did in Chapter 13. I used 23, 1.08, 226.

2. To be effective here, you need to see the entire dog all at once, so zoom out until the entire dog is visible.

3. In this exercise, you want to enhance Ruby's colors — as neutral as they are — so that they're richer against the neutrality of the snow. However, you don't want to intensify the cyan/blue tint of the snow; you want it to be as neutral as possible. Select the Lasso tool (L), and draw a selection around the dog. Stay as close to the edges of the dog as you can.

Go all the way around until you get back to the place where you started drawing. When you connect the beginning and endpoints, the selection is complete.

As you can see, this is easier said than done. Making an accurate selection like this is difficult with the Lasso tool, even if you're using a graphics tablet. (Good luck if you're using a mouse.) The Lasso tool does have good uses. It's great for creating free-form selections that are loose, as you see in later chapters. It just isn't the right selection tool for this job.

4. Remove the selection you just created by choosing Select ➪ Deselect (Command+D/Ctrl+D), or just click somewhere outside the selection with the Lasso tool.

5. Switch to the Magnetic Lasso tool. It's stacked under the Lasso tool. In the options bar, set the tool's options to the following settings: Feather = 0px, Anti-alias = checked, Width = 5px, Contrast = 40,, and Frequency = 40. (You look more closely at these settings in a moment.)

6. Click near the tip of one of the ears to get the tool started. After you click, release the mouse button. Begin outlining the dog again, staying as close to her edges as possible. Notice how much easier you can follow the edge of the contrast between the dog's dark fur and the snow with the Magnetic Lasso. Continue tracing her entire outline until you get back to where you started.

TIP If you have your cursor preferences set to Standard under Preferences ➪ Cursors ➪ Other Cursors, your cursor will look like the icon of the Magnetic Lasso tool. If you want to see the actual width of the tool, press the Caps Lock key. Just remember to press the key again when you finish, because it modifies the way many cursors look. An easier way to accomplish this is to change your cursor preference from Standard to Precise, which allows you to always see the brush size (unless the Caps Lock key is active).

As you trace, notice that fastening points are being laid down by the Magnetic Lasso. These points anchor the selection to the lines and points that separate areas of contrast. If the tool won't place a point where you want one — maybe near the tip of Ruby's white tail or paw or along her back — click to manually insert a fastening point. If a point is placed in a place where you don't want one, press Delete to remove it. Successive points are removed every time you press Delete, so you can back up several points in a row if you need to. If you want to bail and start all over, press Esc.

7. When you complete the selection and get back to the starting point, a small circle appears next to the cursor. This indicates that a click will connect the beginning point with the endpoint, completing the selection. If you have problems closing the selection, try a gentle double-click. Your selection should now look something like Figure 15.6.

NOTE If your gentle double-click is too strong, or not in the right place, the tool thinks you want to start a new selection. If this happens and the selection you just drew disappears, press Esc to make your selection reappear.

NOTE I saved a selection for you in case you have problems getting the kind of selection you want right now. You can load it by choosing Select ➪ Load Selection and then clicking OK.

Notice that the selection in Figure 15.6 isn't perfect. I missed the tip of one of her ears, as well as the edge of her fur in a couple of places. I'll show you how to fine-tune selections in a moment. For now, let's work with what you've got.

FIGURE 15.6

The Magnetic Lasso tool is well suited for selecting a shape that contrasts with its surroundings. Click once to get the tool started, and then let the tool do the rest as you draw. Click to add more fastening points, and use the Delete key to remove unwanted points. A small circle appears next to the cursor when the outline is complete. (If you're using the precise cursor, the tool's icon reappears when the selection is complete.) Click to create the selection.

8. Now that the dog is selected, you can adjust her color independently of the color of the snow. Choose Image ➪ Adjustments ➪ Hue/Saturation (Command+U/Ctrl+U). (Don't use an adjustment layer just yet.) Change the Master Saturation value to 55. Notice that the dog's colors intensify, especially her blue eyes. The white fur begins to look more yellow, which is accurate to true life. (I always realize that Ruby's white really isn't white when I see her in fresh snow.) Make any other adjustment you want to make, and click OK.

9. Now Ruby stands out from the background because her colors are so much richer. Because most of the snow was outside the selection, the color of the snow is still cool. Warm up the color a bit. Invert the selection by choosing Select ➪ Inverse. Now the marching ants are moving around the outside perimeter of the image.

10. I want to desaturate some of the cool colors in the snow. Choose Image ➪ Adjustments ➪ Hue/Saturation. Select Cyan in the Edit drop-down list, and use the eyedropper to sample the colors in the top-right corner of the image. Lower the Saturation value to -100, and click OK.

TIP To temporarily hide a selection, press Command+H (Ctrl+H). This is a good way to see what the changes look like without deselecting the selection. However, don't forget to unhide it when you finish. Otherwise, you may forget it's there and you won't know why weird things are happening later. To unhide it, press Command+H (Ctrl+H) again.

CAUTION Anytime you adjust an image and unpredictable things happen, check to see if you have something selected. Even if you don't think you do, choose Select ➪ Deselect to be sure. Sometimes, something can get selected without realizing it.

The change is very subtle, but I like snow more without the cyan cast. If you had made this adjustment to the entire image — without any selections — Ruby's eyes would have lost their blue color.

Those of you who are following along with the sample file probably see something that doesn't look right. The snow on Ruby's back still has a cyan cast to it. You look at ways to quickly fix that in Chapter 16 when you look at masking.

11. Do one more thing. Choose Filter ➪ Blur ➪ Gaussian Blur. When the Gaussian Blur dialog box appears, type a value of **5** and click OK. This blurs the snow around the dog a bit, making her pop out of the background a bit more.

Using selections (or masks) to isolate areas for selective blurring or sharpening is a very common technique that you revisit later.

As you can see, the Magnetic Lasso tool is powerful, especially in a scenario with edges between regions of contrasting tones like this one. When edges aren't so well defined, it becomes necessary to modify the tool's properties in the options bar so that it accurately follows the edge. The following list highlights some of these settings:

NOTE In order to have an effect, all the settings on the options Bar — except Refine Edge — are applied before the tool is used.

- **Feather:** Used to blur the edge of the selection, creating softer selections. This is discussed in detail in a moment.

- **Anti-alias:** Used to smooth jagged edge transitions. This should be turned on. It's available for the Lasso tools, the Elliptical Marquee, and the Magic Wand.

- **Width:** This specifies the size of the area where edge detection occurs. It specifies the maximum distance from the pointer where an edge will be seen by the Magnetic Lasso tool.

- **Contrast:** Used to modify the Lasso's sensitivity to edge contrast. Higher settings cause the tool to see edges with higher contrast only.

- **Frequency:** Specifies the rate at which fastening points are attached to the edge. Higher settings tend to anchor the selection more quickly.

- **Use tablet pressure to change pen width button:** If you're using a graphics tablet, discussed in Chapter 17, you can click this to quickly turn the pen pressure setting on and off.

- **Refine Edge:** This is an exciting new feature in Photoshop CS3. It is discussed in detail in a moment.

Experiment with each of these settings individually on the `snow_dog.tif` file. Get a feel for how each affects the Magnetic Lasso's selection process. When used properly, this tool creates a selection that's 90 percent complete in just a few moments. Areas that are missed can quickly be added to the selection with more appropriate selection tools.

The Magic Wand tool

The Magic Wand tool — as you probably can tell by its name — is another automated selection tool. It's best suited for selecting colors that are similar to one another. In fact, in the right scenario, few selection tools can match its speed. Follow these steps and play with the Magic Wand a bit:

1. Open the `bird_2.tif` practice file. The goal here is to select the bird as quickly as possible. You could probably select it with the Magnetic Lasso in under a minute.

2. Select the Magic Wand tool (W) from the Tools palette. It's fourth from the top on the single-column Tools palette. It might be stacked under the Quick Selection tool. Set the tool options to the following values: Tolerance = 30, Anti-alias = on, Contiguous = on, and Sample All Layers = off.

   - Tolerance affects the range of similar colors that the tool selects. Low settings restrict the selection to colors that are very similar. High values allow the tool to select a broader range of colors that are less similar. Settings range on a scale of 0 to 255.

   - When Contiguous is checked, only similar pixels that are touching are selected. (Contiguous means that two things are touching, or sharing a common border.) This is a great way to control the Magnetic Lasso's power. Using Contiguous allows you to do things like select a single flower out of a field of similarly colored flowers, as long as their borders aren't touching one another.

3. Click the sky. When you do, everything but the bird is selected. Invert the selection by choosing Select ➪ Inverse, and the job's done. The bird was selected with two clicks.

It's pretty rare for an automated tool to work this flawlessly. It's quite common to combine multiple selections to create the right selection. Look at how you can do this with a single tool:

1. Go back to the `bird_2.tif` file. If any selections are active, deselect them.

2. Try selecting the bird directly with the Magic Wand using the same tool options that you started with before. Click in a couple of darker tones on its chest. As you do, you can see that you can select only small areas at one time. No matter where you click on the bird's chest, you end up with a selection that looks something like the first image in Figure 15.7.

> **TIP**   When you use the Magic Wand tool, you can deselect a current selection by moving the cursor inside the selection and clicking once.

3. Go to the tool options, and deselect the Contiguous option to turn it off. Click the bird's chest again in the same spot. Now more tones are being selected because they no longer need to be touching one another, as shown in the second image in Figure 15.7

4. Try increasing the Tolerance setting. Move it up in increments of 20, and experiment by clicking the bird's chest. The third image in Figure 15.7 shows the selection with a Tolerance setting of 100. Close, but still no cigar.

   You can continue experimenting with increasing Tolerance settings until you eventually stumble across the magic number. Or you can do it much more quickly by building a selection with multiple selections.

FIGURE 15.7

A narrow range of tones is selected because only contiguous tones are being selected (first image). When Contiguous is turned off in the tool options, more tones are selected from the same range (second image). Increasing the Tolerance value allows the Magic Wand to select a greater range of tones. This is the selection with a setting of 100 with Contiguous unchecked in the tool options (third image).

5. Reset the Tolerance value to 30, and deselect any selections. Click the bird's chest. This time, while the selection is active, hold down the Shift key. A small plus sign (+) appears next to the cursor, indicating that another click will add a new selection to the current selection. Click somewhere else on the bird. Notice that more pixels have been added to the first selection.

6. If you continue Shift+clicking different areas of the bird, you eventually get all of it selected. Let's speed up the process. Increase the Tolerance value to 60, and continue Shift+clicking. Now it can be done with three of four clicks.

   It's easy to accidentally select pixels you don't want to select when the tolerance is set this high. If that happens, Alt+click the areas you want to remove from the selection. When you hold down the Alt key, you see a small minus sign (-) next to the icon, indicating that you're about to remove something from the selection.

You also can use the icons on the left side of the options bar, circled in Figure 15.8, with any of the selection tools discussed so far. The advantage to using the keyboard modifier keys is that they're faster. The advantage to using the tool options icons is that you can turn on a setting and leave it turned on. Just remember to turn it off when you finish so you don't get confused later.

FIGURE 15.8

Four icons appear on the left side of the options bar when the Marquee tools, the Lasso tools, or the Magic Wand is being used. The first button is the normal selection mode, the second button adds to the selection, the third button subtracts from the selection, and the fourth button selects only the area of two intersecting selections.

You can learn a couple of important lessons from the previous set of exercises. First, you can always do things in more than one way in Photoshop. Second, one way is often much more efficient than another. In the previous example, the difference was in the selection strategy, rather than the choice of tools. So remember, using the right tool for the job is important, but using that tool in the most efficient way is equally important.

When you're first starting out, these distinctions may not be so clear. Being able to simply get the job done, in some cases, is cause for celebration. That's okay. As you've already seen, you can get to the same place in more than one way. Just allow yourself to continue learning about the main tools you use so you become familiar with their various nuances. Eventually, you'll learn to quickly recognize situations that lend themselves to one particular tool or technique.

The new Quick Selection tool

The Quick Selection tool, introduced in Photoshop CS3, is the latest smart selection tool from Photoshop. This new tool combines the smart technology behind the Magic Wand with the flexibility of a brush-style tool, allowing smart selections to be painted into the image. The Quick Selection tool also does a nice job of creating boundaries around the selected area, providing more defined selection boundaries than selections with the Magic Wand. Follow these steps:

NEW FEATURE The new Quick Selection tool in Photoshop CS3 allows you to create smart selections by painting them in with a paintbrush-styled tool.

1. Open `spring_tulips.tif` from the downloadable practice files on the Web site.

2. Choose the Quick Selection tool from the Tools palette. (It's fourth from the top in the single-column Tools palette.) It's stacked with the Magic Wand. Make sure that Auto-Enhance is selected in the tool options.

TIP If you select Auto-Enhance on the options bar, the boundary of the selection is smoother. It adds some of the selection edge fine-tuning that can be found in the Refine Edge dialog box, which is discussed shortly. This setting also allows the selection to flow more easily toward the edges of the content being selected.

3. Try to select the orange and yellow flowers in the foreground so you can do something to them. Adjust the size of the Quick Selection tool to 100px by clicking on the brush button on the options bar and adjusting the Diameter value from the pop-up menu. Begin painting in the lower-right section of the image. As you paint, notice how the tool seeks similar colors, as shown in the first image in Figure 15.9.

NOTE By default, the Add to Selection button on the options bar is selected, which means that every stroke adds to the last.

4. Continue painting until all of the flowers in front of the fence are selected. Decrease the size of your brush when you get to the edges where the flowers and the fence overlap. If some of the fence is accidentally selected, press Alt while you paint to subtract it. Soon, your selection should look like the second image in Figure 15.9.

As you can see, this tool is quite smart. It can be used to quickly create a base selection that can be fine-tuned with other selection tools.

Strategies for selection success

Each of the selection tools you've looked at so far has strengths and weaknesses. Some tools are smart: One might be good at selecting similar colors, while another is good at finding edges. Other "dumb" tools, like the Lasso, are great when you want complete control over the tool: If you have to quickly draw a loose selection around something, you may not want to use the smarter Magnetic Lasso.

Knowing about these differences — and choosing selection tools based on them — is the foundation of successful selection strategies. After you're comfortable with these differences, you can take your selections to the next level by combining selection tools, based on their strengths, to quickly create perfect selections.

FIGURE 15.9

The Quick Selection tool seeks similar colors as it brushes across the lower-right corner of the photo (first image). You can see how the Quick Selection tool creates defined boundaries as it seeks similar colors. With only a few more strokes, all of the foreground flowers are quickly painted in (second image).

In the previous example, you still have a problem. You can see it in the second image in Figure 15.9. Background areas, showing between and behind the foreground flowers, were also selected when the flowers were selected. You could use the Subtract selection button on the tool options of the Quick Selection tool (or hold down the Alt key) so that you could go back and remove each of these areas from the selection. However, I want to show you a much faster approach that takes only one or two clicks on the image with the Magic Wand tool. Follow these steps:

1. Return to Step 4 in the previous exercise. Select the Magic Wand tool, and set its Tolerance value to 28. Make sure that Contiguous is unchecked so that all similar tones are selected.

2. Alt+click in the large dark area that's just left of the middle of the image. When you do, all the dark areas in the foreground are deselected, as shown in Figure 15.10. If too much is deselected, back up and try again with a slightly lower Tolerance value.

3. If by chance a couple of floating pixels are not deselected when they should have been, Alt+click them, or switch to the Lasso tool and remove them by holding down the Alt key and drawing a loose shape around them.

FIGURE 15.10

The dark areas between and behind the flowers were selected by the Quick Selection tool, along with the flowers. That's okay because they are quickly removed with the Magic Wand tool. One click removed all but one small group of floating pixels below and to the left of the cursor.

This is the key to selection success. You can mix and match tools to quickly piece together a great selection. Begin by using one tool that's suited to quickly building 90 percent of the image. Then use other selection tools to add and remove the bits and pieces they're most suited for working with. This strategy is much more efficient than fiddling with a particular tool's settings, trying to set its preferences so it creates the perfect selection all by itself. Creating a "superstar" selection tool might be fun, but teamwork is much more efficient.

Fine-Tuning Selections

Selecting the right information is the first part of creating a great selection. The second part is adjusting the edge of the selection so that adjustments made to selected pixels blend with the surrounding, nonselected pixels.

Feathering a selection's edge transition

One of the most used methods of modifying a selection's edge boundary is the Feather command. You feather some selections in later chapters, so look at it here. Follow these steps:

1. Open a new file. Choose File ➪ New, and give it the following properties: Width = 6 inches, Height = 4 inches, Resolution = 300, Color Mode = RGB Color/8-bit, and Background = White.

2. Select the Rectangular Marquee tool and use it to create a selection on the left side of the image. (Make sure that the feather value on the options bar is 0px before you draw.)

> **NOTE**   The Marquee tools and the Lasso tools have a Feather setting in their tool options. When this is checked, feathering is applied as the selection is being created. I rarely check this box because I often don't know how much feathering I want until the selection is in place. I'd rather leave this setting at 0px and apply feathering later so I can try a couple of different settings, if needed.

3. Select the Paint Bucket tool (G) from the Tools palette. It's stacked with the Gradient tool, 12th from the top. Click inside the rectangular selection to fill it with the foreground color. (I used black, the default foreground color.)

4. Move to the right side of the image, and draw another selection with the Rectangular Marquee similar in size to the selection on the left.

5. Choose Select ➪ Modify ➪ Feather, and type a value of **30** when the Feather Selection dialog box appears. Click OK. Use the Paint Bucket to fill the new selection with the foreground color. Your image should look something like Figure 15.11.

   I want to point out a couple of things here. First, when the selection is feathered, the angular corners are rounded off. This shows that feathering tends to smooth edges around sharp detail. Second, the feathering takes place on both sides of the marching ants. That means the feathering effect is feathering outward and inward, with respect to the selection boundary.

FIGURE 15.11

The box on the left was created by filling a nonfeathered selection with the Paint Bucket. The box on the right was created by filling a selection that has a Feather Radius of 30 pixels. Notice how much smoother the edge transition is on the box on the right and that the transition is on both sides of the selection.

Feathering a selection allows changes in a selected area to transition into unselected areas. This is extremely useful. You could have used it earlier when you were working on the photo of Ruby in the snow (snow_dog.tif). If you had taken the time to zoom in to the edges of the selection, you would have noticed abrupt changes where the focus goes from sharp to blurred. You can see this in a close-up of the area along the edge of her head in Figure 15.12. This abruptness is always a sign that something digital has taken place. A feather of about 20 pixels would have helped to minimize the abruptness of the change from blur to nonblur, shown in the second image. Go back and give it a try, experimenting with various amounts of feathering.

The amount of feathering for a particular job depends on the size of the file. Thirty pixels is a lot for a small file like the 4 x 6 300 ppi file you just used. On a larger file, like a 16 x 20 or 20 x 30, a feather of 30 pixels would have much less of an effect. Sometimes it takes a little trial and error to find the right amount of feathering. Try one setting and follow through with whatever adjustments you want to make in the selected area. If you don't like the selection boundary transition after your changes, back up and try a different amount of feathering and redo the effect until you find the right formula.

FIGURE 15.12

When you adjusted this image earlier, you didn't feather the selection before blurring the background. The hard transition between the blurred background and the nonblurred dog is easy to see in the first image. When the selection is feathered before blurring, the transition becomes much softer and less noticeable.

You know I'm all about being efficient, so I'm happy to tell you that much of the trial and error just described became history the moment Photoshop CS3 was released. Now there's a new feature that takes the guesswork out of feathering, as well as other selection edge adjustments. That new command is called Refine Edge.

Using the Refine Edge command

You may have noticed that I carefully avoided mentioning the Refine Edge button in the tool options of the tools discussed previously. And you may have noticed the Refine Edge command in the Select menu, right above Modify. Now that you understand how to create selections, let's talk about this new feature, which in my opinion is one of the coolest new things in Photoshop CS3.

When you look at the Refine Edge dialog box, as shown in Figure 15.13, the first thing you notice is that some of the same options that are available when you choose Select ➪ Modify are in the Refine Edge dialog box. Commands like Smooth, Feather, Contract, and Expand have been in Photoshop's Select menu for years. The breakthrough here is that these adjustments can be previewed in a variety of ways before any adjustments are applied. Break this complex command down and look at it piece by piece.

NEW FEATURE The new Refine Edge command takes the refinement of selections to a new level by providing a preview of a selection's modifications while they are being applied.

FIGURE 15.13

The new Refine Edge dialog box in Photoshop CS3 allows you to modify a selection boundary after the selection is in place.

The Refine Edge dialog box features five settings for modifying the edges of a selection. These tools can be used individually or together. They include the following:

- **Radius:** This slider is used to designate the size of the area around the selection's boundary in which changes will occur. This can be increased to create more precise selections around soft detail like hair and fur. (This would have been useful on the snow_dog project you did earlier.)

- **Contrast:** This slider removes any fuzziness in a selection's edge. It's often used to remove any *noise* that's picked up by increasing the Radius setting. (Noise is caused by random fluctuations in pixel values. In its purest sense, it usually looks like film grain.)

- **Smooth:** This slider is used to remove the hills and valleys in a selection's boundary. Higher settings create a smoother edge.

- **Feather:** This slider is used to soften edge transitions on either side of a selection.

- **Contract/Expand:** This slider is used to make a selection larger or smaller.

NOTE There's a very useful area at the bottom of the dialog box, called Description. It gives you a description of the various sliders and viewing options when you hover the cursor over them. If you don't see any descriptions, click the arrow button to show them.

333

In the past, you had Smooth, Feather, Expand, and Contract as options in the Select menu. Using them was anything but intuitive because the effects of changes to these settings couldn't be seen until after the selection process, which resulted in lots of trial and error. When these settings were combined, the results would become even harder to predict. The new Refine Edge command provides an elegant solution to that problem by giving you five ways to preview any modifications to the command's settings.

At the bottom of the Refine Edge dialog box are five preview thumbnails. Clicking one of these buttons changes the way the selection is previewed. Figure 15.14 shows each of those previews. They are described as follows:

> **TIP** Press F while the Refine Edge dialog box is open to cycle through the five preview modes. While in those modes, press X to temporarily hide the preview. Press X again to reinstate it.

- ■ **Standard:** Shows the selection in the usual way with the marching ants.
- ■ **Quick Mask:** Previews the selection as a Quick Mask. Quick Masks are not discussed much in this book, but if you like to use them, you might find this preview setting handy.
- ■ **On Black:** Places the selected area on a black background to isolate it from the rest of the image content.
- ■ **On White:** Places the selected area on a white background to isolate it from the rest of the image content.
- ■ **Mask:** Previews the type of mask that is created by the selection. This is extremely handy when creating masks from selections.

> **CROSS-REF** For more extensive coverage of layer masks, see Chapter 16.

This preview feature is huge. It allows you to create the selection you need without lots of trial and error. It also lets you see how one setting can be used to tweak the modifications of other settings. The biggest drawback I see is that I end up playing with this tool more than I need to because it's so much fun to compare and contrast different edge refinement scenarios.

> **TIP** When you get down to business with this tool, zoom in to take a closer look at the selection's edge. You can use the Zoom tool in the dialog box to click on the image or use the standard keyboard shortcuts for zooming. If you use the Zoom tool and you need to zoom back out, press and hold the Alt key and click on the image. This changes the Zoom tool to zoom-out mode.

Saving and Loading Selections

Sometimes, it takes lots of work to build a complex selection. Several selection tools and techniques might have to be combined to get it just right. You usually don't want to have to redo one of these selections after all that work is done. If you are about to make permanent changes to a complex selection with the tools in Refine Edge, or if you are going to deselect a complex selection, then save the selection in case you want to go back and try a different editing direction. If you're building a quick selection that can easily be repeated — like the Magic Wand selection of the sky in the bird photo in the earlier exercise — then you can easily re-create it if you need it. My rule is that I save a selection if it takes longer than 5 minutes to create. That way, if I need the selection again, I don't have to re-create it or try to remember how I created it in the first place.

FIGURE 15.14

Selections can be previewed in five ways with the Refine Edge command. The previews shown here are in this order: Standard, Quick Mask, On Black, On White, and Mask.

Standard

Quick Mask

On Black

On White

Mask

To save a selection, choose Select ➪ Save Selection. When you do this, the Save Selection dialog box appears, as shown in Figure 15.15. You have three options in the Document pop-up menu as to the location of where the selection will be saved:

- Choosing the current filename allows you to save the selection as part of the current file so you can access the selection later. This is the usual place to save a selection.

- Choosing New allows you to create a new file that contains only the selection. This is a good way to store a selection by itself. I rarely do this, but it's nice to know it's possible.

- If there are other files open and they have the same *pixel dimensions* of the current file, their names appear in the list. You can save the selection to one of those files to transfer it. This is useful when the second document contains the same area that needs to be selected.

TIP

To see a file's pixel dimensions, choose Image ➪ Image Size. The pixel dimensions are the first set of numbers. (The Image Size command is discussed in detail in Chapter 21.)

NOTE

When a selection is saved, it's saved as a channel. If you want to see what a saved selection looks like, go to the Channels palette. It will be sitting at the bottom of the stack.

Loading a selection works pretty much the same way, except in reverse. The dialog box is shown in Figure 15.16. The Document pop-up menu allows you to choose which image you want to work with. The same rule applies. Only images with the same pixel dimensions as the current document appear in the pop-up menu. You can invert the selection as it's loaded by selecting the Invert option.

FIGURE 15.15

The Save Selection dialog box allows you to save complex selections for future use. You can even save a selection from one image to another image by selecting another open file (with the same pixel dimensions) in the Document pop-up menu, or you can save it to a new document by selecting New in the Document pop-up menu.

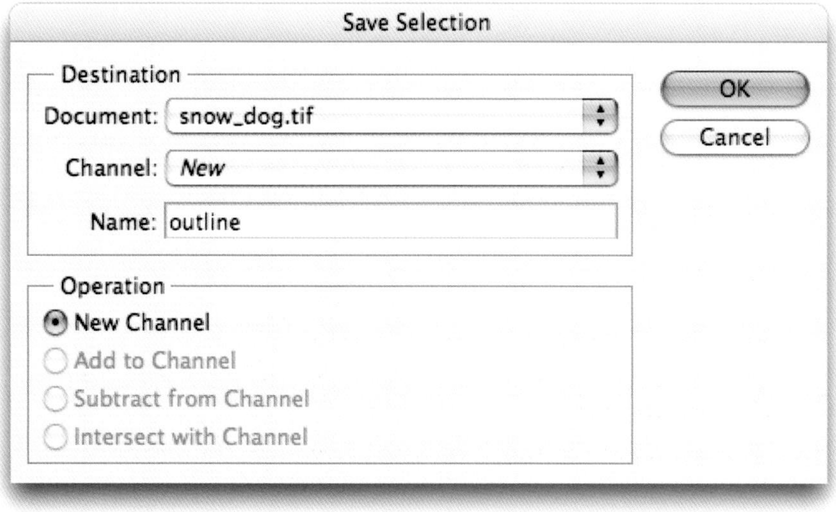

FIGURE 15.16

The Load Selection dialog box allows you to load a selection from the current image or from another open image with the same pixel dimensions. If there are multiple saved selections, they appear in the Channel pop-up menu. The selection can be inverted on the fly by selecting the Invert option.

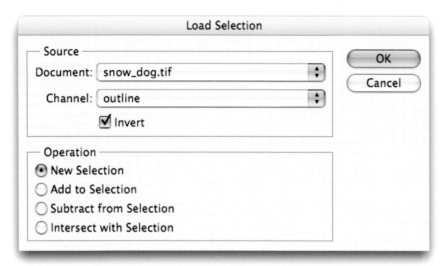

Saving a selection allows you to make a copy of any detailed selection so you have it in the future in case you need it. It also allows you to share a selection with another, similar file. You can retrieve these selections later with the Load Selection command. I tend to work with masks often, so I don't save lots of selections. However, when the need arises, the ability to save and load selections is very handy.

Cutting and Pasting with Selections

You've seen how useful selections are for isolating parts of an image so that local changes can be made to them — tonally or with filters. Selections also are used to isolate something and then copy it somewhere else or remove it altogether. In Chapter 14, you used a selection to copy the young woman by the car to a new layer. Then you positioned this "twin" elsewhere in the image.

Let's revisit that technique with the bird photos you used earlier:

1. Open the `bird_2.tif` practice file.

2. Select the Magic Wand from the Tools palette. Set the Tolerance to 30, and select the Contiguous option. Click the sky.

3. When the entire sky is selected, invert the selection. Choose Select ➪ Inverse or press Shift+Command+I or Shift+Ctrl+I. Now only the bird is selected.

4. You have two options here for creating a duplicate of the bird: copy the original information, or you can cut it. The difference is that cutting leaves a hole behind in the original layer. Copying doesn't affect the original layer. You can see the difference in Figure 15.17.

   Try cutting first. Choose Layer ➪ New ➪ Layer via Cut. The first clue that a new layer has been created is that the marching ants disappear. The second clue it that a new layer, called Layer 1, appears in the Layers palette.

5. Select the Move tool (V) from the Tools palette, and move the bird to the right. When the duplicate bird on Layer 1 is moved, the hole it left behind is revealed. Your image should look like the first image in Figure 15.17.

FIGURE 15.17

In the first image, a new layer is created by cutting a selection from the original layer (Shift+Command+J/Shift+Ctrl+J). This technique leaves a hole in the original layer. In the second image, a new layer is created by copying the selection to a new layer (Command+J/Ctrl+J).

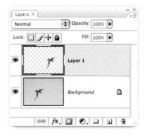

TIP Here's a shortcut I use all the time. When you temporarily need the Move tool, press Command (Ctrl) instead. This key makes the Move tool appear as long as the key is held down. When you release the key, your cursor goes back to the previous tool. This saves lots of time because you don't have to visit the Tools palette as often. (This shortcut to the Move tool doesn't work with all tools. For example, if you're using the Hand tool and you press Command/Ctrl, the Hand temporarily becomes the Zoom tool. It also doesn't work when a selection is active.)

TIP If you want to move the duplicate bird straight to the right, hold down the Shift key as you click and drag. The Shift modifier key restricts the movement of the Move tool to straight lines: up, down, and sideways.

6. Go back to the end of Step 3. Choose Layer ➪ New ➪ Layer via Copy (Command+J/Ctrl+J). Move the duplicate bird to the right. This time, your image should look like the second image in Figure 15.17, with two birds visible.

NOTE Because cutting is destructive, I rarely use it. Instead, I rely on Layer via Copy, or more usually, the keyboard shortcut Command+J (Ctrl+J).

7. Move the duplicate bird to another image. Open the `bird_1.tif` practice file. You should now have two files open. Position the images so you can see both of them at the same time, as shown in Figure 15.18. One way to do this is to go to choose Window ➪ Arrange ➪ Tile Horizontally.

TIP When you use the Arrange command, you also can match all files to the current file's zoom and location by selecting Match Zoom and Location from the Arrange submenu.

8. Click the header of the bird_2 file to make it active. (The header is the top of the image that displays the name of the file.) When the bird_2 file is active, you can see both layers in the Layers palette. To transfer the duplicate bird to the bird_1 file, click and drag the duplicate bird's thumbnail in the Layers palette from its original file into the new file; simply drop it on top of the main image, as shown in Figure 15.18. It's that easy. (You don't have to use any particular tool when doing this.) Go ahead and give it a try. By the way, when you drag a layer from one image into another, the first layer stays behind and a duplicate is created in the second image's Layers palette.

NOTE If these two documents had different color profiles (Adobe RGB1998 and sRGB) and your color management policies were set up as recommended in Chapter 12, a Paste Profile Mismatch dialog box would appear when information was being copied and pasted between them. This is similar to the Profile Mismatch and Missing Profile dialog boxes discussed in that chapter. It's more of a reminder than a warning. If it happens to you, click OK.

TIP If you hold down the Shift key as you drag and drop a layer, the new layer is dropped into the center of the image. Otherwise, it is placed wherever you drop it.

I use this technique when I need the same adjustment layer on two files. Suppose I have two photos that were shot of the same subject at the same time. If I create a Color Balance adjustment layer for one, I can drag it onto the other image instead of building one from scratch for the second image.

FIGURE 15.18

It's easy to move a layer from one file to another. Open both files, and position them so you can see both images. Go to the Layers palette of the image with the layer you want. Click and hold on its thumbnail while dragging it into the second image.

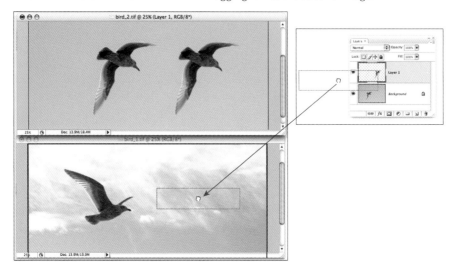

> **NOTE** You also can use the Move tool to move content in the current layer from one image to another without using the Layers palette. I prefer the method I just showed you because it saves having to switch tools. Also, by using the Layers palette to select the layer I want to drag and drop, I can confirm that I'm working with the right layer. This is important when an image has lots of layers.

9. After the duplicate bird is in the new image, you can use the Move tool to fine-tune its positioning.

The two images in this example happen to have the same pixel dimensions. In practice, they don't have to be the same. However, be aware that if the dimensions are different, the incoming layer will change size relative to the difference in sizes between the two files. If you drag a layer from an image with pixel dimensions of 1200 x 800 into an image with pixel dimensions of 2400 x 1600, the incoming layer — the bird in the previous example — will look much smaller in the new image than it did in its original image.

> **NOTE** This size differential isn't the case when dragging and dropping adjustment layers. They resize themselves to fit the entire image's pixel dimensions when dragged into an image with different dimensions.

The general idea when using the technique used earlier is to add a visual element to an image. However, the same technique also can be used to hide a visual element by copying information and placing it on top of the thing you want to hide. For example, you may want to hide an annoying light switch on a wall in the background of an image. Yes, you can do a job like that with a retouching tool like the Clone Stamp, but sometimes it's faster to copy a section of nearby wall and drop it on top of the light switch.

Here's an example of using this method to hide something. In the image in Figure 15.19, the long drawstring hanging down on the right side of the sweater is removed. Follow these steps to see how:

1. Draw a loose selection around the area, as shown in the second frame of Figure 15.19. This selection is used to get the shape you need when you create a copy. The area where the selection touches the edge of the sweater is the most critical part of this selection.

2. Drag the selection to the side so that none of the white drawstring is inside of it, as shown in the next frame of Figure 15.19. With the selection repositioned, you can use its shape to select material to be pasted over the area originally selected.

3. You want the information you copy to blend with the sweater's edge, so soften the edge of the selection with the Feather Command. Press Alt+Command+D (Alt+Ctrl+D) with a value of 1.

> **NOTE** I almost always feather a selection by 1 or 2 pixels when copying and pasting. Otherwise, the hard edge of the selection will show on the edges of the copied information.

4. Copy the selection to a new layer (Command+J/Ctrl+J). A new layer, Layer 1, is created with the exact shape of the selection, as shown in the fourth frame of Figure 15.19. You can see that the 1px feather softened the edges just a bit.

5. Drag Layer 1 to the left with the Move tool so that it's back in the spot where the original selection was created, as shown in the final frame of Figure 15.19. If you look closely, you can still see the shape of Layer 1 along the right edge and the bottom. This is because the area of background that was copied is slightly darker than the area next to the young woman. Ideally, it would blend perfectly with the background.

6. I usually use the Patch tool to clean up something like this. Because the Patch tool works with only one layer, I flatten the duplicate layer back into the Background layer first. After that's done, it takes only two applications of the Patch tool to blend these edges and complete this procedure.

> **TIP** If you're working with an image that has several layers, you may not want to flatten the entire image just to do a bit of retouching. In these cases, you can use the Merge Layers command (Command+E/Ctrl+E) under the Layer menu. The Merge Layers command flattens the current layer with the layer directly below it, while leaving other layers intact.

The entire process took less than a minute and is much cleaner than trying to do this with one of the standard retouching tools because of the large area being covered. This technique won't always work, but when it does, it's hard to beat for speed.

FIGURE 15.19

In this example, the long drawstring on the right side of the image is removed. The fastest way to accomplish that is to use a selection to define the area to be covered (second image). Then use the selection to copy a piece of background to a new layer (third and fourth images). Once that's done, the new layer is positioned over the drawstring and merged back into the Background layer (final image).

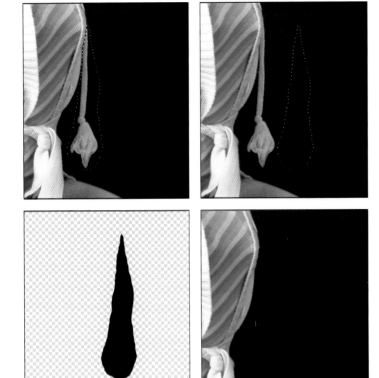

Photo by Dan Christopher

Combining Selections and Filters

Filters are mentioned a couple of times in this book. In fact, you used the Gaussian Blur filter earlier in this chapter. But I never stopped to define exactly what a filter is. Let's take care of that right now.

Filters get their name from their counterpart in the film world. Film photographers have always used glass and other materials in front of their lenses to change the way images are captured by film. For example, photographers used to do things like smear petroleum jelly around the edges of a clear filter to blur the background around someone. With digital capture, most filtering takes place after the image is photographed or scanned. Thank goodness petroleum jelly never has to come near our cameras again!

Photoshop has a large array of filters available under the Filters menu. Some of them are fun and can be used to create cool, creative effects. Those aren't the kind of filters you're concerned with here. You're mostly interested in the more utilitarian filters like Blur and Sharpen, though these techniques can be used with most other filters.

Earlier, in the exercise with Ruby in the snow, a filter is used to blur a selected area of the image. The snow is blurred around her so she'd stand out from it. This is a common technique, especially in the digital age because digital SLRs tend to have a greater depth of field than their film counterparts. When everything's in focus, the viewer may not know what to look at. By selectively adjusting areas of sharpness (or blurriness), you can guide the viewer through the image.

NOTE This blurring technique also can be used to fix an image where the subject isn't as sharp as you want it to be. Select everything around the subject and blur it a bit, causing the subject to look sharper in relation to it.

Figure 15.20 shows the portrait of my friends with their dog. I really like the portrait, but all the sharp detail in the garden behind them is distracting, especially because their skin was smoothed during retouching to give them a softer look. (You look at this portrait in detail in the hands-on retouching project in Chapter 22.)

This problem is solved by following these three main steps:

1. The layer must be copied because blurring permanently affects the pixels. That way, all blurring is isolated to its own layer. If I change my mind later, I can toss it and try something different. (If I think that's a real possibility, I'll save the selection before moving on.)

2. Select the area to be blurred. In this case, a close selection is drawn around the people with the Magnetic Lasso tool and then inverted to select everything around them. (I had to remember to come back and subtract the background area between the man and the dog.) Before moving on, feather the selection by 1 or 2 pixels and adjust the Radius setting in the Refine Edge to soften the boundary of the selection. The second image in Figure 15.21 shows the selection.

FIGURE 15.20

The only thing that bothers me about this portrait is the sharp background that competes with the main subjects.

> **NOTE**   It doesn't make much difference if you feather a selection before or after inverting it.

3. Use a Blur filter to blur the selected information on the duplicate layer. I use the Gaussian Blur filter with a setting of 2.4 and then deselect the selection. The result, the bottom image in Figure 15.21, looks much better because it brings the focus back to the main subjects.

When enhancing eyes in a portrait, similar methods are used to sharpen only the eyes with one of the sharpening filters: Smart Sharpen or Unsharp Mask.

FIGURE 15.21

The problem can be fixed easily by creating a selection around the subjects, inverting it, and then blurring the pixels inside that selection. The final image with the blurred background is much more appealing. (Any major changes like this should always be done on a duplicate layer to maintain flexibility.)

Using Smart Filters in Photoshop CS3

Something that Photoshop users have begged for over the years is a way to use filters nondestructively. When you use a filter on an image layer, the pixels are changed permanently — unless, of course, you're able to go backward in the History timeline. You already know how I feel about making permanent changes like this.

In the previous example, I got around this limitation by duplicating the layer before I applied any filters. This way, if I later decide I don't like the effect, all I have to do is delete the layer. This technique works, but it's less than elegant. The first problem is that when you duplicate layers, you increase the size of the file. Duplicating the Background layer doubles the size of the file. The second issue is that if I do decide later that I don't like the effect of the filter and I want to redo it, I don't always know what the previous filter settings were. I have to start all over and experiment with various settings. When Adobe released Photoshop CS3, it solved both of these problems with a new filter feature named Smart Filters.

NEW FEATURE **Smart Filters is a new feature in Photoshop CS3. Smart Filters allow for the creation of editable filter adjustments that are nondestructive to the image. The filter's settings can be changed at a later date or removed completely.**

When a Smart Filter is used, it becomes part of the layer stack in the Layers palette. Figure 15.22 shows what this looks like when a Smart Filter is used instead of duplicating the layer in the previous exercise. A mask in the shape of the selection appears on the filter's thumbnail because a selection was in place before the filter was used. Clicking the eyeball next to the name hides the filter's effects. Double-clicking the name itself opens the filter dialog box with the settings that were used when the Smart Filter was created. This allows you to make further adjustments if needed. All this flexibility is achieved without a noticeable change to the file's size.

CROSS-REF **Using selections with masks is discussed in Chapter 16.**

NOTE **Smart Filters support all of Photoshop's filters except for Extract, Liquify, Pattern Maker, and Vanishing Point.**

Before going any further with Smart Filters, I need to explain what it is that makes them so smart.

Understanding Smart Objects

Smart Filters work only on Smart Objects. If you have a normal image open and you look in the Filters menu, you won't see a command for Smart Filters. Instead, you see Convert for Smart Filter. If you click that command, the layer that's currently active is converted to a Smart Object.

Smart Objects first appeared in Photoshop CS2. They offer a way to open a file — usually a raw file — as a reference to the original file, rather than a file full of pixels. When you edit a Smart Object, pixels aren't changed because there aren't any pixels to change. The Smart Object acts like a proxy of the original file. In other words, transformation adjustments like scaling and rotating are not destructive to the file.

FIGURE 15.22

When a Smart Filter is created, it appears just below the layer to which it is applied. In this case, because a selection is used, a mask appears in the thumbnail. To edit the filter, click the filter's name. To edit the way the filter blends, click the Blending Options button to the right of the name.

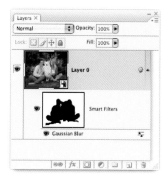

One of the issues with using Smart Objects — especially when considering the objectives of this book — is that Smart Objects don't consist of actual pixels, so retouching tools can't be used on them. If you try to use the Clone Stamp on a Smart Object, the message dialog box shown in Figure 15.23 appears telling you that you have to *rasterize* the Smart Object. The Smart Object must be converted back to pixels — losing its smart capabilities — before the Clone Stamp can be used on it. When the Smart Object is rasterized, all Smart Filter effects become permanent and noneditable.

FIGURE 15.23

Retouching tools can't be used on a Smart Object because they don't contain actual pixels. In order to retouch a Smart Object, it must be rasterized first.

Naturally, you could use the Clone Stamp to clone to another layer by selecting All Layers in the Sample pop-up menu in the Clone Stamp's tool options. But you can't use the Patch tool. Because of that limitation, I don't use Smart Objects/Filters much when I'm working on restoration or retouching projects. However, they do offer a different way of approaching a nondestructive work-flow mentality, so I want to take a closer look at them.

Using Smart Filters

Revisit the portrait of the couple with their dog. This time, Smart Filters are used to blur around them. Follow these steps:

1. Create a Smart Object from this file in one of two ways:

   ▓ Open it as a Smart Object by choosing File ⇨ Open As Smart Object.

   ▓ Open the file, and choose Filter ⇨ Convert for Smart Filters. When this option is selected, a dialog box appears reminding you that the layer is being converted into a Smart Object, as shown in Figure 15.24. If the layer is named Background, it will be renamed because that name is a special name with special properties.

FIGURE 15.24

This dialog box reminds you that you're creating a Smart Object when you choose the Convert for Smart Filters option under the Filter menu.

> **NOTE** A raw file can be opened as a Smart Object by selecting Open in Photoshop as Smart Objects option in the Adobe Raw Converter's Workflow Options dialog box or when opening it into Photoshop from Lightroom.

You can tell that a layer is a Smart Object by looking at the layer's thumbnail in the Layers palette. If it's a Smart Object, it has a small icon on its lower-left corner, as shown in Figure 15.19. When you hover the cursor over this icon, the tooltip shows "Smart Object thumbnail."

2. Create a selection around the subjects and invert it, as you did earlier.

3. Choose Filter ⇨ Blur ⇨ Gaussian Blur. After you like the setting, click OK. The effect is the same as what you got without using a Smart Object. The only difference is in the Layers palette, as shown earlier in Figure 15.19. The Smart Filter appears just below the layer it is affecting.

4. If you want to change the filter's effects, simply double-click the name of the filter, Gaussian Blur. The Gaussian Blur dialog box reopens with the settings used last time still

in effect, as shown on the left in Figure 15.25 This gives you the same kind of flexibility you get with adjustment layers, allowing you to go back and readjust your original setting at any time, as long as the image remains unflattened.

If you double-click the icon to the right of the filter's name, a Blending Options dialog box opens that gives you control over how the filter blends with the layer's content, as shown in the image on the right of Figure 15.25.

FIGURE 15.25

Double-clicking the name of a Smart Filter reopens the filter's dialog with the previous settings still in place (first image). The Smart Filter's Filter Blending Options dialog box allows you to change the filter's blending mode and the opacity of the effect (second image). This dialog box is accessed by clicking the icon to the right of the Smart Filter's name. (You can see the icon in Figure 15.22; it consists of two small black triangles and lines.)

The Blending Options dialog box allows you to lower the opacity of the filter, just like lowering the opacity of a layer. It also allows you to select a different blending mode so you can affect the way the filter's effects blend with the layer's image content. (One of the ways this is used is to select the Luminosity blending mode when sharpening so that any color noise caused by sharpening is eliminated.)

Here's another interesting thing that can be done with Smart Objects. In Chapter 14, I said that adjustment layers can't be made with the color Variations adjustment command. Well, with a Smart Object, you can create a nondestructive, reeditable Variations layer, but you can do the same thing with the Shadow/Highlight command.

Here's how it works. After a Smart Object is created, choose Image ⇨ Adjustments. Notice that all of the adjustment commands are grayed out except for the Shadow/Highlight and Variations commands. If you use one of these commands, it appears below the layer it was applied to, just like a Smart Filter, as shown in Figure 15.26.

FIGURE 15.26

Smart Objects allow you to use the Variations and Shadow/Highlights commands in a nondestructive way. When used with a Smart Object, these two commands appear in the Layers palette just below the layer to which they are applied. Their settings can be readjusted by clicking on their names, just like an adjustment layer.

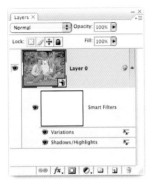

Smart Objects coupled with Smart Filters offer a new way of addressing the age-old problem of making filters nondestructive. The main problem with them here is that when additional retouching needs to be done, the method leaves something to be desired. However, Smart Filters are very powerful if used after all retouching is completed, or in cases where retouching needs are minimal.

Summary

In this chapter, you took a detailed look at selections, one of the most important tools for restoration and retouching. Selections are used to isolate regions of an image so they can be manipulated independently of the rest of the image. This way the final image can be constructed and fine-tuned piece by piece.

Selections are created with a variety of tools, including the Marquee, Lasso, Magic Wand, and Quick Selection tools. Each of these tools can be fine-tuned through its settings in the options bar. Complex selections are created using a new selection to add to or subtract from an existing selection. Even more complex selections are created by combining multiple selection tools and techniques. Each tool is used on the parts of the selection that are most suitable for it.

After a complex selection is in place, its edge can be modified with the new Refine Edge button. Refinements include Radius, Contrast, Smooth, Contract/Expand, and Feather — the most common refinement you do in this book. The Refine Edge dialog box also allows you to select the way the refinements are previewed. This new preview ability enables you to intuitively mix and match settings, creating the perfect selection edge.

After you've invested lots of time in creating a complex selection, you don't want to risk losing it. You can save a selection as part of an image, or as part of any other open image with identical pixel dimensions. This ability allows you to share a selection with a similar file that has the same selection needs. You also can create a new file that contains only the selection for long-term storage.

You looked at how selections are used to copy or remove selected areas from an image. This is one way to duplicate pixels so they can be used to add detail to an image or to hide it. New layers created by copying or cutting also can be shared with other images, no matter what their relative pixel dimensions are.

Finally, you looked at how the filters in Photoshop's Filter menu are used with selections. For the techniques in this book, you mostly work with blurring and sharpening filters, though you use a couple of others on rare occasions. The most exciting thing about filters in Photoshop CS3 is the new ability to use Smart Objects combined with Smart Filters to create nondestructive filters. Because Smart Objects don't contain actual pixel data, retouching tools can't be used directly on them. There are ways to deal with this, but to get the most use from a Smart Filter, you want to take care of all major retouching before turning your image into a Smart Object.

Chapter 16

Creating Flexibility with Layer Masks

So far the Photoshop section of this book has covered several important concepts. Some of them are important because they're encountered more often in a nondestructive workflow. With that in mind, many of these concepts pale in comparison to the concept you learn about in this chapter: layer masking.

When I began using Photoshop many years ago, I heard and read about masks and masking, but I never really understood what they were or how they're supposed to be used. The concept just seemed so abstract. A couple of years later, when I finally understood masking, it completely changed the way I did things from then on.

My goal in this chapter is to help you learn about masking so you can begin using this powerful technique now. I explain exactly what layer masks are, show you how to create them, and then show you how to leverage them by combining masks with some of the things you've already learned in this book. When you're through with this chapter, you'll be ready to take your creativity to a higher level.

Understanding Layer Masks

My neighbors recently had their house painted. Before the painter began spraying the house with paint, he used masking tape and paper to cover all the windows so they wouldn't be painted. This is very much the way selections work in Photoshop. You select only the things you want to paint before you start painting. Everything outside the selection is covered with virtual masking tape and paper. Masking in Photoshop works in a similar way, except that the tape and paper don't have to be applied before the painting begins; they can be applied after the painting is done.

Layer masking is just what it sounds like — masking on a layer. When one layer sits on top of another, part of it can be hidden selectively, and temporarily, with a mask. When the information is hidden, that part of the layer becomes transparent. It would be the same as using the Eraser tool, except that the Eraser is a destructive tool; when something is erased, it's gone. When image information is masked, it can be unmasked if it needs to be revealed again.

The old cliché goes like this: A picture is worth a thousand words. Let's look at how masking works and then come back and dig into the details.

Figure 16.1 shows two completely different images: a young woman by a car and a Japanese garden. The goal here is to combine them into a single image with the young woman in front of the garden instead of the car.

From what you've learned so far, you might think that the best course of action is to use the Magic Wand to select the young woman, copy her to a new layer, and then drag her into the garden image. That would work okay, if the selection were perfect. If you had problems with the original selection and didn't notice them until later, you'd have to back up and start all over again. As I'm sure you can imagine, this kind of technique goes against my philosophy of using a nondestructive retouching workflow.

Here's what I decide to do instead: Combine the two images into a single file with the young woman as the top layer, as shown in the first image in Figure 16.2. I then create a mask and use the Brush tool with black paint to hide everything I don't want to see on the young woman's layer. When I finish painting the mask, the layers and image look like the second image in Figure 16.2.

Look at the layer stack in the second image in Figure 16.2. Notice that a new black-and-white thumbnail is now beside the thumbnail of the young woman on Layer 1. This black-and-white thumbnail is the layer mask I created with the Brush tool. Everywhere I painted around the young woman with black is now hidden from view, which leads to the basic rule of layer masks: Black hides, and white reveals. The beauty of this is that anytime I want to unhide something, I just come back with the Brush tool and apply some white paint to the area I want to reveal.

This concept is simple and powerful. With a layer mask, you can hide and reveal layer information at will. This is the ultimate in workflow flexibility because layer masks are completely nondestructive. Any application of paint on a layer mask can always be undone, as long as the layer is never merged or flattened with other layers.

FIGURE 16.1

I want to combine these images so it looks like the young woman is sitting in front of the garden. I can do it by selecting the young woman and copying her to a new layer, but that technique isn't as flexible as using a layer mask.

Photo by Jerry Auker

FIGURE 16.2

After both images are combined into a single file as individual layers, a mask is created on the top layer. Black on the mask hides information on the layer, and white reveals the layer's information.

Creating Layer Masks

Now that you understand the general idea, do the following masking project so you can get a real feel for layer masking:

1. Open the `78_vette.tif` and the `garden.tif` files from the downloadable practice files on the Web site at `www.wiley.com/go/workflow`. Position them on the screen so that you can see some of both images at once.

2. Click the 78_vette file to make it active. Then go to the Layers palette, and drag the background layer into the garden file. Hold down the Shift key as you drag so the layer is dropped into the center of the image.

3. Now that both images are in the same file, you don't need the 78_vette file, so close it. The `garden.tif` image and its associated Layers palette should now look like Figure 16.3.

FIGURE 16.3

Both images are stacked together in the same file. The layer with the young woman (Layer 1) is on top, so you can't see the garden image below her. The button that looks like a target at the bottom of the Layers palette can be used as a shortcut for creating a layer mask.

4. You're almost ready to start masking. All you need is a mask, which you can create in two ways:

- Choose Layer ⇨ Layer Mask ⇨ Reveal All. (The difference between Reveal All and Hide All is discussed in a bit.)

- Click the Add Layer Mask button, the target-like icon at the bottom of the Layers palette, circled in Figure 16.3.

CAUTION   If you accidentally click the Add Layer Mask button a second time, a vector mask is created. A vector mask is also created if you click this button after creating an adjustment layer. A vector mask appears as a second mask thumbnail, next to the layer mask thumbnail on the Layers palette. You don't use vector masks here, so if you create one by mistake, delete it by dragging it to the trashcan icon at the bottom right of the Layers palette.

Now your Layers palette should look like Figure 16.4 with a white box beside the image thumbnail. This white box, as you saw in Figure 16.2, is a representation of the mask you'll be creating. It isn't the mask itself, just as the image icon in the Layers palette isn't the image itself. It's only a representation of it. The link icon that appears between the two thumbnails signifies that the mask is *linked* with the layer's image content. If you use the Move tool to move the layer's image content, the mask moves too, staying in alignment with the image.

5. Select the Brush tool, and set its Master Diameter to 300px, Hardness to 0%, and Opacity to 100%. Make sure that black is the foreground color. It should be because when you create a layer mask using the two methods shown previously, the color swatches are reset to their defaults — black as the foreground color and white as the background color.

FIGURE 16.4

When a Reveal All mask is created, it appears as a white thumbnail beside the image thumbnail in the Layers palette. (You know that white reveals, so it makes sense that a Reveal All mask is white.)

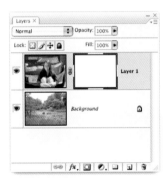

> **NOTE**   When a layer mask is active, you can't select any colors other than black, white, or gray in the Color Picker. Even if you click red in the Color Picker, the swatch on the toolbar is gray. That's because only black, white, and shades of gray can be used on a mask.

6. Start painting around the outer edges of the image. Don't go too close to the young woman just yet. Notice that as you paint, you begin to see the garden layer below. Keep painting until most of the detail around the young woman is hidden, as in the first image set in Figure 16.5.

> **TIP**   When painting a mask with the Brush tool, all painting is done on the image itself, not on the little mask thumbnail.

7. Reduce the size of your brush, and move in closer to the young woman. When you get right next to her, you find that the soft brush doesn't work very well. You can't get right next to her without affecting her, too. Increase the Brush tool's Hardness value to 80 or 90. Try to avoid going to 100 so you still get a soft edge along the outline of the young woman.

8. If you accidentally hide part of the young woman instead of the background, switch your foreground color to white (using the X key or the curved arrow by the swatches) and paint the detail back in. It's that easy.

9. Your image should now look very close to what appears in Figure 16.2. Press the backslash key (\) to take the image into *Quick Mask mode*.

This viewing mode allows you to see all your masking strokes as a red overlay, as shown in Figure 16.6. This is a great way to see exactly where your brushstrokes are. In Figure 16.6, you can see where a spot is missed below her elbow on the left. It wasn't noticeable in the image preview until Quick Mask mode was turned on. You can continue painting while in Quick Mask mode if you want to.

FIGURE 16.5

Information on Layer 1 is hidden as you begin painting with black on the image. This painting is reflected in the layer mask thumbnail on Layer 1 in the Layers palette.

NOTE The red color of the Quick Mask goes back to the days when masks were hand cut, with a razor blade, on orange or red plastic sheets called Amber-lith and Ruby-lith. If you want to use a different color or change its opacity, double-click the mask thumbnail in the Layers palette.

10. When your mask is fine-tuned to your liking, press the backslash (\) key again to go back to normal viewing mode.

TIP If this were a real job, I'd take another few moments to remove some of the distractions in the background, like the two lavender shapes on the right. Remember, if you're going to do this, you have to click the Background layer first to make it active before you can use any retouching tools on it.

To temporarily hide a mask so you can see the image without the effects of the mask, press Shift and click the layer mask thumbnail in the Layers palette. When you do this, a big red X appears on the thumbnail, signifying that the mask is hidden. Click the thumbnail again to unhide the mask.

Another useful viewing option with a mask is to Alt+click the mask. This makes the actual mask appear in the image preview, as shown in Figure 16.7. This mask viewing mode is extremely revealing. Now you can see other areas missed when painting the mask. You may not have noticed them in Quick Mask mode. After taking care of those areas Alt+click again to go back to the normal view.

FIGURE 16.6

Press the backslash (\) key to see your masking on the image while you use the Brush tool. To hide the mask, press \ again. This is a good way to see exactly where your brushstrokes are on the image as you paint them.

Be aware of one more thing when working with masks. When you're painting, or retouching for that matter, you can choose to work on the mask or on the image. This makes sense. Sometimes you want to paint the mask, and other times you may want to paint on the image itself. You can tell which area will be painted on by looking at the thumbnails in the Layers palette.

Click the image thumbnail for Layer 1 in the previous example. When you do this, notice that a small black box appears around the thumbnail. (You can see this in the Layers palette Layer 1 mask thumbnail in Figure 16.5.) Now you can paint on the image itself, or you can use a retouching tool on it. Click the mask thumbnail, and watch the box move back to the mask. (You can see this on the Layers palette thumbnail in Figure 16.4.) Now any painting or retouching that you do is applied to the mask. When a mask is first created, the black box is always around the mask thumbnail, indicating that you can start masking right away.

CAUTION   If you're using a retouching tool on a layer that has a mask and nothing is happening, it probably means that you're retouching the mask instead of the image. To solve this, click the image thumbnail in the Layers palette to make it active instead of the mask.

FIGURE 16.7

Alt+click the layer mask thumbnail in the Layers palette to see the actual mask in the image preview. You can paint on it like this to fix any problems it reveals. When you finish, Alt+click the thumbnail again to go back to the normal view.

Now that you see how easy and powerful layer masking is, let's tie this concept in with some of the other things you've learned so you can see how they all work together.

Using Masks with Selections

At the beginning of the preceding exercise, I suggested an alternate way of handling the project. You could have selected the young woman and then copied her to a new layer. (Or you could have selected her, inverted the selection, and then pressed Delete to delete everything around her, as long as her layer was not named Background.) After that was done, you could have moved her layer into the garden image. If you recall, the main drawback to this strategy is the fact that a move like this is permanent (destructive to pixels). If you did it that way, you'd have to live with that original selection after the young woman was separated from her original background. I'd rather have some options in case I want to make changes later.

Painting a mask with the Brush tool is nondestructive, but it can be time consuming. Also, it isn't always as exact as a selection (as you can see by the sloppy masking job in Figure 16.7). The good news is that the speed and accuracy of a selection can be combined with the nondestructive nature of a mask, to create accurate masks quickly. Follow these steps to see how it's done:

1. If you still have the file from the previous exercise open, click and drag the mask thumb-nail to the trashcan icon at the bottom of the Layers palette. When a dialog box appears asking if you want to Apply or Delete the mask, click Delete.

   Be sure that you don't accidentally grab the image thumbnail. If you do, you'll delete the entire layer instead of just the mask. (If the image is not open, open it and complete Steps 1 through 3 from the preceding steps.) Your Layers palette should look like the Layers palette in Figure 16.3 again.

2. Use the Magnetic Lasso to draw a quick selection around the young woman. Use the Lasso tool to fine-tune the selection by adding and subtracting. It isn't necessary to make this selection absolutely perfect. Just get it close to perfect as quickly as you can. When you finish, feather the selection 1 or 2 pixels to soften its edge.

3. After your selection is in place, it can be used to create a mask. Click the Add Layer Mask button at the bottom of the Layers palette (the icon that looks like a target). A mask is created as soon as you click it, hiding everything on Layer 1 that is outside of the mask.

   This is a much better technique than cutting and pasting for removing the young woman from her background because all the background information is still there. It can be masked back in anytime.

4. Use the Brush to touch-up the mask in any of the spots where the selection wasn't perfect.

CAUTION   Creating a mask from a selection doesn't work if you create the mask the other way by choosing Layer ⇨ Layer Mask ⇨ Reveal All. You have to click the button on the Layers palette or choose Reveal Selection from the Layer Mask submenu (discussed in a moment).

Using a selection is much faster than manually masking out everything around the young woman with the Brush tool. It's not only faster in this case, it's also quite accurate along the edges of the young woman. Keep in mind, though, that you don't have to be this accurate with the initial selection. A loose selection can be used to quickly hide most of the layer, and then the Brush tool can be used to fine-tune the mask. It really depends on the kind of image you're working with. In this example, the crisp outline of the young woman in the original image lends itself to the Magnetic Lasso.

This ability to convert a selection into a mask works both ways: A mask can be loaded as a selection. You may remember back in Chapter 15 that I discussed saving and loading selections, and I noted that a saved selection is saved as a channel in the Channels palette. Well, look at your Channels palette from the preceding exercise. It should look much like the Channels palette in Figure 16.8. This is the same channel that would be created if the selection were saved, rather than converted to a mask.

You've probably already figured this out by now, but to load a mask as a selection, choose Select ➪ Load Selection. When the Load Selection dialog box appears, click OK to load a selection from the channel. You can do this at any time as long as the mask channel is in place.

NOTE **If you modify the mask, the associated channel changes as well.**

FIGURE 16.8

When a mask is created, it becomes its own channel in the Channels palette. This is very similar to what happens when a selection is saved. To load this mask as a selection from the Channels palette, click the indicated button. (You can also load a mask as a selection by Command+clicking/Ctrl+clicking on the mask in the Layers palette.)

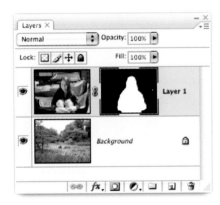
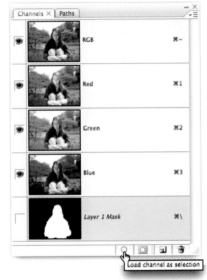

You can load a selection from a mask in two faster ways:

- In the Channels palette, click the Load Channel as Selection button, shown in Figure 16.8.
- Command+click (Ctrl+click) the mask thumbnail in the Layers palette.

TIP **Command+clicking (Ctrl+clicking) any layer content loads it as a selection. In the preceding chapters, you selected a bird and copied it to a new layer. After the bird was isolated on its own layer, it could have been reselected by Command+clicking (Ctrl+clicking) on its thumbnail in the Layers palette.**

As you can see here, selections and masks have a special relationship. This is a great thing to be aware of as you begin to use masks in your retouching workflows.

Comparing Reveal All and Hide All Masks

When you create a new layer mask using the Layer menu (Layer ➪ Layer Mask), your two options are Reveal All and Hide All, as shown in Figure 16.9. The only difference between these two options is the color that's used to fill the mask when it's created:

■ A Reveal All layer mask is filled with white. It's used when a small amount of information is going to be masked out and hidden.

■ A Hide All layer mask is filled with black. It's used when a large amount of information needs to be hidden so that a small amount of information can be revealed by using the Brush tool with white paint.

FIGURE 16.9

You have two options when a layer mask is created via the Layer menu. You can create a Reveal All mask that's white or a Hide All mask that's black. If a selection is active, two more choices appear. You have the choice of revealing or hiding the information in the selection as the mask is created.

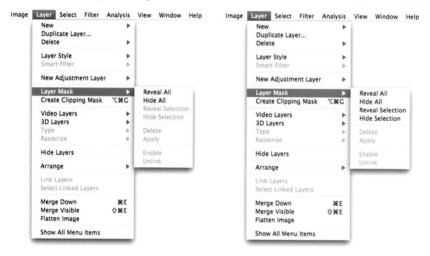

You know that white reveals and black hides information on the layer to which the mask is applied. So it makes complete sense that a layer that reveals all is white and a layer that hides all is black.

CAUTION When you think about masks and the information they reveal and hide, always remember that we're talking about information on the layer that the mask is on, not information that is being seen on layers that are below the masked layer.

Most of the time, you want a mask that reveals all. However, sometimes hiding everything and revealing a small amount of information is faster. For example, I often whiten teeth in a portrait by creating a Hue/Saturation adjustment layer that desaturates the yellows. Then I use the Paint

Bucket to fill the mask with black paint to hide the effect of the adjustment layer. This is the same thing as a Hide All mask. Then I quickly come back and paint the mask white in only the places where the teeth show. This way, the adjustment layer is applied only to the teeth. (You see this technique in Chapter 22.)

TIP To convert a Reveal All mask into a Hide All mask, or vice versa, use the Paint Bucket tool. Fill a mask with white to reveal all, and fill it with black to hide all. You also can fill a selection with paint to affect its area on the mask.

When you create a mask from a selection you have the choice of revealing or hiding the information in the selection by choosing Reveal Selection or Hide Selection from the Layer Mask submenu under the Layer menu, as shown in Figure 16.9. Figure 16.10 shows the difference between these two options when used with a selection.

FIGURE 16.10

In the first example, Reveal Selection is chosen from the Layer Mask submenu. Everything outside the selection is hidden by the mask. In the second example, when Hide Selection is chosen, everything inside the selection is hidden by the mask. The only difference in these images is that the whites and blacks on the mask have swapped positions.

I'll bet you have a question right now. How does the Add Layer Mask button at the bottom center of the Layers palette fit into all of this? Good question. As you saw earlier, when this button is clicked, a Reveal All mask is created. However, you can make it create a Hide All mask instead; simply hold down the Alt key when you click the button to create a Hide All mask. It works the same way with a selection, too. If a selection is active, when you hold the Alt key while clicking the button, the information in the selection is hidden. (I'd hate to tell you how long I used Photoshop before discovering this shortcut!)

Using Masks with Adjustment Layers

Adjustment layers also have a special relationship with layer masks. You may have already noticed it. Whenever you create an adjustment layer, a layer mask is automatically created at the same time. The mask is ready to go; you just have to choose the Brush tool and start painting. Masks are created with adjustment layers because the two are used together extensively.

The image in Figure 16.11 is a portrait of a young man and his musical instrument. A technique that's popular with a portrait like this is to convert everything in the image to black and white, except for the musical instrument. It's reminiscent of a hand-toning effect that film photographers have used since the earliest days of photography. Fortunately, creating this effect with Photoshop is much easier than hand-toning a black-and-white print.

You can use several techniques to create this effect in Photoshop. Some of the solutions are less than elegant because they make permanent changes to the pixels in the image. None of them compare to the ease and flexibility of using an adjustment layer coupled with a layer mask.

To learn how I handle this project, follow these steps:

1. Create a Black & White adjustment layer. (The sliders in this dialog box work much like the grayscale sliders in Lightroom's HSL panel.) This makes the image look like a black-and-white photo. Because it's an adjustment layer, a mask is automatically created.

2. Paint the saxophone with black paint to hide the black-and-white effect of the adjustment layer, allowing the full color of the saxophone to show. (If the musical instrument were a bright color, you could save time by using the Magic Wand to select it before creating the mask instead of painting it in afterward.)

NOTE   **Because there is no image thumbnail on an adjustment layer, you don't need to make sure you're on the mask when painting. If the adjustment layer is the active layer, then you're on the mask.**

The whole process takes about two minutes to create, and it can be removed in a moment by turning off the visibility of the Black & White adjustment layer. Figure 16.12 shows the mask I painted and the Layers palette with the Black & White adjustment layer.

This hand-toning effect is popular in wedding photography. You see it most often in portraits of the bride with her bouquet. Everything in the image is black and white, except for the flowers. The effect causes the flowers to almost jump out of the image.

FIGURE 16.11

A popular technique with a portrait like this is to convert everything except for the instrument to black and white. This is a simple two-step process when using an adjustment layer.

Photo by Denyce Weiler

After the adjustment layer is created, you can paint this mask in a couple of minutes. The color of the musical instrument can be returned to black and white by deleting the mask. Or the image can be returned to full color by turning off the adjustment layer's visibility or completely deleting it.

Combining Selections, Adjustment Layers, and Masks

Now that you have a clear idea of how all of these elements work together, I want to show you one of the ways I most commonly combine the three of them. I always like to have the corners of an image darkened a bit to draw the eye away from its edges. This is something that custom printers have been doing for years in color and black-and-white darkrooms. It's much like the effect of the Vignettes panel in Lightroom's Develop module.

Right now, I want to show you how to use the techniques you've learned so far to darken all the corners of the image at the same time. You're going to do it with a Levels adjustment layer and a mask to keep your workflow flexible. Follow these steps:

1. Open the snow_dog.tif practice file. Adjust the Levels, and make any other adjustments to tone and color that you feel like doing.

2. Select the Elliptical Marquee tool from the Tools palette. Make sure the Feather value is 0px, the Anti-alias option is selected, and Style is set to Normal. Create an elliptical selection that covers most of the central area of the image, as shown in Figure 16.13.

   Remember that you can reposition the selection after it's drawn by placing the cursor inside the selection and then clicking and dragging into position. This way, you don't have to draw it perfectly the first time.

FIGURE 16.13

The first step to darkening all the corners with an adjustment layer is to create a large elliptical selection. This selection is then inverted so that the image surrounding the main subject is selected.

3. After the selection is in place, choose Select ➪ Inverse (Alt+Command/Ctrl+I) to invert it so that the area around the dog is selected.

4. Create a Levels adjustment layer. Change only the middle gray slider. Set it to a value of .50, and click OK. Your image, as well as the mask you created, should now look like the first set of images in Figure 16.14.

   There's a problem here because a step is skipped. I'll bet you know which one. The selection should have been feathered before creating the adjustment layer. I skipped it on purpose because I want you to see the difference.

5. Undo the last step and go back to the end of Step 3 (Command+Z/Ctrl+Z).

6. This time, feather the selection before creating the adjustment layer. Click Refine Edge or press Alt+Command+R (Alt+Ctrl+R) in the Elliptical Marquee tool options. Click the Mask preview button at the bottom right so your selection looks like a mask. Set all Refine Edge values to 0. The hard-edged mask in the preview looks just like the mask for the first image in Figure 16.14.

FIGURE 16.14

In the first set of images, the selection was not feathered before the layer mask was created. You can easily see the effects that a hard-edged mask has on its layer. In the second set of images, the selection was feathered 100px. The feathering creates a soft-edged mask that gradually changes tone.

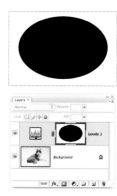

7. Change the Feather value to 100, and click OK. The view goes back to the normal selection view. It's hard to tell that anything has changed.

8. Re-create the Levels adjustment layer, changing only the gray slider value to .50. This time the darkening effect fades as it moves toward the center of the image, as shown in the second set of images in Figure 16.14.

This simple effect combines three of the main Photoshop concepts covered so far: selections, adjustment layers, and masks. This is a good exercise to review whenever you need to refresh your memory about how these three important concepts interact to give you a huge amount of flexibility and control over your editing workflow.

Applying a Gradient to a Mask

As you know, black on a mask hides and white reveals. But what about gray? If you look at the mask in the second set of images in Figure 16.14, you can see that the mask fades from black in the center to white around the edges. The transitional area, created by the feathering, has lots of tones that aren't white or black; they're varying shades of gray. If you compare the mask to the image, you notice that as the gray gets lighter toward the edges of the mask, the effect of the adjustment layer on the image is more revealed.

The first point to make here is that you can paint on a mask with any shade of gray. The darker the shade, the more hidden the layer's information is. This is useful for toning down something without completely hiding it. If you were to create a white Reveal All mask and paint it with 50 percent gray — or better yet, use the Paint Bucket to fill it with 50 percent gray (128, 128, 128) — the layer would be 50 percent hidden. The result is the same as reducing the opacity of a layer filled with 100 percent black to 50 percent.

The second point is that a gradient can be used on a mask to fade it from white to black. The effect is similar to feathering a selection, but it gives you a different kind of control over the mask you create. Here's how that works:

1. Open the snow_dog.tif practice file one last time. (This is the last time you'll see Ruby.) Make any levels or color adjustments you want to make. (If you still have the file open from the preceding exercise, back up to the end of Step 1.)

2. Create a Levels adjustment layer like the one you used in the previous exercise, changing only the gray slider to a value of .50.

3. Select the Gradient tool (G). It's stacked with the Paint Bucket tool, twelfth from the top on the single-column Tools palette. You'll use this tool to draw a gradient on your mask that goes from black to white.

4. Press D to set your color swatches to their default colors of white over black. (When you're on a mask, the default is the opposite of when you are working with the image itself.) Press X to exchange these colors so that the color swatch on top is black (the foreground color) and white is on the bottom (the background color).

5. Go to the options bar to set up the Gradient tool. Click the Gradient Picker pop-up menu, as shown in Figure 16.15, and select the first gradient option: Foreground to Background. Also make sure that the Radial Gradient style is selected, as circled in Figure 16.15.

   Now the Gradient tool will draw a gradient that begins with the foreground color and ends with the background color. As the stroke you draw gets longer, the gradient becomes more gradual. The Radial Gradient mode creates a gradient that radiates in a circular pattern from the center of wherever the gradient is started.

FIGURE 16.15

The Gradient Picker is located on the options bar. Select the Foreground to Background option to make the tool create a gradient that goes from your foreground color to your background color. For this exercise, use the Radial Gradient style (circled).

6. This time, instead of darkening only the corners of the image — something you can do with this tool — you want to draw attention to the dog's face by lightening around it. Click a spot between the dog's eyes, and drag outward a short distance, as shown in Figure 16.16. When you let go of the mouse, a black-to-white radial gradient is drawn on the mask. You can see this mask in Figure 16.16.

   Experiment with shorter and longer strokes so you can see how they affect the image and the mask. Also try adjusting the gray slider value on the Levels adjustment layer to vary the amount of darkening.

> **TIP**   When you use the Gradient tool on a mask, you don't need to undo one gradient before trying another. When a new gradient is created, it replaces the previous one.

As you can see, a mask can be created very quickly with the Gradient tool. You've barely scratched the surface of what can be done with this technique. When the tool is in the Linear Gradient mode — the first mode button in the tool options — it can be used for things like masking the top part of one image with the bottom of another. For example, you can combine an image that has a nice sky with another similar image that has a nice foreground.

FIGURE 16.16

After an adjustment layer is created to darken the entire image, the Gradient tool is used to create a mask with a gradient from black to white. The size of the gradient on the mask is equal to the length of the line drawn with the Gradient tool, as shown in the first image. A short gradient like this lightens a small circular area around the dog's face. Because a gradient is used to create the mask, the transitional boundary from hidden information to revealed information is barely noticeable.

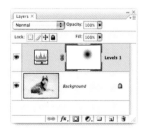

Summary

In this chapter, you learned about layer masking in Photoshop. First, you learned that a mask is used to reveal or hide information on its layer. The main thing to remember here is the basic rule of masking: White on the mask reveals the layer's information, and black on the mask hides the layer's information. You saw how to create masks that reveal all or hide all, and what those two different masks look like.

You also learned that the exactness of a selection can be combined with a mask to create a flexible way to use selections. When a selection is active, you can choose to hide or reveal its contents as you create a mask. You learned that selections and masks have an interesting reciprocal relationship: You can create a mask from a selection as easily as you can create a selection from a mask. You also learned that a saved selection is virtually the same thing as a mask because both become independent channels in the Channels palette.

Next, you saw another way to use adjustment layers by combining them with masks so you can choose which parts of the image are affected by the adjustment layer. Adjustment layers and masks become even more useful when combined with selections. This is a powerful concept that is used often in Photoshop. You will see it again in this book.

Finally, you learned that black and white aren't the only colors used on a mask. Shades of gray are used to control how intense the masking is. A 50 percent gray hides and reveals at the same time by applying masking with a 50 percent opacity — much like adjusting a layer's master opacity. This was demonstrated by using the Gradient tool with a black-to-white gradient to create a localized mask — another useful technique for working with adjustment layers and masks.

When creating a nondestructive retouching workflow, all of these concepts are very important. Make sure that you're comfortable with them before moving on because a clear knowledge of them will serve you well as you learn specific techniques for using them in Part V of this book.

Chapter 17

Using Photoshop's Main Retouching Tools

This chapter focuses on the three main retouching tools in Photoshop: the Clone Stamp, the Healing Brush tool, and the Patch tool. Along the way, you take a couple of side trips to visit some other tools called the Spot Healing Brush and the Liquify filter. By the time you're done, you'll have a complete understanding of how these tools work.

These retouching tools are one of the most important toolsets in the toolbox we call Photoshop. They're used in countless ways to remove imperfections that can be distracting in a photo. Any serious retoucher uses most of them on a daily basis. I encourage you to spend some time exploring them as you move through this chapter because everything you learn here will serve you well when you begin editing your own special images in Photoshop.

Working with Brushes

Some of the tools explored here use what are called *brushes*. A brush is the virtual equivalent of a real paintbrush. It's used to apply colors, tones, and pixel information in a variety of ways for a various number of reasons. Their properties — such as size, hardness, and opacity — can be modified in countless ways to produce just the results that are needed. You begin your exploration of the brush concept in Photoshop with its most basic form: the Brush tool.

Changing brush settings with the options bar and the Brush Preset picker

One basic way of making adjustments to a brush is with the options bar near the top of the screen. Here's how:

1. Create a new file with a blank, white canvas. Choose File ➪ New (Command+N/Ctrl+N). In the New dialog box that appears set the following properties: Width = 6 inches, Height = 4 inches, Resolution = 300, Color Mode = RGB Color/8-bit, and Background Contents = White.

2. This isn't the first time you've needed a new file with these properties. So before clicking OK, click Save Preset. When the New Document Preset dialog box appears, type **4x6 @ 300 white** in the Preset Name text box. Click OK twice, as shown in Figure 17.1.

FIGURE 17.1

After the New file dialog box is completed, a preset is saved when you click Save Preset. When the New Document Preset dialog box appears, give the preset a unique name and click OK.

Now that you've saved these properties as a preset, you can quickly create a file with the same properties in the future by selecting the preset from the Preset pop-up menu in the New dialog box.

> **TIP** Much like Lightroom, you can save presets in a variety of places in Photoshop. You can use them for all kinds of things, from creating new files to saving a set of special properties for a tool. Using presets helps to save time and guarantees that when a particular preset is loaded, the settings are exactly the same every time.

3. Select the Brush tool (B) from the Tools palette. If you don't see the Brush tool in the Tools palette you'll find it stacked with either the Pencil tool or the Color Replacement tool, eighth from the top on the single-column Tools palette.

4. Set your foreground color to black by pressing D (for default foreground and background colors).

5. Before you begin to paint, go to the options bar at the top of the screen, and click the brush sample icon to open the Brush Preset Picker, shown in Figure 17.2. Set the Master Diameter value to 100px, and set the Hardness value to 100%.

TIP A moment ago, you saved a preset for creating new files. Tool presets work in much the same way. You can change the Brush to the preset by choosing the preset's icon in the list. You can save a preset by clicking the Create New Preset button on the pop-up menu, as shown in Figure 17.2. However, with this brush, you don't need to do this. It's already one of the default presets.

FIGURE 17.2

The Brush Preset picker on the options bar provides a quick way to change brush diameter and hardness when the Brush tool is active.

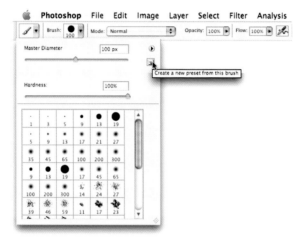

6. Click one side of the new file you opened and drag across the upper part of the white background while holding down the mouse button. You should see a heavy, black line appear on the white background.

TIP If you want the line to be perfectly straight, hold down the Shift key while drawing.

7. Use the Hardness slider on the Brush Preset picker on the options bar to change the hardness to 0% and draw a new line just below the first line.

   Notice that the edges of the line are much softer. Notice also that the line isn't as thick as the first line. The softness of the edge fades in toward the middle of the stroke.

8. Change the Opacity to 50%, and draw a third line below the second line. The new line is just like the previous line except that it's much lighter.

9. Draw another line just like the last one except from top to bottom, as shown in Figure 17.3. Notice that when this line crosses the bottom line, the two strokes combine to create a darker tone that's twice as dark.

   If you want to verify this, use the Eyedropper tool to measure the bottom line where the lines cross and where they don't cross. When I did, the values were 64 and 128, respectively.

377

Recall that you have 256 tones at your disposal (black = 0, and white = 255). The vertical stroke darkened the horizontal stroke by 50 percent.

FIGURE 17.3

Brushes have variable settings like size, hardness, and opacity. Different effects can be achieved by modifying these variables.

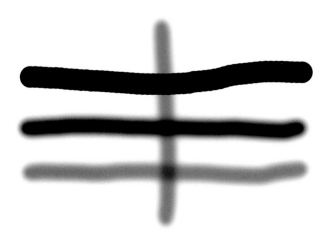

You may have noticed that when two 50 percent opacity strokes cross each other, they don't combine to create 100 percent opacity. That's because each of the 50 percent strokes is simply making the current darkness of the stroke 50 percent darker. Even ten strokes on top of each other don't combine to equal 0 (black). Instead, they equal 1 because no matter how many times you reduce the brightness of the strokes by 50 percent, you can never halve the density to 0.

Here's another useful experiment:

1. Go back to the opening state of the previous file by clicking its thumbnail at the top of the History palette.

2. Set the Brush tool's Master Size to 100px, the Hardness to 100%, and the Opacity to 100%.

3. This time, set Flow to 50% and draw a curvy line across the upper part of the white background.

4. Change the Flow to 25%, and draw a second line below.

   Flow adjusts the rate at which a color is applied as a stroke is drawn. The lower the value, the more spread out the color's application is. With a hard brush, this manifests as overlapping circles, as shown the two top lines in Figure 17.4.

FIGURE 17.4

The Flow setting on a brush affects the rate at which the color is applied. With a hard brush, a stroke looks like overlapping circles. When the brush is soft, the overlapping isn't noticeable.

5. Change the brush's Hardness to 0% and the Flow to 50%, and draw a third line below the first two.

6. Change the Flow to 25%, and draw a fourth line.

7. Change the Flow to 100%, and draw a fifth line at the bottom of the white background.

   Your image should look something like Figure 17.4. Notice that when Flow is lowered with a hard brush, the result is very noticeable. However, when a soft brush is used, the different Flow settings look more like variations in opacity and hardness.

Now that you know all about Flow, I have to tell you that I rarely change it from 100 percent. This section is the last time you change Flow in this book. I included it because I am often asked by students what the Flow setting does.

One more thing to look at in the brush settings on the options bar is the Airbrush setting. This is enabled by clicking the small airbrush icon to the right of the Flow setting (refer to Figure 17.2). When this setting is enabled, paint is continually applied while the mouse button is held down, much like holding a can of spray paint in one place while spraying. Here's how to use the Airbrush setting:

1. Go back to the opening state of the previous file by clicking its thumbnail at the top of the History palette.

2. Set the Brush size to 200 px, Hardness to 50%, Flow to 100%, and Opacity to 50%.

3. Click and hold in one location to paint a soft circle. Notice that no matter how long you hold down the mouse button, the circle doesn't change.

4. Activate the Airbrush feature by clicking the Airbrush button. Now click and hold just as you did above, but in another spot.

   This time, the longer you hold down the mouse button, the more paint is applied, just like an airbrush.

5. Try experimenting with different settings to see what kinds of changes you get. Also try drawing some lines with and without the Airbrush feature turned on.

The results of painting with the Airbrush vary depending on the other brush settings. It's a cool feature to know about when painting with the brush. This feature is available only on the Brush tool and the Clone Stamp tool. You won't use it on the Clone tool when you explore it. However, you return to the Brush tool in Chapter 21 when burning and dodging are covered. That will be a good time to remember the Airbrush feature.

Before moving on to the actual retouching tools, I want to tell you about some great shortcuts you can use when working with brushes. Remember that other tools besides the Brush tool use brushes, so these shortcuts are useful for many of them.

- **To change the brush size, use the bracket ([ ]) keys on your keyboard.** The right bracket makes the brush larger, and the left bracket makes it smaller.

- **To change the hardness in 25 percent increments, press Shift and the right or left bracket.** The left bracket reduces the hardness, and the right bracket increases it. If you are set at 100 percent, pressing Shift+[four times reduces the hardness to 0 percent.

- **To change opacity, use the numbers on the keyboard.** Press 3 to set it to 30 percent or 5 to set it to 50 percent. If you want 55 percent, press 5 twice quickly.

- **To change the brush's flow, press Shift plus the number; Shift+5 equals 50 percent flow.**

- **When the Airbrush feature is active, some of these shortcuts work a little differently.** Pressing numbers on the keyboard changes Flow instead of Opacity. To change the brush's opacity when using the Airbrush, press Shift plus the number. (This is the opposite of when the Airbrush isn't activated.)

Another shortcut I use all the time in Photoshop and other programs is the right-click on the mouse. (I discuss right-clicking for Mac users in the Foreword.) When you right-click in Photoshop, a context-sensitive menu pops up. For tools that use the brush, right-clicking opens the Brush Preset pop-up palette. The only variation is when using the Healing Brush tool or the Spot Healing Brush tool. Because those tools have slightly different brush controls, the context-sensitive pop-up is a little different.

The Brushes palette

With the Brush Preset picker on the options bar and a handful of shortcuts, you can quickly change the main settings on a brush. Sometimes, though, those quick settings aren't enough. When this happens, it's time to go to the Brushes palette.

The Brushes palette, shown in Figure 17.5, is activated by choosing Window ⇨ Brushes, if it's not already showing in the workspace. Each setting in the left Brush Presets menu activates different options on the right. The preview window at the bottom shows how the current selection of settings is affecting the brush.

FIGURE 17.5

The Brushes palette contains a powerful brush engine that allows you to customize every conceivable aspect of a brush. The preview at the bottom of the dialog box shows what a stroke looks like with the current settings.

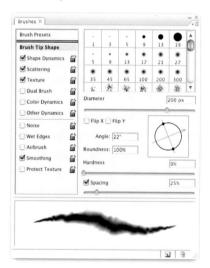

This is where brush power-users come to create their special tools. These people usually are illustrators and painters who use Photoshop in very creative ways. Even though I use Photoshop tools that use brushes, I don't really consider myself one of these power-users. In fact, I rarely go to the Brushes palette because I don't need such sophisticated brushes. I point out the Brushes palette here because I want you to know it exists in case you decide to explore some of the custom settings — and maybe become a brush power-user yourself.

Working with a graphics tablet

I don't know about you, but I can't draw very well with a mouse. Mice are great for moving around and clicking things quickly, but they don't do well when it's time to work on the details. Try using the Brush tool to write your name with your mouse. That's really hard for most people. Mice just aren't built for fine detail and articulation — things that are important when working with many of Photoshop's tools.

This raises another point. Because mice aren't built to be used in the way they're often used, they aren't ergonomic. (I know there are ergonomic mice out there, but they still don't provide the mobility you need.) This can lead to repetitive stress injuries. When mice are used in a very controlling way, the hand muscles tend to get tense, sometimes spreading all the way up our arms and into our necks.

When I really got serious about Photoshop several years ago, I began developing pain in my wrist and neck because I was spending so much time editing. The pain began to diminish the pleasure I was getting from Photoshop. I tried a trackball, but that wasn't any better. After I bought a graphics tablet, my Photoshop life changed. I can now work long hours with much less stress to my body.

> **TIP**
>
> When you spend so much time in front of a computer, be conscious of your working environment. I've met many digital photographers who pour lots of money into their equipment, but never consider the health consequences of working in a non-ergonomic environment. To learn more about ergonomics, see the U.S. Department of Labor's Safety and Health Topics Web site at `www.osha.gov/SLTC/ergonomics/`.

A graphics tablet (see Figure 17.6) consists of a special pen called a stylus and a sensitive tablet that can sense when the pen touches the tablet. Because the action of holding a pen and drawing with it is more natural than using a mouse, the tablet requires much less strain. This natural motion also lends itself to fine articulation and detail work. I often work with mine in my lap to give my arm a rest.

Wacom tablets are the industry standard for graphics tablets. Wacom makes a variety of tablets with different features and sizes under two main lines: Graphire and Intuos. They come in sizes from 4 x 6 inches to 12 x 19 inches. Keep in mind, though, that this is one case where bigger isn't necessarily better. For one thing, a large tablet takes up lots of room on your desk. When moving around the tablet, you have to cover more distance on a large tablet, requiring more hand and arm movement. I have used the 6 x 8 tablet for many years, and I'm completely satisfied with that form-factor.

The pen that comes with a Wacom tablet has two buttons that can be used for right- and left-clicking. In essence, it's like a pen-shaped mouse. You also can click by tapping the tablet; one tap equals one left click, and two quick taps are a double-click. Some of these tablets also come with mice. Personally, I don't care for these mice, so I use a different one that's more ergonomic instead.

Be aware that beginning to use a graphics tablet can be a little disorienting. For one thing, the tablet is mapped to the screen. That is, if the pen is touching the tablet in the lower-left corner, the cursor is in the lower left of the screen. To move the cursor to the top right of the screen, move the pen to the top right of the tablet. This learning curve can take a little time, but it's well worth the effort.

FIGURE 17.6

Wacom tablets come in a variety of sizes. This one is the Intuos 3 6-x-11-inch tablet. The standard size in this range used to be 6 x 8 inches. This one is 3 inches wider to make the form factor match more closely to the wide displays that are being used by so many people today. The 6 x 11 also is more useful for people working with two monitors.

NOTE   You may have noticed that some of the settings in the Brushes palette have a Control setting that allows various features, such as the Shape Dynamics Size Jitter control, to be controlled by pen pressure. These settings are designed to work in conjunction with a graphics tablet. They're more useful for people doing creative painting than for the tasks you do here. I tend to turn these settings to the Off position.

Using the Clone Stamp Tool

The Clone Stamp tool has been with Photoshop since the earliest days. It opened the door to digital retouching as we know it. In essence, the Clone Stamp is used to clone information in an image so that it can be painted into another part of the image. For example, clean skin is *sampled* and painted on top of blemished skin. (You looked at a simplified version of this tool in Lightroom's Develop module in Chapter 7.)

Let's get familiar with this tool and then look at some of the more advanced techniques that are used with it. Follow these steps:

1.   Open the `bird_1.tif` file from the downloadable practice files on the Web site at `www.wiley.com/go/workflow`.

2. Select the Clone Stamp tool (S) from the Tools palette. It's ninth from the top on the single-column Tools palette. Make sure that you're not selecting the Pattern Stamp tool that's stacked with the Clone Stamp.

3. Click the bird's head while holding down the Alt key on your keyboard. (When you press Alt, notice that the cursor changes to a target-like cursor. This is a clue that you are about to sample something.)

4. Set your Brush size to 100px and the Hardness to 0. Make sure the Aligned option is selected on the options bar. Also make sure your Opacity and Flow are set to 100%.

   I tend to work with a soft brush at a setting of 0 until I'm forced to use a harder brush around hard edges.

5. Release the Alt key, and move you cursor to the right side of the image where the sky is mostly empty. Click and begin painting a second bird.

   Notice that two cursors appear as you paint, as shown in Figure 17.7. One cursor is in the area where you're painting, and the other is on the content that's being sampled. As you move the cursor to paint, the sampling cursor follows in alignment, continually updating the information that's being sampled.

> **FIGURE 17.7**
>
> When painting with the Clone Stamp tool, you see two cursors. The cursor on the left indicates where information is being sampled and the cursor on the right shows where the sampled information is being applied. As you paint, the source cursor follows the painting cursor in perfect alignment.

NOTE When the Aligned option is selected, the two Clone Stamp cursors stay in alignment each time you stop and resume painting. When the option is not checked, the sampled pixels from the initial sample area are used for every stroke.

6. After you paint the bird duplicate, it should look something like Figure 17.8.

FIGURE 17.8

The cloning job is complete, but in a few areas I picked up some of the sky around the bird I was sampling, causing some haloing around the new bird.

This image is somewhat forgiving because of the sky and clouds in the background. These soft details lend themselves to blending together. If the background had lots of complicated details, you would have to be more careful about the edges of the duplicate bird blending in.

With that said, there are still a few problems with the duplicate bird in Figure 17.10. A white halo has formed around the bird's tail, beak, and far wingtip caused by clouds around the original bird that were picked up when sampling. You can deal with this in two ways. You could undo the new bird and then repaint it with a smaller brush, especially around the beak and wing. This way works fine, though it can take some trial and error to get just the right size for the job. A faster way to handle this would be to fix the duplicate bird instead of taking the trial-and-error route.

Undoing with the History Brush

Right next to the Clone Stamp tool is another brush tool called the History Brush tool. The History Brush is perfect for solving the problem at hand. The way the History Brush works is that you pick a previous history state from the timeline on the History palette by clicking in the box to the left. After a history state is selected, it can be used to paint that state back into the image. In this case,

385

you want to pick any history state that is previous to the cloning of the bird. By default, the History Brush is set to the opening thumbnail at the top of the History palette, as shown in Figure 17.9, which is exactly what you want.

FIGURE 17.9

Any history state in the History palette can be used for sampling with the History Brush by clicking the box to the left of the history state you want to sample. By default, the History Brush is set to sample the opening state of the image: the thumbnail at the top. You can tell because the History Brush icon is in the box to the left of the thumbnail.

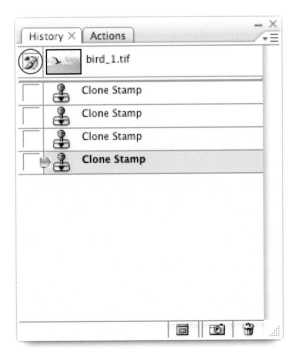

Let's play with the History Brush for a minute:

1. Go back to Step 6 in the preceding set of steps. Select the History Brush (Y) from the Tools palette. It's tenth from the top on the single-column Tools palette. Make sure you aren't selecting the Art History Brush that's stacked with the History Brush.

2. Select a small, soft brush and paint away the halos around the bird by replacing them with the blue that was there before the cloning. Zoom in to make it easier to see what you're doing.

   If your brush is too soft, you'll have a hard time getting a nice edge along the wing because the softness of the brush bleeds over to the wing. Try a harder brush with an opacity of 50 to 75 percent. If you still have problems with the edge of the wing, try reducing the opacity of the History brush to 50 percent to get a better blend along the edge.

3. If you need to paint some of the wing or beak back in, use the History brush. Select the last Clone Stamp history state in the timeline on the History palette by clicking in the box next to it. Don't close the image yet, because you use it again in just a moment.

NOTE Be aware that this tool is tied to the History palette. That means that when the file is closed, all history states are lost. So be sure to use this tool, if necessary, before closing the file.

Cloning from one image to another

You could continue cloning the original bird until the image is full of birds. The problem with this is that each bird would be identical to the first bird so the image wouldn't look very convincing. You can solve that problem by opening another image and cloning a different bird into the first image:

1. Go back to the `bird_1.tif` image that you worked on earlier. If the image is not currently open, open it again.

2. Open the `bird_2.tif` file from the downloadable practice files from the Web site. You should now have two images open. Position them so you can see both images.

3. Select the Clone Stamp (S), and use the Alt key to sample the bird in `bird_2.tif`.

TIP When you work with multiple files it's necessary for an image to be the active image before you can sample from it or paint onto it. To make an image the active image click on it or its header.

4. Go back to `bird_1.tif`, and begin painting the new bird in between the two existing birds. When you finish, your image should look something like Figure 17.10.

As you can see, the Clone Stamp is a versatile tool. You can handle all sorts of retouching issues with it by sampling (copying) part of an image and painting (pasting) the new information into another part of the image — or an entirely different image. Now, with a new feature in Photoshop CS3 that's called the Clone Source palette, the Clone Stamp is even more powerful.

Using the new Clone Source palette in Photoshop CS3

One of the cool new features in Photoshop CS3 is the Clone Source palette, shown in Figure 17.13. This new palette provides a number of features that enhance the performance of the Clone Stamp and the Healing Brush tools:

- **You can save up to five different sample sources** by clicking the Clone Source buttons at the top before sampling with the Alt key.

- **You can t**ransform — rotate or scale — the source material as it's being painted in.

- **An overlay can be displayed** to help with positioning cloned data as it's applied.

FIGURE 17.10

The Clone Stamp tool can be used to duplicate information from one file into another. To do this, sample the content of one file by Alt+clicking, and then paint the new information into the second file.

Try out some of these new features on your bird photos. Saving multiple Clone Source points is pretty straightforward, so the focus here is on the other two features — rotate/scale and the overlay:

1. Open the `bird_1.tif` file from the practice files on the Web site. If the file currently is open from the preceding exercise, close it and reopen it by choosing File ➪ Open Recent ➪ bird_1.tif. Also make sure that `bird_2.tif` is closed.

TIP The Open Recent menu gives you access to the last ten files that were opened or saved. You can change the number of files that appear in this menu in the File Handling preferences in Photoshop's Preferences.

2. Select the Clone Stamp tool, and make the Clone Source palette visible by choosing Window ➪ Clone Source. Select the Show Overlay option.

3. Sample the bird using the Alt key, just as you did in the first exercise with this file. After the sample has been made, the clone overlay appears, as shown in Figure 17.11.

4. When the overlay is positioned where you want it, click and begin painting. If you don't want to see the overlay while you paint, select the Auto Hide option on the Clone Source palette.

    This overlay feature is really nice. It allows you to see what you're cloning before you paint it. The overlay really shines when combined with the rotate/scale feature.

FIGURE 17.11

The new Clone Source palette in Photoshop CS3 provides a number of enhanced controls for the Clone Stamp and Healing Brush tools.

5. Now, undo any cloning you just did. The image should look like it did when it was opened. The sample point you selected previously should still be active.

6. Go to the Clone Source palette and change the scale of the width to 50 percent. Now the sampled data should be half the size in the overlay. Begin painting again. This time the bird is smaller, so it looks like it's farther away — a much more convincing effect than cloning at 100 percent.

> **TIP** A great way to work with the scale and rotation boxes is to use scrubby sliders to change the values. When the Overlay is active, any settings changes are previewed as soon as they're made, which provides an interactive way of finding the best setting for what you need.

7. Type a value of **180** into the Rotation box just below the W and H boxes. Notice that the preview in the Overlay is upside down, which is not such a convincing effect!

8. Try one more setting. Reset all transform settings by clicking the Reset Transform button to the right of the Rotation box, the one with a circular arrow on it. This time, change the width setting to **-100%**. Now the preview is a mirror image of the bird.

Making either the width or height a negative value flips the cloned content on its vertical axis, causing it to display a mirror image, as shown in Figure 17.12.

This new palette adds a huge amount of flexibility to the Clone Stamp tool. Spend some time familiarizing yourself with it now, so that you'll be comfortable with it when the right opportunity presents itself.

FIGURE 17.12

To get a mirror of the cloned source data, change either the width or height value to a negative number.

Working with Tool Blending Modes

As you can see, the Clone Stamp tool is quite useful for sampling information and painting it back into the image in a different spot. In the preceding exercises, you used it to add new visual content to the image. When using this tool for retouching jobs, the thinking is a little different, even though the process is quite similar. With retouching, the objective is usually to hide something in the image by copying information on top of it. For example, when retouching a blemish on someone's face, clean skin is sampled and painted on top of the blemish to hide it. New content is being added to the image, but in a way that it doesn't draw attention to itself.

This sample-and-paint method works quite well when retouching blemished skin in a portrait as long as the skin being sampled is the same color as the area into which it's being painted. If the sampled skin is darker or lighter — even by a small amount — the retouching is noticeable.

When you run into this scenario, you can modify the Clone Stamp tool so that those differences in tone are easier to manage. The main way of gaining control over the Clone Stamp is to change the tool's blending mode.

In Chapter 14, you used layer blending modes to change the way one layer blended with the layer below it. You've probably noticed that the Brush and Clone Stamp tools also have a blending mode drop-down menu on the options bar. It's located just to the left of the Opacity setting (refer to Figure 17.2).

These tool blending modes work in the same way as layer blending modes do, except that they only affect strokes that are painted with the tool, rather than the entire layer. This is extremely useful when working with the Clone Stamp. The two blending modes you're interested in here are the Lighten and Darken modes. Here's what these modes do:

- **The Lighten mode** affects tones that are darker than the sampled tone. Any tones that are lighter than the sampled tone are unaffected.

- **The Darken mode** works in the same way, but with the opposite effect. Tones lighter than the sampled tone are lightened. Tones darker than the sampled tones are unaffected.

Figure 17.13 compares the difference between using the Clone Stamp with the blending mode set to Normal and Lighten. In this example, I'm attempting to tone down the dark blemish in the center of this young woman's forehead; you can see it in the first, unretouched image. In the second image, I sampled the skin just to the left of the blemish and painted it on top of the blemish. I did this in a slightly exaggerated way so that you can see the effect. In the third image, I did everything exactly the same, except that I changed the blending mode on the Clone Stamp to Lighten. Now you can see that only the dark tones of the blemish have been replaced, while the surrounding lighter tones are unaffected.

> **TIP** Another way to gain control over the Clone Stamp tool is to decrease its Opacity so that you're not painting with 100 percent of the sampled tones.

I find this technique to be most useful when working with retouching problems such as flyaway hair. If I'm dealing with light-colored hair against a dark background, I select the Darken mode. If I'm dealing with dark-colored hair against a light background, I select the Lighten mode. This technique also can be used in a variety of other scenarios—like wrinkles and folds in skin. However, in most of those cases, I prefer to use two more powerful retouching tools called the Healing Brush and the Patch tool.

Using the Healing Brush

The Healing Brush tool (J) appeared in Photoshop 7, and it completely changed the way digital retouchers work. (You looked at a simplified version of this tool in Lightroom's Develop module in Chapter 7.) The Healing Brush is similar to the Clone Stamp in that information is sampled by Alt+clicking and then painted into other parts of the image. The big difference is that the Healing Brush attempts to make the sampled data match the lighting and shading of the area to which it's being applied. In other words, it looks at the area where the sampled data is being applied and tries to make the sampled information match the target area. This is huge! Before the Healing Brush, you had to fiddle with the Clone Stamp's blending modes and Opacity setting to get it to work just right. With the Healing Brush, all that trial and error is eliminated.

FIGURE 17.13

In this demonstration, the goal is to lighten the dark blemish in the center of this young woman's forehead (top image). First, I use the Clone Stamp with the blend mode set to Normal. The slightly darker skin that is sampled is too obvious (center image). I undid that cloning and changed the blending mode to Lighten. Now only the darker areas are being affected by the cloning and the retouching is barely noticeable (bottom image).

 Before getting into the nuts and bolts of the Healing brush, I want to show you just how powerful it is. Go back to the image of the young woman. This time, instead of sampling her skin, I'm going to sample the black background to the right and apply it to the blemish, as shown in the first image in Figure 17.13. At first, this might look like I've lost my marbles. However, when I let go of the mouse button, the transparency, lighting, and shading of the black sample is changed to match the skin tones where it's being applied, as shown in the second image in Figure 17.14. If I had sampled the light-colored sweater to the left instead of the black background on the right, the tones would have still blended, but the texture of the sweater would be noticeable.

> **NOTE** Because of this blending capability, the Healing Brush doesn't always do a good job of making a literal copy, like what you were doing with the bird photos earlier.

FIGURE 17.14

The Healing Brush tool does such a good job of blending that it's able to blend the sample of the dark background to the right of the woman into the skin tones nearly seamlessly.

This young woman has plenty of clear skin that I could have sampled instead of the dark background. Sometimes, though, that's not the case. By using any area in the image that doesn't have a strong texture — like the background here — you can build an area of smooth skin that can be used as a sample area for further retouching.

Even though the Healing Brush is a brush tool, the options for setting it up are a little different than the Clone Stamp or the Brush tool. The first thing you notice is that it doesn't have an Opacity setting. This can be a bit disconcerting at times. (I show you how to deal with it in a moment.) Another big difference is that the Brush pop-up menu on the options bar isn't the same. Figure 17.15 shows what it looks like.

Something else you might have noticed is that when the Healing Brush is selected, all the options on the Brushes palette are grayed out. That means that you can't use the Brushes palette with this tool. The few features that are available have been moved to the pop-up Brushes menu in Figure

17.15. You already know about the Diameter and Hardness settings, so let's look at the other options on this menu:

- **Spacing controls the distance** between the marks that are laid down when a brush stroke is made. The value is a percentage of the size of the brush. When higher values are used, the brush stroke skips along, laying down a series of dots rather than a solid line. I seldom raise this any higher than 1 percent, which is the lowest value.

- **Angle controls the rotation** of the long axis from horizontal. This setting can be used to create a chiseled effect.

- **Roundness controls the ratio** between the long axis and the short axis of the brush. The lower the value, the more linear (rather than round) the brush is.

- **The Size pop-up menu** allows you to use pen pressure on a graphics tablet to vary the size of the stroke. The harder you press, the bigger the stroke. In Figure 17.15, you'll notice a warning icon just to the right of this setting, which indicates that a graphics tablet is not currently connected to the system.

- **The Brush Preview** allows you to see changes to the shape of the brush when values for Angle and Roundness are modified. You also can click and grab sections of this display to interactively change settings.

FIGURE 17.15

The Brush pop-up menu for the Healing Brush is different than the Clone Stamp's pop-up menu. The main thing that's missing is an Opacity slider.

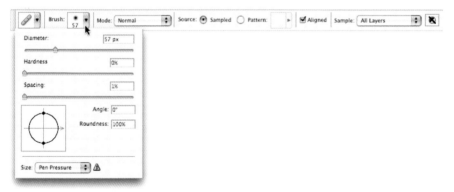

Now that I've explained these settings, I want to tell you that it's pretty rare for me to change them. I find that I can accomplish what I need to do by working mostly with Diameter and Hardness. In fact, I always retouch with a graphics tablet, yet I turn off pen pressure because I want to control brush diameter with a fixed setting, rather than the pressure of my pen.

The Healing brush also has a Blending Mode pop-up menu on the options bar, though the options are more limited than with the other brush tools. These additional settings on the options bar are worthy of note:

- **Source determines where source data comes from.** When set to Sampled, the Alt key is used to sample image information. When set to Pattern, a pattern from the Pattern pop-up menu (which is activated when this is selected) is used. I always leave this set at Sampled. (I cover the Sample settings when I talk about retouching multiple layers.)
- **Aligned is the same as the Aligned setting in the Clone Stamp options.** When this option is selected, sample points are aligned with the brush as it moves. When it is deselected, the original selection is used for every new stroke.

The new Clone Source palette, which you explored when the Clone Stamp was discussed, also can be used with the Healing Brush. I find the overlay settings to be quite useful here, too.

As demonstrated earlier, the Healing Brush is a powerful tool. However, the blending features that make this tool so powerful also can cause it to fail miserably in certain circumstances. Whenever this tool is used in an area where there's a big difference between light and dark tones, it gets confused. This confusion manifests itself as a smear in the image.

Go back to the image of the young woman. Imagine that I want to retouch something on the edge of the white hood she's wearing. I sample the white area to the left and paint a stroke along the edge of the hood. When I do this, the tool wants to blend my stroke with the underlying tones. But it gets confused because it doesn't know if I'm interested in the light tones or the dark tones, so it gives me a little of each—a dark smear, as shown in Figure 17.16.

There are two ways to deal with this scenario. The first is to switch to our old friend, the Clone Stamp tool. The other is to use a selection to isolate the area so that tones outside of the selection are not used in the Healing Brush's calculations.

Busting Dust with the Spot Healing Brush

The Spot Healing Brush is a close cousin to the Healing Brush. They're both stacked together, along with the Patch tool and the Red Eye tool. The Spot Healing Brush has the same blending abilities as the Healing Brush. The main difference is that sampling isn't done with the Alt key. This tool automatically creates a sample from around the area that's being retouched, much like the Spot Removal tool in Lightroom's Develop module, except that you can't adjust the area the Spot Healing Brush samples from. This can cause some problems when detail you don't want to sample is being sampled. The Spot Healing Brush works best in areas that are low in detail, such as backgrounds. This tool is most useful when cleaning up dust on scans, or removing dSLR sensor dirt from a background.

 The first image in Figure 17.17 shows a photo of my mother that was taken many years ago. It has a number of dirt and mold spots in the sky and on her dress. The Spot Healing Brush is the perfect tool for handling these spots because of the lack of detail in these areas.

FIGURE 17.16

The powerful Healing Brush tool can be fooled easily when it's used along an edge with strong contrast. This confusion appears as a smear in the image.

To quickly remove these spots, I select the Spot Healing Brush, adjust the brush size so that it's a little bigger than the spots I'm removing, and simply click them to remove them. The second image shows what the image looks like after about two minutes of work with the Spot Healing Brush. Retouching doesn't get much faster than this!

Two of the tool options for the Spot Healing Brush to note are Proximity Match and Create Texture:

- **Proximity Match** uses pixels around the selection to generate the sampled data.
- **Create Texture** uses the pixels in the selection to create a texture that is used to fill the area being painted.

For the example in Figure 17.19, each of these settings worked equally well. However, if you don't like the results of one setting, try the other.

Using the Patch Tool

As useful as the Healing Brush is, I prefer to use the Patch tool for a large percentage of my retouching. The Patch tool is stacked with the Healing Brush and the Spot Healing Brush, and it works in a very similar way. The main difference is in the way image information is sampled and applied. This tool uses a selection instead of a brush. A selection is drawn and then dragged to the area to be sampled. When the mouse button is released, the sampled information fills the original selection and blends it in the same way as the Healing Brush does. To see how this tool works, follow these steps:

1. Open the `portrait_1.tif` file from the downloadable practice files from the Web site.

2. Select the Patch tool (J) from the Tools palette. It's stacked with the Healing Brush, seventh from the top on the single-column Tools palette. Make sure that Source is selected on the options bar next to Patch.

> **TIP** To quickly select a tool that's stacked underneath another tool, press Shift along with the tool's shortcut key to cycle through the stacked tools. In this case, press Shift+J. (To make this work, be sure to select the Use Shift for Tool Switch option in Photoshop's General preferences; it is already selected by default.)

3. In this example, we want to tone down the lines under the woman's eyes. Click and draw a selection around the lines under the right eye, as shown in the first image in Figure 17.18. Keep the selection a little loose around the outside so it's not too close to the detail that's being removed.

FIGURE 17.17

This old photo has several dirt and mold spots in the sky and on her dress. These can be removed in a number of ways with the retouching tools in Photoshop, but the Spot Healing Brush is the fastest. With only a couple of minutes' work, the spots are removed.

FIGURE 17.18

Fixing the lines under this young woman's eyes is a perfect job for the Patch tool. A selection is drawn around the area with the Patch tool (first image). The selection is moved to an area with clean skin (second image). When the mouse button is released, the pixels from the clean skin are pasted and blended into the original selection (third image). Because the blend is a little too strong, the Fade command (fourth image) is used to reduce the Patch tool's effect to 60 percent.

TIP Selections can be created using any of the selection tools covered in Chapter 15. You just have to switch back to the Patch tool to use it after creating the selection.

4. Move the cursor so it's inside of the selection. Notice that a small box appears next to the cursor as in the first image of Figure 17.18.

   When the cursor is inside of the selection, you can click and drag the selection to the area you want to sample. If the cursor is outside of the selection, a click erases the selection and begins a new one.

5. Click inside the selection and hold down the mouse button while dragging it to the top of her forehead where the skin has the least amount of texture, as shown in the second image in Figure 17.18. Don't get too close to the hairline.

   As you move the cursor, you'll notice that the original selection under the eye is constantly being updated with the information that's inside the second cursor. This preview is extremely useful when patching an area that contains detail such as lines or patterns. Using the preview, you can line up these patterns before releasing the mouse button.

6. When the selection is in place, release the mouse button. When you do, the information in the original selection is replaced with the information from the second selection. Choose Select ➪ Deselect (Command+D/Ctrl+D) to deactivate the selection. Now you can see that the lines under the eye have been eliminated, as shown in the third image in Figure 17.18.

   The only problem with what you just did is that the effect is too strong. Even though this woman is young, she should still have some definition under her eye to give it shape. Because the Patch tool — like the Clone Stamp — doesn't have an Opacity setting as an option, you have to use something else to reduce the effect of the tool.

7. Go back two steps in the History palette's timeline. You should now be at the point where the selection was first created with the lines showing under her eye. Drag the selection to the skin at the top of her head, and release the mouse button — just as you did in Steps 5 and 6 previously.

8. Before you do anything else, choose Edit ➪ Fade Patch Selection (Shift+Command+F/Shift+Ctrl+F) to open the Fade dialog box. Move the slider to the left until you see just enough of the lines reappear to give the eye socket some shape, as shown in the fourth image in Figure 17.18.

   The Fade command allows you to fade the last thing that you did so that you can select the opacity you want. This is also how you adjust the opacity of strokes painted by the Healing Brush. When retouching portraits, I use the Fade command constantly.

> **TIP** The Fade command can be used after just about anything you do in Photoshop. I find this extremely useful. It allows me to overdo something and then fade it back to the point where I like it. The key to using Fade is that it must be the very next thing you do. For example, if you deselect the selection first, the Fade command under the Edit menu is grayed out.

> **NOTE** Instead of using Fade, you could do all retouching on a separate layer and then lower the opacity of the layer. However, the Fade command allows you to adjust the opacity of individual actions instead of everything on the layer at once.

9. I want you to see how powerful this tool is. Back up again to Step 3 using the History palette. This time, drag the selection to the dark background in the top right of the image and release the mouse button. When you do, notice that the background tones are blended in to match the skin tones — very much like the Healing brush. The effect is even softer than when you sampled the skin on her forehead because the background doesn't have as much texture as the skin you sampled earlier. Use the Fade command to tone it down.

10. Follow the same procedures to retouch the lines under the left eye.

The tool options for the Fade command on the options bar are fairly simple. On the left, just to the right of the Tool Presets box, are four small buttons. These allow you to modify your selection by adding to it or subtracting, just like the tool options for the main selection tools.

To the right of these buttons are two radio buttons that control what area is being patched. There are two settings: Source and Destination. When Destination is selected, the information from the selection you first draw is dragged and dropped when you move the selection — sort of the opposite of the effect of selecting the Source button. This can be quite useful when working quickly to clean up a background. When you select the Transparent option, only the texture of the sample area is used as a sample. None of the color and tone information is sampled.

You should be aware of a couple of things when using the Patch tool. Quite often, you need to do a little cleanup around the edges of the patched area with the Healing Brush, or the Patch tool itself, so that the edges blend a little better, especially when patching large areas. Another issue with the Patch tool is that it suffers from the same smudging problem as the Spot Healing Brush when patching areas that are near edges of high contrast or the edge of the image frame.

Fixing Red Eye

The Red Eye tool first appeared in Photoshop Elements, Photoshop's little brother. The tool was brought into the full version of Photoshop with the release of Photoshop CS2. The Red Eye tool, which is stacked with the Healing Brush, offers a quick and efficient way for dealing with red eye.

This tool works much like the Red Eye tool in Lightroom's Develop Module. In fact, for the purposes of this book, red eye should be removed during the production phase of the workflow. However, there are times when a red eye slips through the Production Workflow without being fixed. That's why I want to spend a moment exploring it here.

As I mentioned in Chapter 7, red eye is caused by light reflecting off the retina and bouncing back into the lens of the camera. It usually appears when a camera's flash is on the same plane as the lens. The effect is more pronounced in subjects who have gray or blue eyes, as well as children.

Figure 17.19 shows a photo of my two dogs, Hazel and Ruby. Whenever I point a camera with an on-camera flash at Ruby, the Husky on the right, I get red eye. (I've noticed this with other blue-eyed dogs as well.)

FIGURE 17.19

Photoshop's Red Eye tool makes fixing red eye a snap. With the Red Eye tool, a selection is drawn around the eye. When the mouse button is released, the red disappears.

To fix this, I draw a selection with the Red Eye tool that encompasses the eye, as shown in the second image. Because this tool works only on red, I don't have to be very careful with the selection. After the selection is in place, I release the mouse button and the red eye is instantly eliminated, as shown in the third image in Figure 17.19. Something that would have taken a bit of doing with other techniques a few years ago now takes less than a minute with the Red Eye tool.

NOTE Because this tool works with the color red, I was able to use it to remove a piece of Ruby's red collar that was poking out through her fur.

The Red Eye tool has only two options: Pupil Size and Darken Amount. By default, both of these are set to 50 percent. Try adjusting these values if you're not getting the results you want.

Retouching with Layers

In Chapter 14, using layers to create flexibility in the workflow by isolating permanent changes to individual layers is discussed. The main reason for doing this is to minimize the destructive nature of some of the things you do in Photoshop. "Destructive" may seem like a harsh term when you are, in fact, making the image better. What the term really refers to is the fact that original pixel data is being replaced by something else. After that happens, it may not be possible to undo the change.

As you probably understand by now, any retouching tool that samples pixel data from one part of the image and paints/drops it into another part of the image is destructive by its very nature — pixels are being permanently altered. After those tools have been used and the image has been closed, those changes can't be undone. Therefore, you must learn various retouching strategies that protect the original properties of the underlying image.

The most fundamental way of accomplishing this is to duplicate the layer that's being retouched — quite often the Background layer — and doing all retouching on it instead of the original layer. That way, if you don't like something, you can remove it — or the whole layer — and begin again by duplicating all or part of the original layer.

Sampling multiple layers

In recent versions of Photoshop, Adobe has addressed this issue by adding limited multilayer retouching. This feature has been taken to a whole new level with the release of Photoshop CS3. In the tool options for the Clone Stamp, the Healing Brush, and the Spot Healing Brush, you may have noticed the Sample pull-down menu, which hasn't been discussed yet. This menu allows you to choose which layers are being sampled. You have these three options, as shown in Figure 17.20:

- **Current Layer:** Only pixels from the current layer are sampled.
- **Current & Below:** Only pixels from the current layer and below are sampled.
- **All Layers:** All layers are sampled.

FIGURE 17.20

Now you can have more control over layers when sampling for cloning or healing by selecting which layers are being sampled. Adjustment layers can be specifically ignored by clicking the button just to the right of the Sample pull-down menu.

NEW FEATURE The Clone Stamp, the Healing Brush, and Spot Healing Brush have a new setting in their tool options that allows for much greater flexibility when using retouching tools with multilayered images. When Current & Below is selected in the Source pop-up menu, any layers above

the current layer are ignored. Additionally, a new button on the right allows you to ignore adjustment layers when sampling.

In Photoshop CS2, the options were limited to all layers or the current layer. The choice was made in CS2 by clicking in a check box next to Sample All Layers. The extra option of Current & Below allows you to arrange the layers you're working with so you sample only the layers you're interested in. After the retouching is done, the layers can be rearranged if needed.

One of the most popular ways of using this multilayer sampling ability is to create an empty layer above the layer to be retouched so that all new retouching is added to the empty layer. Let's try it:

1. Open the `bird_1.tif` practice file.

2. Create an empty layer above by choosing Layer ⇨ New ⇨ Layer and then clicking OK. The new layer, Layer 1, is added to the top of the layer stack and becomes the active layer.

3. Select the Clone brush from the Tools palette, and change Sample to All Layers. Also, make sure that the blending mode is set to Normal.

4. Let's clone the bird onto a separate layer. Set the brush's Diameter and Hardness to the settings of your choice. Alt+click to sample the bird, and begin painting it into a new place in the sky.

   When you finish, the image should look like one of the preceding exercises, with two birds in the sky. The difference is that the cloned bird is on Layer 1. Let's verify it.

5. Click the eyeball icon next to the Background layer to hide the layer. Now the cloned bird should look something like Figure 17.21.

FIGURE 17.21

When you select Sample All Layers in the Sample pop-up menu, you can place cloned data on its own layer using the Clone Stamp. This can be verified by turning off the visibility of the Background layer.

The important thing here is that the Background layer is undisturbed, which can be verified by turning its visibility back on and turning off the visibility of Layer 1. This is an effective way of quickly isolating retouching done with the Clone Stamp, the Healing Brush, or the Spot Healing Brush.

Ignoring adjustment layers

Another setting in this new feature is a button just to the right of the Sample pop-up menu that allows you to ignore adjustment layers when cloning or healing. When all layers are being sampled and adjustment layers are present, the effect of the adjustment layers is duplicated. This is really easy to see by doing a simple experiment. Follow these steps:

1. Open a new file by choosing File ➪ New, and give it the following properties: Width = 6 inches, Height = 4 inches, Resolution = 300, Color Mode = RGB Color/8-bit, and Background = White. If you created the "4x6 @ 300 white" preset in the New dialog box earlier in this chapter, use it to quickly create this file.

2. Choose Edit ➪ Fill, and select 50% Gray from the Contents pop-up menu. At this point, you should be looking at a gray Background layer.

3. Create a Levels adjustment layer by choosing Layer ➪ New Adjustment Layer ➪ Levels, and change the middle, gray slider to 1.48. Don't change the white-point slider or the black-point slider. When you click OK, the gray of the image gets lighter.

4. Make the Background layer active again by clicking it.

5. Select the Clone Stamp (S) tool from the Tools palette, and change the brush diameter to 200px. You can use the Hardness setting of your choice. Make sure that the Blending Mode is set to Normal and Opacity is 100 percent.

6. Choose All Layers from the Sample pop-up menu on the options bar, and make sure the Ignore Adjustment Layers button is not clicked.

7. Choose any spot you want, and Alt+click to sample it. Scoot the cursor over a bit, and paint a small circle. When you do this, notice that the circle you just painted is lighter than the gray you sampled. That's because the lightening effect of the Levels adjustment layer was doubled when it was sampled.

8. The way this used to be dealt with was to turn off the visibility of any adjustment layers when sampling all layers. Let's try it. Click the eyeball icon next to the Levels layer. You don't even need to resample because you already have a sample loaded. Just paint another circle. This time, you can't see your painting because it's the same color as the sample.

9. Turn the Levels layer visibility back on. On the options bar, click the Ignore Adjustment Layers button and paint again. The painted gray is the same tone as the sampled gray. The effect is the same as turning the adjustment layer's visibility off.

The inadvertent sampling of adjustment layers when all layers are selected for sampling has thrown many a novice retoucher for a loop because he or she didn't realize that the adjustment layer's effects were being multiplied. Now that you know what this problem looks like, you can take appropriate action, like clicking the Ignore Adjustment Layers icon on the options bar.

I imagine you've already guessed what my biggest problem is with this technique for retouching on a separate, empty layer. These options aren't available with my favorite retouching tool, the Patch tool. I use the Patch tool extensively when retouching, so I duplicate the main layer and do most of the retouching on that duplicate layer instead of using an empty layer. The biggest difference is that duplicating an image layer increases the size of the file more than using an empty layer for retouching.

Body Sculpting with the Liquify Filter

Photoshop has a highly specialized retouching tool called the Liquify filter. This tool is so specialized that I rarely use it. However, when conditions are right, few retouching tools can match the Liquify filter's abilities.

The Liquify filter works by distorting the image with tools like Warp, Pucker, and Bloat. The Liquify filter is located in the top section of the Filters menu, accessed by choosing Filter ➪ Liquify. Figure 17.22 shows the Liquify dialog box. As you can see, the Liquify filter is complex. On the left is a set of tools that affect the filter's distortion in different ways. On the right side are a number of options for fine-tuning the effects of those tools.

FIGURE 17.22

On the left of the Liquify filter's dialog box is a set of tools with names like Warp, Pucker, and Bloat. On the right are various tool options that are used to fine-tune the way the tools on the left affect the image.

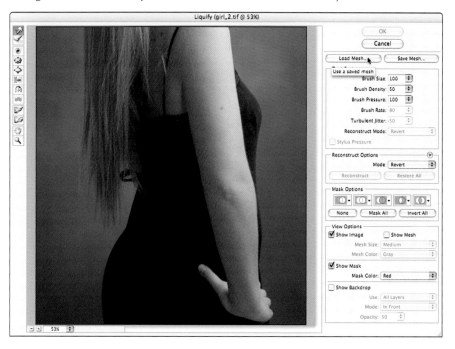

I could write an entire chapter about the Liquify filter. My goal here is to introduce it so that you're aware of it. I hope you'll be inspired to explore this filter further after you see what you can quickly accomplish with it.

In this example, the woman in Figure 17.22 doesn't like the way her dress looks because the camera angle distorted it. She felt that it was sticking out farther than it does in reality. This is the sort of problem that the Liquify filter is well suited for solving. The goal here is to distort the image so that the protruding fabric is minimized.

For this job, I selected the Push Left tool from the Tools palette on the left, sixth from the top. The Push Left tool moves pixels to the left when you click and drag straight up. When the cursor is dragged downward, the tool moves pixels to the right. Here, I want to move the pixels around her bottom to the right, so I drag the tool downward while holding down the mouse button. The first image in Figure 17.23 shows the effect of dragging and moving pixels to the right. The second image shows what the woman looks like after the stroke is completed. This was all done with a single stroke.

FIGURE 17.23

As the Push Left tool is dragged downward, pixels under the brush are moved to the right. Using only a single downward stroke, this problem is solved.

This filter works so well here because the background is simple. The image lends itself to being liquefied. If the background contained lots of detail — like an outdoor portrait in a garden — adjustments like this would require more work. As it is, the only area that needs to be cleaned up with the Clone Stamp or Healing Brush is where the bottom tips of her hair were also distorted to the right. This kind of cleanup is quite common when using the Liquify filter.

TIP   Use Liquify's Freeze tool to paint a mask onto areas you don't want to affect. You also can use an existing mask.

NOTE   The Liquify filter is a resource hog. If you're working on a large file, it can take quite a while to load and execute. When working with a large file, use a selection to isolate the area being worked on before opening the Liquify filter. That way, only the selected area is loaded into the Liquify filter's dialog box, which speeds up the process quite a bit.

Again, you're barely scratching the surface of what this filter is capable of. I encourage you to spend time exploring it in more depth. When you get playful with it, you can create some really interesting and creative visual effects.

Summary

This chapter introduced a number of retouching tools and some of the ways in which they're used. At the heart of some of these tools are brushes that can be modified almost endlessly. You started off by looking at brushes in general to get the concept of how brushes are modified and fine-tuned using the Brush pop-up menu on the options bar and the Brushes palette. Learn to use the most basic setting for these brushes before becoming dazzled by the cool, custom brushes that can be created with the Brushes palette.

Then you looked at some of the tools that use brushes, like the Clone Stamp, the Healing Brush, and the Spot Healing Brush. You found that the Clone Stamp is useful when literal duplicates need to be created and that the Healing Brush is most useful when you need to blend retouching strokes. The Spot Healing Brush is best suited for quickly removing spots.

You then explored my favorite retouching tool, the Patch tool, which is a close cousin to the Healing brush. This tool uses selections for sampling and pasting pixel information from one part of an image to another. You should learn to use the Fade command with this tool to get the most from it.

You saw how easy it is to use the Clone Stamp and the Healing Brush/Spot Healing Brush on a separate layer by selecting which layers are sampled in the Source setting on the options bar. This allows you to isolate retouching strokes to their own layer. The only drawback to this technique is that it isn't available with the Patch tool.

Last, you took a quick look at the powerful Liquify filter. In the right scenario, this tool can be hard to beat when compared with other retouching tools and techniques. Remember, if you're working with a large file, you can speed up the process by using a selection to isolate the area you want to work on before invoking the Liquify filter.

Chapter 18

Using Photoshop Actions with Lightroom

One of the most powerful things about Photoshop is one of the least used. I'm referring to the ability to automate just about anything you can do in Photoshop so that you only have to click a button or two to perform specific tasks. There are several automation tools in Photoshop, but the main tool is called an *action*. A Photoshop action is merely a recording of sequential editing steps that can be played back on any file. Before Lightroom, these actions were the only way to create a workflow-friendly environment when dealing with large numbers of files — especially non-raw files.

In Chapter 9, I mention that Lightroom provides a way to use these powerful actions when exporting files, allowing you to perform the action's editing steps on the files after they're exported. This ability allows you to add editing steps to your workflow that can be done in Photoshop, but not in Lightroom. For example, you could create an action in Photoshop that adds a large copyright symbol to proof files when they're being exported from Lightroom. In this chapter, you look at how that's accomplished. But before you can do that, you need a basic understanding of how actions are created and how they're ordinarily used in Photoshop. Be aware that this is only intended as an introduction to actions and automation in Photoshop. If the topics covered here pique your curiosity, you can learn much more about them in Photoshop's help menus.

IN THIS CHAPTER

Understanding how Photoshop actions and droplets can automate common tasks

Using droplets to allow Lightroom and Photoshop to work together

Understanding Actions and Droplets

Actions are accessible in the Actions palette, as shown in Figure 18.1. If you have trouble locating it, choose Window ⇨ Actions.

FIGURE 18.1

The Actions palette is usually grouped with the History palette. Like many other palettes, the most necessary functions are performed with the buttons at the bottom of the palette. Other commands are located in the palette menu.

Actions palette menu

Begin recording

Stop playing/recording   Create new set

Play selection

Create new action

When you look at the Actions palette you notice that Photoshop comes loaded with some predefined actions called Default Actions that allow you to do all kinds of things. This group is called an *action set*. Photoshop comes with other predefined action sets that are located at the bottom of the palette menu, which is opened by using the button below the palette's Close button. To make the actions in these action sets accessible you need to load the sets into the Actions palette. In Figure 18.2, you can see the different sets of predefined actions at the bottom of the palette menu. Click any of these action sets to add them to your Actions palette. Each set appears as a folder that can be collapsed when the actions in it aren't needed. In Figure 18.2, you can see that the Image Effects action set has been added.

CAUTION   Choosing Button Mode from the palette menu turns the actions in your palette into colored buttons that are used to quickly identify specific actions. Be aware that when the Actions palette is in Button mode the buttons at the bottom of the palette aren't visible.

FIGURE 18.2

Photoshop comes with a number of action sets designed to address different types of editing needs. Click on any of these sets in the Actions palette menu to load them into the palette.

Commands
Frames
Image Effects
Production
Text Effects
Textures
Video Actions

These preloaded actions seem useful at first, but to be honest, I rarely use them and know very few people who do. To harness the true power of actions you need create your own custom actions to carry out repetitive tasks that are common to your specific workflow.

Creating an action

Actions are easy to create. You simply tell Photoshop to record everything you do and save those steps. Create a simple action that you can use to place a copyright symbol ((c)) in the middle of a 4 x 6 file. Doing this ensures that any proof prints made from these files are clearly labeled with the copyright symbol, making them unsatisfactory for reproducing if they fall into unscrupulous hands.

NOTE If you want a copyright symbol action for images with dimensions other than 4 x 6 (Web images, for example), follow these steps using a test file that is the correct dimensions. You'll also have to reduce the font size accordingly.

TIP I always tell my clients to create an action when they find themselves doing the same thing over and over. The action can be temporary, meaning that it's used for a specific set of photos and then discarded, or it can be a permanent addition to your custom action set.

The Actions palette has a Record button, a Play button, and a Stop button — just like a little tape recorder. And that's exactly how it works. Specific steps on a sample file are recorded and then played back on other files. Follow these steps:

NOTE An action is very similar to a macro in other software, such as Microsoft's Word or Excel.

1. Create a new file. Choose File ⇨ New, and give it the following properties: Width = 6 inches, Height = 4 inches, Resolution = 300, Color Mode = RGB Color/8-bit, and Background = White. If you created the "4 x 6 @ 300 white" preset in the New File dialog box earlier, use it to quickly create this file.

2. You're going to use white type so you need to change the background layer's color so you can see the type. Choose Edit ⇨ Fill. When the Fill dialog box opens choose 50% Gray from the Contents Use menu and click OK to fill the layer with 50 percent gray.

3. Before you record a new action, create an action set for your custom actions so they don't get mixed in with the default actions. This makes it easier to find them later. Go to the Actions palette and click on the Create New Set button at the bottom of the palette. Name the new set My Actions and click OK. (This name can always be changed later by double-clicking it in the Actions palette.)

TIP After you accumulate some custom actions it's a good idea to save your personal action set and burn it to a CD. That way if your computer dies, you won't loose all of your special actions. To save your action set select it and choose Save Actions from the palette menu. (You can load your saved action set into another computer by choosing Load Actions.)

4. Collapse any of the default action sets that are open because you don't need them.

5. Now it's time to create your action. Select any tool from the Tools palette (other than the Type tool) and click the Create New Action button. The New Action dialog opens, as shown in Figure 18.3. Name the action Copyright Symbol. Be sure to choose My Actions from the Set menu.

   The Function Key menu is used to assign a shortcut key to your action, which you don't need here. The Color menu is used to assign a color when working in Button mode.

FIGURE 18.3

The New Action dialog box allows you to name your action and choose in which action set it will be stored.

6. You're ready to begin. Click the Record button. Now every step will be recorded as part of the action. Follow the next steps exactly; otherwise your action may not work correctly later.

7. Select the Type tool (T) and click in the center of the image to activate the tool in the image. Go to the Tool Options bar and set the following attributes for the Type tool. Change the font to Times New Roman. Change the font size to 200 pt on the options bar. Click on the colored swatch on the options bar and change the text color to white.

8. Now you can create the copyright symbol. Press Alt+G (Mac) or Alt+0169 on the numeric keyboard (Windows) to create a copyright symbol. When you see the copyright symbol, click the Commit Edits button of the right side of the Tool Options bar. It looks like a check mark. (The circle with a diagonal line through it is used to cancel edits.)

9. Use the Move tool to position the symbol in the center of the image.

10. Go to the Layers palette. Notice that the type is on its own layer. Reduce the opacity of the type layer to 30 percent by clicking in the Opacity box and typing **30**. I added a drop shadow to mine so that if it gets positioned on a light area of the photo the dark shadow will make it visible. If you want to add one, choose Layer ➪ Layer Style ➪ Drop Shadow. Adjust the sliders in the dialog box until you like the shadow and then click OK.

11. You're almost done. You just need to flatten the text layer into the background layer. Choose Layer ➪ Flatten Image.

12. You need to record a step that saves the file, otherwise, when you run it on groups of files they will all open in Photoshop and stay there. Choose File ➪ Save As and save the file as

a JPEG with Quality of 12 to your Desktop. Name it `Test.jpg`. You can throw it away when you finish this exercise.

13. Okay, all of the steps you need are recorded so stop recording before doing anything else. Click the Stop button on the Actions palette. You can also close the 4 x 6 copyright test file you just created.

Your new action should look like the Copyright Symbol action in Figure 18.4. Notice that each step is recorded as part of the action. You can see where I clicked the twirly beside Set current layer to reveal the exact settings for that individual step.

The settings you used in this exercise are general. Try creating variations of this action for different types of work. Experiment with the font size, color, and layer opacity. Also try adding a drop shadow by choosing Layer ⇨ Layer Style ⇨ Drop Shadow. (If you use a drop shadow, instead of lowering the layer's Opacity value, try lowering its Fill value to preserve the opacity of the shadow. A value of 0 shows the drop shadow effect without the type.)

FIGURE 18.4

The new Copyright Symbol action is now in the My Actions action set. Here the action is expanded so you can see each step. The third step, Set current layer, is expanded so you can see the exact settings that were used to create the action.

NOTE   The difference between an action and a preset is that a preset is used to record the current set of conditions. For example, when you create a Develop preset in Lightroom you choose the settings you want to record in the preset. An action allows you to turn on a recorder that makes a record of almost anything you do once the recording begins.

Playing an action

Now it's time to test your action to see if it does what it's supposed to do. To play an action on an open file, select the action in the Actions palette and click the Play button at the bottom of the Actions palette.

CAUTION   Be sure the name of the action is selected, rather than one of its individual steps, before running it. Otherwise only the step that's selected, along with any subsequent steps, will be performed.

You need to test your action on a file that has been sized to 4 x 6 inches at 300 ppi. Open a suitable file, select the Copyright Symbol action, and click the Play button at the bottom of the palette. When you do, Photoshop will re-create all of the stored steps in the action on the current file, placing a large copyright symbol in the middle of the image, as shown in Figure 18.5. (Be aware that this file will overwrite the Test.jpg file you saved to the Desktop because of the Save As step.)

TIP   If your action doesn't do what it's supposed to do, check the action's steps in the Actions palette to see which one it's having problems with. The problem step will be the one on which the actions stop.

Actions become more powerful when they can be run on several files at the same time. This is called *batching*. You're not going to get into batching actions right now because I want to focus on using Lightroom to run your Copyright Symbol action on several files at the same time. But keep in mind that you can batch an action in Photoshop by choosing File ➪ Automate ➪ Batch in Photoshop. You can also batch an action on a group of files directly from Bridge by choosing Tools ➪ Photoshop ➪ Batch. The process is very similar to creating a droplet.

Working with droplets

An easy way to run an action on a group of photos is to turn the action into a *droplet*. A droplet is an automatic way of batching an action. It allows you to turn an action into an icon that can be placed anywhere on your computer. When you want to run the action on a file, or a whole folder of them, you merely drop the file or folder directly onto the droplet. Photoshop doesn't even have to be open because this amazing little icon opens Photoshop, if necessary, and performs all of the action steps on every file.

Create a droplet from your Copyright Symbol action. Follow these steps:

1. Choose File ➪ Automate ➪ Create Droplet. The Create Droplet dialog box appears, as shown in Figure 18.6. (This dialog box is very similar to the Batch dialog box.)

2. Select a place to save the new droplet to by clicking Choose. I choose to save it to my Desktop so that I have easy access to it when I transfer it to Lightroom. Name the droplet Copyright Symbol Droplet.exe and click Save.

3. In the Play section, choose your action set (that is, My Actions) and the Copyright Symbol action. Be sure to select the Suppress File Open Options Dialogs option so that all file opening happens behind the scenes.

   Also select the Suppress Color Profile Warnings option in case the files you want to process are not in the same color space as your working space. (Otherwise the action may stop every time a file opens while Photoshop checks with you to see how you want to handle the profile mismatch.) All color space issues will be handled in accordance with the way you set up your color management policies in the Color Settings preferences. Select the Include All Subfolders option if you want to process images contained in subfolders.

FIGURE 18.5

This detail shows the copyright in place in the center of the photo. It's translucent because you reduced the opacity of the type layer. The drop shadow keeps it from blending with the light areas on her legs.

CROSS-REF Color management policies are discussed in Chapter 12.

4. Choose Save and Close from the Destination pull-down menu so that the new files over-write the files placed on the droplet instead of creating a duplicate set in another folder. (Normally, I don't advocate overwriting files, but in this case you will be exporting files from Lightroom that are designed to be overwritten.) Also select the Override Action "Save As" Commands option so that when files are saved they aren't saved with the same name you used on your sample file when you created the original action.

5. Click OK.

FIGURE 18.6

Use the Create Droplet dialog box to convert the Copyright Symbol action into a droplet. Click Choose to create a name for the droplet and to choose where to save it.

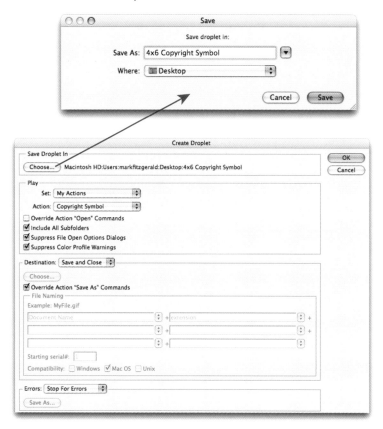

 The droplet is created almost instantly. Use a folder of test images to try it out. Simply click and drag the folder and drop it onto the droplet. (Now you know where these cool gadgets get their name!)

Automating Lightroom with Photoshop Droplets

Now that the droplet is created and working to your satisfaction, it's time to finish the process by linking the new droplet with Lightroom. To do that you need to add it to a special folder that Lightroom uses for storing the export droplets. Follow these steps:

1. Open Lightroom and select a random photo in the Library module.

2. Position Lightroom so it doesn't cover the entire Desktop. You want to be able to see your copyright droplet on the Desktop because you'll need it in a moment.

3. Click the Export button on the left side of the screen, below the left-hand panel set in the Library module (File ➪ Export). When the Export dialog box appears, go to the Post-processing area at the bottom. Select Go to Export Actions Folder Now from the After Export menu. This opens the Mac Finder/Windows Explorer, with Lightroom's special folders in it. Find the Export Actions folder, shown in Figure 18.7, and double-click on it to open it.

FIGURE 18.7

When you choose Go to Export Actions Folder Now from the Post-processing section of the Export dialog box the Mac Finder/Windows Explorer window opens with all of Lightroom's special folders. Double-click on the Export Actions folder to open it.

CROSS-REF Exporting from Lightroom is discussed in detail in Chapter 9.

4. Now you need to locate your Copyright Symbol droplet on the desktop and drag it into the Export Actions folder you just opened. When it's there close Mac Finder/Windows Explorer.

   If you prefer, you can use a second Finder/Explorer window for locating and moving the droplet. You can also copy and paste it instead of moving it if you want to keep a copy on your desktop that can be stored with other droplets you create.

5. Now when you go to the After Export menu you see the droplet is permanently listed in the menu because you placed it into the Export Actions folder, as shown in Figure 18.8. Whenever you export files for 4 x 6 prints and you want to add a copyright symbol to the image, you can select this droplet for automatic post-processing in Photoshop after Export. For now, you can click Cancel on the Export dialog box to close it.

NOTE For this copyright droplet to work correctly you need to choose **Resize to Fit** in the Image Sizing area of the Export dialog box. Then choose **Width** and **Height** from the menu and set both the width and height values to **6 inches** and set resolution to **300 ppi**. If you don't do this, and you run the droplet on full-sized files, the copyright symbol will be too small.

FIGURE 18.8

When droplets are placed into the After Export Actions folder, they show in the After Export menu in the Post-processing section of Lightroom's Export dialog box.

Droplets allow you to harness the power of Photoshop when exporting files from Lightroom. If you think about all of the different ways you can use them to add additional editing steps to exported Lightroom photos, you'll soon realize that the possibilities are endless.

Summary

Actions are one of the most powerful workflow features in Photoshop because they allow you to record almost any sequence of steps that can be played back later on different files. You took a very brief look at them here by creating your own Copyright Symbol action.

When an action is converted to a droplet it gives the action the ability to be activated from outside of Photoshop. This remote activation is the key that allows you to link actions to Lightroom's Export dialog box. When a droplet is added to the Export Actions folder it's listed in the Post-processing After Export menu where you can choose it when exporting photos.

If this is your first experience with actions and droplets, I recommend that you explore them more deeply in Photoshop's help files. They are very useful when used in conjunction with Photoshop. And when they're paired with Lightroom's Export dialog box they open all sorts of automatic post-processing options that aren't possible with Lightroom alone.

Part V

Putting the Tools to Work

In the last several chapters, you've explored a number of Photoshop concepts, tools, and techniques. Now it's time to make sense of how they're used to solve typical workflow issues and problems. You begin by taking closer look at what the term *retouching* means and why it's important. Then you look at how the Creative Workflow is managed by breaking it down into four main parts. Understanding these parts makes it easier to envision the entire Creative Workflow as a whole.

As you move through Part V, you see the tools put to work solving some of the most common portrait retouching issues. Even if you don't shoot portraits, you will learn a lot from here because these techniques are used to solve most retouching issues, no matter what kind of subject matter you shoot.

Then you explore the necessary steps to finishing an image. I show you a nondestructive method for burning and dodging your photos so that you can control areas of tone within the image. Then I explain resolution and why it's important to understand when you change the size of an image. I also cover professional sharpening strategies and the differences between inkjet and lab printing.

Finally, we put the workflow into motion by working on a downloadable practice photo together. You'll have the opportunity to work side-by-side with me while I take a portrait photo through the entire Creative Workflow. If you work through the process, by the end of this part you'll understand exactly how Photoshop is used to take your special images to the next level during the Creative Workflow.

Chapter 19

Creating Strategies for Success

When we jumped into the Photoshop section of this book we didn't stop to discuss the Creative Workflow. That's because it makes more sense to get some of the basic tools and concepts out of the way first. Now that you're ready to put those tools and concepts to work, you need to take a moment to consider the Creative Workflow and how it's implemented.

I image you're beginning to realize that Photoshop's retouching tools are a key element in the Creative Workflow. That's because retouching is used to improve images in countless ways. In this chapter, you take a closer look at what is meant by retouching and how it fits into the four phases of the Creative Workflow. Let's begin by defining what we're talking about when we say retouching.

What Is Retouching?

When most people hear the word *retouching*, they usually think about portrait retouching. It's no wonder. In the days before digital, when photographers were shooting film, the things that could be done in standard postproduction were quite limited. A film-based workflow had two basic types of retouching: film retouching (mostly medium and large format negatives) and print retouching. Film retouching was done with dyes applied to the negative, and print retouching was done with pencils, dyes, and sprays applied to the print. Print retouching was often necessary after film retouching to blend both steps because of the limited abilities of the film retouching. These techniques were usually reserved for portrait photos to reduce wrinkles and remove blemishes. Any other manipulation took place in the darkroom and was considered custom printing, not retouching.

> **NOTE** Naturally, high-end retouching at the time involved film masking and airbrushes, but that kind of work was expensive and usually not available to the average professional photographer.

Today, the term *retouching* has taken on a whole new meaning. When I looked up the word at Wikipedia.com, the online encyclopedia directed me to a section titled "Photo Manipulation." The definition was "the application of image-editing techniques to modify photographs, through analog or digital means." Clearly, the term has been redefined to fit modern photographic tools and procedures. The line between film retouching and print retouching has vanished, as has the line between retouching and darkroom work. That's because images can be improved in countless ways during the postproduction process using Photoshop and other digital tools. Now it's all part of the same process that takes place with a digital file, before any prints are made, if they're even needed.

> **NOTE** Post-production (or simply known as) refers to anything that's done to an image after its initial creation. This broad term refers to things like cataloging, archiving, and printing, as well as retouching.

As these boundaries disappear, the term retouching has come to broadly refer to just about any image manipulation that can be done to a digital file. Even though the variety of problems solved with retouching may be open-ended, the tools, techniques, and procedures used are very much the same for most of those problems. You look at some of those tools and techniques in Part IV. The goal of this chapter is to discuss the path to workflow success, rather than the shoes one should wear when walking the path.

Adding Value with Retouching

Retouching is about more than tools and techniques. It's about a process to improve an image beyond what was capable at the time the image was captured by the camera. This process is central to the idea behind the Creative Workflow. Sometimes, the process consists of fixing problems and mistakes. But in its purest form, retouching and the Creative Workflow are about taking an image to the next level of quality and personal expression.

Photographers who understand the retouching process know that their job is only half done when they click the shutter, because they can add so much value to the image during the postproduction process. The image in Figure 19.1 is from the photo shoot I imported into Lightroom in Chapter 5 and organized in Chapter 6. The original photo in the first frame is a nice shot of this couple and their dog. Many people would be happy to have a photo of themselves like this. However, after a little more than an hour of retouching, this image is transformed into something special — completing my vision of what I want from this portrait.

FIGURE 19.1

A little more than an hour's retouching transforms this portrait into what I envisioned when I shot it.

Here's a list of some of the things I did to increase the value of this image.

CROSS-REF **We work together with this image in Chapter 22, so you'll have a chance to see some of these changes in action.**

- **I removed a number of distractions** from the background and foreground, including dead flowers in the bushes and on the ground. Also, I removed and toned down bright, distracting plants and leaves because they tended to pull the viewer's eye away from the subjects.

- **I did a little facial retouching** on both of the people, including smoothing their skin. (I didn't have to touch the dog!)

- **I darkened and lightened specific areas** to balance out tonal discrepancies, which is called burning and dodging.

CROSS-REF **You look at burning and dodging in Chapter 21.**

- **I blurred the background** to add separation between it and the main subjects.

- **I darkened all the corners** to keep the viewer's eye focused on the center of the image, rather than its edges.

For a professional photographer, the extra hour spent with an image like this means more money. It also means that the final image is beyond what the average photographer produces. It has become a true creative expression of the individual who crafted it. If you're a professional photographer, this ability to take images to the next level during the Creative Workflow is a way to set yourself apart.

Retouching, and the Creative Workflow add value to all kinds of images. Figure 19.2 shows before and after versions of another project. The goal with this project was to be more literal in my creative interpretation of the scene while using the retouching tools.

Here's a list of some of the things I did with this photo to increase its value.

- **I removed all of the distractions** that were in front of the building, such as light posts and wires.

- **I corrected the distortion** (caused by the wide-angle lens) by straightening the vertical lines. This is a necessity with architectural photography.

- **I darkened the left side of the building** so it doesn't stand out as much.

- **I darkened all corners** to keep the viewer's eye within the frame.

(If you want to explore this image more, it's used as a hands-on project in my book *Photoshop CS3 Restoration and Retouching Bible*, also published by Wiley.)

FIGURE 19.2

Even though the before and after versions of this image are strikingly different, the integrity of the subject remains untouched. It looks like someone literally removed a layer of distractions to reveal the building below.

Photo by Seattle Photography, Inc.

Even though the goal with each of the images in Figure 19.1 and Figure 19.2 was to improve them, the retouching process was different for each. With the portrait in Figure 19.1, the goal was to tone down distractions and soften a number of elements in the image. Because of the nature of the image, I didn't have to worry about changing the reality of the scene. While removing distractions, such as dead leaves, I didn't have to be very careful about where I sampled from, as long as everything blended together. When people look at this image, they don't care what the bushes look like — whether this is a depiction of the reality of the scene. What they want to look at are the people — and the dog, of course. And when they look at those subjects they aren't concerned if dead leaves are gone, some wrinkles were removed, and the skin was softened.

My goal as a photographer with this project was to capture the personalities of this couple and their dog. My primary goal as a retoucher was to make the image pleasant to look at by removing distractions and creating an environment where the viewer's eye is drawn to the main subjects. I had lots of creative license while doing that, which is one of the attractions of this image and what really makes it a custom portrait.

The goal of the photographer of the building image in Figure 19.2 was to get a good photo of this hotel. He did an excellent job. I've stayed at this hotel is in downtown Seattle a few times. I can tell you that this photo was taken from the one place where the hotel isn't surrounded by other buildings. And the photographer was able to shoot this on a day with a beautiful sky — which can be quite a feat in Seattle!

As a retoucher, my objective with this building image was similar to the portrait in Figure 19.1. I wanted to make a nice image even better by removing distractions. However, the process of doing that was very different from my process for Figure 19.1. With this project, not altering the underlying qualities of the building was important; the interpretation had to be a literal interpretation. If I changed something, such as removing a window, the change would be instantly noticeable. The effect of the retouching needed to appear more like someone peeled off a layer of distractions without significantly changing the look of the building.

Whether or not you're a professional photographer — or whether you photograph people or buildings — these skills are essential. They allow you to completely explore your creative vision. This is very empowering because when you fully understand the process, you will be able to visualize how it will affect your image before your finger presses the shutter button. After you have this ability to pre-visualize the retouching process, it forever changes the way you shoot.

Managing the Creative Workflow

The Creative Workflow in Photoshop can vary widely depending on the image being edited and its intended final use. That, combined with the complexity of Photoshop, can sometimes make the Creative Workflow difficult to manage. Therefore, it pays to step back and consider the workflow from a distance. When you do so, you find many commonalities. Let's look at some of these key points to consider when thinking about the Creative Workflow.

Planning ahead

With any Creative Workflow project, you should take some time to evaluate the project and formulate a mental plan of the actions you need to take. Think about where the image is and where you want to take it. Visualize the outcome. After you have that picture in your mind, ask yourself these questions:

- Does that timeframe fit into the time you're willing to allot for the project? How long will it take to move the image from where it is to where you want it to be?

- Does the project fit your skill set? Will you be able to accomplish what needs to be done with what you currently know? Don't be afraid to take on a challenge or two, but be careful about getting in over your head and making commitments that are hard to fulfill.

- Will you need to learn something new in order to accomplish the project? If so, take the time to seek out the resources you need in order to make the project a success. Every time you learn to use a new tool or technique, you can add one more tool to your toolbox.

- What are the intended uses of the image? Will it be an inkjet or photographic print? If so, what size? The retouching process for an image being printed as a 30 x 40 is much more demanding than the process for an 8 x 10 because every flaw will be seen at 30 x 40. If the image is for commercial use, will it be used in a magazine or a Web site? Again, how big will it be?

Knowing the answers to some of these questions will help you to know how you want to handle the project. After that plan is put together, it's time to do the work.

The four-phase Creative Workflow

When you looked at Lightroom's Production Workflow earlier in this book you found that you were able to break the workflow down into three main parts: import and organize, basic editing, and output. These steps were easy to visualize because of Lightroom's layout. The parts of the Creative Workflow aren't always as distinct from one another , and they often overlap. With that in mind, here are the four phases of the Creative Workflow:

- **Phase 1 — Adjusting image fundamentals:** This is where the foundation for a successful project begins. Brightness, contrast, and color are adjusted to their optimal settings. Even if these settings were adjusted previously in Lightroom or Adobe Camera Raw, they're reevaluated at this time. Other things that might fall into Phase 1 are preliminary cropping, straightening, and preliminary size adjustment.

- **Phase 2 — Fixing distractions:** This phase is the core of the retouching process. It's where all the hard work is done. As you can see in Figures 19.1 and 19.2, the things done here run the gamut from toning down wrinkles to removing telephone poles.

- **Phase 3 — Controlling the viewer's experience:** After all the distractions are handled, creative techniques are used to produce the type of visual experience you want the viewer to have. Some of the techniques used here are nonstandard cropping, selective sharpening and blurring, as well as burning and dodging.

- **Phase 4 — Output and archiving:** Prints can be output with a variety of printers and media. Output files are prepared accordingly. After all of the work is done it pays to archive the master retouched file so that you can find it again later if necessary. Otherwise you may have to repeat all of the creative workflow process later if you need to output the file again.

CROSS-REF File organization and archiving are discussed in Chapter 3.

Each of these phases must be considered during the process. For example, when I'm adjusting the brightness and contrast of an image in Phase 1, knowing that it will be cropped to a horizontal panorama in Phase 3 is helpful. That way, if I'm having difficulty with tones at the top of the image, I can ignore them because they'll be cropped out later.

Another thing to remember is that sometimes more than one phase is being addressed at the same time. When I removed the bright plants above and to the right of the woman in Figure 19.1, I was removing something distracting as well as controlling the viewer's experience by removing something bright that was pointing away from the subjects.

Some images require different mixtures of these four phases. The portrait in Figure 19.1 mostly requires Phase 2, with a healthy amount of Phase 3. The building in Figure 19.2 needs plenty of Phase 1 before all the work in Phase 2 can begin. Very little of Phase 3 is needed.

Knowing when to stop

Knowing when to stop working on an image is just as important as knowing how to begin. I've consulted with lots of professional photographers and digital assistants to teach them these skills. Quite often, they call me in because they've lost control of their retouching workflow. When we sit down and begin to deconstruct their workflow, they quickly see that they tend to spend too much time on things no one will see. Don't get me wrong. I'm all about perfecting an image. However, if its final use is going to be an 8 x 10 inkjet print and you're zoomed in to 200 percent (see Figure 19.3) and retouching every pore in someone's skin, you're probably wasting your time. (You may even be wasting your time if the image is going to be a 30 x 40 photographic print, but will be mounted on canvas and hung high on a wall where people can't get close to it.)

I know this is a difficult pill for some people to swallow. They take comfort in knowing that every detail is managed. I understand this. If you're working on a labor of love, then by all means go for it. But if you're a busy professional, or if you have other important images you want to work on, you'll have to learn to use your time efficiently.

One of the things at play here is that with film we were never able to see the image larger than it would be printed. The things we saw were the film and the print itself. It was impossible — or at least prohibitively expensive — to micromanage a retouching project at the level some people do today. With digital, the ability to view the image at extreme magnification has skewed the viewing environment. Remember that as you work. Zoom in when you need to, but avoid the temptation to do unnecessary work.

FIGURE 19.3

It's okay to zoom in close to work on important details like eyes. Just be sure that your time is well spent on details that are visible in the final print.

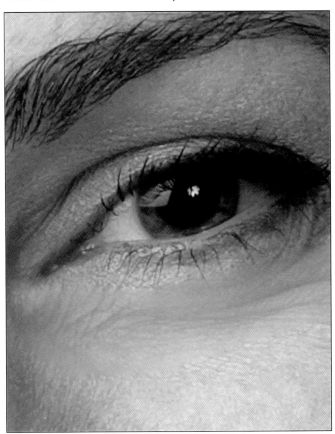

Strategies for Retouching Multiple Images

I want to briefly mention retouching multiple images, as shown in Figure 19.4, because I get asked about it all the time. The conversation usually goes something like this: "I photographed a high school student for her senior photos. Her mother ordered several different poses, which is great. However, the girl's skin needs lots of retouching. Several of the poses are similar, so can I retouch them all at once, or can I automate the retouching so that after I do it on one image, I can easily apply it to the others?"

As you saw with Lightroom's Develop module and Adobe Camera Raw, it's possible to use versions of the Clone Stamp and the Healing Brush on one file and then synchronize those same changes with other files. It sounds good in theory, but the image content of each of the images has to be identical for these tools to work satisfactorily. About the only time this feature is useful is when you're dealing with sensor dust that falls in exactly the same place on consecutive images. Even then, the surrounding image content needs to be consistent for this to work on every image — for example, a bunch of product shots with sensor dust on the white background.

You can automate retouching with Photoshop actions, but again the retouching steps you record would be occurring in exactly the same places on every image. Any variations in image content would have a serious effect on the retouching of different images.

FIGURE 19.4

Doing similar retouching on multiple images is made easier if you take notes and limit the amount of work you do on the first image, and share tonal and color changes with adjustment layers.

So what it boils down to is this: If you're faced with a scenario like the high school senior shoot just outlined, you'll have to retouch each one of the images individually. When you work on a project like this, three key things can make the process flow more efficiently:

- **Take notes as you retouch the first image**, especially if you plan to work on parts of the project in different sittings. I can tell you from experience that it's frustrating to not remember what you did to the first image when it comes time to work on the next one.

- **Try to limit the amount of work you do**, especially when working on the first image. If you set a high standard, be prepared to stick to it with the rest of the images. As long as you're ready to follow through, it's okay. (Limiting your work makes the recommended note-taking process much easier.)

- **Use adjustment layers to share any adjustment settings**. After an adjustment layer (such as a Color Balance layer) is created, it can be dragged onto another image. Even if the second image's color needs are a little different, you already have a starting place that's consistent with the first image. Also, it's okay if the images are sized differently because adjustment layers cover the entire image no matter what its size is.

If you keep these three tips in mind, the process of retouching multiple images of the same subject will go more smoothly.

Summary

In this chapter, retouching is finally defined. You saw that it's about fine-tuning an image and taking it to a higher level, adding value to it along the way. This added value is what separates a custom image from a nice photo.

The Creative Workflow is divided into four phases. Each of these phases is used to manage different creative aspects of the image. Retouching tools and techniques are central to the first three phases; therefore these phases often overlap when specific retouching tasks are being carried out.

There are a great number of possibilities with Photoshop in the creative workflow. Therefore, it becomes extremely important to manage the workflow. The first step in that management process is to get a bird's-eye view of the project, allowing you to get a feel for what's required. The next step is to consider each of the phases in the four-phase workflow so that you get an idea of how they impact one another. Finally, know when to stop. Look for the point of diminishing returns where additional retouching has little effect on the quality of the final image.

Finally, you looked at strategies for retouching multiple, similar images. This may not happen often, but when it does, these strategies will save you time and make your life easier.

Chapter 20

Solving Special Portrait Retouching Problems

Even though the kinds of problems solved by retouching run the gamut, much of the focus in the retouching world today is in portrait retouching. Photographers and retouchers often ask me about how to handle these special kinds of challenges, so I decided to devote a chapter to the most common issues, such as swapping heads, replacing missing eyes, and smoothing wrinkled clothing. Keep in mind that the techniques discussed in this chapter can be used on a wide range of subject matter beyond portraits.

Because the goal of this chapter is to share my overall strategies for dealing with these issues, I don't focus closely on the details of every step. Instead, I show you how a group of similar concepts are used to solve a variety of common portrait retouching problems. We begin with a technique that sounds extreme, but is often one of the easiest — swapping heads.

Swapping Heads

Not long ago, when photographers were shooting film, the option of switching someone's head from one image to another was a daunting task, even under the best of circumstances. Because of this, it was rarely an option for the average portrait photographer.

With digital photography and Photoshop, the ease of performing head swaps has changed modern portraiture. It's no longer necessary to make sure everyone in a group is perfect in a single exposure when photographing a group. The photographer just has to make sure she gets plenty of exposures of each pose with at least one good picture of each person. Then each person in the group can pick the exposure where he or she looks best. The retoucher simply brings all the best heads together into a single, perfect group portrait.

> **NOTE** Swapping heads — and even entire bodies — is a very common technique today. I worked on one family portrait where I completely changed three people's bodies and the heads of two other people.

Though this technique is most often used to combine individual expressions for group portraits, it's not limited to them. Figure 20.1 shows two images of a young man. He liked the way his hands are positioned in the image on the left, but he wanted a more serious face like the one in the image on the right. With Photoshop, that's no problem.

This procedure is very straightforward. I simply copy the head in the second image to its own layer and then drag it into the first image. The whole process with this particular set of images is facilitated by the fact that his body position and the background are very consistent. The only wrinkle is that the head is larger in the second image.

FIGURE 20.1

Replacing this young man's head in the first frame with the head in the second frame creates the perfect combination of hand position and facial expression.

Let's look how easy this head swap is:

1. I use the Lasso tool to draw a loose selection around his head in the second image. I always prefer to keep a selection like this fairly loose so I can fine-tune the copied material with a mask after it's in the main image. This means I don't need to feather the selection.

    After the selection is in place, I copy the information inside it to its own layer, as shown in the first frame of Figure 20.2, by pressing Command+J (Ctrl+J).

TIP If the man's head were in exactly the same position on both of these images, I would only copy his face from the second image, instead of his entire head.

2. After the head is on its own layer, I grab its thumbnail in the Layers palette and drag it into the main image, positioning it over the original head. When I lower the new layer's opacity to position the new head, I can see that it's a little too big, as shown in the second frame of Figure 20.2.

FIGURE 20.2

After the new head is on its own layer, it's dragged into the main image and placed on top of the original head. When the new layer's opacity is lowered, it's easy to see that the new head is a little bigger than the old head.

3. I need to scale this young man's head so it's the correct size for the image. To do that, I choose Edit ⇨ Transform ⇨ Scale. The Transform command is used to adjust different aspects of the geometry of any layer, except for the Background layer. (If you want to transform the Background layer, change its name to anything other than Background.) You can also transform multiple layers by selecting all of them in the Layers palette before invoking the command. The Transform menu options include Scale, Rotate, Flip Horizontal, and Flip Vertical.

When the Transform command is in use, an adjustment box appears around the edges of Layer 1, as shown in Figure 20.3. I can scale the layer by clicking and dragging any of the *control handles*, the small boxes at the corners or the sides of this box. However, one of the things I need to be careful about here is that I don't change the proportions (aspect ratio) of the new head layer when I scale it. So I hold down the Shift key to lock the aspect ratio of the layer as I scale it by dragging one of the corner control handles.

NOTE This isn't the first time you've encountered the Shift key in a role like this. You may have noticed by now that the Shift key is always used as a modifier key to lock proportions or to make a drawing tool draw a straight line.

I reposition the layer a couple of times as I scale, to realign the eyes. I use them as a registration point because I know that when the eyes on Layer 1 line up with the eyes on the Background layer, the scale will be correct, as shown in the first frame of Figure 20.3.

FIGURE 20.3

I scale the head with the Transform command until the eyes are the same size in both versions of the head. Then I raise the Opacity of the new layer back to 100 percent. Even though the eyes are aligned with the bottom layer, the shoulder line is out of registration.

4. After the scale is correct, I press Enter to accept it and complete the Transform command. Then I return the Opacity of Layer 1 to 100 percent, as shown in the second frame of Figure 20.3. I turn the visibility of Layer 1 off and on a couple of times to check my work. (Use the Esc key to cancel out of the Transform command if you don't like what you're getting and you want to start over.)

> **TIP** When changing the size of a new layer like this, you should always scale down in size. When layer information is scaled up, it tends to diminish in quality as the pixels are spread apart, especially when the size is changed substantially.

5. The new head looks good, but it's sitting a little too low. The eyes on the layer were aligned with the old head, which was positioned looking downward. I can solve this problem in two ways: I can mask out everything below the chin on the new layer, or I can simply reposition the new layer a little higher. This is a better solution because the eyes will be in the right place because his head isn't tilted downward in Layer 1. It also is faster. I drag the layer upward until the collar of his jacket matches on both sides. Now I can just barely see the edges of Layer 1 against the Background layer.

6. I create a mask and use a soft brush around the edges of the image to blend the edges of the new layer with the layer below it, as shown in Figure 20.4.

FIGURE 20.4

A bit of quick masking around the outer edges of the new layer blends it with the Background layer in no time. You can see by the mask in the Layers palette that I didn't have to mask the lower section because the collar and shoulders are in perfect alignment.

> **TIP**   These two exposures were identical. If there was a tonal or color discrepancy — for example, if the new layer was a little darker and greener — I would have adjusted the new layer before flattening.

If I hadn't stopped to record my steps, this head swap would have taken about two or three minutes to complete. Even if it took a little longer, it would still have been worth it because it's what made the customer happy.

Replacing Missing Eyes

Human eyes are some of the most complicated things to retouch. They're not only rich with intricate detail, they also are the first things people look at when they view a well-designed portrait. Because they are so important to the viewer, you must always make sure that a portrait subject's eyes look their best. That can be a tall order when one or both eyes are obscured or completely missing.

Closed eyes: Replacing missing eyes with donor eyes

One of the hardest things a retoucher can be asked to do is to replace a missing eye. Eyes go missing for a variety of reasons; sometimes people blink right when the exposure is being made, and sometimes light reflects off their glasses, causing what are called *glass-glares*.

When you're faced with having to replace missing eyes, the best-case scenario is to have another set of eyes that can be used as donors. Naturally, it's best if those eyes actually belong to the subject and were photographed similarly with the same kind of lighting and exposure. The direction the head is facing also makes all the difference here.

> **NOTE**   I have been known to "borrow" someone else's eyes to fix missing eyes caused by glass-glare in a large group photo (a group of 50 people, for example). You can get away with this only when the heads are so small that seeing detail in the eyes is difficult. Even so, try to match the eye color if you know it because sometimes that's all that can be seen in a group photo.

Figure 20.5 shows two photos of the same young woman. For the moment, imagine that these two photos are the only ones the photographer shot during the session. Because the woman has such a pretty smile, the only way to salvage this job is to combine the eyes from the nonsmiling face with the smiling face.

This job looks pretty straightforward. Most things between the two photos are consistent. Both have the same lighting, and the angle of the head is very similar. The only real difference is that the head is a bit larger in the second image. The procedure is much like the head swap discussed in the preceding section; I copy the eyes from the donor image and drag them into the target image.

FIGURE 20.5

In this exercise, the eyes in the second image are used as "donor eyes" for the first image. The procedure is much like the head swap.

Here's the lowdown on how I approach this project:

1. I make a loose selection around both eyes in the second image.

2. I copy both eyes in the second image to a new layer and drag that new layer into the first image.

3. I lower the opacity of the new set of eyes so I can see the underlying layer. I use the eyebrows as a reference point to align both layers.

4. Because the new eyes are bigger, I choose Transform ➪ Scale to scale them down to the correct size while holding the Shift key down.

5. The new eyes are a little dark because the image they came from was a bit darker, so I use Levels to lighten them a tad.

6. I finish by using a layer mask to mask out everything I don't need on the new eye layer, leaving only the eyes and some of the skin around them. You can see what this looks like in the first frame of Figure 20.6.

FIGURE 20.6

The first image shows what the new eyes look like after they're in place. The second image shows what this woman's eyes really look like when she's smiling like this.

Something still doesn't look right in the new image. The eyes are too wide open for someone who's smiling so much. We intuitively notice it because it just doesn't look right. I included the second image in Figure 20.6 to show you what this woman's eyes really look like when she's smiling. It isn't possible to make the first image in Figure 20.6 look like the second one, but I can improve it.

NOTE   When we smile, we tend to tighten our eyes, which completely changes their appearance. Some famous portrait artists only make portraits of unsmiling people. They do this because they want to capture as much of the eyes as possible because they are the central theme of the portrait.

I use the Transform command to scale the new layer containing the eyes, (Edit ⇨ Transform ⇨ Scale). When the transform bounding box appears around the eyes layer I click the control handle at the top of the box and drag downward, as shown in the first image in Figure 20.7. This time I don't use the Shift key because I want to change the aspect ratio. The scaling action compresses the height dimension of the eyes. When I'm finished, they look more realistic. (Some might argue that they look better in this portrait than the squinting, natural eyes in the second image in Figure 20.6.)

NOTE   You may have noticed that I used the Transform command twice on the eye layer. I want you to know that transforming a layer more than once isn't considered a best practice. It's better to perform all transformations during one use of the command to avoid any artifacting due to the effect of the command on the layer's pixels. (You can even revisit the Transform menu and select a different transformation such as Rotate while the command is active.) I used it in two separate applications here to demonstrate my point.

440

The Transform command comes to the rescue again. I use it to squish the eyes a bit so they lose some of their oval shape.

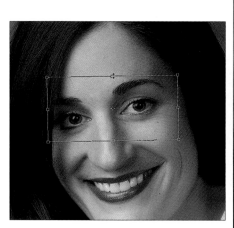 

This project looked like a no-brainer on the surface because the two images are so similar. But after seeing the new eyes in context, something looks funny. The thing to walk away with here is that eyes are very tricky to work with. When you're doing a project like this, try to find donor eyes that match the expression of the main image. Follow your gut instinct when you see them in the context of the new image. If something doesn't look right, try to figure out why.

Glass-glares: Rebuilding without donors

Glass-glares are the bane of retouchers everywhere. They represent one of the most common difficult retouching problems that a portrait retoucher is likely to run into. Glass-glares are caused by light — often coming from the photographer's strobes — reflecting off the portrait subject's glasses. When they're severe, they'll completely obliterate the eye, as well as anything else behind the glass like eyebrows and skin.

I've seen glass-glares in studio portraits where the whole surface of the glasses was a blown-out reflection of the photographer's umbrella. This shouldn't be happening in the digital world. If you're photographing someone with glasses in the studio, check your exposures often. If you see that the glasses are reflecting light you can use an old studio trick to eliminate them. Tilt glasses downward ever so slightly so that the glass isn't parallel to the camera lens and lights. Be careful, though, because if you tilt too far, it becomes obvious.

TIP If you see glass-glares when you're shooting, take the time to go back and reshoot. It will be much faster — and look much better — than using Photoshop to fix the problem.

Sometimes, tilting still won't do the trick. This is true when you're shooting outside with natural light. If you can't control glass-glares when you're shooting, you can cover yourself by having the model remove his or her glasses for a couple of frames every time you change poses. That way, you'll have a set of donor images to use if you need to borrow some eyes. Working with donor eyes like this is about the cleanest way of retouching glass-glares.

With that said, severe glass-glares still happen, and they have to be dealt with. Figure 20.8 shows a nice portrait of a high school senior with some pretty serious glass-glares. The way I'd normally handle a retouching problem like this would be to look at all the other photos from the session to see if I could find an eye or two to act as donors. I've used this strategy many times — in some cases building eyes from different parts of assorted images. It's tedious work, but it can save a portrait.

These glass-glares were caused by natural light that was reflected in the glasses. This is the only photo I have, so I have to reconstruct the eyes using only information contained within the image. (If you find yourself in a situation like this, have the model remove her glasses for a couple of shots so that you have some clean eyes to drop into the image later.)

Photo by Ted Miller Jr.

For this example, imagine that this is the only photo I have so it's all I have to work with. Before I even begin a job like this, I want to know something about how the image will be used. In this case, the client wants a 5 x 7 print with minimal cropping. This means that her head — from the top of her hair to the bottom of her chin — will only be 1.5 inches in height on paper; the eye itself will be only 0.05 inches. That small size makes this project doable. If it were going to be printed larger, or if it were being cropped closer, it would be much harder to reconstruct these eyes convincingly.

This glass-glare removal procedure is complex and detailed. I break it down here into general steps so you can follow my thinking as I work on this image:

1. First, I need to reconstruct one eye so I can use it to rebuild the other eye. The eye on the left is in the best shape, so I begin with it. I use the Clone Stamp to sample areas of skin that are similar to what I think should be underneath the glare. I don't worry if I'm off in tone a little in this first pass because I'll come back and fine-tune if I need to. The objective is to get some detail into the glare areas. I use parts of the eye on the lower left to rebuild the upper-right area of the eye, as shown in the first frame of Figure 20.9. I work with the image zoomed in close, using short brush strokes with the Clone Stamp.

2. I look for opportunities to extend lines like the upper and lower eyelids. If some of these details were showing in the right eye, I'd try to sample them from there. I also pay attention to catch lights. It's hard to tell where they should be, so I have to improvise. After I get most of the area filled in, I do some fine-tuning.

> **TIP** Because all the retouching is on a duplicate layer, I can hide it occasionally to compare my work with the original. This is a good indictor to let me know if I'm on track.

3. Now that the tones are similar, I use the Patch tool to blend them together better. I also use the Clone Stamp at 50 percent opacity to do some blending around the edges. I then clone the shadow along her nose because there should be one inside the glasses, as shown in the second frame of Figure 20.9.

> **TIP** I often find it useful to look at some real eyes when doing a project like this, even if they're in the mirror.

4. Now that the left eye is looking good, I can copy it and use the copy for the right eye. I draw a loose selection around it and then copy it to a new layer. Before I can move it into place on the right side, I have to flip it horizontally so that it's oriented correctly. To do that, I choose Edit ➪ Transform ➪ Flip Horizontal. Then I use the Move tool to drag it into place on the right side, as shown in the first frame of Figure 20.10.

5. After the new eye is in position, I use a mask to remove everything around it that I don't want, trying to salvage as much a possible from the underlying eye. I use a soft brush with its opacity set to 50 percent to get better blending of my strokes.

6. When you look at the first image in Figure 20.10, you probably notice something strange. The girl looks cross-eyed because the right eye is backward; the catch light is on wrong side. If her pupils were more visible, it would look even weirder.

   Here's how I solve this problem. Now that the right eye is mostly reconstructed, I go back to the left eye and sample it with the Clone Stamp. (I make sure that Current & Below is selected next to Sample on the options bar so that I can sample from the Left Eye layer and paint on the Right Eye layer.) Then I clone the iris area from the left eye onto the right eye, as shown in the second frame of Figure 20.10. Now the eye is looking in the right direction. Essentially, I unflipped the orientation of just the central part of the eye.

FIGURE 20.9

A project like this is all about finding good sampling opportunities. In the first image, I use the good parts of the left eye to rebuild the rest of it. In the second image, I duplicate the shadow by the nose by sampling the lower section.

FIGURE 20.10

After the left eye is complete, I copy it to a new layer. I have to flip it horizontally with the Transform command before I can move it into place. Even though the eye is flipped, it still looks weird because it's looking the wrong way. In the second frame, I'm using the center part of the left eye to re-create the central part of the right eye to unflip its orientation.

CAUTION Copying and flipping an eye to replace another eye is risky. The only way to make it convincing is to go back and reclone the iris and pupil area so that the eye looks in the right direction.

7. The eyes are starting to look pretty good, but the lack of dark pupils bothers me. To solve this, I create a new layer above the new eye layer and name it Pupils. Then I use the Brush tool to paint a small black pupil in the center of each eye. Because these two paint spots are on their own layer, I have lots of control over them. I take advantage of this control by changing the layer blending mode to Soft Light. That way, any catch lights that are below the paint will show through it.

   I use the same technique on another new layer set to Normal blending mode to use white paint to add a couple of very light catch lights. Because catch lights aren't always in the same position in both eyes, I'm sure to vary them a bit. I then lower the opacity of the layer so they're very translucent. I also use the Gaussian Blur filter to smear them a bit.

8. Next, I add a burn and dodge layer and use it to add some contour to the eye sockets and to darken areas where I think the glasses frame would cast a shadow. (I discuss burning and dodging in detail in the Chapter 21.)

9. I then use the Clone Stamp to tone down some of the reflections on the frames of the glasses. Sometimes these can be as bad as the glass-glares themselves.

NOTE Sometimes, the glare on the frame is worse than the glare on the glass. It doesn't always have to be completely removed, but it does have to be toned down.

10. Now it's a matter of fine-tuning. This step can take as long as all the previous steps combined because this is where everything comes together. I repeatedly turn the visibility of all new layers off and on so I can compare the new and old images. This is a good way to spot anything that doesn't look right. I'm working at 100 percent zoom, so I occasionally zoom out to 50 percent to see the image closer to its actual size. This always puts things into perspective. I also remind myself that the eye in the finished print will be very small.

TIP The most important step in a project like this is to walk away from it and do something else for a while. When you come back, you can see the project from a fresh perspective and know immediately if it isn't working.

   Don't be afraid to back up and try again at this point. Sometimes, you need a couple of tries with a complicated project like this. Just save your layers from the first attempt so you can compare both attempts. You may even find that you can combine parts of your first attempt with parts of your second attempt to get it right.

Figure 20.11 shows the final portrait and the layer stack in its Layers palette. Notice that I used a Curves adjustment layer with a mask on the top layer to darken the edges of the image.

Use this technique only as a last resort. If you do attempt it, be sure to give yourself plenty of time to work on it. Also, don't be afraid to fail as you search for the best path to making the image work.

FIGURE 20.11

Here's the final image with the new eyes in place — quite an improvement over the original in Figure 20.8. I also included the layer stack so you can use it to review my steps.

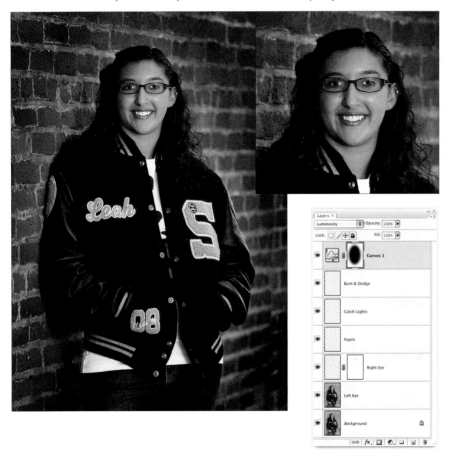

Removing Braces

When it comes to a portrait, teeth are almost as important as eyes. Retouchers are often asked to repair broken and missing teeth. One of the hardest things a retoucher can be asked to do is remove braces. At least with eyes, it's possible to find donor eyes in another image. With teeth, that's rarely an option. It's left to the retoucher to determine what the teeth should look like without braces. (I know a couple of photographers/dentists who would probably be very good at this.)

CROSS-REF You learn how to whiten and lighten teeth in Chapter 22.

The young lady in the portrait in Figure 20.12 has a pretty smile that's being obscured by her braces. My job as a retoucher is to use as much of the existing teeth to rebuild the missing teeth. This is a tall order here because some of her teeth are completely hidden. The good news is that the two front teeth are completely free of braces, which gives me plenty of material to sample.

FIGURE 20.12

Braces removal is much like rebuilding eyes. You have to work with what's there to create what isn't there. In this case, I'm fortunate that the two front teeth are braces-free.

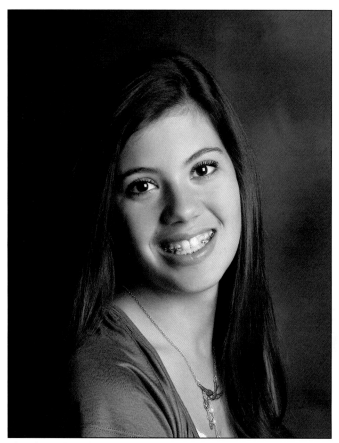

Photo by Emily Andrews

The process for this project is very similar to the process detailed in the preceding example, so I'll only hit a couple of high points. First, I fix the easy problems, like the teeth next to the clean front teeth, by cloning parts of the two front teeth with the Clone Stamp, as shown in Figure 20.13. I work with a soft brush unless I'm near the edge of a tooth. When I am, I raise the Hardness value closer to 60 percent.

FIGURE 20.13

I begin this process by removing some of the easy stuff by sampling the clean front teeth. This allows me to build up new sample areas.

After I have some teeth reconstructed, I begin using them to reconstruct other teeth. This process takes a while because several teeth have to be created from scratch. When everything starts coming together, I make another pass to fine-tune any problem areas.

TIP Because all the retouching is on a separate layer, I can hide it occasionally to compare my retouching to reality.

The first frame in Figure 20.14 shows what the teeth look like when they're mostly reconstructed. They're getting close, but they still look too flat. To remedy this, I add a burn and dodge layer and use a small, soft brush with the Brush tool to shape the teeth by darkening the shadow sides with black paint and lightening the highlight sides with white paint. This helps to make them look more believable, as shown in the second frame of Figure 20.14.

FIGURE 20.14

The reconstructed teeth look too flat in the first image. A burn and dodge layer is used to shape them by darkening the shadow sides and lightening some of the highlight sides of the teeth. They look more three-dimensional in the second image.

Figure 20.15 shows the finished portrait. Like the project with the glass-glares, this one requires lots of time and patience. When you're doing a project like this, be sure to step away from it once in a while to give yourself a chance to see it from a different perspective. Don't be afraid to try again if you don't like what you get the first time.

When you get drawn into a complicated project like this, it's easy to lose your point of view and go past the point of what's needed. Keep the final use of the image in mind as you work. If you bite off more than you can chew and find it's beyond your current ability, be willing to chalk it up to the learning process and move on.

FIGURE 20.15

Here's the finished portrait without the braces. Though a project like this can be difficult, when it works, it's worth the effort.

Fixing Wrinkled Clothing

So far, we've focused on facial retouching. But a complete retouching job covers the entire image. Sometimes, the clothes in a portrait require more attention than the face. The portrait in Figure 20.16 looks great, except that the woman's shoulder looks funny because of the wrinkle in her jacket. Fortunately, this is easy to fix. All I need to do is copy a piece of jacket, drop it into the shoulder area, and then blend it all together. Here are the four steps I take to quickly solve this retouching problem:

1. First, I draw a selection outlining where I want the sleeve to be, as shown in the first frame of Figure 20.17. The line from her shoulder to her collar has to approximate what I want the shoulder line to look like. The inner part of the selection doesn't have to be as exact. Because the shoulder line is a bit soft, I feather the selection 1px.

2. I drag the completed selection to a fairly clean part of the jacket, as shown in the second frame of Figure 20.17. I'm looking for an area that doesn't have lots of detail like seams or shadows. When the selection is in place, I copy it to a new layer (Command+J/Ctrl+J). Now I have a piece of jacket that I can use as a patch.

3. I use the Move tool to drag the new layer into position so it's covering the space I want to fill, as shown in the first frame of Figure 20.18. I'm careful to line it up because I'll be merging it in the next step.

4. After the new layer is in place, I merge it back into the background layer, (Command+E/Ctrl+E). Now I just need to use the Patch tool to clean up any seams that are left, as shown in the second frame of Figure 20.18. When I'm finished blending, the image looks like Figure 20.19.

This simple fix took only a few minutes, yet it adds so much to the image. If a pattern on the clothing had been involved, the process would have been more complicated, but still very doable. It would have just taken a little more time and patience.

FIGURE 20.16

The face in this portrait only needs a little retouching. The more important issue that needs addressing is the fold in the woman's jacket along the shoulder. It makes her shoulder look out of place.

Photo by Dan Christopher

FIGURE 20.17

First, I create a selection that is close to the shape I need to fill. Next, I drag the selection to an area of the jacket that's suitable for duplicating.

FIGURE 20.18

When the selection is in place, I copy the selected area to its own layer and use the Move tool to position it in the area where I first drew the selection. When I like the way everything lines up, I merge the duplicate layer back into the Background layer. Then I use the Patch tool to quickly clean up any traces of the merge, as shown in the second image.

FIGURE 20.19

A few minutes of work makes all the difference in this portrait without even touching the face.

Smoothing Skin

In the early days of Photoshop, blemish removal was a main topic in books like this. Now Photoshop's retouching tools have become much more sophisticated with the addition of tools like the Spot Healing Brush and the Patch tool, so blemishes aren't such a big problem. My guess is that by now you have a clear understanding of how those tools are used to clean up blemished skin. Instead of talking about how to remove pimples, I want to discuss the question I get asked most when it comes to skin: "What's the best way to smooth skin?"

One thing about modern digital cameras is that they see everything. When someone is photographed with a high-end dSLR, you can see every pore in her skin. Sometimes, this is too much. In the world of portrait retouching, the word *porcelain* has become quite popular when describing the desirable skin texture in a portrait. Lots of portrait photographers want the subjects in their portraits to have skin almost as smooth as porcelain. Naturally, this term means different things to different people. Some retouchers really pour it on, while others only introduce a hint of skin smoothing.

Whether you want a lot or just a little, you essentially have two different ways of smoothing skin in Photoshop. One is to use a blurring filter on a duplicate layer and then mask it so the blur shows only on the skin. The other is to use a plug-in that's specially designed to smooth skin. Let's look at both techniques.

Using the Surface Blur filter to smooth skin

Before you use this technique, or any other skin smoothing technique, be sure to take care of basic facial retouching like large blemishes and bags under the eyes. That way, your retouching gets blended during the smoothing process.

The portrait in Figure 20.20 is one you've already seen in this book. This young woman has nice skin to begin with, but the photographer wants the portrait to have more of a high-fashion look. I used these steps to smooth her skin with a filter and a mask:

FIGURE 20.20

The photographer who made this portrait wants it to have a high-fashion look. Skin smoothing will definitely help achieve the look he's after.

1. I make a duplicate of the main retouching layer — after the primary retouching has been completed — to use for blurring. I rename this layer Blur.

2. Photoshop has several blurring filters under the Filter ⇨ Blur submenu, as shown in the first frame of Figure 20.21. I want to use the Surface Blur filter. When I click it, the Surface Blur dialog box appears, as shown in the second frame of Figure 20.21.

FIGURE 20.21

Surface Blur is one of Photoshop's newer filters. It's located at the bottom of the Blur submenu. When the dialog box opens, you use the two sliders to adjust the amount of blur while preserving edge detail.

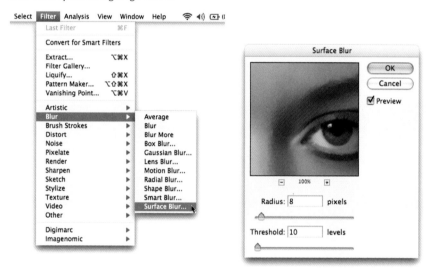

The Surface Blur filter is one of Photoshop's newer filters. It was introduced in version CS2. The filter is designed to protect edge detail while blurring everything else. It has two sliders: Radius and Threshold. (As is the case with most filters, the values used with these sliders depend on the size of the image file.)

- **Radius** controls the amount of blur. It specifies the size of the area being sampled for blurring. Higher values result in more blurring.

- **Threshold** controls the range of tonal values being considered for blurring. Lower values preserve more edge detail.

I set the Radius value to 8 and the Threshold value to 10. This is a little strong, but because the effect is on its own layer, I can tone it down by reducing the layer's opacity.

TIP Alternate between zoom amounts of 100 percent and 50 percent when smoothing skin. The 100 percent view allows you to see the effect on each pixel, while the 50 percent view is usually closer to the actual size of the image.

CROSS-REF Optimal zoom levels are further discussed in Chapter 21.

3. The blur on the skin looks better, but everything else is blurred, too. To remedy this, I create a layer mask that hides everything on the Blur layer (Layer ⇨ Layer Mask ⇨ Hide All) and then come back with the Brush tool and white paint to reveal only the areas of skin where I want blurring to show. I have to be sure to paint all the skin — such as hands and fingers. I also have to be careful around detail like the hair in front of her face and her necklace, as well as her eyes. Figure 20.22 shows the final effect. It's pretty close to what I'm looking for, but it needs a bit of touchup before it's perfect.

TIP This is a good time to use the backslash (\) key to see the painting in Quick Mask viewing mode.

FIGURE 20.22

Here's the final effect of smoothing skin by using the Surface Blur filter with a mask. It looks pretty good but still needs a bit of touchup.

This smoothing strategy works well as long as you don't mind doing some masking and a bit of touchup. Experiment with it on a couple of portraits until you get a feel for the effect. After you understand the concept, you'll find many different ways to apply it for softening — or sharpening — specific areas of an image.

Smoothing skin with a plug-in

A *plug-in* is supplementary software designed to work with Photoshop. Plug-ins allow you to do all kinds of things that can't be done as easily — or at all — in Photoshop. Plug-ins work within Photoshop, so using them as part of your workflow is seamless.

My favorite skin-softening plug-in is Portraiture by Imagenomic. This software does the best job of skin smoothing I've seen from a plug-in. The dialog box for Portraiture is shown in Figure 20.23. This powerful filter provides a huge amount of control over the smoothing process. For one thing, I can use the eyedropper to select the exact color of the skin. This is important because the filter affects only the range of skin colors I define. That's why its smoothing effect doesn't affect things like eyes and teeth. However, if I don't feel like fiddling with the dials, I can use one of the presets in the pop-up menu at the top left, which is what I'll do now.

FIGURE 20.23

The Portraiture plug-in by Imagenomic provides lots of control over skin smoothing. I tend to start with one of the presets, shown at the top left, and then fine-tune the settings to dial in the effect.

For the project here, I used the Smoothing Normal preset on a duplicate layer. The final effect is shown in Figure 20.24. If you compare Figure 20.24 to Figure 20.22, you'll see that the smoothing is cleaner in Figure 20.24, especially around the hair in front of her face. It also was much faster to create.

The one thing to be aware of with this filter is that it works on similar colors. So any color that's similar to the selected skin tone is affected. You may not be able to see it in this book, but the flesh-colored stripes on the woman's blouse have been blurred along with the skin. That isn't a problem here because I ran the filter on its own layer, so I can go back and do some quick masking to hide the effect on the clothing.

FIGURE 20.24

Here's the final effect of using the Smoothing Normal preset in Portraiture. Notice how much cleaner the skin smoothing is around the hair in front of the model's face than the image in Figure 20.22.

This is intended only as an introduction to this powerful filter. I wanted to mention it here because it's one of the most exciting retouching plug-ins I've run across in a while. If you want to know more, visit the Imagenomic Web site at www.imagenomic.com.

Summary

This chapter started with one of the most common special retouching tasks that portrait photographers are asked to do — a head swap. In that example, you saw just how easy it is to replace someone's head with a head from another image, creating the perfect portrait. If you're a portrait photographer, keep this in mind when shooting. Always be sure to cover yourself, especially when shooting groups, so that you have plenty of heads and expressions to choose from for every pose you shoot.

Repairing and reconstructing eyes raises the retouching difficulty level several notches. The first eye project you looked at was fairly straightforward. I replaced closed eyes with a set of donor eyes from a similar image. Even though the new eyes were a close match, you saw that they still didn't fit the woman's expression. I was able to scale the eyes and get a usable image, but it would have been better to use donor eyes that more closely matched the expression in the target image.

In the second eye project, you looked at complex glass-glares. This project was extremely difficult because of the lack of raw material. If this image were going to be printed bigger or cropped closer, I may have not even attempted it. The same is true for the braces project. Be willing to explore difficult projects like these, but honor your limits. Know when to pass on a project that's beyond your comfort level.

The project with the wrinkled jacket was a reminder that portrait retouching extends beyond the head. When you're working on an image, look at clothing to see if you can remove any distractions like shiny buttons or distracting wrinkles.

Skin smoothing adds a finished look to a portrait. I showed you two ways to approach skin smoothing. Work with one of these methods until you get a feel for it. Experiment until you find the amount of smoothing that works best for you. You don't have to go for the full porcelain effect, but use a little smoothing to blend retouching and give the skin a softer glow.

Each project you looked at in this chapter — except for skin smoothing — had one major concept in common. Missing information was reconstructed with existing information. You probably realize by now that using various techniques for "copying" and "pasting" is how most retouching is done. It's all about utilizing a bunch of sophisticated tools and techniques to leverage what we have, to create what we need.

Chapter 21

Adding Finishing Touches

Y ou're nearing the end of the creative workflow. Only a few things need to be done to at this point to prepare a file for output. This chapter begins by looking at burning and dodging — a procedure that's used to modify the tonal ranges of different regions of an image. You're going to take a close look at the best way to do it nondestructively.

Then you look at adjusting image size and cropping. During that discussion you delve into the mysterious realm of resolution and how it affects image size by experimenting with a practice file. You'll be surprised at how easy this concept is to understand when you see it in action.

The Lightroom section of this book included a discussion about sharpening. I broke it down into three different types: capture, creative, and output. When discussing Lightroom, you concentrated on capture sharpening. In this section, you look at how the two other types of sharpening are accomplished during the creative workflow.

A high percentage of photos that make it this far into the creative workflow are generally intended for printing. Because of that, you take a close look at printing with inkjet printers and printing at a photolab. The information presented here will help you get the best printed output possible from your files when you choose one of these printing options.

Burning and Dodging to Balance Tones

Burning and dodging isn't necessarily a finishing touch. In Chapter 20, it is used to modify local tonal areas while retouching eyes and teeth. In the broadest sense, though, burning and dodging is used to complete the final

463

look of the finished image. The objective is to creatively guide the viewer's eye through the print by controlling the tonality of important — and less important — areas of the image.

Burning and dodging in the traditional darkroom

The terms *burning* and *dodging* refer to techniques that have been used in chemical darkrooms since the earliest days of photography. When printing a negative onto a piece of light-sensitive paper with an enlarger, the longer the light hits the paper, the darker the tones on the paper become. When an area of a print needs to be darker than the rest of the print, the printer makes a second exposure onto the paper. During that second exposure, he holds a sheet of cardboard with a small hole between the enlarger and the printing paper, allowing the light to hit only the area to be darkened. This way, he controls where the additional light strikes the paper. This process is called burning-in or burning.

Dodging is the opposite. If something needs to be lighter than the rest of the print, the printer uses a tool to block some of the light passing from the enlarger to the printing paper. This way, he holds back some of the light from hitting the sensitive paper; less light means lighter tones on the print.

In the days of the traditional darkroom, burning and dodging was a hit-and-miss operation. You never really knew how well you did until the photo paper was developed a few minutes later. (In the world of professional photolabs before digital, that was often several hours later.) Fortunately, the process is much easier and more controllable in the world of digital imaging and Photoshop.

Burning and dodging without Photoshop's Burn and Dodge tools

Photoshop CS3 has two tools in the Tools palette called the Burn and Dodge tools. These two tools have been part of Photoshop for a long time. However, I won't discuss them because I rarely use them. In fact, I don't know many serious Photoshop users who do. I don't like to use these tools for two reasons. First, these tools can be difficult to control, especially for someone new to photo manipulation. I know one or two people who have spent time mastering the tools, but I don't think it's worth the time because of the second problem with these tools: They're destructive to the image.

When Photoshop's Burn and Dodge tools are used, they permanently change pixels in the image. If you change your mind tomorrow, you can't undo their effects. The only way to isolate the effects of these tools is to duplicate a layer and use them exclusively on that duplicate. This is one of the least flexible ways of isolating burning and dodging to an independent layer because it still isn't easy to make modifications later. Also, duplicating a full image layer can double the size of a file.

Let's look at an alternative method for burning and dodging that doesn't use the standard Burn and Dodge tools. Follow these steps:

1. Open the practice file `downtown_portland.tif` from downloadable practice files on the Web site (`www.wiley.com/go/workflow`). This photo, shown in Figure 21.1, was shot from Portland, Oregon's famous Rose Garden. The view is looking back toward

downtown Portland with Mt. Hood in the background. In the first frame, there's quite a discrepancy between the dark tones of the trees and foliage in the foreground and the light tones on the mountain in the background, which is barely visible. If you attempt to darken the entire image to make the mountain more visible, the overall tonality becomes too dark.

The goal here is to balance the tones in this image by darkening the mountain and its foothills, as well as some of the buildings downtown, while maintaining the tonality of most of the greenery in the foreground, as shown in the second frame of Figure 21.1.

2. Add a new layer by choosing Layer ➪ New ➪ Layer (or click the New Layer button on the bottom of the Layers palette). Double-click on the new layer's name and rename it **Burn & Dodge**.

3. Change the blending mode of the Burn & Dodge layer on the Layers palette to Soft Light. You select this from the drop-down menu at the top of the Layers palette.

CAUTION The painting on a burn and dodge layer is affected by any adjustment layers above it. If you have an adjustment layer that's applying a strong tonal correction, place the burn and dodge layer above it so it will be unaffected by the adjustment layer.

4. Select the Brush tool from the Tools palette and change its size to 100 pixels to begin. (Change the size as you work so that it suits the area where you're working.) Decrease the Hardness value to 0 percent, set the Opacity to 25 percent, and make sure Flow is 100 percent. You're going to be painting with black and white, so make sure the color swatches on the toolbar are set to their defaults by pressing D. (Remember that you can use the X key to swap the colors of the foreground and background swatches.) Here's how it works: Paint with white where you want to lighten parts of the image, and paint with black to darken. Begin with black.

5. Begin painting the mountain and the foothills in front of it. Try not to paint the buildings just yet. Notice that the darkening effect is stronger on the darker tones of the hills in the foreground than it is on the mountain. That's because the mountain is so much lighter.

The effect should be slightly noticeable. This is the reason you're working with such a low opacity on the Brush tool. It's much better to reach the desired tonality by building up a couple of strokes than it is to try to nail it with one stroke at a special opacity.

NOTE Though you're painting with white and black paint, the effect is different from working with a layer mask. In this case, you're painting content onto the layer instead of using a mask to modify existing content. (You can mask your painting on the Burn & Dodge layer with a layer mask if you want to.)

6. Increase the Opacity of the Brush tool to 50 percent and paint the mountain and the distant foothills to darken them a bit more. Occasionally, turn the Burn & Dodge layer's visibility off and on to check your work.

TIP Feel free to experiment with higher Opacity settings on the Brush tool. Just be advised that lower settings are often the best place to start.

FIGURE 21.1

In this first photo of downtown Portland, Oregon, Mt. Hood is barely visible in the background. If the overall tonality is adjusted to darken the mountain, the foreground tones would be too dark. This problem is solved in the second image by darkening the mountain, as well as some buildings and the upper part of the sky with a burn and dodge layer.

7. When you're happy with the mountain, decrease the Brush Opacity to 15 percent and paint some of the buildings to darken them.

> **TIP** If you don't like some of your burning and dodging, use the Eraser to remove any painting from the Burn & Dodge layer and try again with the Brush tool. (Yes, this is one of those rare times when using the destructive Eraser tool is okay.)

8. Most of the light tones are beginning to come into line. Now see what you can do about some of the dark foliage in the middle foreground. Change the Brush color to white (X) and paint some of the dark areas in the foreground. Don't lighten any of the foliage that's near the edge of the frame.

9. This image is almost ready. The only thing that still bothers me is that the sky is so light. I don't like the way it draws the eye away from the main subject matter. Switch the color back to black (X). Change the brush size to 500 px and increase the Opacity to about 40 percent. Paint across the top of the image and down both sides of the sky. The objective here is to darken all of these edges, helping to contain the viewer's eye within the frame. Build up the strokes at the top and sides so that the tone darkens as it gets closer to the edge of the frame.

   I add this finishing touch of darkening corners and sides to almost every image during the Creative Workflow — just as I did in when custom printing in a film-based, wet darkroom.

> **TIP** If you plan to crop the image much, you'll have to revisit this layer after cropping to check the edges. If some of your darkening was removed, add more to balance the image.

10. Just for grins, change the layer blending mode back to Normal. The image should look something like Figure 21.2. This is a good way to check your strokes to see if you missed something obvious. This also reinforces the idea that all of your brush strokes actually added layer content in the form of paint.

When burning and dodging, be aware that if the detail is already gone from a blown-out highlight, no amount of burning will bring it back. The same goes for detail completely lost to a shadow. If you try to recover it, you'll end up with a ghostly gray area.

Because your burning and dodging is on its own layer, you have lots of control over it. You can go back and make modifications to the painting on the layer by erasing some of it or adding more. You also can lower the layer's opacity if you want to tone down the overall effect. And, of course, you can delete the layer and begin again, all without permanently changing the underlying image.

Before moving on, here's a quick review of this easy, nondestructive burning and dodging technique:

1. Create an empty layer above the main image layer(s).
2. Change its blending mode to Soft Light.
3. Use the Brush tool at a low opacity. I usually begin with 15–20 percent, increasing the value only when I can't see any effect. Paint with black to darken and white to lighten.

FIGURE 21.2

This figure shows what happens when the layer blending mode set back to Normal. Now the paint strokes are completely visible. If you begin to burn and dodge and you see strokes like this, it means you forgot to set the Burn & Dodge layer's blending mode to Soft Light.

TIP Setting up a Burn and Dodge layer is a perfect job for an action. Create one that records the three earlier steps so that it prepares the Burn and Dodge layer for you whenever you need one. You can even add steps that select the Brush tool and set the painting colors to default, as well as automatically renaming the layer to Burn and Dodge for easy identification.

Changing an Image's Resolution and Size

Quite often it's necessary to change an image file's resolution and/or size. Doing so seems straightforward; however, I've seen many photographers do one or both of these operations incorrectly. The problem usually stems from a lack of understanding about image resolution and how it affects image size.

CAUTION Always save a master file with all layers before changing size or cropping. Otherwise it may be hard to backup and resize the file for a different output use later.

Demystifying resolution

One of the things that can be the hardest to get your head around when you start down the digital path is resolution. This confusion is compounded by the fact that there are two different kinds of resolution in the digital world. One is *dots per inch*, and the other is *pixels per inch*.

Dots per inch (dpi) refers to the number of dots per inch that an inkjet printer is capable of applying to a sheet of paper. It can range from 720 to 2800 and more. The closer these dots are to each other, the more they blend together forming continuous tones on the print. Naturally, this depends on the paper that's being printed on. If the paper is porous watercolor paper, the dots soak in and blend just fine at lower dpi settings like 720. On glossy photo papers, a higher setting — such as 1440 — is needed because the ink dries on the surface. About the only time people discuss dpi is when they are talking about a printer.

When we're talking about resolution in digital photography, we're usually thinking about pixels per inch (ppi). This refers to the distance between the pixels that make up digital images. Pixels per inch is an important setting because it determines what digital images look like when they're displayed and printed. Sometimes a lower value is desirable, and other times a higher value is preferred.

TIP Keep in mind that people often use the terms dpi and ppi interchangeably, saying dpi when they really mean ppi. If they're not specifically talking about a printer's output, then they probably mean ppi.

If you have an image file that's 150 ppi and you need to convert it to 300 ppi for printing, converting the image reduces it to half its size. An 8 x 10 becomes a 4 x 5. Let's explore why that happens.

Doing the simple math

I know I just said the dreaded *M* word, but please keep reading because in the next few paragraphs I show you how to use simple math to understand what Photoshop is doing when you resize your photo files. Let's start with getting a better handle on how resolution works. Follow these steps:

1. Choose File ➪ New, and create a new file with the following attributes: Width = 2 inches, Height = 2 inches, Resolution = 300, and Color Mode = RGB Color, 8-bit. The New dialog box shown in Figure 21.3 shows these settings.

FIGURE 21.3

Use these settings in the New dialog box to set up a sample file for this exercise.

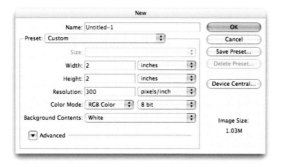

2. When the file opens in Photoshop, choose Image ⇨ Image Size (Alt+Ctrl+I). Notice that the dimensions are the same as what you specified with the New File command.

3. For the first part of your experiment, uncheck the Resample check box.

   Notice that the Pixel Dimensions area at the top of the Image Size window goes gray when Resample is turned off. That means that the number of pixels being used in your image is fixed at 600 x 600 pixels. You come back to this in a moment.

4. Change the resolution setting to **150**. Notice that the size of the image goes from 2"×2" to 4"×4", as shown in Figure 21.4.

   You're changing the distance between pixels as you modify the resolution of the file. You have fixed overall pixel dimensions of 600 x 600. When you set your resolution to 300 pixels per inch, the math dictates that the image is 2"×2" (2" x 300 ppi = 600 pixels).

   When you set your resolution to 150 ppi, the image must become 4"×4" in size (4" x 150 ppi = 600 pixels).

FIGURE 21.4

When Resample is turned off, Resolution affects Document Size and vice versa. However, no new pixels are added and none removed because the actual Pixel Dimensions cannot be changed.

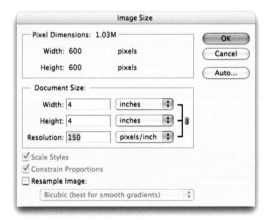

Resizing and resampling

In the last example, you were asked to turn off Resample because Resample has a special function that affects the math involved in resizing an image. With Resample turned off, the Pixel Dimensions remain fixed. Any change to Resolution affects Document Size and vice versa. Let's see what happens when Resample is turned on:

1. Create the same sample file again: 2"×2" at 300 ppi.

If you still have the Image Size window open from the preceding example, you can reset it to the settings it had when you opened it by holding down Alt and clicking Reset (where the Cancel button used to be). (This works with almost every dialog box where you see a Cancel button.)

2. This time, leave the Resample box checked. (Click it if it isn't already checked.)

3. Change the Resolution to **150**.

   Notice that the Image Size remains at 2"×2". What did change was the Pixel Dimensions at the top of the window. They went from 600 x 600 to 300 x 300.

4. Change the Resolution to **600**. Now the Pixel Dimensions changes to 1200 x 1200, but the Document Size remains fixed, as shown in Figure 21.5.

FIGURE 21.5

When Resample is turned on, changes to Resolution or Document Size affect Pixel Dimensions only. Pixels are added or removed to accommodate the changes. This can be seen in changes to Pixel Dimensions at the top of the window.

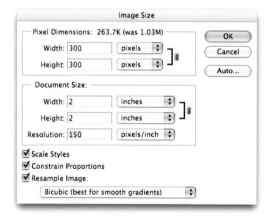

When Resample is turned on, modifications to Resolution or Document Size in the Image Size window affect only the Pixel Dimensions. What's happening is that when you make the document smaller or reduce its resolution, resampling takes pixels from the image to make it smaller. This is called *downsampling*.

If you make the Document Size larger or increase the Resolution, resampling adds pixels to the image. This is called *upsampling*. You can verify that this is taking place by looking at the file size readout next to Pixel Dimensions. 21.4, the file size was 1.03MB. In Figure 21.5, it becomes 263.7Kb. Fewer megabytes mean fewer pixels.

Keep in mind that adding lots of pixels to an image can affect the image's quality. Photoshop is pretty good at upsampling, but only so much can be done. Lots of guesses need to be made on Photoshop's part when deciding what color to make a new pixel. The quality of the outcome depends on the size and quality of the original file. When a quality file is used it's easy to double or even triple the size of the file. However, if you push it too far and try to upsample an image beyond Photoshop's capabilities, you can hit a point of diminishing returns where quality begins to suffer. For projects that require massive upsampling beyond Photoshop's abilities, look to a plug-in like Genuine Fractals by onOne Software (`www.ononesoftware.com`). This plug-in uses fractal math to accomplish some amazing upsampling feats.

So remember, if you only want to change the resolution of the file, uncheck Resample. If you need to make the image smaller or larger, then Resample must be checked.

Sometimes it's necessary to change the document size and resolution at the same time. For example, suppose you have a file that is sized to 8"×10" at 250 ppi, and you need to change it to a 4"×5" at 300. Making this change with the Image Size command requires two steps. Both steps can be carried out in one use of the Image Size command:

1. Create a new file by choosing File ➪ New; make the file measure 8"×10" at 250 ppi.
2. Open the Image Size dialog box by choosing Image ➪ Size (Alt+Ctrl+I).
3. Deselect the Resample Image option, and change the resolution to **300**. Notice that the Document Size changes to 6.67 x 8.33 because you're moving the pixels closer together.
4. Select the Resample option, and change the Document Size Width to 4 inches.
5. Click OK.

   Now you have a file that is 4"×5" at 300 ppi.

Using the correct image interpolation method

There's one more wrinkle to throw at you before moving on. In the previous examples, you probably noticed a box next to Resample Image in the Image Size dialog box, as shown in Figure 21.6.

This box allows you to change the *image interpolation* that's used when you resample an image. Different interpolation settings affect the way new pixels are assigned color based on the surrounding pixels. You have five choices:

- **Nearest Neighbor:** Fast, but not very precise; best for illustrations with edges that are not anti-aliased rather than photos
- **Bilinear:** Medium quality results
- **Bicubic:** Slower but more precise; produces smoother graduations than the two previous methods

■ **Bicubic Smoother:** Based on Bicubic interpolation, but designed for enlarging images

■ **Bicubic Sharper:** Based on Bicubic interpolation, but designed for reducing image size

The two interpolation methods that interest us most are Bicubic Smoother and Bicubic Sharper. These are the two you'll use almost exclusively when resampling images in Photoshop. When you're upsampling, or increasing the number of pixels in an image, choose Bicubic Smoother. When you're downsampling, or decreasing the number of pixels, choose Bicubic Sharper.

FIGURE 21.6

Image interpolation gives you different options with the kind of math that's used when you resample an image. Be sure to use the appropriate method for the type of sizing you're doing.

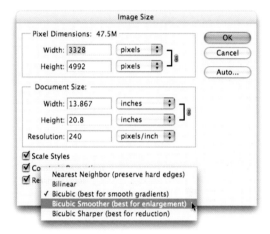

NEW FEATURE With earlier versions of Photoshop, you had to remember what these two interpolation methods did. Now in CS3, a short description appears behind Bicubic Smoother and Bicubic Sharper in the Image Size dialog box to remind you when to use them. Thank you, Adobe!

These two resampling interpolations, introduced in Photoshop CS, allow much cleaner resampling of images. Before they were introduced, upsampling was done in a different way. Something known as the Ten Percent Method was common. Ten percent increments were used to increase the size of a file with the Bicubic interpolation method. The process was repeated, ten percent at a time, until the image was close to the desired size. This process was used as a way of dealing with the limitations of the Bicubic interpolation. Now with Bicubic Smoother, the Ten Percent Method is no longer needed. Jumps of 100 percent and more can be done in one step.

Using the Crop Tool

Because cropping in Photoshop is considered destructive — it can't be undone later — I always leave master image files uncropped. That's why I waited until now to discuss this basic tool. There are two ways to use the Crop tool. It can be used to crop to a predetermined size (like 5 x 7), or it can be used to create a custom crop to suit special needs. Let's investigate this tool. Follow these steps:

TIP You looked at cropping in Lightroom's Develop module. When you plan to create a master file it's best to undo any final cropping in Lightroom before opening the file so you can leave your options open. There's nothing worse than doing a couple of hours of work on an image in Photoshop and then deciding that you wish you hadn't cropped something out in the early stages of the workflow.

1. Open the `beach_dog.tif` from the downloadable practice files on the Web site. Before doing anything, look at the document size of this image so you know what you're working with. Choose Image ⇨ Image Size (Alt+Command+I/Alt+Ctrl+I). This file's size is 7.787 inches by 11.68 inches at 300 ppi.

2. Select the Crop tool (C) from the Toolbox; it's fifth from the top on the single-column Toolbox. Go to the options bar at the top, and click the Clear button to clear any settings from the Crop tool's options. When all settings are cleared, the tool is ready to handle any kind of special cropping.

3. Click near the upper-left area and drag downward to the lower right. Notice that you can create any aspect ratio you want while dragging. This is similar to unlocking the aspect ratio on Lightroom's Crop tool. When you let go of the mouse button you use the control handles at the sides or corners of the selection to change the dimensions of the cropping boundaries.

TIP If a setting called *Snap* is turned on, you may be having trouble with the cropping selection trying to jump to the image boundary when you work near the boundaries of the image. Snap allows the cursor to move in smart ways so that it quickly lines up with other things in the image. Sometimes, though, it's not smart enough. To solve this problem, choose View and click Snap to deselect it. (This is one of the few commands you can access while the cropping selection is active.)

4. Click anywhere inside the cropping selection to drag and move it to a different location. (This is a little different than dragging the image as you did in Lightroom.) You can also use the cursor keys to nudge the box a small amount.

5. You have a problem with this image because the horizon isn't straight. Fortunately this is easy to remedy during the cropping operation. Simply move the cursor outside of the cropping selection until it turns into a curved, double-headed arrow icon. Now you can click and drag to rotate the crop box to any orientation. Try to match the line of the horizon with the top line of the crop box, as shown in Figure 21.7.

TIP The rotation is centered around the crosshair in the center of the crop box. If you want to rotate around a different area — like a corner — move the crosshairs to that location.

6. When you like the crop, press Enter or Return. If you want to bail out and begin again, press Esc.

You can also commit a crop by clicking the check mark button on the options bar. And you can cancel the cropping action by clicking the Cancel button beside it. (A third way is to right-click and choose from the contextual menu.)

FIGURE 21.7

You can rotate the cropping box so that you straighten the image as it's being cropped. To do this, move the cursor outside of the box until the cursor becomes a curved double arrow and then click and drag upward or downward.

This free-form cropping works fine when you don't need a specific size, but most often at this point in the workflow you do. Trying to create an exact size with the Crop tool like this is very hard to do. It's more a matter of trial and error and lots of luck. Fortunately, you can specify a particular size before cropping. Try this again and crop to a specific size. Continue where you left off after Step 6, and follow these steps:

7. Return the file to its opening state by clicking the image icon at the top of the History palette.

8. Go to the options bar and type **5** in the Width field and **7** in the Height field. Type **300** in the Resolution field, which is the most common resolution for printing.

TIP If the reading beside the numbers says something other than "in" (inches), then your ruler preferences are set to something other than inches. This is easy to fix. If the ruler isn't currently visible, choose View ⇨ Ruler (Command+R/Ctrl+R), right-click the ruler, and select Inches. (I like to leave the Ruler visible because it's useful for other things, too.)

9. Draw your crop box again. This time notice that the aspect ratio is locked and that there are no control handles at the top, bottom, or sides. Rotate the crop until you like it and then commit the crop. Now you have a file that's sized for 5 x 7 at 300 ppi. This is a little different from the Lightroom crop because you're specifying an actual size with pixel dimensions. Final sizing doesn't happen in Lightroom until the file is exported or opened directly into Photoshop.

CAUTION By default the Crop tool uses bicubic resampling to change the size of the image. When you decrease the size you're downsampling, and when you increase the size you're upsampling. If you need to increase the size more than 10–15 percent, it's best to use the Image Size command with the Bicubic Smoother option to increase the image size before final cropping.

Professional Sharpening Strategies

Chapter 7 introduces sharpening and why it's important for digital files. In that section, three different types of workflow specific sharpening are discussed: capture sharpening, creative sharpening, and output sharpening. That chapter focuses on capture sharpening, which is applied by the camera on non-raw files and applied during Lightroom editing (or ACR) for raw files. In this section, I discuss how sharpening is applied for the two other types of sharpening. First, let's review what we're talking about:

- **Creative sharpening** is used to fine-tune an image creatively by selectively modifying the sharpness of selected areas of the image. When I use the term *sharpening* here, I am also referring to its opposite, *blurring*, which is the lack of sharpness. What that means is that creative sharpening can be used in the same image to sharpen something of interest, such as someone's eyes, and to blur something else, like the background around the subject.

  The main thing to understand about creative sharpening is that its effect is relative to the rest of the image. The goal isn't to make part of the image perfectly sharp. The goal is to make part of the image stand out from its surroundings by sharpening it or blurring the detail surrounding it.

- **Output sharpening** is overall sharpening that's designed to prepare an image for output, such as printing or onscreen viewing. This sharpening is applied to the entire image with the intent of getting it ready for a particular output option. One of the things to understand here is that size matters. A file that's being prepared for printing as a 5 x 7 requires a completely different sharpening scenario than the same file being prepared for a 16 x 20. Otherwise, if the sharpening on the 5 x 7 looks great, the 16 x 20 will not be sharp enough.

CAUTION Something you want to avoid when possible is sharpening an image for output, changing its size, and then resharpening for a new output size. Sharpening on top of previous sharpening adversely affects the image by introducing unwanted *artifacting*—distortions introduced by the digital process—causing image details to look "crunchy" instead of smooth.

This means that any creative sharpening will be further sharpened during the output sharpening process. Knowing this is important because it means you need to avoid overdoing the amount of creative sharpening.

NOTE Keep in mind that sharpening is not used to fix severely blurred images. It's used to compensate for some of the effects of digital capture—whether by camera or scanner.

No matter if you're doing creative sharpening or output sharpening, one of Photoshop's two sharpening tools is used: the Unsharp Mask (USM) and the Smart Sharpen filters. These filters are very similar to one another. Let's compare and contrast them as you explore how they're used.

TIP Remember that both these filters can be used as Smart Filters, as discussed in Chapter 15.

Using the Unsharp Mask filter

People are often confused when it comes to using the Unsharp Mask (USM) filter because the name is totally counterintuitive. Why would someone want to use something named *unsharp* to sharpen an image? The reason this sharpening filter has such an odd name is that it refers to a sharpening method that was used before digital was an option. In that method, a negative that needed to be sharpened was duplicated. The duplicate negative was intentionally created just a bit out of focus. The two negatives—the original and the new one—were then sandwiched together slightly out of registration and then printed. The effect increased contrast around edge detail and made the resulting print look sharper. This is the same way the Unsharp Mask and the Smart Sharpen filters work.

NOTE You may notice that there are some other sharpening filters in the Sharpen menu. One is named Sharpen and another is Sharpen More. One would think that these are the main sharpening tools, but they aren't. They are blunt instruments that can't be controlled. In the many years that I've been using Photoshop, I've never used either of these.

The Unsharp Mask dialog box, shown in Figure 21.8, is found in the Filter menu (choose Filter ⇨ Sharpen ⇨ Unsharp Mask). This filter doesn't detect edge detail per se; instead it looks for pixels that have different tonal values than surrounding pixels. It then increases the contrast of those surrounding *edge pixels* causing the lighter pixels to get lighter and the darker pixels to get darker. This is what creates the sharpening halos discussed in Chapter 7. The sliders in the USM dialog box are used to control how these halos are created. Let's take a closer look at them.

FIGURE 21.8

The Unsharp Mask filter has been the main sharpening tool in Photoshop for many years. Sharpening is accomplished with this filter by balancing the settings of the three sliders.

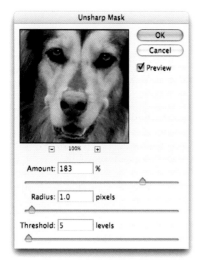

- **Amount:** The Amount slider is used to control the amount of contrast between differing pixels, which affects edge contrast. Higher values equal more contrast and lower values equal less contrast.

- **Radius:** This slider is used to determine the number of pixels that are changed when the filter sees tonal variation. Higher values increase the size of the halos and cause the sharpening to be obvious. The Radius slider is the most important slider here. Exercise caution when using it because too high of a value creates sharpening halos that are too noticeable. Too high of a Radius value combined with a high Amount value causes the image to look over-sharpened.

  Keep in mind that this value is going to vary depending on the subject matter. A lower value works best with photos rich in edge detail, while higher values can be used for photos that don't have as much detail in them.

CROSS-REF See the sharpening discussion in Chapter 7 for more on how image content affects sharpening values.

- **Threshold:** The Threshold slider is used to determine how different in tone the surrounding pixels need to be before they're considered edge pixels, causing them to be sharpened. For example, a value of 5 affects only neighboring pixels that have a tonal difference of 5 or more (on a scale of 0 to 255). The default value of 0 causes all pixels in the photo to be sharpened.

NOTE Apply creative sharpening to a duplicate layer in the master layered file or use a Smart Filter. This ensures that any sharpening can be undone later by discarding or modifying the layer.

Using the Unsharp Mask requires a bit of a balancing act among these three sliders. The best way to understand their use is to take the USM filter for a test drive. Follow these steps:

1. Open `high_desert_flower.tif` from downloadable practice files on the Web site and zoom to 50 percent. This photo has lots of edge detail on the main subject, with little edge detail in the background.

NOTE A couple of times in this book you are asked to zoom to 50 percent when evaluating an image. This is because Photoshop does a much better job of rendering a file to the screen at zoom ratios of 25 percent — in other words, 25 percent, 50 percent, and 100 percent. You can't really judge an image when it's zoomed to any zoom ratio that isn't a multiple of 25.

2. Choose Filter ⇨ Sharpen ⇨ Unsharp Mask to open the Unsharp Mask dialog box. Type **200** for Amount, **1.0** for Radius, and **0** for Threshold. Notice that this sharpens much of the edge detail on the flower.

   I find that low Radius and Threshold settings and higher Amount settings are usually the best place to start when using the Unsharp Mask. Then adjust the Radius and Threshold values to match the subject content of the photo.

TIP Though the USM dialog box has a preview window, you won't be using it. It's much better to use the actual image for evaluation purposes. So go ahead and drag the dialog box to the side so you can get a good look at the flower.

3. Now increase the Threshold setting to **10** and notice that the sharpening tapers off. This is especially noticeable on the crown of the flower. That's because only edge pixels with a tonal difference of 10 or more are sharpened.

4. Increase the Amount value to **300**. The sharpening increases, but it's still more subtle than the Step 2 setting.

5. Now increase the Radius value to **2**. Notice how much this small adjustment affects the flower's edge detail. It's beginning to look too crunchy, which means it's over-sharpened.

6. Decrease the Amount value to **200** again. The crunchiness is reduced, bringing the edge contrast back into line.

As you can see, there isn't necessarily an exact set of sharpening values for this image because of the way these settings affect one another. This photo would benefit from the settings in Step 2 or Step 6. Something else to notice here is that the out-of-focus bee is still out of focus, even though its edges are sharpened.

> **TIP**   Sometimes sharpening causes a color shift. When this happens, it's easy to fix. If the sharpening is applied to a duplicate layer, change the layer's blending mode to Luminosity. If the sharpening is applied to the main image layer, choose Edit ➪ Fade and change the Mode to Luminosity in the Fade dialog box. (Just remember that Fade must be the very next step after sharpening is applied.)

Using the Smart Sharpen filter

One of Photoshop's newer filters is the Smart Sharpen filter introduced in version CS2. This filter is considered smart because it treats various regions of the image differently based on the content of those regions. The Smart Sharpen filter attempts to sharpen only the areas of the image that have detail without affecting areas that don't. This is different from the USM that affects all areas of the image equally. Figure 21.9 shows the Smart Sharpen dialog box. This dialog box doesn't have a Threshold slider because it isn't needed. It also has some controls that aren't in the USM. Let's take a closer look:

FIGURE 21.9

The Smart Sharpen filter is one of Photoshop's newer filters. Its more sophisticated dialog box allows you to address a number of sharpening issues within the photo. When the Advanced radio button is selected, the Shadow and Highlight tabs are revealed.

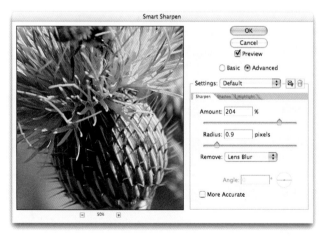

- **Amount** and **Radius:** Function the same as the sliders in the Unsharp Mask.
- **Remove:** A cool feature that adjusts the way the filter works, depending on the problem. The pop-up menu has three options: Gaussian Blur, which is the same algorithm used by

the Unsharp Mask; Lens Blur, the best choice for most digital camera files; and Motion Blur, which attempts to compensate for blur caused by motion during the exposure. When Motion Blur is selected, the Angle setting is activated. This allows you to input the direction of the motion that caused the blur. For example, if the blur is from a sideways motion during the exposure, use a value of 0.

- **Advanced:** Gives you more control by allowing you to work with the shadows and highlights independently of the rest of the image. You can use Fade Amount to adjust the amount of sharpening and Tonal Width to restrict your adjustments to the shadows or the highlights. This is quite useful when you have lots of noise in the shadows that you don't want to sharpen.

- **More Accurate:** Selecting this option makes the filter provide a more accurate removal of blurring, but the process takes longer.

NOTE The only thing I don't like about this filter is that the dialog box is huge, which can make it hard to see the image while using the filter — especially when working on a computer with a smaller display.

As mentioned earlier, creative sharpening is used to differentiate parts of the image from one another using either of these filters. This is accomplished by using masks and/or selections when sharpening (or blurring) those parts. For example, if you want to sharpen someone's eyes, create a feathered selection around the eyes before opening the sharpening filter.

TIP Selective blurring can be used to help a photo whose sharpness isn't up to snuff. Say you have a photo of someone in a garden, but the overall focus is *soft*. If you blur the garden in the background and not the person, the person will look sharper because of his or her relationship to the more blurred background. That's why this is still considered creative sharpening.

After all creative sharpening is done and the file is sized to its final dimensions, another sharpening pass must be made to prepare the file for printing, or any other kind of output such as Web display. This is an important step that can make or break a great image.

Sharpening for output

A moment ago, I discussed the need to zoom to a multiple of 25 percent when sharpening. There's a reason I choose 50 percent instead of 25 or 100 percent. That's because this percent is usually the zoom ratio that comes closest to approximating the actual size of the printed image on your screen. One would think that zooming to 100 percent would display the image at its actual size. However, because a computer monitor isn't capable of displaying an image at 300 ppi it has to spread the pixels out to the resolution it can display — usually between 70 and 90 pixels per inch. (That's why 72 ppi is a common resolution for photos intended for the Web.) This causes a photo with a resolution of 300 ppi to look bigger on the computer monitor than the actual print. If you're viewing at 100 percent while sharpening, you probably will be disappointed in the results because your preview doesn't match reality.

The optimal zoom ratio can vary from system to system. Here's how to find out which zoom multiple of 25 percent is best for your particular viewing environment:

1. Choose View ⇨ Rulers to turn on the rulers. Figure 21.10 shows a photo with the rulers displayed. If your rulers are already turned on, you don't have to do this.

Choose View ⇨ Rulers to display a ruler at the top and left side of an image. This is useful when you want to get an idea of how big the display is in relation to the actual size of the image.

2. With the rulers showing, hold a real ruler up to the screen while zooming the image. When the file's ruler and the real ruler match, the file is displayed at its actual size. Because you want a multiple of 25 percent, try 25 percent and 50 percent to see which is closest to reality. On all of my monitors, 50 percent is a little bigger than reality and 25 percent is a little smaller. I use 50 percent because an image that displays a little bigger is easier to look at and evaluate.

NOTE   When sharpening for the Web, zoom to 100 percent to display the image at actual size because the output is intended for a computer monitor.

Following the previous guidelines helps to ensure that the sharpening you see on your screen more closely matches the final output size. However, be advised that there are a couple of other variables that come into play.

- **Display versus Print:** Even in a perfect world the sharpness shown on a monitor won't always translate to printed output. That's because the way a computer displays an image is different than the way the image looks on paper. In fact, different monitors can look different. When I first switched from a CRT monitor to a flat panel monitor I noticed that everything looked sharper on the new monitor. That's because of the resolving power of this newer style of LCD monitors.

- **Printing Processes:** Different kinds of printers and printing paper affect the way an image looks. Prints on glossy paper always look a little sharper than prints on matte. Some inkjet papers, such as fine-art papers, are very absorbent and really soak up the ink, which diminishes the effects of sharpening.

- **Size Matters:** Sharpening is dependent on the dimensions of the print. That's why it's important to do all final cropping and sizing before output sharpening is applied.

The thing to take away from this is to experiment with your intended output until you're comfortable predicting how your computer's display translates onto a printed image.

Making Prints from Your Files

After a file is sized and sharpened it's ready to print. This section looks at the two most popular printing options: inkjet printing and printing at a photolab.

Inkjet printing with the new CS3 Print command

Inkjet printing has come a long way since its early days. The output from modern printers rivals traditional photographic printing in quality and longevity. Additionally, the variety of printing papers is way beyond the narrow range of traditional printing. The downsides are the cost per print and the amount of time involved, especially when the color doesn't match like it's supposed to. However, for many people, these issues are outweighed by the convenience and control of using an inkjet printer.

Understanding the settings

When someone asks me to help solve an inkjet color-matching issue, I usually find that the problem is an incorrect driver setting. That's because the correct driver settings are what allows Photoshop and the printer to have an intelligent conversation. If any one of these is set incorrectly, the chances of a good color match become slim.

Figure 21.11 shows the new Print dialog box. Some of these settings are more important than others. Let's go over them from left to right:

NEW FEATURE Photoshop CS3 has combined the Print and Print with Preview options from CS2 into one useful Print dialog box. This helps to solve much of the confusion people had with printing in Photoshop CS and Photoshop CS2.

FIGURE 21.11

The new Print dialog box in Photoshop CS3 has everything in one user-friendly place. The description box on the lower right provides useful descriptions of all the settings in the column above it when the cursor hovers over them.

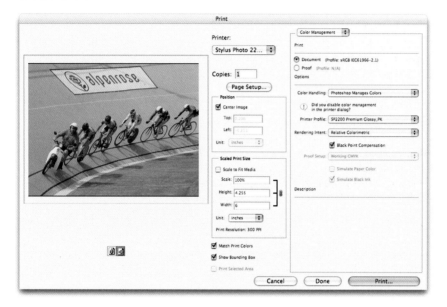

- The Preview window allows you to see how the image is positioned on the paper. This preview is very useful because it alerts you to sizing errors — which has saved me a number of times. Something new about this preview is that it now functions as a color preview when Color Management settings are changed. (The Match Print Colors option must be selected for this function to be active.)

- The information in the middle of the dialog box is mostly self-explanatory. I stay away from using the Scaled Print Size section unless I'm doing a quick print. Normally, I think it's best to have all sizing done before getting to the Print dialog box — otherwise how can I trust that my sharpening is optimal.

  If Bounding Box is selected, a black box outlines the image. The corners of the box can be used to resize the image. Again, I don't recommend using this to resize an image.

The Color Management section on the right is where the important settings are. Let's break them down. (If you don't see a heading that says Color Management at the top right of your Print dialog box, click beside Output and select Color Management from the drop-down menu.) These are your choices:

NOTE Notice that as you hover the cursor over different sections of the Color Management area, a contextual description appears at the bottom of the screen. Use this to learn more about the options here.

- **Document:** Selecting this option informs Photoshop of what the starting color profile is for the document. In this case, it's sRGB color. Be sure this radio button is selected.

- **Color Handling:** This tells Photoshop whether you want it to handle color management or if the printer will be taking care of color. I prefer to let Photoshop manage the color unless I'm using *RIP* software with the printer. Photoshop is much smarter than most printers when it comes to color management.

  If you have a newer printer you can try managing the color with the printer. Try it both ways and see which color handling method you prefer. Just be aware that if you choose Printer Manages Color from the Color Handling menu, the rest of the Color Handling area is grayed out. You'll have to use the printer driver to manage color instead of Photoshop's Print dialog box.

NOTE RIP software replaces the driver software that comes with a printer. Its primary function is to make the interface between you and the printer — and the computer and the printer — more flexible and powerful. One of the primary advantages to using a RIP with your printer is that it's very good at handling color. RIP software also does a great job with black-and-white printing. One of my favorites is ImagePrint by ColorByte (`www.colorbytesoftware.com`). The software isn't cheap, but it pays for itself in no time if you do lots of inkjet printing.

- **Printer Profile:** If this setting is wrong, all bets are off for consistent color matching. By default, this is set to the color space that the image is currently in — in this case, sRGB. For the most part, that's useless information. Photoshop is already aware of the file's color space. What it needs to know is something about the conditions of the printer where the file is being sent. This is where a profile is selected that describes the printer's paper and the ink that will be used to make the print.

  Figure 21.12 shows part of the Printer Profile pop-up menu. Photoshop comes with a bunch of canned profiles. Also, new printer profiles are installed on your system when a new printer is installed. These printer-specific profiles allow you to match Photoshop to the type of printer, ink, and paper you're using.

FIGURE 21.12

The Printer Profile drop-down menu has a long list of profiles. Some of these were installed as part of Photoshop, and others were installed with new printers. The section shown here shows the profiles that are associated with my Epson printer.

All the profiles in Figure 21.12 that begin with SP2200 are profiles that came with my Epson 2200 printer. Each of these profiles describes a particular paper and ink combination used by the printer. Selecting the correct one informs Photoshop about the specific printing environment. In this case, I point to an Epson 2200 profile for Premium Glossy paper with Photo Black ink.

> **TIP**   If you don't see profiles for your printer, or you don't understand what the names of your profiles mean, contact your printer's manufacturer or download them directly from your printer's Web site.

■ **Rendering Intent:** This tells Photoshop what system to use for mapping colors from the computer to the printer. This helps to compensate for differences between the color space of Photoshop and the printer's color space. Photographers tend to work with Relative Colorimetric and Perceptual. The difference is that if some colors in the file are outside the range of reproducible colors, the Perceptual rendering intent tries to manage those *out-of-gamut* colors by bringing them into gamut while preserving the relationship of all of the colors as it compensates. In some cases that means that in-gamut colors will shift. On the other hand, the Relative Colorimetric rendering intent keeps most in-gamut colors as they are and moves only the out-of-gamut colors into the new gamut.

> **NOTE**   According to Adobe, the Relative Colorimetric rendering intent is the standard rendering intent for printing in North America and Europe.

Sometimes, changing this setting affects colors, and sometimes, it doesn't. It really depends on the image and the printing environment. If the Match Print Colors option is selected, any changes in Rendering Intent are reflected in the preview.

■ **Black Point Compensation:** Selecting this option helps to map the black from the image in Photoshop to the black that the printer is capable of printing. It's usually best to leave this checked.

The two key settings here are Color Handling and Pinter Profile. Let Photoshop manage the color and give it useful information to describe the intended printing environment.

The third key setting has to do with the printer's settings. (You won't get to this dialog box until you click Print in the Print dialog box.) Now that Photoshop knows what to do with the file, you need to tell the printer to play dumb and don't try to manage the color. If Photoshop and the printer are fighting over color management, there's no predicting what the result will be. This setting is going to vary from printer to printer, as well as between Mac and Windows platforms. Look for a check box in your printer driver settings called No Color Correction or something similar.

In Figure 21.13, I set the printer's resolution to 1440 dpi (dots per inch). As mentioned earlier in the section on resolution, this setting determines how closely the dots of ink are laid down on the paper. The higher the number, the closer the dots. When printing on matte or glossy paper it's best to use 1440 so that the dots are close enough that they form a continuous tone — you can't see the space between the dots. If 720 is used on glossy paper you could end up with some jagged lines.

FIGURE 21.13

You can see where I set up the printer driver for the type of paper I'm using. This is also where I set the printer's resolution to 1440 dpi. This tells the printer how much ink to apply to the paper.

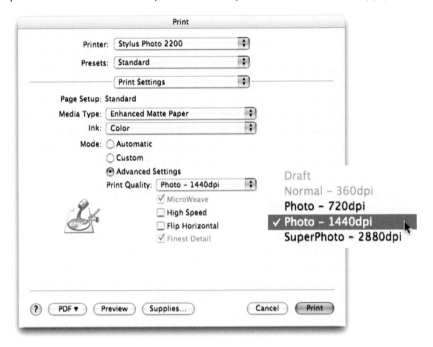

When printing on fine-art papers that are absorbent it's okay to use 720 because the ink soaks into the paper and fills in the space between the dots. Using 720 instead of 1440 saves ink because fewer dots are being printed. The higher setting of 2880 is intended to bring the dots even closer together. However, you'll have a hard time discerning the difference between 1440 and 2880 without a magnifying glass. The main difference is that twice as much printing ink is used. If you can't see the difference, why use more ink?

Evaluating the print

The goal with printing — whether it's done on an inkjet printer or by a lab — is to match the way the image displays on the monitor as closely as possible. Naturally, if the monitor isn't calibrated and profiled, it will be hard to determine whether the print is a match to the file. I have seen cases where a photographer's color matching problems disappeared when she calibrated her monitor.

The other key to determining if the print is a match to the display is to be sure that the print is being viewed under a daylight-balanced light source. If the print is being viewed under normal household light (incandescent), it appears warmer than it really is. If it's being viewed under florescent light, it appears cooler. If you aren't using daylight balance, you can't accurately evaluate the print's color.

> **TIP** Be sure to give inkjet prints time to completely dry before making a critical analysis of their color. Absorbent papers dry faster than less-absorbent papers.

Printing at a lab

As mentioned earlier, inkjet printing isn't for everyone. It can be time consuming and expensive. Most photographers I know, especially the professionals, have their printing done by professional photolabs. Here are some of the main advantages to printing at a lab:

- **Real photo paper:** Although there's nothing wrong with using quality inkjet papers and inks, some people are not comfortable with them. Photolabs use the same types of printing paper that they've always used. This gives you the opportunity to have your photos printed on papers like Kodak's Metallic or Fuji's Crystal Archive papers.

- **Finishing services:** Full-service labs offer a wide range of finishing services such as dry mounting and canvas mounting, as well as matting and framing.

- **Professional color management:** This is often the number one reason for using a lab, especially for photographers new to color management. That's because the people who work in photolabs, especially pro labs, are experts at seeing and correcting color. You can save time and improve your quality by letting them take care of your final color corrections until you're comfortable taking over the task.

When you work with a new lab it's very important to ask lots of questions before placing your first order. That way you'll know exactly how to prepare your files. Find out exactly what the lab prefers. For example, what color space does the lab use — sRGB or Adobe RGB (1998)? Knowing the answer to this question allows you to make sure that you use the same color space when editing, enabling you to better predict what the final color will look like when the prints are made. If you deliver files that are in the wrong color space the lab will manage the color space conversion (usually automatically), which can produce unpredictable results.

> **TIP** If the lab has custom profiles for its printers, ask for them and instructions on how to apply them to your files in Photoshop so you can manage the conversion process yourself. Doing this with a calibrated monitor is the best way to accurately predict final printed color.

> **CROSS-REF** See Chapter 12 for a discussion of color spaces.

Another question to ask is: Does the lab prefer JPEG or TIFF files? Most prefer JPEG, but I know of some labs that work with both. If you're delivering TIFF files, be sure to flatten them before taking them to the lab. Also, if you're working with 16-bit files, be sure to change the files to 8-bit. To do this, choose Image ➪ Mode ➪ 8-bits/Channel.

Some labs prefer that you deliver files that are completely prepared for printing — that is, sized and sharpened — while others simply want a full-sized JPEG file. I always prefer to manage these variables myself, especially when I order large prints. I want to know that the image is cropped exactly as I want it cropped and that sharpening is done the way I like it. However, if you don't have the time or the experience to make these decisions, let the lab do it for you. When you're more comfortable with your workflow, you can take on some of these duties yourself.

The most important thing to consider when working with a lab is communication. Discuss your needs and expectations with the lab before placing an order. Make sure that it is willing to listen. When problems occur and your expectations aren't met, be sure to find out why. If the problem is related to your workflow, listen to suggestions from lab personnel. These technicians work with lots of photographers so they see many of the same mistakes. If they point one out to you, thank them and consider modifying your workflow to fix it. If the lab is doing something wrong be sure to let the lab personnel know so they have the opportunity to fix the problem. If the lab isn't willing to do so, start looking for another lab.

NOTE When working with a pro lab it's always useful to develop a relationship with a specific contact person. After this person gets to know you and your work, they'll be able to keep an eye your orders and generally give you better service.

Saving and Archiving Files

Although organization and archiving are discussed in Chapter 3, I just want to reiterate the importance of saving all files that are created during the Creative Workflow. That goes for layered master files that are saved before final sizing and cropping, and files that have been completely prepared for printing. Be sure to save these files to the appropriate folder in your organizational system. Think about updating all of those folders in Lightroom with the Synchronize Folder command.

TIP Add the print size to the end of the filename for printing files so that you can easily identify them later.

After all files are in place take the final step of archiving them. If you're working on a large project, burn all of the files and folders to a DVD and file it away as extra insurance. I can tell you from personal experience that it isn't any fun to have to re-create files that were previously created when they could have been backed up so easily.

Summary

This chapter began by looking at how burning and dodging is carried out in the Creative Workflow. Photoshop provides Burn and Dodge tools, but I prefer not to use them because they're destructive to an image's pixels. This goes against the philosophy of flexibility and nondestructiveness. Because of that, I presented an alternative way of creating a Burn and Dodge layer that isolates all burning and dodging and prevents it from permanently affecting the image's pixels.

One of the most fundamental, yet least understood, aspects of digital photography is resolution. You took a detailed look at it here and went through a couple of exercises so that you could see the difference between changing a file's resolution and resampling it when working with the Image Size command. I also discussed interpolation methods so that you know which is appropriate for enlarging or reducing the size of a file.

In theory, Photoshop's Crop tool is similar to the Crop tool in Lightroom's Develop module. Both allow you to crop to a specific size, though in Lightroom that size is a proportion rather than final dimensions. The main difference is that the Crop tool in Photoshop makes permanent changes to the file. Because of that, it's a good idea to save a master file before doing any cropping.

You took a detailed look at sharpening in this chapter by exploring the Unsharp Mask and the Smart Sharpen filters. Each of these filters does a good job, though the Smart Sharpen filter is more powerful because it's smarter about the detail that gets sharpened, and it offers more controls to apply that sharpen for different image scenarios. No matter which of these tools is used for final sharpening, it's important that the file is at its final dimensions before sharpening is applied. Ways to ensure that the image display on your monitor is at its optimal setting so that you can accurately evaluate sharpening onscreen were also discussed.

Most photos that go through the Creative Workflow are intended for printed output. The focus was on the two primary output methods for photographers: printing with an inkjet printer and working with a lab. You explored Photoshop CS3's new Print dialog box and looked at the key settings in this dialog box. If you have problems with the color of your inkjet output, be sure that all of these settings are correct. When you work with a lab, be sure to ask lots of questions so that you'll be able to deliver top-quality files.

Chapter 22

Putting the Creative Workflow into Action

The last several chapters were devoted to exploring the Photoshop tools and techniques used in the Creative Workflow. As you saw, there are many similarities and analogies to the tools and techniques used in Lightroom for the Production Workflow. The main difference between the Production and Creative workflows is that the production workflow is designed to get you to the Creative Workflow. Whereas the Creative Workflow allows you to take an image in any direction you desire. It's much more open-ended because the opportunities and choices are countless when working in Photoshop. The main job of the Ccreative Workflow is to manage these choices so that they're made at the appropriate time.

This chapter puts all of the pieces of the Creative Workflow in place by working on a practice image. As you do, you see how the Production and Creative Workflows link together to form the entire post-production work-flow. You also see how easy it is to quickly transform an average photo into a special image that becomes a personal expression of the photographer. When you learn to do this, it takes your photography to the next level. You'll be able to envision this process and know what's possible before you even click the shutter.

Evaluating the Project

The Creative Workflow picks up where the Production Workflow leaves off. So go back to one of the images used in the Lightroom portion of this book, as shown in Figure 22.1. You may recall that it's from a portrait session I did with my friends and their dog relaxing in the garden.

FIGURE 22.1

This nice photo of a couple relaxing in the garden with their dog is one of the images used in the Lightroom portion of this book. In this chapter, you're going to fine-tune this image and prepare it for printing. During the process, you'll be retouching the people's faces and removing all of the distractions circled in the background.

NOTE   These techniques apply to many different types of images. I'm using this particular image because it presents many of the usual problems that need to be solved during the Creative Workflow. Even if you don't typically work with portraits, please take the time to work through this chapter. When you experience the techniques I show you, you'll instantly see how they can be used in your own work.

Imagine for a moment that I just finished the Production Workflow portion of this project. All of the important photos from the session were shown to the clients with a slide show presentation. They chose this image as the one they want to hang on their wall. They want a 20 x 24 print mounted on canvas. They chose that size because they already have an antique frame they want to use with it. Having this knowledge is important. Now I know the image is being enlarged to a size where detail is easier to see so I want to retouch carefully. However, the fact that the print will be mounted on canvas means that some of that detail will be diminished due to the texture of the canvas.

CAUTION The file used will be very large by the time it's done, tipping the scales at a little under 400MB. If you're working on a system with limited resources, be prepared to wait for some of the filters to run. (It will help to turn off any other applications while working on this file.) I thought about reducing the size of the image, but I want to handle this file the same as I normally would if I were preparing it for printing.

Now that you know how the image will be used, let's take a closer look at it so you can evaluate the process:

- The light stand in the background on the right is easy to remove, but it will probably be cropped in the final version. The window frame showing behind the subjects bothers me more, even though it's part of the real scene. We'll go ahead and remove it.

- Some of the plants in the background are distracting. The bright green leaves on the right will be near the frame of the cropped image, so we'll want to do something about them. We'll also want to remove all of the dead flowers in the bushes and on the ground.

- The people need some basic retouching to tone down wrinkles and smooth their skin. The man's hair is a bit too dark against the dark background on the side, making it hard to distinguish the edge of his hair. We'll need to lighten it with some dodging. (If I had only shifted my position to the side a bit before shooting, I could have made sure a lighter portion of background was behind him.) We'll also lighten and whiten both people's teeth, something I do to almost every portrait.

- The clothes are okay. I don't see any wrinkles that are screaming at me so we'll leave them alone. There are some loose threads here and there, as well as a spot on the man's knee. We'll take care of all of them during general retouching.

- The overall sharpness is good, but I want to blur the background around the subjects a bit to add some separation. The juxtaposition will make the subjects stand out and look sharper. I also want to darken the background around them to add some drama to the scene.

- Cropping and sizing this image will be straightforward because we are working with a common print size. However, we'll have to increase the size of the image a bit to fit that final print size by resampling it.

- The scene is evenly lit and the exposure is decent. All in all, this file gives us a decent starting point.

NOTE Although this is a portrait, you can make a similar list for a photo with nearly any subject matter. The idea is to analyze the image to identify its strengths and weaknesses. Being able to identify these traits is as important as knowing how to work with them.

This list equals one to two hours of work. Most of that work will take place in Phase 2 of the workflow where the majority of retouching is handled. Before we can begin retouching, though, we need to make sure that the all of the fundamentals are in place so that when we begin doing the hard work we'll know we're building on a solid foundation.

NOTE   The process on which you're about to embark will convert this nice portrait into a family heirloom, vastly increasing its perceived value.

Phase 1: Adjusting Fundamentals

Quite often, a file that's already been adjusted in Lightroom needs little attention to its fundamentals when opening it into Photoshop. It depends mostly on whether the actual file was evaluated in Lightroom, or whether it was synchronized with the settings on a different file. (In the first case, the file's attributes are evaluated; in the second, arbitrary edits are made based on similarity.) Let's get to work. Follow these steps:

1. Open `R_and_K049.dng` from the practice files on the Web site. This is a raw file saved in Adobe's DNG format, so it should opened from Bridge into Adobe Camera Raw. The Lightroom adjustments made to it in Chapter 7 should still be in effect.

NOTE   You can open the file from Lightroom, but you won't be able to set all of the workflow options you need. So go ahead and use Bridge and ACR for this example. If you need a refresher on Bridge, see Chapter 11.

2. When the ACR dialog box appears, click and hold on the Crop tool on the toolbar at the top and select Clear Crop from the pop-up menu, as shown in Figure 22.2. You're removing the Lightroom cropping because I don't want to limit your choices at the beginning of the process by making a permanent change now. Cropping is addressed at a more appropriate time in the workflow.

FIGURE 22.2

Click on the Crop tool to open a Cropping menu. Choose Clear Crop to remove any cropping applied in Lightroom.

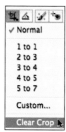

3. Decrease the Clarity value to **0** for the same reason. You can add contrast later if you want to. Also reduce Vibrance to **0**.

> **TIP** When you open a raw file that's been adjusted in Lightroom, take the opportunity to be sure that the Lightroom adjustments are the best adjustments for that file. If they aren't, modify them now or completely turn them off. For example, it might be better to undo any spotting before opening the file so that the retouching can be done with more appropriate tools in Photoshop. If you're working with a non-raw file — or if you're opening a raw file directly from Lightroom — you'll have to undo these changes in Lightroom before opening the file in Photoshop.

4. Make sure the clipping previews are activated. Notice that the highlight clipping preview indicates that some extreme highlights are being clipped on the woman's hair and on one of the dog's ears. These are small areas that can be toned down with retouching later if necessary. I prefer to take that approach instead of affecting the entire image with the Recovery slider now because I don't like the way the slider flattens overall contrast. (When working in the Creative Workflow I use the Recovery slider, as well as the Fill Light slider, only when necessary because they affect the entire image.)

5. There's more room for adjustment on the shadow end of the tonal scale. I increase the value of the Blacks slider to **8** to deepen some of the blacks in the background. If I notice shadow clipping on the subjects, I would lower the value until it disappears. The color looks good, but if you want to modify it, or any of the tones, go ahead and do that now.

6. Zoom to 100 percent and check the darkest shadows in the background for noise. You shouldn't see any, but this would be the time to make adjustments in the Detail panel if you need to. Also check any bright, backlight highlights (like the woman's hair or the bright plants in the background) for color fringing around the edges. I don't see any here, but if you do, use the Chromatic Aberration sliders in the Detail panel to remove it.

7. Click the Workflow Options Hyperlink at the bottom center of the ACR dialog box. When the dialog box opens, fill it out as shown in Figure 22.3 and click OK. Here are the settings I use and why I selected them:

FIGURE 22.3

The Adobe Camera Raw Workflow Options dialog box allows you to create the kind of file you want from a raw file. Fill it out the way it is shown here for this project.

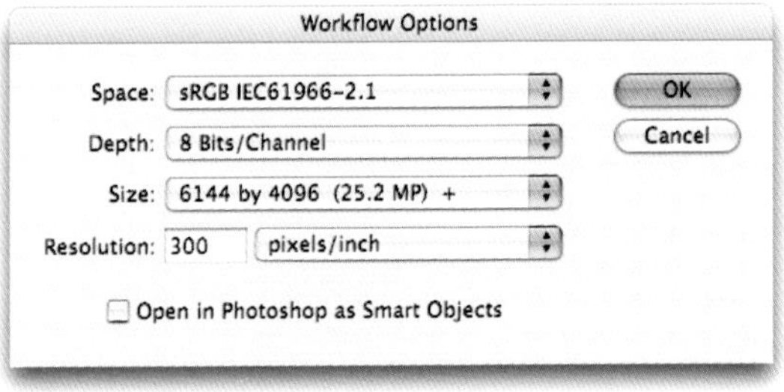

■ **Space:** The professional lab I'm planning to use for printing prefers sRGB files so it makes sense for me to do my editing in that color space. Otherwise, I may see colors during editing that can't be printed by the lab's equipment — which can be frustrating.

■ **Depth:** I use 8 Bits/Channel because this image isn't in need of heavy-duty retouching or massive tonal and color adjustments. Choosing 16 bits would double the file size with little added advantage, especially when you consider that most pro labs won't accept 16-bit files. (A 16-bit version of this final layered file would be pushing 750MB before you flatten the layers later to prepare the file for the lab.)

■ **Size:** The largest size (25.2 megapixels) is used here. This is smaller than what you need for your final size, but it gets you close. Using ACR to do this first resize allows it to be done with the raw data. (This is the setting that isn't available when opening a raw file from Lightroom.)

■ **Resolution:** Because I know I'll need 300 ppi for printing later, I establish that final resolution now.

8. The file is ready to open. Click Open Image to open it. If an Embedded Profile Mismatch dialog box appears, choose to use the embedded profile.

CROSS-REF See Chapter 12 for a discussion on profile mismatch errors.

NOTE By the time you're finished with this file you're going to be using three different filters, combined with their own masks, on this image for different effects. I'd like to use Smart Filters, but working with multiple Smart Filters and multiple masks is tricky. Additionally, with a project like this it's common to find additional retouching later on. When working with Smart Filters you need to convert the layer to a Smart Object, which makes retouching the layer impossible unless it's converted back — completely negating the usefulness of a Smart Filter.

Because this is a raw file, it had to go through Adobe Camera Raw on its way to Photoshop. This allowed you to address most of the image's fundamentals before opening it. If this were a non-raw file, you would use the Levels or Curves adjustment layers to adjust tonal issues and the Color Balance and/or Hue/Saturation adjustment layers to adjust color. Also use adjustment layers if you decide to make additional adjustments to overall tone or color after opening this image. For example, if you want to bump up the overall Saturation, use a Hue/Saturation adjustment layer at the top of the layer stack.

TIP Remember that the main goal while working in the Creative Workflow is to always work in a nondestructive way. That means that any Levels, Curves, or color adjustments that are made during Phase 1 — and in later phases — are done with adjustment layers.

Phase 2: Fixing Distractions

Now that the fundamentals are out of the way, you can start having some fun with this photo. Before you begin retouching, though, I want you to take a moment to get a feel for what the image will look like after it's cropped.

The image won't be cropped now; I just want you to get a feel for the final cropping so you don't waste time retouching details that will be cropped later. You can always retouch those details later if you decide to print the image full frame because you'll be saving a master file before any final cropping. Follow these steps:

1. Pick up where you left off with Step 8 earlier. Be sure that your ruler is displayed, (Command+R/Ctrl+R) and that it displays inches. If it doesn't, right-click on it and choose Inches from the menu. Also make sure your zoom level allows you to see the entire image (Command+0/Ctrl+0).

2. Select the Crop tool (C) and type **24** into the Width field and **20** into the Height field. The resolution doesn't matter at the moment, because you won't be cropping yet. You only want to take a look. (Keep in mind that if you were cropping, it would be important to type 300 into the Resolution field even though the image is already at 300 ppi. Otherwise, Photoshop will most likely change the resolution to something other than 300 ppi.)

3. Click near the top left of the image and drag downward to the bottom right. Create a cropping selection that encloses the image from top to bottom and that's centered on the couple, as shown in Figure 22.4. (Remember that you can reposition the cropping selection by moving the cursor inside of the selection and then clicking and dragging.) I tried to balance the space between their outer knees and the edge of the frame.

4. The cropping selection now gives you an accurate preview of the final cropping. Here's the cool part: Click on the vertical ruler to the left and drag a guide out to the right edge of the selection. Click on the ruler again and drag a second guide to the right edge of the selection. Now you can cancel the cropping selection by pressing Esc. The two guides stay in place, indicating where the eventual cropping will take place. Now you know that anything outside those guides, like the light stand, doesn't need to be retouched.

TIP   To hide guides, press Command+H (Ctrl+H), (Hide). This also works with selections. If you hide a selection, be sure to reveal it again or you may forget about it. To reveal a hidden feature, use the keyboard shortcut again.

Cleaning up the background

Now that the image fundamentals are optimized it's time to move into Phase 2 of the Creative Workflow. You begin by cleaning up the background. Pick up where you left off with Step 4 and follow these steps:

5. Before you start retouching, duplicate the background so that all retouching is isolated to its own layer. Click and drag the Background layer in the Layers palette to the Create a New Layer button at the bottom of the palette. Double-click on the layer's name and rename it **Retouching**.

TIP   Always duplicate the main image layer before beginning any retouching. The untouched Background layer is used for comparison so that you can check any work against it.

FIGURE 22.4

Use the Crop tool to define an approximate future cropping area and then drag vertical guides from the ruler to the vertical edges of the cropping selection. When you cancel the cropping operation, both of the guides stay in place as a reminder where the eventual edges of the image will be.

6. Begin with the distractions by removing all of the dead leaves in the background behind the man. Use the Patch tool to loosely select each dead leaf and replace it with suitable background information. Though this is a very forgiving background, be sure to find sample leaf details that roughly match the targeted area. Remember, you don't have to be true to nature, you just don't want the retouching to be noticeable. (If you have trouble with the Patch tool smearing, use the Clone Stamp tool instead, or use the Clone Stamp to blend any smearing that occurs.)

TIP I like to work in full-screen viewing mode when doing a project like this. Press F to cycle through the four modes. I also like to hide the palettes whenever possible by pressing the Tab key. Press the Tab key again to reveal the palettes.

7. When the leaves behind the man are looking good, move down to the ground and remove the dead leaves and twigs near his legs and feet. (Remember, you can press the Spacebar at any time to temporarily activate the Hand tool for navigation purposes.) Quickly scan the rest of the background to see if there are any other distractions.

TIP Occasionally turn the visibility of the Retouching layer off and on to check your work.

8. Now that the easy stuff is out of the way, you can tackle some of the larger background retouching issues. Focus on the light-colored window frame that runs horizontally above the dog, and vertically above and to the right of the woman, as shown in the first frame of Figure 22.5. Begin working with the Patch tool on the section above the dog. Work on

small sections of the frame until it's mostly obscured, as shown in the second frame of Figure 22.5. Be sure to line-up details like stems and leaves when possible. If a Patch application isn't quite perfect, clean it up with additional Patch tool work.

9. Occasionally switch to the Clone Stamp tool when you need to sample details accurately. Work with a soft brush to add stems or leaves. I used the Clone tool to remove the bright leaf that was sticking up behind the dog's right ear. You can see where I sampled the ferns above and extended them to the edge of the ear. This works better than the Patch tool because of the issue with the Patch tool smearing near the edge of the ear.

TIP Work with the Patch tool when you can, but if you see smudging, switch to the more literal Clone Stamp tool. If you have trouble blending details with the Clone Stamp, consider lowering the brush opacity when trying to blend two different types of detail.

FIGURE 22.5

The goal is to hide the window frame behind the subjects in the first image. In the second image, the Clone Stamp tool is used to cover it with ferns. You can see that I'm sampling some of the retouching that I already did to obscure more of the wall.

10. Use the Clone Stamp with a very soft brush to begin removing the vertical post by sampling and pasting the dark areas beside it. When the post is gone, come back with the Clone Stamp and paint in some flowers. I used the rotate section of the Clone Source palette to change the orientation of the flowers and ferns as I painted them, as shown in Figure 22.6. I set mine to 30 degrees. This keeps them from looking like duplicates. Just remember to set it back to 0 before moving on.

FIGURE 22.6

I used the Rotate the clone source feature of the Clone Source palette to rotate these flowers 30 degrees while cloning them. This makes cloning less obvious and allows me to position the flowers the way I want them.

> **TIP**
>
> Remember that dragging the cursor as you paint hides traces of your strokes better than clicking in a static position.

11. Make one more check of the background for any other distractions. I removed the small group of red flower buds in the top-right corner because they were so bright in the background. I also removed a few of the bright leaves above and to the left of the man's head. Go ahead and make a quick retouching pass over the clothing. Look for anything that needs to be removed, like the spot on the man's inside knee.

The image is looking pretty good now. Check yours by hiding the retouching layer. The changes should be noticeable. You're about to begin facial retouching. But before you do, save the master file as a PSD and with the following name: **R_and_K049-Master.psd**. Follow the organizational rules laid out in Chapter 3 for the correct place to save a master file. Be sure to stop occasionally and save this master file as you continue to work in the case of any computer malfunctions.

Softening blemishes and wrinkles

While removing the distractions from the background you had lots of leeway when sampling. Now that you're moving to the main subjects, you need to work more deliberately. Pick up where you left off with Step 11 and follow these steps to soften blemishes and wrinkles:

12. Zoom to 50 percent and center the woman's face on the screen. Select the Patch tool and draw a selection around the line under her eye on the right and drag the selection to a clean section of skin. I used an area on her forehead, as shown in the first frame of Figure 22.7. Immediately, choose Edit ⇨ Fade Patch Selection and decrease the fade to 65 percent. Fading like this keeps the retouching more realistic by allowing some of the original lines to show through.

FIGRUE 22.7

In the first frame, I retouched lines under the eye by using the Patch tool to sample clean skin from the forehead. Then I faded the Patch tool to 65 percent using the Fade command. In the second frame, I used the same technique to retouch lines by the corner of the eye. Here it's important to keep the right edge of the upper sample selection close to the edge of the hair, similar to the target selection below, to avoid smearing.

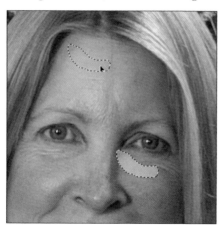

13. Draw a second selection around the lines near the corner of her eye, as shown in the second frame of Figure 22.7. Drag the selection upward, keeping the right edge aligned with the edge of the hair. This prevents the Patch tool from smearing when working along a line like this. Fade this application of the Patch tool to about 65 percent.

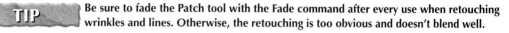

TIP Be sure to fade the Patch tool with the Fade command after every use when retouching wrinkles and lines. Otherwise, the retouching is too obvious and doesn't blend well.

14. Continue working your way around the woman's face with the Patch tool, removing any lines, blemishes, or facial shine. Large areas like the forehead need to be broken down into separate applications of the tool. Use the Fade command when necessary to bring back some detail. As larger areas of skin get cleaned up, you can select larger areas to work with.

The goal here is to prepare the skin for final smoothing. Keep in mind that the smoothing will help to blend minor imperfections in the skin and in your retouching technique.

15. Select the large area on her chin where the skin looks a little bumpy. Sample the forehead skin and then fade to about 50 percent to bring back some details.

16. I like the woman's smile lines, but I want to tone them down. Select them all and use the clean skin on her forehead for sampling. Be sure to fade enough to bring back the character of her smile.

17. When you finish with the woman's face, do the same procedure on the man. Begin with the lines on his forehead so that you can have a clean area of skin to use for sampling. When you get to the lines below the man's eye on the right, try selecting all of them and dragging the selection to the forehead for sampling, as shown in Figure 22.8. The trick to making this work is to not select too close to the edge of his face on the right. Fade the Patch tool to about 55 percent.

FIGURE 22.8

The Patch tool is used to retouch all of the lines under the man's eye at once. Be careful about drawing the original target selection too close to the edge of his face, or you'll get smearing from the difference in contrast. This large area needs to be faded to blend it better.

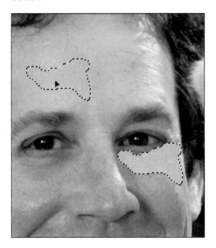

18. Use the same techniques with the lines above his right eye. When you get to the top section of his forehead, by his hair, you have to switch to the Clone Stamp to control the smearing issues. Decrease the Opacity of the tool to about 65 percent to help with blending.

NOTE This man's skin is rougher than the woman's. Some of that is due to razor stubble. My goal in retouching him is to not make his skin as smooth as the woman's. Therefore, I tend to use lower fade percentages with him.

19. I want to work with all of the lines below the man's chin with one selection of the Patch tool. If I try to break it into smaller parts, I may have trouble with smearing. Even if doing all of the lines at once isn't perfect, I can fade it and blend it in with the Clone Stamp.

One of the problems with creating a selection this big is that the man doesn't have enough clean skin to use for sampling. Fortunately, that's not a problem here because the woman's skin is already clean. I can use it for sample material, as shown in Figure 22.9. The difference in skin color doesn't matter because the tool only samples the texture. After a bit of fading and some touch up around the edges, it's hard to tell what the original looked like. I use this technique again to clean up the rest of the rough skin on his neck.

> **TIP** Keep in mind that you'll be smoothing the skin in a few moments, which helps to blend facial retouching into un-retouched areas.

FIGURE 22.9

The Patch tool is so powerful that it can be used to retouch lines on the man's neck by sampling the already retouched skin on the woman's face. The tool compensates for the tonal and color differences. Naturally, I have to fade the effects of this tool and do a little touch up, but this works much better than trying to address every line individually with the Patch tool.

20. Quickly remove any bright shine from the teeth because it's distracting. Select the Clone Stamp and zoom to 100 percent magnification. Work with a soft, small brush (10 px) at an Opacity of 80 percent and begin toning down or removing any distracting shine. You come back a little later to whiten them.

> **TIP** No matter what kind of image you're working with, always look for insignificant bright spots that are distracting. Remove them or tone them down to enhance the viewing experience.

The skin is ready for smoothing, but before you do that take one more look at the image for retouching. Something that bothers me on the right side of the image is that there are a couple of bright green branches that lead the viewer's eye out of the frame. I'm all about trying to keep the eye inside the frame, so I want to remove those subtle distractions, which are circled in Figure 22.10.

21. Zoom to 50 percent and use the Clone Stamp at 100 percent Opacity and a soft brush to clone the two distractions out of the image. (This can be considered Phase 3 retouching because you're attempting to control the viewer's experience.) Scan the entire image one more time to see if there's anything else you want to remove with retouching, like the wrinkle on the woman's ankle and the loose thread by the mans neck.

FIGURE 22.10

I want to remove these two branches because they are so bright and near the edge of the intended final crop. Distractions like this tend to lead the viewer's eye out of the image.

Smoothing skin and blending retouching

Now that the facial retouching is complete it's a good idea to smooth the skin a bit to blend the retouching. Skin smoothing also adds a finished look to a portrait like this one. Pick up where you left off with Step 21 and follow these steps to smooth the skin in the sample portrait:

22. You're about to turn down a different road, so save your master file again. Duplicate the Retouching layer by choosing Layer ➪ Duplicate Layer. Name the new layer **Smooth Skin**.

23. You can run a filter to smooth the skin and blend your retouching. Choose Filter ➪ Blur ➪ Surface Blur. Type a value of **7** for Radius and **8** for Threshold and click OK. The resulting blur may seem a bit strong, but remember that it's on its own layer, so the layer opacity can be reduced to lessen the effect. In fact, quite often it's better to overdo a filter on a layer like this and then fine-tune the effect with the layer opacity.

NOTE You can try using the Gaussian Blur filter instead, which gives you a slightly different effect than the Surface Blur filter. See which you prefer.

24. The entire layer is blurred, so use a mask to hide the blurring where you don't want to see it. Because that means you need to hide most of the image, use a Hide All mask to do most of the work. Choose Layer ⇨ Layer Mask ⇨ Hide All. Now all you need to do is mask the blur back in wherever you see skin.

25. Zoom to 100 percent, and select the Brush tool (B). Set the Opacity to 70 percent, the Hardness to 0 percent, and the Flow to 100 percent. Set the foreground color to white (D) and begin painting the skin with a fairly large brush, about 100 px. Reduce the size of the brush when necessary. Decrease the Opacity when you work around edges to blend the transition between blurred and nonblurred details. Be sure to paint all exposed skin, including arms, legs, and hands. Be careful not to paint any details like lips and eyes to keep them sharp. If you do accidentally paint them with white, come back and paint them with black. (I often do this anyway with details just to be sure I didn't accidentally blur something I want to keep sharp.) Figure 22.11 shows the Layers palette at this point in the project.

NOTE The D key sets the color swatches to their default colors. The X key is used to swap (exchange) those colors between the foreground and background swatches.

FIGURE 22.11

Here's the Layers palette so far with my three layers. You can see the masking I did on the Smooth Skin layer so that the blurring is only seen in the areas painted white.

TIP Press the backslash (\) key if you want to check your mask. You can also Alt+Click on the layer mask in the Layers palette to display your mask. You won't be able to see your brush strokes in the context of the image, but at least you can see if you missed any obvious spots. Alt+Click the mask again to return to the normal view.

26. Now that you can see the effect, zoom to 50 percent check to see if you want to dial back the effect of the blur by reducing the Opacity of the layer. I lower the Opacity to 75 percent.

Whitening and lightening teeth

Now that the facial retouching is almost complete it's easy to see that the teeth need some attention. Follow these steps to whiten and lighten them:

27. Add a Hue/Saturation adjustment layer to the top of the layer stack by choosing Layer ➪ New Adjustment Layer ➪ Hue/Saturation. Name the layer **Teeth** when the New Layer dialog box opens. You're going to use this layer to remove the tint from the teeth.

    When the Hue/Saturation dialog box appears, choose Yellows from the Edit menu. When you do, the eyedropper icons become active. Use the first eyedropper, the Eyedropper tool, to click on the man's teeth to define the shade of yellow you're interested in. Lower the Saturation value to -40 to remove some of the yellow. Raise the Lightness value to 10 to lighten the teeth a bit, then click OK.

28. Once again, the adjustment affects the whole layer — just like the Surface Blur filter did. You need to create a Hide All mask (black) but the adjustment layer already created its own Reveal All mask, (white). Not a problem because it's easy to convert a Reveal All mask to a Hide All mask — and vice versa — with the Paint Bucket. Select the Paint Bucket tool (G) and select black as your foreground color. Click anywhere inside the image to fill the mask with black and hide the effects of the layer. (Use white paint to convert a Hide All mask to a Reveal All mask.)

29. Select the Brush tool and select white as your foreground color (X). Choose an Opacity value of 100 percent and paint the teeth with a small soft brush to add the desaturation and brightening effects of the Teeth adjustment layer. If you feel that the effects are too strong — or not strong enough — you can revisit the settings in the adjustment layer by double-clicking it. (This same technique is often used with a Levels or Curves adjustment layer to whiten and lighten the whites of someone's eyes. I could use it here with another Hue/Saturation adjustment layer to modify the hue of the man's skin tone to make it match the woman's more tanned skin tone.)

> **TIP**   **If this couple's teeth were very different from one another, I would use separate Teeth layers for each of them.**

This photo is looking very nice. All you need to do is add a few finishing touches and it will be ready for output.

Phase 3: Controlling the Viewer's Experience

You just used a selective blurring technique that uses a mask to soften the skin in your photo. Let's use a similar technique to blur the background around the subjects.

Selectively blurring the background

Pick up where you left off with Step 29 and follow these steps:

1. Pick up where you left off in Step 29. Make another duplicate of the Retouching layer and name it **Blurred Background**.

2. Choose Filter ⇨ Blur ⇨ Gaussian Blur. When the dialog box appears, type a value of **6** and click OK.

3. Create a Reveal All mask by choosing Layer ⇨ Mask ⇨ Reveal All. Zoom in and use the Brush tool with black paint to hide the blur on the main subjects. When you work around their edges — where the subject edge meets the blurring effect — use an opacity of 50 percent or lower to help blend the transition. Use a lower opacity to lessen the blur effect on the grass in front of the subjects because it shouldn't be as blurred as the area behind them. Because this effect is on its own layer, you can modify the layer's opacity to lessen the effect.

Creative burning and dodging

In Phase 1 you adjusted the overall tonality of the photo. Now it's time to modify tones on a local level. Follow these steps to use the burn and dodge technique you learned about in Chapter 21 to complete Phase 3 for this photo:

4. Create a burn and dodge layer by adding a new empty layer to the top of the stack and changing its blending mode to Soft Light. Name the new layer **Burn & Dodge**. Select the Brush tool and set the foreground color to black.

5. Work with a large brush (about 700 px) with an opacity of 20 percent and a hardness of 0 percent. Also be sure that Flow is set to 100 percent. Begin darkening the edges of the image by painting with black. Start by painting the corners and then work your way inward, overlapping your strokes so that they're darker near the edge. The idea is to darken all edges of the print, while fading the darkening inward, toward the subjects so that it's less noticeable. Remember that we will be cropping where the guides were placed earlier, so imagine that they represent the edge of the image.

NOTE   Darkening the edges and corners of an image helps to keep the viewer's eye on the inner portions of the image.

The upper right needs little darkening, while the grassy corners at the bottom, as well as the central area in front of the subjects, needs to be darkened more. Darken the tops of the tall flowers in the background more than the lower sections. Figure 22.12 shows the burning on my photo and the strokes that created it.

NOTE   I darkened the dog's nose and snout to give it a bit more punch.

6. While you're on the Burn & Dodge layer, check the rest of the image to see if there are any other areas that need local darkening or lightening. I don't like the way the man's hair on the side of his head blends into the dark background. Use white paint to lighten his hair on the Burn & Dodge layer a bit. Be careful not to go too light, otherwise his hair begins to look grayish.

7. When all burning and dodging is complete the file is ready to be sized and sharpened for output. Be sure to save the master file now before you move forward because you will be making permanent changes in the next section.

This figure shows the Burn & Dodge layer with a white background behind it. Notice that the areas that were burned more are darker. (It was necessary to change the blending mode back to Normal for this demonstration.)

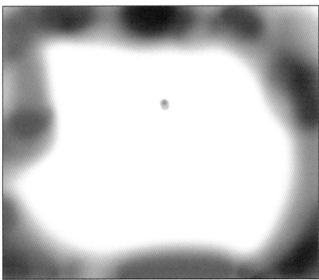

Using snapshots to compare before and after versions

I always like to compare my before and after images to see how I'm doing. With a bunch of layers, it becomes harder to do because several need to be turned off to reveal the original Background layer. Here's a cool way to compare your before and after images using snapshots:

8. Remember the Snapshots feature in Lightroom's Develop module? Well, there's also a Snapshot button on the bottom of the History palette. It looks like a small camera. Click it now to create a snapshot of the current state of your file. The new snapshot is added to the top section of the History palette, just below the icon of the opening state of the image, as shown in Figure 22.13. Name the snapshot **After** by double-clicking on its name.

9. Turn off the visibility of every layer except for the Background layer by clicking the eyeball icons next to them. When only the Background layer is visible, create a second snapshot and name it **Before**.

 Unlike the history in Lightroom, Photoshop's history is volatile. All history, including snapshots, is deleted when you close the file.

Now you can quickly compare the before and after versions of the image by selecting the appropriate snapshot from the History palette, shown in Figure 22.13. Use this opportunity to determine if you need to adjust the opacity of any of the layers to dial in their respective contribution to the overall image.

FIGURE 22.13

Use snapshots to compare different history states of an image. To create a snapshot, click the camera button at the bottom of the Layers palette. (The snapshot at the top was created when the file was opened. Clicking on it reverts the file's history to that opening state.)

Something to be aware of when using snapshots is that when you're ready to get back to work it's not only necessary to click on the After snapshot; you also have to click on the last history state (the one on the bottom of the stack) in the History palette. Otherwise, when you begin working again, all of those saved history states are replaced by history state of the next editing action you take. This isn't a huge deal; you just lose some of your history states.

Phase 4: Preparing for Output and Archiving

Now that the master file is complete you're ready to prepare this file for printing. That process entails two steps: final sizing and sharpening.

Final cropping and sizing

Pick up where you left off with Step 9 previously and follow these steps:

1. Select all of the layers in the Layers palette except for the Burn & Dodge layer. Do this by clicking on the Background layer and then Shift+clicking on the Teeth layer, which is just below the Burn & Dodge layer on top. Choose Layers ⇨ Merge Layers (Command+E/ Ctrl+E). This merges the selected layers into one layer, while preserving the Burn & Dodge layer so that you can reevaluate it after cropping.

> **NOTE** Normally, I wouldn't merge these layers just yet. I'm doing it here because we're about to increase the size of this already large file. Merging these layers helps to reduce the size of the practice file so that it might be more manageable on your system.

2. Select the Crop tool and click the Clear button on the options bar to clear all of the tool's settings. You want to crop the area inside of the guides you placed earlier (you already know they're proportional to the 20 x 24 aspect ratio). Click at the top left of the image where the left guide is and drag downward to the lower-right corner to complete the cropping selection. The cropping selection should look just like it did early in the process when you placed your guides. Press the Return (Enter) to commit the crop.

3. You don't need the guides anymore so choose View ⇨ Clear Guides.

4. Choose Image ⇨ Image Size to open the Image Size dialog box. I'm planning to make a 20 x 24 print from this file so I want to size it up now to its final size so that I can add final sharpening.

   Currently the document size is 16.3 x 13.6. (Your size may vary slightly, depending on where you placed your guides. However, the size should be close to mine.) Be certain that the Resample Image option is checked, and then change the Document Size Width value to **24** inches. The Height value should automatically change to 20, or close to it, as shown in Figure 22.14. (If the value is lower than 20, try changing it to 20 and see if the width falls into line.) Choose Bicubic Smoother for the rendering intent because it's designed for enlarging images, and then click OK.

> **NOTE** You could have used the Crop tool with the exact dimensions typed into the tool options to get the file to its final size and skipped Steps 3 and 4. But by default the Crop tool doesn't use the Bicubic Smoother rendering intent. When resizing and upsampling an important file like this, it's best to do it right, even if that entails a couple of extra steps.

5. Take a quick look at your burning and dodging now that the image is cropped and sized. Make any necessary modifications and then choose Layer ➪ Flatten Image. (This is where I would normally flatten all layers if it hadn't already done so in Step 1.)

FIGURE 22.14

After the image is cropped to the correct proportion, you can use the Image Size dialog box to change the dimensions to the final size of 20 x 24. Be sure to select Bicubic Smoother when increasing the size of an image.

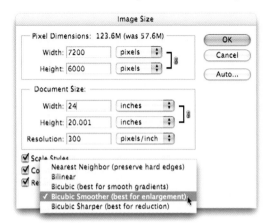

Sharpening for output

Now that your image is at its final size you can apply sharpening for output. Follow these steps to use the Smart Sharpen filter:

6. Now all you have to do is sharpen this image and it will be ready to print. Zoom to 50 percent and choose Filter ➪ Sharpen ➪ Smart Sharpen. When the Smart Sharpen dialog box appears, grab it by its gripper bar at the top and scoot it to left, halfway off the screen so you only see the controls, allowing you to see the image better, as shown in Figure 22.15. Set Remove to Lens Blur and select the More Accurate option.

TIP   I often hide all palettes by pressing the Tab key before opening this filter. This allows me to see the image with less clutter around it.

Experiment with the Amount and Radius sliders to try a few different combinations. Check and uncheck the Preview box to compare the current setting to no sharpening. Press the Spacebar to access the Hand tool for panning the image while the dialog box is open. Remember that higher Radius values tend to amplify any effects of the Amount slider. I settled on 400 percent for Amount and 1.0 for Radius.

> **TIP**   It's always a good idea to make one more quick check for retouching after sharpening an image. If any minor artifacting is introduced by the filter, you can remove it now. It's also a good idea to reevaluate the overall tones in the image because sharpening can affect contrast and brightness.

FIGURE 22.15

The Smart Sharpen dialog box takes lots of screen real estate. Scoot it to the left so that you can see its effects on your image instead of relying on the dialog box's preview window.

7. The file, shown in Figure 22.16, is ready for printing. Save it as `R_and_K049-20x24.tif` and place it into the appropriate finals or printing folder, as discussed in Chapter 3. If you plan to create any other sizes for printing, say an 8 x 10, for example, you need to back up to Step 1 instead of using the Crop tool on this sharpened file. That way when you get to Step 6 the sharpening will be appropriate for an 8 x 10.

Archiving all files

When you put this much work into creating a file you need to be sure to archive all files prepared for printing — as well as the layered master file. You can either store them on a backup hard drive or burn them all to a CD/DVD (I usually do both).

It's amazing how many photographers go through all of the work in this chapter, but neglect to make backups of these important files. I can tell you from personal experience that there's nothing worse than losing important files that you poured your time into. Even if you have the original raw file backed up, redoing all of the Creative Workflow can be a daunting task. Sometimes, even remembering what you did to the image the first time is a challenge.

TIP Throughout this book I've offered many tips for your consideration. If you only remember one tip, be sure that it is to archive all files at the end of a project.

FIGURE 22.16

Here's the final image, ready for printing. Compare it to the before image in Figure 22.1.

Summary

This brings you to the end of the Creative Workflow and this book. You've covered an amazing amount of ground. As a review of this chapter, I'd like to reiterate some of the more salient points you encountered while exploring the Creative Workflow.

The main point to embarking on the Creative Workflow journey is to fine-tune and optimize an image so that it looks its best. This is done by managing various parts of the image — eliminating distractions and enhancing the important aspects of the main subject. The process is presented as a workflow because many of these steps need to be carried out in a particular order. Also, so many options are available that it's important to manage the choices by defining the process. Naturally, the fine points of this workflow look different for different types of imagery. However, no matter what kind of subject matter you shoot, nearly every image will benefit from this process.

The central concept to creating a smooth-flowing Creative Workflow is to use layers and masks to isolate every important change that's made to the image. Doing so creates a huge amount of control and flexibility over those changes. It allows you to preserve the original Background layer for comparison purposes — or in case you want to back up to it again to redo a copy you made earlier.

This chapter took you through the same process I've used on countless images with all sorts of subject matter. Though the photo in this project was a portrait, these techniques can be used to fine-tune and perfect just about any photo. The key to making them work for you is to learn to see the weaknesses and strong points in your photos. When you're able to do this, it will change the way you shoot because now you know what's possible during the creative portion of your post-production workflow.

Index

SYMBOLS AND NUMERICS